MAGILL'S LITERARY ANNUAL 2023

*Essay-Reviews of 150 Outstanding Books
Published in the United States During 2022*

With an Annotated List of Titles

Volume II
M-Z
Indexes

Edited by
Jennifer Sawtelle

SALEM PRESS
A Division of EBSCO Information Services, Inc.
Ipswich, Massachusetts

GREY HOUSE PUBLISHING

Cover photo: Leonardo Cendamo/Getty Images

Copyright © 2023, by Salem Press, a Division of EBSCO Information Services, Inc. All rights in this book are reserved. No part of this work may be used or reproduced in any manner whatsoever or transmitted in any form or by any means, electronic or mechanical, including photocopy, recording, or any information storage and retrieval system, without written permission from the copyright owner. For permissions requests, contact permissions@ebscohost.com.

Magill's Literary Annual, 2023, published by Grey House Publishing, Inc., Amenia, NY, under exclusive license from EBSCO Information Services, Inc.

For information contact Grey House Publishing/Salem Press, 4919 Route 22, PO Box 56, Amenia, NY 12501.

∞ The paper used in these volumes conforms to the American National Standard for Permanence of Paper for Printed Library Materials, Z39.48-1992 (R2009).

Publisher's Cataloging-In-Publication Data
(Prepared by The Donohue Group, Inc.)

Names: Magill, Frank N. (Frank Northen), 1907-1997, editor. | Wilson, John D., editor. | Kellman, Steven G., 1947- editor. | Goodhue, Emily, editor. | Poranski, Colin D., editor. | Akre, Matthew, editor. | Spires, Kendal, editor. | Toth, Gabriela, editor. | Sawtelle, Jennifer, editor.
Title: Magill's literary annual.
Description: <1977->: [Pasadena, Calif.] : Salem Press | <2015->: Ipswich, Massachusetts : Salem Press, a division of EBSCO Information Services, Inc. ; Amenia, NY : Grey House Publishing | Essay-reviews of ... outstanding books published in the United States during the previous year. | "With an annotated list of titles." | Editor: 1977- , F.N. Magill; <2010-2014>, John D. Wilson and Steven G. Kellman; <2015>, Emily Goodhue and Colin D. Poranski; <2016>, Matthew Akre, Kendal Spires, and Gabriela Toth; <2017->, Jennifer Sawtelle. | Includes bibliographical references and index.
Identifiers: ISSN: 0163-3058
Subjects: LCSH: Books--Reviews--Periodicals. | United States--Imprints--Book reviews--Periodicals. | Literature, Modern--21st century--History and criticism--Periodicals. | Literature, Modern--20th century--History and criticism--Periodicals.
Classification: LCC PN44 .M333 | DDC 028.1--dc23

FIRST PRINTING
PRINTED IN THE UNITED STATES OF AMERICA

For Reference

Not to be taken from this room

CONTENTS

Complete Annotated List of Contents. vii

The Man Who Could Move Clouds—*Ingrid Rojas Contreras* 367
Mean Baby—*Selma Blair*. 371
The Memory Librarian—*Janelle Monáe, Alaya Dawn Johnson, Danny Lore,*
    Eve L. Ewing, Yohanca Delgado, and Sheree Renée Thomas 376
Memphis—*Tara M. Stringfellow* 381
Moon Witch, Spider King—*Marlon James*. 386
Moth—*Melody Razak*. 391
Mother Noise—*Cindy House*. 396
The Movement Made Us—*David J. Dennis Jr. with David J. Dennis Sr.* . . . 400
My Seven Black Fathers—*Will Jawando*. 405

The Naked Don't Fear the Water—*Matthieu Aikins* 410
A New Name—*Jon Fosse*. 415
Night of the Living Rez—*Morgan Talty* 420
Nightcrawling—*Leila Mottley* 425
The Nineties—*Chuck Klosterman* 429
Nona the Ninth—*Tamsyn Muir*. 434
Notes on an Execution—*Danya Kukafka*. 439
Nothing Burns as Bright as You—*Ashley Woodfolk* 444
Nothing More to Tell—*Karen M. McManus* 449
Now Is Not the Time to Panic—*Kevin Wilson* 454

The Ogress and the Orphans—*Kelly Barnhill* 458
Olga Dies Dreaming—*Xochitl Gonzalez*. 462
Otherlands—*Thomas Halliday* 467
Our Missing Hearts—*Celeste Ng*. 472

Properties of Thirst—*Marianne Wiggins* 476

The Rabbit Hutch—*Tess Gunty*. 480
Red Paint—*Sasha taqʷšəblu LaPointe* 485
Rise—*Jeff Yang, Phil Yu, and Philip Wang*. 490
River of the Gods—*Candice Millard*. 494
Rogues—*Patrick Radden Keefe* 499

The School for Good Mothers—*Jessamine Chan* 504
Sea of Tranquility—*Emily St. John Mandel* 509
Seeking Fortune Elsewhere—*Sindya Bhanoo* 513
Serious Face—*Jon Mooallem*. 517

Seven Empty Houses—*Samanta Schweblin* 521
The Seven Moons of Maali Almeida—*Shehan Karunatilaka* 526
Shy—*Mary Rodgers and Jesse Green* 531
Siren Queen—*Nghi Vo* 536
Small World—*Jonathan Evison*. 541
Solito—*Javier Zamora* 546
The Song of the Cell—*Siddhartha Mukherjee* 551
South to America—*Imani Perry* 556
The Stardust Thief—*Chelsea Abdullah*. 560
Stay True—*Hua Hsu* 564
Stories from the Tenants Downstairs—*Sidik Fofana* 568
The Summer of Bitter and Sweet—*Jen Ferguson* 573
Swim Team—*Johnnie Christmas* 578
The Swimmers—*Julie Otsuka* 582

Take My Hand—*Dolen Perkins-Valdez*. 587
Tell Me Everything—*Erika Krouse*. 592
Thank You, Mr. Nixon—*Gish Jen* 596
This Time Tomorrow—*Emma Straub*. 601
This Woven Kingdom—*Tahereh Mafi* 606
A Thousand Steps into Night—*Traci Chee* 611
Time Is a Mother—*Ocean Vuong*. 615
A Tiny Upward Shove—*Melissa Chadburn* 619
Tomorrow, and Tomorrow, and Tomorrow—*Gabrielle Zevin* 623
The Trayvon Generation—*Elizabeth Alexander* 628
The Treeline—*Ben Rawlence*. 633
True Biz—*Sara Nović*. 638
Trust—*Hernan Diaz* 643
The Twist of a Knife—*Anthony Horowitz* 647

Under the Skin—*Linda Villarosa*. 652

The Verifiers—*Jane Pek* 657
Victory. Stand!—*Tommie Smith and Derrick Barnes*. 662
The Violin Conspiracy—*Brendan Slocumb*. 667
The Vortex—*Scott Carney and Jason Miklian* 672

Walking the Bowl—*Chris Lockhart and Daniel Mulilo Chama* 677
The White Girl—*Tony Birch* 682
The World Keeps Ending, and the World Goes On—*Franny Choi*. 687

CONTENTS

Yonder—*Jabari Asim* 691
You Don't Know Us Negroes and Other Essays—*Zora Neale Hurston* 695
Young Mungo—*Douglas Stuart* 700

Category Index 705
Title Index 711

COMPLETE ANNOTATED LIST OF CONTENTS

VOLUME I

Afterlives 1
    Nobel Prize winner Abdulrazak Gurnah's epic novel explores the impacts of colonialism on the lives of a handful of characters in East Africa from the early 1900s to the 1960s.

Ain't Burned All the Bright 5
    Ain't Burned All the Bright, *the second collaboration between award-winning young adult author Jason Reynolds and artist Jason Griffin, is an art book and a poem, illustrating the anguish of a multigenerational Black family in the summer of 2020. Quarantined (and one infected) because of the deadly COVID-19 virus, the family members react to news reports of Black people being killed and brutalized by police.*

All Down Darkness Wide 10
    Seán Hewitt's memoir, All Down Darkness Wide, *recounts the author's experience in a relationship turned upside down by a period of suicidal depression. Told through flashbacks to this period in his life, Hewitt weaves a story that attempts to account for the harm that can be done when one is forced to hide the most important parts of oneself, including mental illness and sexual identity.*

All My Rage 14
    In Sabaa Tahir's contemporary novel, Pakistani American protagonists and estranged best friends Noor and Salahudin navigate their senior year of high school while confronting racism, financial hardships, and family crises in the California desert.

All the Flowers Kneeling 19
    All the Flowers Kneeling, Paul Tran's debut collection, explores the experiences of a young, queer, transgender Vietnamese American dealing with the aftermath of abuse and imperialist violence, seeking acceptance, hope, and a way of making sense of their past.

All This Could Be Different 23
    A 2022 National Book Award finalist, Sarah Thankam Mathews's All This Could Be Different *chronicles a young lesbian woman's professional travails, her platonic and romantic relationships, and her struggles with her traditional Indian family.*

Also a Poet: Frank O'Hara, My Father, and Me 28
    Writer Ada Calhoun's hybrid memoir Also a Poet: Frank O'Hara, My Father, and Me *is both an attempt to finish a biography of the poet Frank O'Hara that her father had begun over forty years prior and an examination of the relationship between her and her father, the lapsed poet and art critic Peter Schjeldahl.*

Babel: Or the Necessity of Violence: An Arcane History
    of the Oxford Translators' Revolution. 32
    In this dark and violent historical fantasy novel, R. F. Kuang constructs an alternate version of 1830s England to offer thought-provoking commentaries on academia, race, colonialism, and empire. It focuses on a Chinese immigrant-scholar who, along with three of his cohorts, learns how to harness the magical and destructive powers of silver-working while studying at Oxford University's vaunted Royal Institute of Translation, colloquially known as Babel.

Bad Mexicans: Race, Empire and Revolution in the Borderlands 37
    Bad Mexicans *offers an account of the origins of the twentieth-century Mexican Revolution that focuses on the efforts of Ricardo Flores Magón, whose work was carried out primarily within the borders of the United States and helped to lead to the downfall of the long-serving dictator Porfirio Díaz. This lens enables Hernández to explore US involvement in Mexico in the years leading up to the revolution and the treatment of Mexicans in the United States.*

Big Girl 42
    Big Girl *is a fraught but triumphant coming-of-age story about a resilient young girl and her besieged Black community, both under intense pressures to become thin, colorless versions of themselves.*

Black Cake 47
    Black Cake *(2022) is an intergenerational and multicultural story of a Caribbean woman's survival, the secrets she keeps her entire life, and how she chooses to reveal them to her adult children after her death.*

Black Cloud Rising 52
    Black Cloud Rising *tells the fictionalized story of the real-life Sergeant Richard Etheridge, who was freed from bondage and joined the Union Army's African Brigade in 1863. Etheridge is best known for his post-war military service commanding a unit that served as a forerunner of the Coast Guard, but* Black Cloud Rising *illustrates how Etheridge's character was forged through his experiences as a sergeant leading other men recently freed from enslavement in combat.*

COMPLETE ANNOTATED LIST OF CONTENTS

Blank Pages and Other Stories 56
    Bernard MacLaverty's short story collection Blank Pages and Other Stories *explores quiet moments of human connection in the face of despair and the ways in which people move through loneliness in an isolating world.*

Bliss Montage 60
    Bliss Montage, *by Ling Ma, is a kaleidoscope of moments set against the danger and violence women—in this case mostly Chinese American women—experience in the world. Protagonists range from ex-girlfriends to daughters to expectant mothers, all of whom are trying to make sense of their place in the world and navigate sticky situations, told through Ma's vivid prose.*

Body Work: The Radical Power of Personal Narrative 65
    Part craft book, part memoir, this acclaimed best-selling essay collection examines the many challenges and rewards of personal narrative writing. Drawing on extensive research and her experiences as both an author and teacher, Melissa Febos offers practical tips and keen insights into the transformative power of the medium.

The Book Eaters 70
    A haunting tale of motherhood and loyalty, Sunyi Dean's The Book Eaters *follows a woman who dares to break away from her restrictive family of supernatural entities.*

Book Lovers 75
    A story that challenges the stereotypical way in which female characters and love are presented within the romance genre, Book Lovers *is the third romance novel by* New York Times *bestselling author Emily Henry.*

The Books of Jacob: Or: A Fantastic Journey across Seven Borders, Five Languages, and Three Major Religions, Not Counting the Minor Sects. Told by the Dead, Supplemented by the Author, Drawing from a Range of Books, and Aided by Imagination, the Which Being the Greatest Natural Gift of Any Person. That the Wise Might Have It for a Record, That My Compatriots Reflect, Laypersons Gain Some Understanding, and Melancholy Souls Obtain Some Slight Enjoyment 80
    In The Books of Jacob, *the Nobel Prize–winning Polish author Olga Tokarczuk presents a novel of epic proportions chronicling the career of Jacob Frank, an eighteenth-century Jewish heretic who proclaimed himself a messiah and led a religious movement that won thousands of adherents.*

Booth 85
    Karen Joy Fowler's epic, generation-spanning novel Booth *focuses on a specific, tragic era of United States' history, the lead-up to and eventual start of the Civil War, and the experiences of the Booth family—including John Wilkes Booth—within those times. Told from the perspectives of several members of the Booth family, the novel creates a patchwork of experiences preceding one of the most infamous moments in American history: the assassination of President Abraham Lincoln.*

The Bullet That Missed: A Thursday Murder Club Mystery 90
    The Bullet That Missed *is the third installment of English author Richard Osman's best-selling mystery series* The Thursday Murder Club. *Elderly, amateur sleuths Elizabeth, Ron, Joyce, and Ibrahim have found a new cold case—the unsolved murder of a Kent TV reporter named Bethany Waites—and, in pursuing it, uncover a much larger web of deceit.*

Buster Keaton: A Filmmaker's Life. 94
    In Buster Keaton, *the noted biographer James Curtis presents a definitive and appreciative account of the life of the great twentieth-century silent film comedian Buster Keaton. Curtis covers Keaton's life in great detail, from his early days as a child vaudeville performer to his final years.*

Call Me Cassandra 99
    This novel by award-winning Cuban writer Marcial Gala tells the story of a boy growing up in 1970s Cuba who sees himself as the reincarnation of the doomed prophet Cassandra from Ancient Greek myth. It explores issues of identity, fate, and violence in unusual and compelling ways.

Calling for a Blanket Dance. 103
    Oscar Hokeah's debut novel, Calling for a Blanket Dance *(2022), follows the growth and development of Ever Geimausaddle, an Oklahoman of Cherokee, Kiowa, and Mexican heritage, as related by members of his family.*

Camera Man: Buster Keaton, the Dawn of Cinema, and the Invention
    of the Twentieth Century 108
    In Camera Man, *the veteran film critic Dana Stevens presents an appreciative study of Buster Keaton that attempts to place the man and his work in the context of his times. Stevens sees Keaton, a comedic star of silent films during the twentieth century, as a figure whose tumultuous career reflected key cultural and technological trends of the time.*

The Candy House 113
    A sequel to the Pulitzer Prize–winning A Visit from the Goon Squad *(2010), Jennifer Egan's* The Candy House *examines ideas about human connectivity, relationships, technology, and memory.*

COMPLETE ANNOTATED LIST OF CONTENTS

Carrie Soto Is Back 118
Taylor Jenkins Reid solidifies her status as a leading voice in popular fiction with this suspenseful and emotionally powerful 1990s-set drama, which centers around the post-retirement comeback of a legendary female tennis champion.

Civil Rights Queen: Constance Baker Motley and the Struggle for Equality . . . 123
Tomiko Brown-Nagin's biography explores the life of Constance Baker Motley, an influential civil rights attorney and the first Black woman to be appointed a US federal court judge.

The Colony 128
The Colony, Irish novelist Audrey Magee's Booker Prize–nominated novel, explores the harms and complexities of colonialism. In it, an arrogant English painter visits a remote Irish island in 1979, at the same time a French linguist is staying there, during the height of the bloody sectarian conflict in Northern Ireland known as the Troubles.

Companion Piece 133
Novelist Ali Smith follows up her acclaimed Seasonal Quartet with a fifth companion novel exploring the nature of freedom and constraint and what it means to live in post-Brexit Britain during the COVID-19 pandemic.

Constructing a Nervous System 137
Literary critic Margo Jefferson's unorthodox memoir combines remembrance, personal reflection, quotation, and analyses of various artistic works to bring to life a portrait of the author's imaginative life.

Corrections in Ink 141
In this gritty and unflinchingly honest debut memoir, investigative journalist Keri Blakinger, who was once addicted to drugs and spent almost two years in prison for heroin possession, examines her own rise, fall, recovery, and redemption, providing harrowing revelations about the inhumane conditions and gross inequities inside US prisons.

Customs 146
Solmaz Sharif's second book of poetry explores the experiences of exile and of moving between borders, filtered through the author's experience as an Iranian American.

The Daughter of Doctor Moreau 150
Silvia Moreno-Garcia's eighth novel, The Daughter of Doctor Moreau, *is a fresh take on H. G. Wells's nineteenth-century tale of a man facing dire consequences for the arrogance of delving into forbidden science.*

Daughter of the Moon Goddess.............................. 155
    A thrilling fantasy novel inspired by the myth behind the Chinese Mid-Autumn Festival, Daughter of the Moon Goddess *places a feminist spin on the legend, examining the bond between mother and daughter and the sacrifices we make to save a loved one.*

Deaf Utopia: A Memoir—and a Love Letter to a Way of Life............ 159
    Nyle DiMarco, who was born into a large family of Deaf people, here recounts in an impressively cheerful and uplifting book the challenges he has faced during his life but also the real joy he feels every day in living as a Deaf person.

Demon Copperhead... 164
    Barbara Kingsolver's tenth novel tells the story of a boy growing up poor and orphaned in rural Appalachia. An intelligent survivor, he becomes a sympathetic guide to a landscape abandoned by the modern economy and ravaged by drugs, where real hope seems scarce.

Dinosaurs.. 169
    Dinosaurs, *a novel by award-winning author Lydia Millet about a wealthy man seeking absolution from his privilege, is a meditation on how to be good in a world defined by disaster and doom.*

The Door of No Return.. 173
    Told in lyric verse, Kwame Alexander's The Door of No Return *brings the horrific realities of the slave trade front and center in a manageable way for young readers who are learning about this tragic history.*

Ducks: Two Years in the Oil Sands............................ 177
    In this graphic memoir, artist and writer Kate Beaton recounts her two years working in the oil sands of Alberta, Canada. While determined to use the job to pay off her college loans, she struggles with loneliness, the sexist attitudes of management and her male coworkers, and the disturbing information she learns about the oil industry's impact on the environment and Canada's Indigenous population.

Easy Beauty.. 182
    Chloé Cooper Jones's first full-length work, the memoir Easy Beauty, *explores the concept of beauty from classical times to the present, as it relates to public perceptions of, and her internal thoughts about, her disability.*

COMPLETE ANNOTATED LIST OF CONTENTS

Either/Or 187
    A sequel to Batuman's 2017 novel, The Idiot, Either/Or *follows Selin Karadağ over her sophomore year at Harvard University and her summer traveling in Turkey as she reflects on the events of her freshman year and continues her journey of self-discovery.*

Fellowship Point 192
    Alice Elliott Dark's second novel, Fellowship Point, *explores lifelong friendship, family legacies, and the power of place as two older women fight to preserve their land in coastal Maine.*

Free: A Child and a Country at the End of History 197
    Political theorist Lea Ypi presents a beautifully written memoir of her early life in Albania as the country's strict communist regime came to an end. She compellingly documents the suffocating atmosphere of a totalitarian state as seen through the eyes of an innocent, as well as the chaotic attempt to transition to a market economy.

Gathering Blossoms under Fire: The Journals of Alice Walker, 1965–2000 . . . 202
    Gathering Blossoms under Fire *is an edited collection of journal entries from the Pulitzer Prize–winning American writer Alice Walker.*

Half American: The Epic Story of African Americans Fighting World War II
    at Home and Abroad. 207
    In this engagingly told history, Matthew F. Delmont offers a comprehensive look at the experiences of Black Americans during World War II, chronicling their various indispensable roles in the war effort both at home and abroad while experiencing pervasive racial segregation, prejudice, and violence.

Happy-Go-Lucky 212
    In Happy-Go-Lucky, *a collection of eighteen semiautobiographical essays, humorist David Sedaris delves into his fraught relationship with his father, the COVID-19 pandemic, and several other topics, all with his signature empathy, humor, and absurdity.*

The Haunting of Hajji Hotak and Other Stories 217
    The twelve stories in The Haunting of Hajji Hotak *revolve around a village called Deh-Naw in the Logar province of Afghanistan, though many are set in California. Fantastical, strange, and surreal, Jamil Jan Kochai's stories grapple with a history of generational violence in surprising ways.*

Heartbroke. 221
    Heartbroke, *Chelsea Bieker's dark and powerful first collection of short fiction, offers a poignant yet unsentimental portrait of lost souls and broken hearts set against the beautifully bleak backdrop of California's Central Valley.*

Her Country: How the Women of Country Music Became the Success
   They Were Never Supposed to Be. 226
   In Her Country: How the Women of Country Music Became the Success They Were Never Supposed to Be, *music journalist Marissa R. Moss chronicles the pitfalls and obstacles faced by women in country music who dared to step away from tradition and sexist standards. Told through a vivid narrative, the book provides a rich history of women in the modern country music world, from the 1990s to the 2020s.*

His Name Is George Floyd: One Man's Life and the Struggle for Racial Justice . . 231
   In His Name Is George Floyd, *journalists Robert Samuels and Toluse Olorunnipa use primary sources and hundreds of recorded interviews with family members, lawmakers, activists, and others to understand the life of George Floyd within the context of the political, social, economic, educational, and legal policies and practices that impacted him and other Black people in the United States.*

Horse 237
   With multiple, interwoven narratives spanning nearly two centuries, Horse *presents a fictionalized odyssey centered around the life and legacy of a real-life nineteenth-century racehorse. Taking on weighty issues of race, art, science, and social unrest, the novel emphasizes the importance of perseverance and following one's passion.*

How to Raise an Antiracist 242
   Written by renowned American author and scholar Ibram X. Kendi, How to Raise an Antiracist *is a guide for parents and teachers on how to educate children about racism and, in turn, protect them from its harmful impact.*

The Hurting Kind 246
   Ada Limón's sixth poetry collection, The Hurting Kind, *finds the writer in familiar territory: uncovering the deeply personal within the frame of the natural world, laying devotion upon the seemingly ordinary, and revealing its extraordinariness. Written during the pandemic, her poems call the reader back to the body, back to the earth, with moments of wonder made deeper by pain.*

I Cried to Dream Again: Trafficking, Murder, and Deliverance 250
   Activist Sara Kruzan's memoir, written with the assistance of veteran writer Cori Thomas, chronicles her abusive childhood, descent into sex work as a trafficking victim, conviction for murder, and imprisonment for life without possibility of parole. The narrative, which concludes with her ultimate release from prison after nearly two decades, provides insight into not only the flaws of the American criminal justice system and the horrific realities of sex trafficking but also the human capacity to move beyond trauma.

COMPLETE ANNOTATED LIST OF CONTENTS

I Must Betray You. 254
    Set in communist Romania in late 1989, I Must Betray You *follows Cristian Florescu, a seventeen-year-old high school student who is blackmailed by the "Securitate," the regime's secret police, to become an informer. Living in a society where isolation and fear reign supreme, Cristian hopes to expose to the world the reality of Romania, a country in the throes of revolution.*

If I Survive You. 259
    If I Survive You, *the debut short-story collection by Jonathan Escoffery, follows a Jamaican American family living in Florida and explores issues of identity and belonging.*

I'll Show Myself Out: Essays on Midlife & Motherhood 264
    I'll Show Myself Out is a tragicomic memoir of new motherhood. In this collection of essays, Jessi Klein, a comedian, writer, and producer, explores topics ranging from details of the physical trauma following childbirth, to the psychological challenges of changes to the body, to the disconnect of rosy social images of motherhood versus the struggles of its daily realities.

I'm Glad My Mom Died 268
    I'm Glad My Mom Died is a memoir written by actor, singer, writer, and director Jennette McCurdy about her traumatic youth. Based on her one-woman show, it is her first book.

An Immense World: How Animal Senses Reveal the Hidden Realms around Us . . 273
    The second book by journalist Ed Yong, An Immense World *is a guide to sensory biology and the different ways that animals experience life on Earth.*

The Impossible City: A Hong Kong Memoir. 278
    The Impossible City chronicles the coming of age of a young woman dealing with both personal difficulties and the upheavals of postcolonial Hong Kong while documenting the vibrant—and possibly vanishing—culture of the city in the late twentieth and early twenty-first centuries.

Index, a History of the: A Bookish Adventure from Medieval Manuscripts to the
    Digital Age. 282
    In Index, a History of the, *Dennis Duncan chronicles the history of the index from the development of alphabetic order to the emergence of computerized indexing technology thousands of years later.*

Inheritance: A Visual Poem 287
    Inheritance *presents an illustrated version of a poem by acclaimed writer Elizabeth Acevedo that originated as a spoken word piece. It uses the subject of Black hair to explore the complicated ancestral legacy and present-day impact of Afro-Latinidad heritage, and Dominican identity in particular.*

The Invisible Kingdom: Reimagining Chronic Illness 291
    Meghan O'Rourke's memoir The Invisible Kingdom: Reimagining Chronic Illness *takes on the author's experience with mysterious autoimmune syndromes and disease, chronicling her fight to be taken seriously by the medical establishment and find relief, if not a cure, to her debilitating issues. Taking into account the work of writers like Christina Crosby and Susan Sontag and the research and opinions of countless medical doctors, it strives to provide a detailed look at the barriers facing so many people with illness that presents itself inside rather than out.*

The Kaiju Preservation Society 296
    John Scalzi's The Kaiju Preservation Society *follows a startup marketing executive who, after being demoted and then fired during the COVID-19 pandemic, takes a job with a mysterious animal rights organization whose mission is to save strange, secret creatures living in a parallel world.*

Kaikeyi 300
    A reimagining of the Hindu epic the Ramayana, Kaikeyi *tells the ancient story through the lens of a character commonly portrayed as a villain, Rama's stepmother, Kaikeyi.*

Killers of a Certain Age 304
    Best known for her best-selling mysteries set in Victorian England, author Deanna Raybourn's novel Killers of a Certain Age *is a contemporary thriller featuring a cast of female assassins in their sixties. After forty years of killing Nazis, drug lords, and dictators, the assassins are set to retire, when they find that they have become the targets of their former organization.*

Last Call at the Hotel Imperial: The Reporters Who Took On a World at War . . 308
    Historian Deborah Cohen traces the careers of four American foreign correspondents whose work shaped public opinion and marked a significant era of journalism in the United States in the period leading up to and during World War II.

The Last Slave Ship: The True Story of How Clotilda Was Found,
    Her Descendants, and an Extraordinary Reckoning 313
    The Last Slave Ship, *a history by award-winning environmental journalist and filmmaker Ben Raines, weaves together a complex captivating saga of criminal deception, and a legacy of trauma, recovery, and resilience in telling the story of the discovery of the Clotilda, the final ship to bring enslaved Africans to the United States.*

COMPLETE ANNOTATED LIST OF CONTENTS

The Last White Man 318
    Pakistani author Mohsin Hamid's fifth novel, The Last White Man, *explores intimate and sensitive issues of identity and perception through a world in which people have begun mysteriously exhibiting different racial characteristics.*

Left on Tenth: A Second Chance at Life 323
    In this tender and humorous memoir, best-selling author and screenwriter Delia Ephron takes readers on a journey of loss, love, and hope as she chronicles her near-fatal battle with an aggressive leukemia after losing her first husband to cancer and unexpectedly finding love again at age seventy-two.

Legacy of Violence: A History of the British Empire. 328
    Historian Caroline Elkins documents the extreme measures political leaders in Britain used to sustain its empire during the late nineteenth and twentieth centuries in the face of growing independence movements in colonial territories around the globe.

Lesser Known Monsters of the 21st Century 333
    Lesser Known Monsters of the 21st Century *is a collection of surreal and fantastical short stories that hold up a warped mirror to modern life, dealing with technology and uncertainties about the future as well as timeless themes of grief and the search for human connection.*

Lessons 338
    The novel Lessons *follows one man's life over the course of more than sixty years of history, tackling existential questions of time, relationships, trauma, and meaning.*

Lessons in Chemistry. 342
    The best-selling novel Lessons in Chemistry, *which has been published in some forty countries, tells the story of a female chemist named Elizabeth Zott intent on bucking the chauvinism and misogyny of the male-dominated scientific community in mid-twentieth-century America. After Elizabeth reluctantly agrees to host an educational television cooking show, she becomes a source of inspiration and empowerment to other women.*

The Letters of Thom Gunn 346
    Thom Gunn was not only a major post-war British poet but also a key figure in the growing gay rights movement in twentieth-century society and literature. The selections from his thousands of letters collected in The Letters of Thom Gunn *provide much valuable information about the poet's life and work.*

Liberation Day 351
    In Liberation Day, *a 2022 collection of short stories by award-winning author George Saunders, characters try and fail to break free from oppressive systems.*

Lost & Found 356
    This memoir explores an interval in the author's life during which her father succumbed to his final illness and the author also met and eventually married her partner. Through these important life markers of grief and celebration, Kathryn Schulz explores the concepts of lost, found, and "and"—the latter representing living with the coexistence of both "lost" and "found."

Lucy by the Sea 361
    Lucy by the Sea, an examination of loneliness, love, and friendship, follows a long-divorced New York couple who escape the pandemic to shelter in a remote house in coastal Maine.

VOLUME II

The Man Who Could Move Clouds 367
    Ingrid Rojas Contreras's first memoir, The Man Who Could Move Clouds, is a story about family inheritances, including trauma, mystery, and genetics, and how each generation processes the last. Told through the author's perspective following an accident that left her with temporary amnesia, this book excavates the life of her mother, grandfather, and the family gift (an ability to tap into the mystical and ghostly) with curiosity, wonder, and compassion.

Mean Baby: A Memoir of Growing Up 371
    Selma Blair's debut as a writer, Mean Baby: A Memoir of Growing Up, is the story of her life so far, which reveals much previously unknown information surrounding her development as a person and growth as an actor.

The Memory Librarian: And Other Stories of Dirty Computer 376
    The Memory Librarian and Other Stories of Dirty Computer is a literary extension of lead author Janelle Monáe's 2018 album and short film, Dirty Computer. In five short stories by Monáe and five coauthors, gender nonconformists resist the memory standardization efforts of New Dawn, a totalitarian regime in an Afrofuturistic dystopia.

Memphis 381
    Memphis, set against the backdrop of a city in flux, follows the story of a family of strong Black women. The characters contend with troubled relationships and internal struggles, as well as events of world-changing significance, as they attempt to survive—and even thrive.

Moon Witch, Spider King 386
    The second volume in the Dark Star Trilogy, Moon Witch, Spider King traces the life of Sogolon, the titular Moon Witch, from girlhood through the events of the preceding novel.

COMPLETE ANNOTATED LIST OF CONTENTS

Moth. 391
    Moth, *an intensely dramatic work of historical fiction, vividly depicts the life of one Brahmin family before and after the violent partition that established India and Pakistan as two independent nations in 1947.*

Mother Noise 396
    Mother Noise *is a memoir about writer and artist Cindy House's experiences with addiction as well as her life in recovery as a mother.*

The Movement Made Us: A Father, a Son, and the Legacy of a Freedom Ride . . . 400
    The memoir of civil rights leader David J. Dennis Sr., written with his son, journalist David J. Dennis Jr., focuses on the elder Dennis's role in the Freedom Rides and voter registration efforts in Louisiana and Mississippi in the early 1960s. The Movement Made Us: A Father, a Son, and the Legacy of a Freedom Ride *also includes a recounting of the efforts of Dennis and his son to reach an understanding of their relationship and the impact of the father's work on that of his son.*

My Seven Black Fathers: A Young Activist's Memoir of Race, Family,
    and the Mentors Who Made Him Whole 405
    This inspirational memoir by attorney, civil rights activist, and local government leader Will Jawando chronicles how he navigated the pains and triumphs of life as a Black male in the United States with the help of seven Black men who mentored him over the years. His experience also sheds light on broader issues of race, family, and masculinity in society.

The Naked Don't Fear the Water: An Underground Journey with
    Afghan Refugees 410
    In The Naked Don't Fear the Water, *the distinguished foreign correspondent Matthieu Aikins presents a compelling account of his undercover journey on the migrant trail from Afghanistan to Europe with his friend Omar, a former interpreter with the Canadian and United States armed forces in Afghanistan who hoped to escape war and poverty and make a new life in the West. Aikins' book is both a tale of danger and survival and a penetrating meditation on the moral, political, and economic crisis resulting from the mass movement of people in a disordered world.*

A New Name: Septology VI–VII 415
    A New Name *is the final installment of Norwegian author Jon Fosse's seven-volume* Septology *series that explores ideas surrounding art, God, and the human experience.*

Night of the Living Rez 420
 Morgan Talty's first full-length work; Night of the Living Rez *(2022), collects a dozen linked stories, most published individually between 2017 and 2020, as told from the changing perspective of a young boy on the Penobscot Indian Island Reservation in Maine who seeks answers to questions about his purpose and existence.*

Nightcrawling 425
 Seventeen-year-old Kiara struggles to support herself, her brother, and the child of a neighbor. When she gets pulled into a legal case involving a group of police officers, her life is turned upside-down, forcing her to determine the true meaning of family.

The Nineties. 429
 In The Nineties, *distinguished journalist and author Chuck Klosterman presents a penetrating analysis of the last decade of the twentieth century. Mixing political and cultural commentary, he deftly analyzes a decade that, because of the digital revolution that took off in the early twenty-first century, may often seem more distant than it actually is chronologically.*

Nona the Ninth 434
 In Nona the Ninth, *the third installment in the* Locked Tomb *series, a young woman with amnesia navigates life in a besieged city while her companions attempt to discern her true identity.*

Notes on an Execution 439
 Danya Kukafka's second novel, Notes on an Execution, *traces the path of an individual as he evolves from neglected child to serial killer to Death Row inmate.*

Nothing Burns as Bright as You. 444
 In her 2022 young adult novel Nothing Burns as Bright as You, *acclaimed author Ashley Woodfolk uses poetic prose to tell the story of an intense, impassioned, and troubled first love affair.*

Nothing More to Tell 449
 In Nothing More to Tell, *Karen M. McManus presents an engaging murder mystery aimed at a young adult audience. Returning to her old prep school after an absence of almost four years, student journalist Brynn Gallagher begins investigating the murder of a popular teacher that was never satisfactorily resolved; her efforts threaten to expose old secrets and lead to danger and romance.*

COMPLETE ANNOTATED LIST OF CONTENTS

Now Is Not the Time to Panic... 454
 Set in the sleepy southern town of Coalfield, Tennessee, Now Is Not the Time to Panic *is a coming-of-age story, told from the perspective of teenager Frances (Frankie) Budge as she experiences a life-altering summer in which she and her friend Zeke's seemingly insignificant creation sends the whole town of Coalfield, and beyond, spiraling into unimaginable territory.*

The Ogress and the Orphans... 458
 The town of Stone-in-the-Glen was once a beautiful and happy place, but after the library and several other buildings burned down, the people fell into despair. A group of orphan children and a friendly ogress, however, remain hopeful and loving, eventually showing the townspeople that being a good neighbor can make a change for everyone.

Olga Dies Dreaming.. 462
 Debut novelist Xochitl Gonzalez's first book follows two Puerto Rican siblings living in New York as they weigh their personal lives against their larger family and social obligations.

Otherlands: A Journey through Earth's Extinct Worlds............... 467
 In Otherlands: A Journey through Earth's Extinct Worlds, *paleobiologist Thomas Halliday takes readers back in time, exploring the often-unrecognizable environments of long-past eras and the creatures that thrived within them.*

Our Missing Hearts.. 472
 Celeste Ng's third novel, Our Missing Hearts, *is a story about the power of love during crisis. As the United States begins to experience extreme political upheaval in a dystopian near-future, Bird is a shy and awkward child who must learn to live without his mother as his father turns ever more inward.*

Properties of Thirst.. 476
 Award-winning author and Pulitzer Prize finalist Marianne Wiggins writes about World War II, the Los Angeles water wars, and Japanese internment in her 2022 novel Properties of Thirst.

The Rabbit Hutch.. 480
 Tess Gunty's debut novel, The Rabbit Hutch, *offers a wide-ranging and highly assured look at the lives of a handful of characters living in a declining Midwestern city.*

Red Paint: The Ancestral Autobiography of a Coast Salish Punk 485
   Interweaving personal life experiences with ancestral history, Coast Salish writer and artist Sasha taqʷšəblu LaPointe explores loss, healing, and the enduring spirit across generations of women in her memoir, Red Paint. The author also probes the wounds of her ancestors, exploring the intergenerational burdens of trauma and the path toward healing.

Rise: A Pop History of Asian America from the Nineties to Now 490
   Rise brings together a wide range of contributors and draws on a number of different genres to tell the story of Asian America and its culture over the last thirty years.

River of the Gods: Genius, Courage, and Betrayal in the Search
   for the Source of the Nile 494
   Writer Candice Millard presents a compelling account of the turbulent relationship between explorers Richard Francis Burton and John Hanning Speke in their nineteenth-century quest to locate the source of the Nile River.

Rogues: True Stories of Grifters, Killers, Rebels and Crooks 499
   Veteran journalist Patrick Radden Keefe's Rogues: True Stories of Grifters, Killers, Rebels and Crooks gathers together twelve memorable long-form nonfiction pieces originally published in the New Yorker exploring people's motivations, behavior, and morality in a variety of situations, including criminal ones.

The School for Good Mothers 504
   Jessamine Chan's debut novel, The School for Good Mothers, imagines a world in which negligent mothers are forced to attend a prison-like school in hopes of winning back their children. Drawing on real-world policies, Chan's impressive and devastating dystopian satire offers a glimpse of a near-future dominated by incarceration, surveillance, and perpetual punishment.

Sea of Tranquility 509
   Emily St. John Mandel's sixth novel, Sea of Tranquility, combines elements from metafiction and speculative fiction to provide fresh twists on familiar time-travel tropes.

Seeking Fortune Elsewhere 513
   Seeking Fortune Elsewhere is the debut short story-collection from journalist Sindya Bhanoo. Centered largely around characters who are of South Indian descent, the stories touch on topics ranging from aging to parenthood to the strains and rewards of living in a new country while also keeping an eye on the past.

COMPLETE ANNOTATED LIST OF CONTENTS

Serious Face. 517
 Writer Jon Mooallem's first book of essays collects twelve of his pieces previously published in the New York Times Magazine, as well as one newly written essay, that explore a variety of offbeat subjects with curiosity and empathy.

Seven Empty Houses 521
 Seven Empty Houses by Samanta Schweblin explores themes of loneliness, love, and isolation through the guise of seven houses and apartments. Drawing on both familial intimacy that strains those closest to each other and the relentless passing of time, this collection understands that sometimes strangeness is what breaks a person, but sometimes a stranger is the one to save us.

The Seven Moons of Maali Almeida 526
 The Seven Moons of Maali Almeida is a ghost story set amidst the backdrop of the Sri Lankan civil war. It is the second novel by the award-winning Sri Lankan writer Shehan Karunatilaka.

Shy: The Alarmingly Outspoken Memoirs of Mary Rodgers. 531
 In this exceptionally candid memoir, noted composer, author, and philanthropist Mary Rodgers offers insight into her own remarkable life as well as a wealth of juicy details about the many famous people she knew. Her incisively witty recollections, bolstered by extensive notes from coauthor Jesse Green, provide a unique view of the world of twentieth-century American musical theater.

Siren Queen 536
 Seamlessly blending fantasy and reality, Siren Queen presents a unique take on the golden age of Hollywood, focusing on a Chinese American actor who stops at nothing to become an immortal silver screen star.

Small World. 541
 Spanning 170 years of American history, this epic and ambitious novel tracks the intersection of four modern families and their nineteenth-century ancestors as they struggle to find hope, meaning, and purpose in a rapidly changing world.

Solito 546
 In the memoir Solito, award-winning author Javier Zamora chronicles his journey from El Salvador to the United States as an unaccompanied nine-year-old.

The Song of the Cell: An Exploration of Medicine and the New Human 551
 The Song of the Cell, by Pulitzer Prize-winner Siddhartha Mukherjee, explores the past, present, and future of cellular biology and its implications for one day eradicating cancer and other diseases.

South to America: A Journey below the Mason-Dixon to Understand
the Soul of a Nation 556
    Imani Perry's National Book Award–winning work South to America: A Journey below the Mason-Dixon to Understand the Soul of a Nation, *combines cultural criticism, travelogue, and memoir to present a sociopolitical history of the Southern United States.*

The Stardust Thief. 560
    Loulie al-Nazari is the Midnight Merchant, known as a dealer in magical relics which she tracks with her mysterious bodyguard, Qadir. After a brief meeting with the Sultan's youngest son, she is coerced into chasing after a legendary lamp containing one of the last of the jinn kings. The ensuing journey is filled with mystery, adventure, and tragedy.

Stay True 564
    In his debut memoir, Stay True, *Hua Hsu recounts the unlikely friendship he struck up with Ken, a gregarious, confident young man who seemed his polar opposite, while they were attending the University of California, Berkeley, in 1990s California. When tragedy struck, Hsu turned to writing to excavate his grief.*

Stories from the Tenants Downstairs 568
    Stories from the Tenants Downstairs *is a collection of interconnected short stories that explore gentrification, class struggle, and aspiration. It is the debut book from American author Sidik Fofana.*

The Summer of Bitter and Sweet 573
    The young adult novel The Summer of Bitter and Sweet *tells the story of a Métis teenager named Lou whose last summer before leaving for college does not turn out as she had planned. After an old friend returns to the area, she begins to recognize not only how much she has changed but the extent to which her life has been based on lies. Author Jen Ferguson explores themes of family, friendship, sexuality, and trauma throughout the book.*

Swim Team 578
    Swim Team, *a middle-grade graphic novel from illustrator Johnnie Christmas, follows a young girl named Bree as she faces her fear of swimming and learns to build lasting friendships. The book also explores the history of racism and segregation that continues to shape access to the sport of swimming.*

The Swimmers 582
    The Swimmers *is a slim, stunning novel that meditates on the nature of aging, dementia, and identity, as well as mother-daughter relationships.*

COMPLETE ANNOTATED LIST OF CONTENTS

Take My Hand. 587
    Take My Hand, best-selling author Dolen Perkins-Valdez's third novel, is a work of historical fiction that examines the involuntary sterilizations of Black girls and women that happened in the United States in the 1970s.

Tell Me Everything: The Story of a Private Investigation 592
    Part reportage and part memoir, Elizabeth Krouse's Tell Me Everything: The Story of a Private Investigation *chronicles the novelist and short-story writer's work as a private investigator on a landmark sexual assault case involving a college football team in the early 2000s as well as how sexual abuse has affected her personally.*

Thank You, Mr. Nixon 596
    Thank You, Mr. Nixon is a collection of interlinked short stories that explore the cultural relationship between the United States and China. Featuring a rotating cast of characters—ranging from elderly parents to preteen children—the collection spans generations and continents attempting to understand geographic and political divides.

This Time Tomorrow 601
    In This Time Tomorrow, *best-selling author Emma Straub considers life and familial love in a time-bending story that is both funny and poignant. When a woman named Alice Stern, the daughter of the famous science-fiction novelist Leonard Stern, turns forty, she finds herself thrust back in time to the day of her sixteenth birthday. Alice must figure out how she got there, and what choices she must make to change the course of her life.*

This Woven Kingdom. 606
    In Tahereh Mafi's young adult fantasy novel, equal parts love story and political scheming, Alizeh, a jinn with special powers working secretly as a maid, accidentally meets the human crown prince of Ardunia, Kamran. Once their worlds collide, their curiosity and feelings about each other grow while the kingdom of Ardunia is thrown into turmoil.

A Thousand Steps into Night 611
    Set in a world inspired by Japanese mythology, A Thousand Steps into Night *is a fantasy novel by the best-selling American author Traci Chee.*

Time Is a Mother 615
    Ocean Vuong's second collection of poetry, Time Is a Mother, *finds the writer grappling with the 2019 death of his mother. Combining poignant descriptions and moments with a modernist sensibility, the poems blend perspective and create an atmosphere of timelessness as Vuong imagines both the past—near and distant—and a future spent without her.*

A Tiny Upward Shove. 619
    A Tiny Upward Shove, journalist Melissa Chadburn's gut-punch of a debut novel, is shocking for its brutal violence but also its vivid beauty. In it, a teenager named Marina, who is selling sex to maintain her heroin addiction, is murdered by serial killer Willie Pickton. In her dying moments, she reaches out to the aswang, a mysterious and vengeful spirit from Filipino folklore.

Tomorrow, and Tomorrow, and Tomorrow 623
    Gabrielle Zevin's 2022 novel, Tomorrow, and Tomorrow, and Tomorrow, *is an emotionally absorbing story about video game designers making it big in the late 1990s and early 2000s. Zevin follows main characters (MCs in gaming parlance) Sadie, Sam, and Marx through worlds both virtual and real to tell a story about the importance of play, the creative process, and the power of true friendship.*

The Trayvon Generation 628
    The Trayvon Generation is a treatise about the generational impact of White supremacy and anti-Black racism on the lives of Black families with a focus on Black youth under the age of twenty-five that author Elizabeth Alexander defines as the Trayvon Generation.

The Treeline: The Last Forest and the Future of Life on Earth 633
    In The Treeline, *author Ben Rawlence focuses on a deep study of seven tree species of the boreal forest in an effort to bring greater clarity to the fundamental habitat changes already underway due to climate change. This work of ecojournalism is a call to action as well as a sobering account of the irreversible damages that are already underway.*

True Biz 638
    True Biz is a coming-of-age story that celebrates the American Deaf community while examining the sociopolitical challenges it continues to face within the hearing world. It is author Sara Nović's third book.

Trust 643
    Across four interconnected but contradictory narratives, Trust *follows the story of the marriage of an elite New York City couple and probes themes of truth and fiction, morality and finance, and mental illness.*

The Twist of a Knife 647
    The author's fictional alter ego Anthony Horowitz is arrested for the murder of a theater critic who panned his new play, forcing him to ask for help from Daniel Hawthorne, a detective with whom Horowitz had previously collaborated on three true-crime novels based on Hawthorne's investigations.

COMPLETE ANNOTATED LIST OF CONTENTS

Under the Skin: The Hidden Toll of Racism on American Lives and
  on the Health of Our Nation. 652
   In Under the Skin, *Linda Villarosa provides a comprehensive and well-supported investigation into systemic racial disparities that have roots in slavery and continue to impact African Americans' medical care, overall health, and living conditions.*

The Verifiers. 657
   Set in New York City, Jane Pek's debut novel, The Verifiers, *is a complex murder mystery involving the online matchmaking industry.*

Victory. Stand!: Raising My Fist for Justice 662
   Victory. Stand! Raising My Fist for Justice *presents the inspiring life story of the athlete and activist Tommie Smith in a graphic novel format aimed at young adult readers. Centered around the 1968 Olympic Games, at which Smith won a gold medal and raised a gloved fist on the podium in an iconic protest for civil rights, the book also covers Smith's childhood and later life with particular attention to issues of racial justice throughout.*

The Violin Conspiracy 667
   Unfolding after the theft of a Stradivarius violin, owned by Ray McMillian, The Violin Conspiracy *follows the frantic and global search for the violin while Ray continues to prepare to compete in the important Tchaikovsky Competition in Moscow. Alongside the narrative of the theft, the novel unspools Ray's family history and his struggles to be recognized as a high-performing Black professional in the majority-White world of classical music.*

The Vortex: A True Story of History's Deadliest Storm, an Unspeakable War,
  and Liberation. 672
   The Vortex *offers a "novelistic" account of one of the deadliest storms in history—a 1970 cyclone that devastated much of Bangladesh, at the time part of Pakistan known as East Pakistan, and set the stage for Bangladeshi independence.*

Walking the Bowl: A True Story of Murder and Survival among
  the Street Children of Lusaka. 677
   This nonfiction work examines the tenuous experience of impoverished children living in one of the world's fastest-growing cities. Despite being a carefully researched anthropological study, it has the gripping narrative arc of a novel, painting detailed portraits of several young people who find themselves connected to a murder investigation.

The White Girl 682
    Aboriginal artist Odette Brown lives in fear that the Welfare Board will take her light-skinned, blonde granddaughter, Sissy, away from her, especially when Odette begins to experience health problems. Set in a small Australian town in the 1960s, Tony Birch's novel follows Odette as she searches for a way to protect the one person she has left.

The World Keeps Ending, and the World Goes On 687
    The World Keeps Ending, and the World Goes On *explores the concept of apocalypse, bringing together history and speculative futures to contextualize the many issues facing the world today and imagine how humanity might cope with or even overcome them.*

Yonder. 691
    The novel Yonder *offers a powerful evocation of the horrors of slavery and the promise of freedom while focusing on the humanity of enslaved people.*

You Don't Know Us Negroes and Other Essays 695
    Henry Louis Gates Jr. and Genevieve West have chosen fifty of acclaimed author Zora Neale Hurston's essays in this collection, covering issues such as folklore, art, race, gender and politics. Though many of the essays were previously published, there are several pieces that appear for the first time in this volume.

Young Mungo 700
    Douglas Stuart's second novel focuses on the story of Mungo Hamilton, a sensitive teenager living on the margins of society in Glasgow, Scotland, as he navigates young love and family dysfunction.

The Man Who Could Move Clouds

Author: Ingrid Rojas Contreras (b. 1984)
Publisher: Doubleday (New York). 320 pp.
Type of work: Memoir
Time: Largely the 1940s–the present day
Locales: Colombia, Mexico, the United States

Ingrid Rojas Contreras's first memoir, The Man Who Could Move Clouds, *is a story about family inheritances, including trauma, mystery, and genetics, and how each generation processes the last. Told through the author's perspective following an accident that left her with temporary amnesia, this book excavates the life of her mother, grandfather, and the family gift (an ability to tap into the mystical and ghostly) with curiosity, wonder, and compassion.*

Principal personages

INGRID ROJAS CONTRERAS, the author, a native of Bogotá, Colombia, later living in the US who suffers temporary amnesia after a collision between her bike and a car door
MAMI, her mother, a healer who also suffered temporary amnesia as a young girl after falling down an empty well
NONO, her maternal grandfather, a well-known and well-respected healer
NONA, her maternal grandmother, who suffered through her marriage to Nono, a known philanderer
XIMENA, her older sister, who does not take part in or believe in the family tradition of magic and medicine
TÍA PERLA, her aunt; her mother's sister, who works with Mami to disinter their father's body in Colombia
FABIÁN, her cousin, who joins the sisters and Ingrid in their quest to disinter Nono

Ingrid Rojas Contreras's second book and first memoir, *The Man Who Could Move Clouds* (2022), is many things: a history of her mother's family and her own immediate family, specifically a history interested in the many ways her mother's family taps into the mystical as healers in Colombia; an account of her struggles following a bike accident that left her with temporary amnesia that sometimes reoccurs years later; and an exploration of the unseen side of human experience. Told through chapters that bounce between timelines, Rojas Contreras's story is as interested in how a family's

Ingrid Rojas Contreras

history informs its present as it is in all of the details that add up to make a life, never discounting how much those small moments, like a conversation between mother and daughter across borders, matter or how the effects of violence take possession of one's body without one seeing it happen. Seamlessly moving from 2000s and 2010s United States—during which Rojas Contreras is an adult living in Chicago and San Francisco—and 1940s–90s Colombia—during which the stories of her grandparents and parents, as well as her own and her sister's early lives, are described in poignant detail—*The Man Who Could Move Clouds* reveals the mystery that is there to be discovered in every small moment.

The Man Who Could Move Clouds opens simply, with Rojas Contreras providing the reader with an overview of herself and her family and a recounting of the bouts with temporary amnesia both she and her mother had experienced in their lives. When her mother, as a young child, fell down a long well and remained in a coma for several weeks, she awoke with gifts that allowed her to see ghosts and hear voices, making her an invaluable addition to her father's business as a healer. Rojas Contreras herself also relates experiencing a period of post-amnesia dreaming, after which her aunts eagerly await any reports about her own gifts that may have come from the jarring event of her own accident, but she does not have them. She additionally uses this moment to introduce the reader to the extreme violence that surrounded her family in Bogotá and the efforts they took to escape when their family became the target of kidnappings when she and her sister, Ximena, were young girls. Following this introduction, Rojas Contreras skillfully lets each chapter introduce a deeper aspect of the story. The reader learns about Rojas Contreras's grandfather, Nono, a healer who traveled through the Colombian countryside for months at a time, leaving his wife at home to care for their growing family while he committed infidelities. They also learn about the gifts that have been passed down through the family for years. In one chapter, "The Well," the story of her accident is braided with her mother's and the mystical occurrences around each. In a series of chapters in the memoir's second section, titled "Exhumation," Rojas Contreras recounts the story of her birth, the early days of her parents' marriage, and the death of her grandfather. Always circling back, she creates something of a whirlpool effect through her structure, giving the reader larger pieces of the puzzle before swirling back into the past, illuminating each story with greater detail.

Two of the book's greatest strengths include its rich cast of characters. Though Rojas Contreras is at the center of this story, the reader is made to understand that she is nothing without the pieces she has received from those who came before her, particularly her mother. Because of the richness and humanity of these characters, including her grandfather, grandmother, various aunts and uncles, cousins, and parents, the tension around the magical happenings in her family and in Colombian culture at large is more profound. Positioning her family within the lens of colonialism and recounting the steps taken by the Spanish when they arrived in South America to convert people to Catholicism by torture or any other means necessary, Rojas Contreras is able to make this piece of her family's history—the tradition of healers and the danger the family faces as a result of this practice—as important as any other. Rojas Contreras herself vacillates between belief and skepticism, sometimes taking her father's side of science and, at others, taking in the wonder of her mother's world. The family is split, with her sister and father as nonbelievers in her mother's family's ways. Rojas Contreras is often at the center, wanting to believe but leaning in their direction. However, around every corner is a new ghost—her mother often summoned spirits to babysit Rojas Contreras and her sister when her parents went out—a new vision carrying the family forward in some way, a new warning meant to protect. For example, ahead of Rojas Contreras's bike accident, which happens as she is running an errand to pick up a new silk black dress she has had altered, her mother calls her, warning her daughter that this dress will make her a widow. Rojas Contreras recounts that although the dress did not make her a literal widow, it did make her dead to herself for a period as she tried to piece back together who she was. During a moment of reflection later on, Rojas Contreras remembers being in her apartment surrounded by the swaths of silk that made up her dress, which in turn created a black circle around her, one similar in appearance to the dark hole her mother fell down as a young girl.

The driving plot line of the memoir is the family's secret plan to exhume the body of Nono, who has come, in dreams, to Rojas Contreras, her mother, her Tía Perla, and a few other family members, requesting to be moved. The plan must be kept secret from others, despite the fact that Rojas Contreras and her mother are planning to spend three months in Colombia to complete the task. This plot opens up the family's story, told to Rojas Contreras by family members. Long nights spent hatching the plan in backyards in Colombia melt into tales involving Nono. For example, his daughters recount his funeral. One of Nono's special gifts was the ability to move clouds, in addition to his skill as an entrepreneur despite being illiterate. At his funeral, a single rain cloud appears over his grave as the service is taking place, shocking his family, who look around at the bare sky above the rest of the graveyard. Since his death, his grave has become a pilgrimage site for family and townspeople who ask him for favors. This, the sisters believe, is the reason he wants to be moved: to be released from the responsibility of performing tasks and miracles for the living. Each piece of the plan has appeared in the dreams of one of the family members called to perform the exhumation, leading them to the final resting place for his ashes. Even here, Rojas Contreras's struggles with belief add a beautiful tension as she listens to the stories of her family and dedicates herself to the plan, even though she does not feel these gifts herself.

The Man Who Could Move Clouds, which became a finalist for the National Book Award for Nonfiction, was positively received by critics overall for its thought-provoking musings on the interrelated impacts of stories, family, politics, and history.

Writing for the *New York Times*, Miguel Salazar noted that though the memoir could feel thin at times when dealing with themes of colonialism and Colombian history, Rojas Contreras's control of the oral history told vis-à-vis her family makes for an exciting prospect. Salazar wrote, "Contreras has forced into the public record a collective identity of clairvoyants and spiritualists—beginning with Nono—that she has pieced together from the disintegrating fragments of her own familial past. In the process, she has written a spellbinding and genre-defying ancestral history." The anonymous *Publishers Weekly* reviewer praised the author's engaging writing style, calling her prose "mesmerizing" and the book itself a "lyrical meditation," while noting that it contains a powerful message about the importance of remembering and understanding the past. Similarly, in a review of the book for *BookPage*, Priscilla Kipp described Rojas Contreras's writing as "enchantingly poetic" and lauded her ability, through this memoir, to make the history of her family and her country "more immediate and personal."

Author Biography
Ingrid Rojas Contreras is the author of the 2018 novel *Fruit of the Drunken Tree* and the memoir *The Man Who Could Move Clouds* (2022). Her work has been featured in a variety of publications.

Melynda Fuller

Review Sources
Boshier, Rosa. "'The Man Who Could Move Clouds' Is a Memoir Full of Magic. Review of *The Man Who Could Move Clouds*, by Ingrid Rojas Contreras. *The Washington Post*, 11 Aug. 2022, www.washingtonpost.com/books/2022/08/11/ingrid-rojas-contreras-memoir-review/. Accessed 4 Jan. 2023.
Chaffa, Mandana. "Temporality and Memory in *The Man Who Could Move Clouds*." Review of *The Man Who Could Move Clouds*, by Ingrid Rojas Contreras. *The Ploughshares Blog*, 12 July 2022, blog.pshares.org/temporality-and-memory-in-the-man-who-could-move-clouds/. Accessed 4 Jan. 2023.
Kipp, Priscilla. Review of *The Man Who Could Move Clouds*, by Ingrid Rojas Contreras. *BookPage*, 12 July 2022, www.bookpage.com/reviews/man-who-could-move-clouds-ingrid-rojas-contreras-book-review/. Accessed 17 Jan. 2023.
Review of *The Man Who Could Move Clouds*, by Ingrid Rojas Contreras. *Kirkus*, 20 Apr. 2022, www.kirkusreviews.com/book-reviews/ingrid-rojas-contreras/the-man-who-could-move-clouds/. Accessed 4 Jan. 2023.
Review of *The Man Who Could Move Clouds*, by Ingrid Rojas Contreras. *Publishers Weekly*, 15 Apr. 2022, www.publishersweekly.com/9780385546669. Accessed 4 Jan. 2023.
Salazar, Miguel. "Descended from Shamans and Ghost Whisperers." Review of *The Man Who Could Move Clouds*, by Ingrid Rojas Contreras. *The New York Times*, 6 July 2022, www.nytimes.com/2022/07/06/books/ingrid-rojas-contreras-the-man-who-could-move-clouds.html. Accessed 4 Jan. 2023.

Mean Baby
A Memoir of Growing Up

Author: Selma Blair (b. 1972)
Publisher: Alfred A. Knopf (New York). Illustrated. 320 pp.
Type of work: Memoir
Time: 1972–the present day
Locales: Detroit, Michigan, and environs; New York City; Southern California

Selma Blair's debut as a writer, Mean Baby: A Memoir of Growing Up, *is the story of her life so far, which reveals much previously unknown information surrounding her development as a person and growth as an actor.*

Principal personages
SELMA BLAIR, the author, a film and television actor
MOLLY ANN COOKE, her mother, a judge
ARTHUR SAINT BLEICK, her son, born in 2011
ELLIOT BEITNER, her father
MIMI, her sister
LIZZIE, her sister
KATIE, her sister
JAMES TONER, an English teacher who encouraged her to try acting
AHMET ZAPPA, son of musician Frank Zappa, her husband 2004–06
JANA KOGEN, her agent
JASON BLEICK, a clothing designer, Arthur's father

The author of *Mean Baby: A Memoir of Growing Up* (2022) is a bona fide celebrity. An actor, Selma Blair began appearing on large and small screens in the mid-1990s and has worked almost constantly in her chosen profession ever since. By the turn of the twenty-first century, she had hit her stride as a regular (as Zoe Bean) on the television series *Zoe, Duncan, Jack & Jane* (1999–2000), and she had given featured performances in such popular films as *Legally Blonde* (2001) and *Hellboy* (2004). As an actor, she forged friendships among some of the biggest names in the industry. Along the way, she also acquired a reputation for sometimes bizarre behavior, often attributed to binge drinking. *Mean Baby* does not deny nor excuse such issues but concentrates more on discussing the reasons behind her actions, which are founded in factors over which she has had no control. As the author notes, "We are all in search of a story that explains who we are.... We are made not only by the stories we tell ourselves but by the tales of others—the stories they tell us, and the stories they tell about us."

Blair's sincere, entertaining, anecdotal, and frequently humorous story begins, as memoirs generally do, with her birth. In the first of three parts, readers learn she was raised in Jewish traditions in a suburb of Detroit, Michigan, from the time she was born in 1972. She was the youngest of four daughters born to Molly Ann Cooke, a beautiful, ambitious, fashionable woman who "could be simultaneously affectionate and hurtful." (Upon requesting to know what was on the menu for dinner, she relates that her mother would sometimes answer with "poison.") Though many in her life came to refer to her as "mean baby," reportedly on account of the judgmental looks she seemed to adopt from the outset, the latest arrival in the household, in fact, had no formal name during her first several years of life, other than "Baby Girl Beitner."

Selma Blair

Tracing her behavior as a child, Blair theorizes that this lack of identification might partially have accounted for her occasional mean streaks, such as the desire to bite someone, a practice continued from childhood into adulthood. She was eventually, at preschool age, named Selma (Bat Sheva, "battlefield," in Hebrew) after a late friend of her mother. "Blair" ("helmet of god," in Hebrew) was added in honor of a Michigan politician and judge.

Despite such early drawbacks, Blair details that she adored her mother and wished to be like her. As a child, she adopted her mother's habit of using alcohol as a "salve." In Blair's particular case, she used alcohol to quell the strange leg pains, fevers, depressions, and other mysterious, troubling physical and mental sensations she began experiencing as a young girl. (The possibility that she was suffering from multiple sclerosis, a condition that affects the brain and spinal cord and can cause a multitude of physical symptoms, is presented early and referred to throughout the memoir.) She got drunk for the first time, on Passover wine, at age seven. There would be many further episodes of intoxication.

Part 1, "Signs," is peppered with lines that demonstrate the author's observational skills, such as this: "We play the parts we are given. We become the stories that are told about us. . . . As adults, we pull our childhoods with us wherever we go." Or, this statement: "Adults are just like you, but older." The first section follows Blair through Hebrew school into prestigious Cranbrook Kingswood High School, where she resisted the inappropriate advances of a school administrator. At the same institution, an English teacher first suggested she should audition for a school play, and she was ultimately cast as a lead in T. S. Eliot's *Murder in the Cathedral*.

The second part, "Questions," continues Blair's story through higher education (at Kalamazoo College and the University of Michigan) and her emergence as an actor. Though the section highlights her professional advancement, it also details her significant personal retreats and is considerably downbeat for a star on the rise. She describes becoming more devoted to alcohol—"I didn't drink for attention; I drank to disappear"—following injuries sustained in a horse riding fall, and several brutal sexual assaults perpetrated while she was intoxicated. She attempted suicide for the first time during this period. Beginning to consult psychics, she was told, "You will have a horrible disease and will die a horrible death." An eye doctor mentioned she had optical neuritis, a nerve inflammation symptomatic of a serious, chronic condition. She went into rehab for the first, but not the last, occasion.

At the same time, Blair continued working to become an actor. She took acting classes in New York for college credit before moving there upon graduation. While workshopping scenes, she was noticed by agent Jana Kogen, who signed her and sent her out on auditions. After numerous auditions, she landed her first professional role on a children's television series in 1995, and soon she was cast in a feature film. Upon the advice of her agent, she headed west to California. There, she met and befriended numerous individuals who would become influential in her career—the late Carrie Fisher, Sarah Michelle Gellar, Reese Witherspoon, Claire Danes, Jake Gyllenhaal, Kate Moss, Britney Spears, and many others. She attended parties alongside guests like George Lucas, Michael Keaton, Robert Downey Jr., Meg Ryan, and David Duchovny. She graced the cover of Vanity Fair in an Annie Leibovitz portrait session and was the first female actor to make the cover of Italian Vogue. At the age of thirty-two, she married (in a ceremony conducted at Fisher's house) musician Frank Zappa's son, Ahmet; by the time she was thirty-four, they had divorced.

The third part of *Mean Baby*, "Answers," covers Blair's life during the decade of the 2010s. This section focuses on chronicling two major events in the author's life. First, is the birth (after around thirty-seven hours of labor) of her son, Arthur Saint Bleick, in 2011, which gave her new purpose. The second is her deteriorating physical condition—characterized by confusion, short-term memory loss, exhaustion, numbness and frequent falls, and an increasing reliance on alcohol (including a highly publicized incident in which she passed out aboard a commercial airliner). Finally, in 2018, her medical issues were properly diagnosed as multiple sclerosis and subsequently treated, providing hope for the normalization of her future life.

Critical reaction to *Mean Baby* was overwhelmingly positive and often centered around Blair's authoritative ability to describe deeply personal, painful experiences and struggles while maintaining a relatable, often lighter, and even optimistic tone. Frances Ryan, writing for the *Guardian*, noted that the memoir was "written with warmth and candour" and called attention to Blair's "self-awareness, wit and charm," admitting, "I laughed out loud more than I cried." In a review for the *Los Angeles Times*, Jessica Ferri agreed with that assessment, deeming Blair "a talented writer" and declaring *Mean Baby* "no frothy celebrity memoir." Likewise, Jennifer LaRue, writing for the *Washington Post*, described Blair's memoir as "intensely self-aware and cheerfully self-revealing" and pointed out the author's "chatty, confiding tone" that makes readers feel as though they are spending time with a "smart and, yes, slightly bratty new friend."

Despite the general acclaim for *Mean Baby*, there were a few gently critical comments, mostly related to errors that beginning writers typically commit. One such is an internal flaw in the text that no reviewers mentioned or commented about: the tendency, especially in the memoir's later stages, to fall back on tired cliches—"scared to death," "watch like a hawk"—rather than devising fresh similes and metaphors to make comparisons, as though the author's fully charged battery with which her story began had been drained of energy. The unnamed critic providing a review for Kirkus, for example, praised the "sharp, memorable account . . . that will have wide appeal to both fans and general readers alike" but also mentioned that the narrative "occasionally meanders." The wandering narrative is the result of an episodic, rather than a strictly chronological, approach to the biographical information presented that is, overall, still engaging and effective if, at times, a bit distracting. The reviewer for the New York Times, Susan Burton, expanded upon a shared perceived flaw that the memoir's middle section, which dwells upon the author's relocation to Southern California and its aftereffects, sags somewhat in comparison to the rest of the book. "Once Blair makes the cross-country move," Burton wrote, "her book loses some of the spell cast by the early section." This is a valid objection, since Part 2 consists largely of brief scenarios in which Blair interacts in various ways with a succession of name-dropped fellow celebrities. The real benefit of this section is in the revelations about the character of individual stars exhibited in their relationships with her. Most are shown to be sympathetic, kind, generous, and quite forgiving about the author's sometimes outrageous behavior, even before its origin was finally determined and publicly announced.

These are fairly minor quibbles about a memoir that must be deemed courageous for its willingness to expose less-than-flattering truths about the author's periodic lack of control, especially given the high social standards constructed around and placed upon Hollywood celebrities. Blair admits not only to alcohol abuse but also to incontinence as well as bouts of being unable to walk or speak. Her initial effort at writing demonstrates an ability to recognize dramatic situations and the verbal skills to describe them for the edification and entertainment of others. *Mean Baby* seems like it could be the first chapter in what could be a distinguished writing career unfolding alongside her acting performances.

Author Biography
Actor Selma Blair accumulated multiple screen credits and earned critical praise for her work since landing her first professional acting role in the mid-1990s. *Mean Baby: A Memoir of Growing Up* is her first full-length published book.

Jack Ewing

Review Sources
Burton, Susan. "When It Comes to Labels, Selma Blair Will Write Her Own." Review of Mean Baby: A Memoir of Growing Up, by Selma Blair. *The* New York Times, 15 May 2022, www.nytimes.com/2022/05/15/books/review/mean-baby-selma-blair.html. Accessed 30 Oct. 2022.

Ferri, Jessica. "Review: What Selma Blair's Memoir Has to Teach Us All about Self-Medication." Review of Mean Baby: A Memoir of Growing Up, by Selma Blair. Los Angeles Times, 3 June 2022, www.latimes.com/entertainment-arts/books/story/2022-06-03/review-what-selma-blair-memoir-has-teach-us-all-about-self-medication. Accessed 30 Oct. 2022.

LaRue, Jennifer. "Selma Blair Shares Stores of Abuse and MS, but She Doesn't Want Pity." Review of *Mean Baby: A Memoir of Growing Up*, by Selma Blair. *The Washington Post*, 15 May 2022, www.washingtonpost.com/books/2022/05/15/selma-blair-memoir/. Accessed 30 Oct. 2022.

Review of Mean Baby: A Memoir of Growing Up, by Selma Blair. Kirkus, 17 May 2022, www.kirkusreviews.com/book-reviews/selma-blair/mean-baby/. Accessed 30 Oct. 2022.

Review of Mean Baby: A Memoir of Growing Up, by Selma Blair. Publishers Weekly, 18 May 2022, www.publishersweekly.com/9780525659495. Accessed 30 Oct. 2022.

Ryan, Frances. "Mean Baby by Selma Blair Review—Negotiations with Adversity." Review of Mean Baby: A Memoir of Growing Up, by Selma Blair. The Guardian, 5 July 2022, www.theguardian.com/books/2022/jul/05/mean-baby-by-selma-blair-review-negotiations-with-adversity. Accessed 30 Oct. 2022.

The Memory Librarian
And Other Stories of Dirty Computer

Authors: Janelle Monáe (b. 1985), Alaya Dawn Johnson (b. 1982), Danny Lore, Eve L. Ewing, Yohanca Delgado, and Sheree Renée Thomas
Publisher: Harper Voyager (New York). 336 pp.
Type of work: Novel
Time: Near future
Locale: Little Delta; Freewheel

The Memory Librarian and Other Stories of Dirty Computer is a literary extension of lead author Janelle Monáe's 2018 album and short film, Dirty Computer. *In five short stories by Monáe and five coauthors, gender nonconformists resist the memory standardization efforts of New Dawn, a totalitarian regime in an Afrofuturistic dystopia.*

Principal characters
SESHET, the Director Librarian and loyal employee of New Dawn
JANE 57821, a rebel who is committed to empowering and rescuing women from New Dawn's control
RAVEN, a nursing student trying to juggle love, employment, and her academics while not drawing attention from New Dawn
AMBER, a college student who feels responsible for holding her family together following her mother's experiences with New Dawn
BUG, a young artist who lives in Freewheel

By design, *The Memory Library and Other Stories of Dirty Computer* centers characters who are Black, queer, trans, and nonbinary. Marked as social deviants by the ruling New Dawn organization, the protagonists in each of the five stories in the collection resist the regime. Though it is not exactly clear who or what New Dawn is or are, members identify as both human and artificial intelligent agents that operate as mechanisms of control within the totalitarian state. As Leah von Essen said in her review for *Booklist*, "Monáe and her five collaborators paint a picture of a technocapitalist dystopia ruled by an organization that monitors the memories of its populace. While the New Dawn erases the memories of 'deviants' to create a standardized future, underground, gender-nonconforming rebels fight back by remembering, sharing, storytelling, and creating."

Janelle Monáe (Courtesy HarperCollins Publishers)

The Memory Library begins with its namesake, a short story by Alaya Dawn Johnson and Monáe. In this story readers are introduced to the city of Little Delta and the main characters Seshet and Alethia 56934, a trans woman. The number following Alethia's name is an indication of a checkered past. Seshet on the other hand, is the Director Librarian of the Little Delta Repository within the New Dawn and not only adheres to the laws of the land, but she also plays a vital role in upholding the expectations of the dystopian world's governance. Those who refuse to conform to these expectations are referred to as "dirty computers" by the New Dawn and their misbehavior is met with physical attacks, imprisonment, and memory erasure. In quick succession Seshet must grapple with her identity as director librarian and as a woman who may be willing to engage in risk and resistance for a woman she believes she has just met. "The Memory Librarian" raises questions about the way memories shape experiences and identity, which memories are permitted and by whom, and which memories are wiped clean.

"Nevermind," coauthored by Danny Lore, is the second story in *The Memory Library*. The story takes its title from Nevermind, a gas the New Dawn deploys to cleanse dirty computers of their souls and memories. Building upon the first story, "Nevermind" gives readers a rich understanding of the Little Delta's underworld and humanizes its inhabitants through the story of Jane 57821, one of several dirty computers and rebels who live outside the authority of New Dawn at the all-female commune known as the Pynk Hotel. Through colorful and engaging descriptions readers learn the ways in which the residents of the Pynk Hotel fight for survival and seek to protect one another physically, while also protecting their access to create and consume art by allowing creative freedom that harken back to the days of old. Who controls content consumption, who defines clean, what is clean enough, and how thin is the line between current events and memories are all questions for readers to reflect on.

"Timebox," the third short story in *The Memory* Library, is coauthored by Eve L. Ewing. Raven is a nursing student who recently moved into a new apartment with her girlfriend, Akilah. Although they are New Dawn residents, the state does not play a prominent role in their story. While unpacking and settling into their new shared space, Raven discovers that the pantry in their kitchen has an unexplainable relationship with time. Not trusting her instincts because she knows she is exhausted, she enables Akilah to experience this phenomenon as well. The women agree to keep this information private until they determine what is best for them as well as what may benefit the masses. Akilah does not necessarily uphold her end of the bargain and decides it would be best if they went public with this magical pantry. The story explores the value of time, the best way to use it, and whether it is best measured by quantity or quality.

The fourth short story in *The Memory Librarian*, coauthored by Yohanca Delgado, is "Save Changes." In this story we meet sisters Amber and Larissa (Larry) whose mother, Diana, was part of a rebellion when the New Dawn captured her and wiped her memory—and her interest in life—clean. Prior to his passing, the girls' father gave Amber a stone that possessed the power to reverse time. With the stone around her neck, Amber was committed to protecting her family and ensuring they maintained a low profile. Larry, on the other hand, believes life is for the living and parties with others who are not afraid of New Dawn. Eventually, when Larry convinces Amber to venture out and live a little, the sisters join free-spirited revelers at a party to remember. This story urges readers to think about how often they wish to turn back time, but also poses the question of whether they would really do so if they could.

The Memory Librarian wraps up on a perfect high note with "Timebox Altar[ed]," coauthored by Sheree Renée Thomas. A pleasant read that focuses on four young people and the role of hope in their lives, the story takes place in Freewheel, an area that is mostly unpatrolled by New Dawn. The four children have survived countless challenges including, but not limited to, parental imprisonment, parental death, poverty, and hopelessness. Through the art of Bug, the youngest of the four, they are gifted a glimpse into the future through magic and imagination. It will be up to them to retain these memories and work to understand how memories can be futurist, not only past tense.

In April 2022, *The Memory Librarian* debuted to stellar reviews and as a New York Times Best Seller. Critics celebrated this book for its creativity in general and especially for the way it not only centers, but celebrates, LGBTQ, feminine, nonbinary, and Black characters predominantly in five short, speculative, futurist tales. Each story has a way of leading readers down a road of self-reflection and planning for their futures. As is the case with most well written texts, readers may find themselves with more questions than answers. Unfortunately, a few of the questions may not be about personal journeys; rather they are about the characters, plot and other details left ambiguous in *The Memory Librarian*. In a review for the *New York Times*, Stephen Kearse states "Science fiction has historically—and often unfairly—been mocked for investing more brainpower into explaining elaborate systems than fleshing out the people who live within them, but 'The Memory Librarian' fumbles both pursuits. There's so little explanation of the basic mechanisms of New Dawn's rule that the downtrodden main characters are deprived of agency and nuance." Be that as it may, this is a book of hope and joy in the most unlikely of places. As Edward Segarra wrote for *USA Today*, "By reframing aspects of social life and identity, which can often feel convoluted and heavy, in a heightened, dystopian context, Monáe reveals the simplicity of our shared humanity. 'The Memory Librarian' shows us the future can be an unnerving reflection of our unexamined vices, but we can also plant the seeds for a brighter tomorrow."

Though the stories are not necessarily page turners and some of the characters could have been better developed, *The Memory Librarian* is absolutely a book that elicits both joy and hope. As the genre of science fiction continues to expand in its representation of Black characters and diverse plots, it is a respectable leap into the world of literature by Monáe, who continues to live out of this world, seemingly without fear or boundaries.

Authors' Biographies
Janelle Monáe is a Grammy Award–nominated singer-songwriter, actor, producer, and founder of the Wondaland Arts Society record label. Their albums include *The ArchArachnoid* (2010), *The Electric Lady* (2013), and *Dirty Computer* (2018). They have appeared in the films *Moonlight* (2016), *Hidden Figures* (2016), *Harriet* (2019), and *Antebellum* (2020). *The Memory Librarian* is their first book.

Alaya Dawn Johnson's first novel, *Racing the Dark*, was published in 2007. *The Summer Prince* (2013), her debut YA novel, was long listed for the National Book Award for Young People's Literature, while her second YA novel, *Love Is the Drug* (2014) won the Nebula for Best Young Adult Novel. She is also the author of the novel *Trouble the Saints* (2020) and the story collection *Reconstruction* (2021), among others.

Danny Lore is a queer, Black writer from Harlem. A noted writer and editor who works across several mediums such as novels, comic books, podcasts, they have had their short fiction published by FIYAH, Podcastle, Fireside, Nightlight, and EFNIKS.com. Their five-issue comic series, *Queen of Bad Dreams*, was published in 2019.

Sociologist, cultural organizer, and award-winning writer Eve L. Ewing is an associate professor at the University of Chicago. She is the author of *Electric Arches* (2017), a collection of poetry, essays, and visual art; *Ghosts in the Schoolyard: Racism and School Closings on Chicago's South Side* (2018), nonfiction; *1919*, Afrofuturist poems that explore the 1919 Chicago Race Riot; *Maya and the Robot* (2021), a children's novel; and Marvel Comics' *Ironheart* series (2020), among others.

Yohanca Delgado is a Wallace Stegner Fellow (2021–23) and a National Endowment for the Arts recipient (2022). Her work has been published in anthologies, including *Best American Short Stories* 2022, *The O Henry Prize Stories* 2022, and *The Best American Science Fiction and Fantasy 2021*, as well as *The Paris Review*, *One Story*, *Story*, *Time*, and the *New York Times Magazine*. She is an assistant fiction editor at *Barrelhouse*, a 2021 Emerging Critic at the National Book Critics Circle, and a member of the inaugural Periplus Collective mentorship program.

Sheree Renée Thomas is the bestselling and award-winning author of the hybrid collections *Shotgun Lullabies*, (2011) and *Sleeping Under the Tree of Life* (2016); the prose collection *Nine Bar Blues: Stories from an Ancient Future*; and the Marvel novel adaptation *Black Panther: Panther's Rage* (2022). She is also the editor of two World Fantasy Award–winning anthologies, *Dark Matter: A Century of Speculative Fiction from the African Diaspora* (2000) and *Dark Matter: Reading the Bones* (2004).

LaShawnda Fields

Review Sources

Essen, Leah von. Review of *The Memory Librarian and Other Stories of Dirty Computer* by Janelle Monáe, Alaya Dawn Johnson, Danny Lore, Eve L. Ewing, Yohanca Delgado, and Sheree Renee Thomas. *Booklist*, 1 Mar. 2022, www.booklistonline.com/The-Memory-Librarian-And-Other-Stories-of-Dirty-Computer/pid=9758542. Accessed 23 Jan. 2023.

Kearse, Stephen."Janelle Monáe's Queer, Afrofuturist Literary Debut". Review of *The Memory Librarian and Other Stories of Dirty Computer* by Janelle Monáe, Alaya Dawn Johnson, Danny Lore, Eve L. Ewing, Yohanca Delgado, and Sheree Renee Thomas. *The New York Times*, 19 Apr. 2022, www.nytimes.com/2022/04/19/books/review/janelle-monae-the-memory-librarian-and-other-stories-of-dirty-computer.html. Accessed 23 Jan. 2023.

Miller, Stuart. "'I Knew There Were More Stories to Tell': Why Janelle Monáe Returned to Writing Sci-Fi." Review of *The Memory Librarian and Other Stories of Dirty Computer*, by Janelle Monáe, Alaya Dawn Johnson, Danny Lore, Eve L. Ewing, Yohanca Delgado, and Sheree Renée Thomas. *Los Angeles Times*, 21 Apr. 2022, www.latimes.com/entertainment-arts/books/story/2022-04-21/i-knew-there-were-more-stories-to-tell-why-janelle-monae-turned-to-sci-fi-stories. Accessed 23 Jan. 2023.

Segarra, Edward. "The Memory Librarian: Janelle Monáe Tackles Technology and Queerness in Afrofuturist New Book." Review of *The Memory Librarian and Other Stories of Dirty Computer*, by Janelle Monáe, Alaya Dawn Johnson, Danny Lore, Eve L. Ewing, Yohanca Delgado, and Sheree Renée Thomas. *USA Today*, April 2022, www.usatoday.com/story/entertainment/books/2022/04/19/janelle-monae-takes-us-to-future-with-the-memory-librarian/9505644002/. Accessed 23 Jan. 2023.

Memphis

Author: Tara M. Stringfellow
Publisher: The Dial Press (New York). 272 pp.
Type of work: Novel
Time: 1937–2003
Locale: Memphis, Tennessee

Memphis, set against the backdrop of a city in flux, follows the story of a family of strong Black women. The characters contend with troubled relationships and internal struggles, as well as events of world-changing significance, as they attempt to survive—and even thrive.

Principal characters

JOAN, an aspiring young artist who suffers a childhood trauma
MYA, her bright and sensitive younger sister
MIRIAM, her strong-willed mother
JAXSON, a.k.a. Jax, her father, who serves in the military
AUGUST, her aunt, who runs the most popular hair salon in the area
DEREK, her troubled cousin
MISS DAWN, a wise, elderly woman
HAZEL, Miriam and August's mother
MYRON, Hazel's doting husband, a police officer
MAZZ, Jaxson's friend and fellow military man
BIRD, Jaxson's twin brother
STANLEY, the kindly German Jewish immigrant who runs the local deli

Memphis (2022), the debut novel from poet and former lawyer Tara M. Stringfellow, could be considered a bildungsroman of sorts—while it follows some of its individual characters as they grow and mature, the book also traces the journey of a whole family, the Norths, as it evolves through three generations. The perspective changes from chapter to chapter, with the narrative voice alternating between Hazel, the matrilineal head of the clan; her daughters, August and Miriam; and Joan, one of Miriam's two daughters. Joan's chapters are told in first person, a technique that serves to position her as the book's central figure without detracting from the insight gleaned into the other characters. The time frame also fluctuates, with chapters set, in an unchronological fashion, in select years stretching between 1937 and 2003.

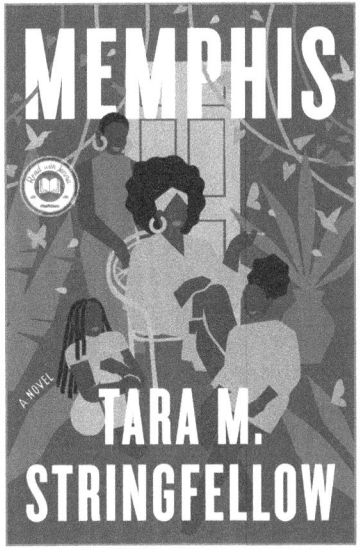

In the early pages of *Memphis* it is 1995, and Miriam has decided to escape her moody and volatile husband, Jaxson (generally known as Jax), a Marine. The reader discovers in subsequent chapters that the impetus for her escape occurs after she angers him by wearing a gold dress and red shoes to a military ball at which all of the other spouses, per tradition, are wearing black or white gowns, and he becomes physically abusive. She flees the North Carolina military base where they live, along with her daughters, Joan, then ten years old, and Mya, who is seven, headed for her childhood home in Memphis.

Miriam's family house in Memphis had been built by her father, Myron, the area's first Black police detective. The reader later learns that he was later lynched by his White colleagues, leaving Hazel widowed and his unborn daughter without a father. Although he had been a responsible family man who unquestionably doted on his wife, some reviewers characterized Myron as the first in the book's long list of men who have let down their families in some way.

Tara M. Stringfellow

The lovingly landscaped house is now home to Miriam's aunt August, who runs a popular hair salon in the rear of the building, and her troubled adolescent son, Derek. Derek's presence makes the house a less-than-perfect refuge for Miriam and her daughters. The reader soon discovers that during a visit when Joan was a toddler, Derek had physically traumatized her. A sensitive and artistically gifted young girl, Joan remains emotionally traumatized by the incident, which has also driven an additional wedge between Miriam and Jax, who blames his wife for not better protecting their daughter. Still, with few other options for housing and Memphis itself exerting a strong pull, Miriam remains there. She and August carefully delineate boundaries, and Joan and Mya never venture into their cousin's territory. The families are forced, however, to share the kitchen, and communal dinners are a source of bitter tension until the late 1990s, when Derek is arrested.

The murder of Hazel's husband, Miriam's abuse at Jax's hands, and Joan's traumatic experience in childhood are far from the only trials and tribulations suffered by *Memphis*'s characters. Many of their troubles stem from simply being Black in the United States. Hazel, for example, was born in 1921, according to a helpful family tree included in the book, and she was subject to all the racism and injustice that growing up in the Jim Crow South entailed. In one particularly chilling scene from when she is a young girl, she acts defiantly in front of a White police officer and is forced to flee from his threat of violence. Later, as she is working in her mother's dressmaking shop, Myron bursts in to propose to her, and a White patron becomes hysterical at the presence of a Black man, casting a pall on what should have been a wholly romantic moment. Later yet, as a newlywed, she visits the police station where Myron works and is automatically assumed to be posting bail for an incarcerated male she knows.

Persevering through obstacle after obstacle, the widowed Hazel ultimately becomes a nurse and instills in Miriam and August a staunch belief that they should never count on a man to survive. When August's desire to attend college is derailed by the need to care for an increasingly troubled Derek, she instead launches a beauty parlor that develops into a pivotal meeting spot for her neighborhood's Black female residents. When Miriam is forced to earn her own living after leaving North Carolina, she struggles, like her mother, to graduate from nursing school, often falling asleep on a stack of textbooks. Her drive to attain a practical job with which to support her daughters makes it difficult for her to understand Joan's desire to become an artist. She is much more simpatico with Mya, who has an enviable affinity for science and aims to attend medical school. Joan, however, finds something of an escape from her childhood trauma in sketching everything around her, from the butterflies that flit around the porch of her house to the hands of Miss Dawn, an elderly local woman respected for her sagacity and good advice.

Memphis itself functions, intriguingly, almost as a colorful character in its own right throughout the book. Through Stringfellow's writing, the reader watches it change from the bucolic locale where Myron built a home and planted its yard with his own hands to a place fighting a scourge of brutal violence. Readers learn, as well, of the city's rich history and role in the civil rights movement. Hazel, working as a nurse by the mid-1960s, witnesses the mangled bodies of the two garbage collectors whose accidental deaths led to a pivotal strike for better conditions and compensation for Black sanitation workers. The strike drew the support of Martin Luther King Jr., who arrived in Memphis for the first time in March 1968 and the following month went on to give the now-iconic speech in which he declared, "I've been to the mountaintop." Memphis was also the site of his assassination the following day.

Such attention to time and place helped *Memphis* generate considerable advance buzz and incite a bidding war among multiple publishers, reportedly landing Stringfellow a high advance—an impressive feat for a writer who had previously published only poetry. Some sources contended that Stringfellow's own compelling background was responsible for some of the publishing world's excitement. Hazel was inspired by her own grandmother, one of the first Black nurses in Memphis, and Myron was drawn from her grandfather, a World War II veteran who went on to become the first Black homicide detective in Memphis. Like Myron, he was killed by his own unit, and his death was covered as a murder by several local Black papers.

Memphis became a national best seller and drew largely laudatory reviews. Many critics admired Stringfellow's adroit juggling of themes both tragic and joyful—mirroring the way in which the characters contend with those themes in their own lives. "Storytellers often pair beauty with trauma as if they are two sides of the same coin. Stringfellow manages to avoid those trappings while also separating Blackness from trauma, two things also too often paired and fetishized in pop culture and media," Aaron Coats wrote in an assessment for the *Chicago Review of Books*. "She highlights the importance of acknowledging Black beauty as it exists on its own, and how it prevails in the face of adversity." In a review for the *Washington Post*, Ron Charles also praised the author's ability to wrestle with dichotomy, noting that Stringfellow "has a lush, romantic style that's often the only counterweight to the grim details of her story."

An occasional critic quibbled with some of Stringfellow's choices but ultimately found the logic and wisdom behind them. Charles, for example, wrote, "The novel's scrambled chronology initially feels like a challenge, but the chapters are clearly dated and named as they move to focus on a grandmother, her daughters and her grandchildren. Readers will come to see that Stringfellow is demonstrating the erratic movements of history, the false starts and reversals and, yes, the moments of progress that are reflected in our haphazard march toward realizing King's vision for America." Similarly, Kia Corthron, reviewing the book for the *New York Times*, concluded that despite some flaws, *Memphis* serves as a "rhapsodic hymn to Black women" that is well worth reading.

It was also commonly noted that *Memphis* is, poignantly and fittingly, dedicated to one young witness to that haphazard march of progress. In a poetic message to Gianna Floyd, the daughter of George Floyd, a Black man who was killed by Minneapolis police officers in 2020, setting off widespread protests, Stringfellow begins by writing, "i wrote you a black fairy tale / i understand if you not ready." Continuing, she notes, "just fine this book ain't going / nowhere this book gon be right here / whenever you want it."

Author Biography

A Fulbright Fellowship semifinalist and former attorney, Tara M. Stringfellow has also written poetry. Her work has appeared in a variety of forums, including *Women Arts Quarterly Journal*, *Collective Unrest*, and *Jet Fuel Review*. *Memphis* is her debut novel.

Mari Rich

Review Sources

Charles, Ron. "*Memphis* Traces Decades of Black Americans' Trauma and Triumph." Review of *Memphis*, by Tara M. Stringfellow. *The Washington Post*, 12 Apr. 2022, www.washingtonpost.com/books/2022/04/13/memphis-tara-stringfellow-book-review/. Accessed 19 Jan. 2023.

Coats, Aaron. "Visions of Black Beauty in *Memphis*." Review of *Memphis*, by Tara M. Stringfellow. *Chicago Review of Books*, 24 June 2022, chireviewofbooks.com/2022/06/24/visions-of-black-beauty-in-memphis/. Accessed 19 Jan. 2023.

Corthron, Kia. "*Memphis* Is a Rhapsodic Hymn to Black Women." Review of *Memphis*, by Tara M. Stringfellow. *The New York Times*, 5 Apr. 2022, www.nytimes.com/2022/04/05/books/review/memphis-tara-m-stringfellow.html. Accessed 19 Jan. 2023.

Hankin, Tara M. Review of *Memphis*, by Tara M. Stringfellow. *BookPage*, 5 Aug. 2022, www.bookpage.com/reviews/memphis-tara-m-stringfellow-book-review/. Accessed 1 Feb. 2023.

Kramer, Pamela. Review of *Memphis*, by Tara M. Stringfellow. *Bookreporter*, 14 Apr. 2022, www.bookreporter.com/reviews/memphis. Accessed 19 Jan. 2023.

Mannion, Una. "*Memphis*: Honours the Strength, Creativity and Resilience of Black Women." Review of *Memphis*, by Tara M. Stringfellow. *The Irish Times*, 9 Apr. 2022, www.irishtimes.com/culture/books/memphis-honours-the-strength-creativity-and-resilience-of-black-women-1.4839061. Accessed 19 Jan. 2023.

Moon Witch, Spider King

Author: Marlon James (b. 1970)
Publisher: Riverhead (New York). 656 pp.
Type of work: Novel
Time: Nearly two hundred years ago–the narrative present
Locale: The North lands, the South lands

The second volume in the Dark Star Trilogy, Moon Witch, Spider King *traces the life of Sogolon, the titular Moon Witch, from girlhood through the events of the preceding novel.*

Principal characters

SOGOLON, a.k.a. Moon Witch, the protagonist, who possesses a strange power she refers to as "wind (not wind)"
MISS AZORA, the operator of a brothel in Kongor
MISTRESS KOMWONO, a noblewoman who takes Sogolon into her household
KEME, a marshal in the Fasisi Red Army and a lion shapeshifter, later Sogolon's lover and the father of her children
YÉTÚNDE, Keme's first wife and the mother of his eldest children
KWASH KAGAR, Kwash Moki, and Kwash Dara (a.k.a., the Spider King), kings of the North lands
THE AESI, chancellor to the kings of the North lands, a powerful being with the ability to alter memories
EMINI, a princess and the sister of Kwash Moki
THE BOY, the rightful heir to the throne of the North lands
LISSISOLO, a princess, the sister of Kwash Dara, and the mother of the Boy
NSAKA NE VAMPI, a bounty hunter, Sogolon's great-great-granddaughter, and a conspirator in the plot surrounding the Boy
BUNSHI, a water sprite and a conspirator in the plot surrounding the Boy
THE TRACKER, Mossi, the Leopard, Fumeli, Sadogo, and Venin, Sogolon's companions in the search for the Boy

Published in 2022, *Moon Witch, Spider King* is the second book in Marlon James's Dark Star Trilogy, a fantasy series launched in 2019 with the acclaimed novel *Black Leopard, Red Wolf,* a finalist for the National Book Award. That earlier novel book tells the story of a man named Tracker who, following a number of hardships, embarks on a quest through a fantastical version of Africa in search of a missing boy of great importance. His companions in that quest include shapeshifters, mercenaries,

Marlon James

and a woman named Sogolon, also known as the Moon Witch, who is shown to possess strange powers but about whom little else is revealed. With *Moon Witch, Spider King*, James shifts the reader's focus to Sogolon herself, uncovering a personal history and complex motivations of which Tracker, with his limited perspective and deeply held preconceptions of both women and witches, would have been largely unaware.

Moon Witch, Spider King begins more than a century prior to *Black Leopard, Red Wolf*, when Sogolon is a young girl living with three older brothers. Blamed for killing their mother in childbirth and causing their father's subsequent insanity, she is imprisoned in a termite mound and subjected to a great deal of abuse throughout her childhood. After plotting her escape for some time, Sogolon succeeds in escaping her family and is soon found by the brothel operator Miss Azora, who takes her to a brothel in the city of Kongor. She later joins the household of Mistress Komwono, a wealthy noblewoman who has lived in Kongor since being exiled from the city of Fasisi on the order of the king's sister, Jeleza. While in Mistress Komwono's household, Sogolon comes to realize that she possesses an unusual magical power, a pushing force that she begins to refer to as "wind (not wind)." She initially has little control over this power, as she discovers when she accidentally kills Mistress Komwono's husband after he attacks her.

Following the death of her husband, Mistress Komwono is summoned back to Fasisi, and Sogolon joins the party traveling to the city. Their journey is overseen by a man named Keme, a marshal in one of Fasisi's armies, in whom Sogolon takes an interest. Upon arriving in Fasisi, the group encounters Emini, daughter of the ailing king, Kwash Kagar, and her brother, the crown prince Likud. The most formidable power in the city is the Aesi, the king's chancellor, who is believed to have been an eternal presence in the kingdom; no one can remember where he came from or when he assumed his position, nor can anyone recall a time before his arrival. Under Kwash Kagar and the Aesi's rule, the fear of witchcraft has become rampant in Fasisi, and many women have been accused of witchcraft and killed. To help locate witches, the crown has brought in a Sangoma, or witch finder, and his Sangomin companions, a group of children with an array of strange, magical gifts. Such children, referred to as mingi children in *Black Leopard, Red Wolf*, will be familiar to readers of that earlier novel, in which Tracker raises a group of mingi children as his own. The Sangomin of *Moon Witch, Spider King*, however, are nothing like the persecuted innocents that Tracker encounters. Rather, they are deadly menaces who run amok in Fasisi, harming the city's residents and facing little resistance. Perhaps even more disturbing is the fact that no one in Fasisi remembers Jeleza or acknowledges that Kwash Kagar ever had a sister; yet, one of the city's greatest military commanders wears a marriage necklace despite having no wife, and he calls for Jeleza in his sleep.

As both Sogolon and the reader discover, the Aesi possesses the ability to alter minds and erase memories of specific people, a power he has used to subvert the traditional line of succession in the North Lands. Traditionally, each king's heir was the firstborn son of his eldest sister, the King Sister, rather than one of his own children. With Jeleza erased from existence, the throne instead passes to Likud, who takes on the name of Kwash Moki following his father's death. As Sogolon is able to resist the Aesi's mind-altering power, she remains aware that something is amiss even after joining the household of the princess Emini, who does not remember Jeleza but, as sister of the new king, does remember her rightful role in the line of succession.

Soon Emini is banished from the city, and Sogolon joins her on the journey toward the nunnery at Mantha, a facility where men of the royal family have long sent women they wished to be rid of. As they travel to Mantha, however, the Sangomin children attack the caravan and kill all but Sogolon, who fights back against the attackers. She is later found by Keme, who, because of the Aesi's powers, no longer remembers her or the slain princess. With nowhere else to go, Sogolon moves into Keme's home, where he lives with his wife, Yétúnde, and their children. Over time, she integrates into the household and begins a relationship with Keme, who had been hiding his identity as a lion shifter. She bears him several children, some of whom inherit his shapeshifting abilities. She likewise hones her fighting skills, participating in competitive donga fights under the identity of No Name Boy.

Although the ordinary people of Fasisi forgot Sogolon upon her departure for Mantha, the Aesi did not, and he attacks her home after realizing that she is still alive. She uses her wind (not wind) to kill him, but his defeat will not be a permanent one: as Sogolon later learns, the Aesi is a godlike being who will be reborn eight years after each time he is killed. Twelve years after his rebirth, he will "reset the world," causing all those who remember his past incarnation to forget him and enabling his return to the post of king's chancellor. Though immune to the Aesi's direct mental manipulation, Sogolon is not immune to the reset, and she forgets about the Aesi for many years following an unsuccessful attempt to kill him after his rebirth. During those years she establishes her reputation as the Moon Witch, a champion of women and an enemy of predatory men. After many years, a group of conspirators recruit Sogolon as a participant in their plan to restore the traditional line of succession to the North. The plan hinges on the survival of a child born to Lissisolo, Kwash Dara's King Sister, who has herself been exiled to Mantha. Following the birth of Lissisolo's child, known only as the Boy, the group seeks to hide him from Kwash Dara and the Aesi until he can safely assume the throne.

It is not until part four of *Moon Witch, Spider King* that Sogolon's story intersects with the events of *Black Leopard, Red Wolf*. After the plan to protect the Boy goes very wrong, Sogolon joins a group of searchers tasked with finding him, Tracker among them. Recounting the search and its aftermath from a new perspective, the novel not only sheds light on Sogolon's actions during periods of the narrative in which the companions are separated but also provides an alternative understanding of Tracker.

Sogolon describes him as a "boy who don't realize he still just a boy" and at times criticizes him for his limited understanding of the forces at work in their world. The intersection of *Moon Witch* and *Black Leopard* is also interesting as the more than one hundred years of historical context leading up to this point demonstrates how the events of Sogolon's early life have led to the present circumstances and how the world of the series has changed over the course of Sogolon's lifetime. Likewise apparent is the extent to which some things—namely, the Aesi's hold over the North and its kings—have remained the same throughout that period. As Sogolon tells an inquisitor near the end of the novel, Tracker "don't even know that this tale is not just bigger than him, but one hundred seventy and seven years older." Thanks to Sogolon, however, the reader is aware of this historical context and has a fuller understanding of both the world James has created and the threat the novel's most frightening beings may pose to it.

Reviews of *Moon Witch, Spider King* were largely positive, with many critics commenting approvingly on the novel's contributions to the Dark Star Trilogy as a whole. The anonymous reviewer for *Publishers Weekly* described the work overall as "brilliant," while the critic for *Kirkus* described James's take on the fantasy genre as "deeper and more profoundly innovative" than that of most other writers and characterized Sogolon's narrative voice as "witty, richly textured, and musically captivating." In a review for *NPR*, Alex Brown described the novel as "a rare sequel that is better than the first" and expressed particular appreciation for the ways in which Sogolon navigates the patriarchal society in which she lives and challenges the misogyny of the novel's other characters, including Tracker. Writing for *Locus*, Gary K. Wolfe likewise praised the character of Sogolon, noting that she "turns out to be a much fuller, more expansive character than Tracker ever was." Some reviewers critiqued elements of the novel, including its pervasive violence, and *Guardian* reviewer Anthony Cummins noted that the work can at times become confusing due to "James's relaxed attitude to (for example) using three different names for the same character in a single paragraph." However, Cummins identified the series' narrative arc as a compelling one, writing that "anyone who stays the course through all this probably won't want to miss the final instalment to come."

Author Biography
Marlon James is the author of several critically acclaimed, award-winning novels, including the *Black Leopard, Red Wolf* (2019), a New York Times Best Seller and finalist for the 2019 National Book Award, and *A Brief History of Seven Killings* (2014), winner of the 2015 Man Booker Prize and the Anisfield-Wolf Book Award for fiction, among other honors.

Joy Crelin

Review Sources

Brown, Alex. "*Moon Witch, Spider King* Is a Rare Sequel That Is Better Than Its Predecessor." Review of *Moon Witch, Spider King*, by Marlon James. *NPR*, 15 Feb. 2022, www.npr.org/2022/02/15/1080058279/moon-witch-spider-king-is-a-rare-sequel-that-is-better-than-its-predecessor. Accessed 31 Oct. 2022.

Cummins, Anthony. "*Moon Witch, Spider King* by Marlon James Review – The Lion, the Witch and the Lost Child." *The Guardian*, 28 Feb. 2022, www.theguardian.com/books/2022/feb/28/moon-witch-spider-king-by-marlon-james-review-the-lion-the-witch-and-the-lost-child. Accessed 31 Oct. 2022.

Ivey, Eowyn. "Marlon James's Moon Witch Tells Her Side of a Haunting Story." Review of *Moon Witch, Spider King*, by Marlon James. *The New York Times*, 14 Feb. 2022, www.nytimes.com/2022/02/14/books/review/marlon-james-moon-witch-spider-king.html. Accessed 31 Oct. 2022.

Review of *Moon Witch, Spider King*, by Marlon James. *Kirkus*, 30 Nov. 2021, www.kirkusreviews.com/book-reviews/marlon-james/moon-witch-spider-king/. Accessed 31 Oct. 2022.

Review of *Moon Witch, Spider King*, by Marlon James. *Publishers Weekly*, 17 Dec. 2021, www.publishersweekly.com/9780735220201. Accessed 31 Oct. 2022.

Wolfe, Gary K. Review of *Moon Witch, Spider King*, by Marlon James. *Locus*, 18 Feb. 2022, locusmag.com/2022/02/gary-k-wolfe-reviews-moon-witch-spider-king-by-marlon-james/. Accessed 31 Oct. 2022.

Moth

Author: Melody Razak
Publisher: Harper (New York). 368 pp.
First published: *Moth*, 2021, in Great Britain
Type of work: Novel
Time: February 1947–December 1948
Locales: Delhi, India

Moth, an intensely dramatic work of historical fiction, vividly depicts the life of one Brahmin family before and after the violent partition that established India and Pakistan as two independent nations in 1947.

Principal characters

ALMA, the protagonist, eldest daughter of a Brahmin family
ROOP, her younger sister
BRAHMA, a.k.a. Bappu, her father, a professor at Delhi University
TANISI, a.k.a. Ma, her mother, a professor at Delhi University
DAADEE MA, her grandmother, Bappu's mother
FATIMA BEGUM, Roop's ayah, who is Muslim
COOKIE AUNTIE, a.k.a. Lakshmi, her wealthy, liberated aunt; Bappu's twin sister
DILCHAIN-JI, the family's cook

Melody Razak's first novel, *Moth*, is a graphic and deeply intimate portrayal of a family living through the upheaval wrought in conjunction with the August 1947 Partition of India, the sudden ending of British rule of the Indian subcontinent, which was divided into the independent states of majority-Hindu India and majority-Muslim Pakistan. Spanning the period between February 1947 and December 1948, a time of sectarian violence and mass displacement of people across the subcontinent, *Moth* casts light on the ways Indian women's vulnerable status worsened during Partition. In so doing, the novel suggests a truth that extends beyond India, that women holding less power and lower status than men experience the most egregious suffering and loss during times of chaos, lawlessness, and societal breakdown. Religious traditions, cultural expectations, issues of caste, ethnicity, and gender all figure significantly alongside sectarian politics in shaping this family story, which is by turns sweet, humorous, and horrifying.

After a chilling prologue describing an impending infanticide, the novel opens into the nighttime serenity of Pushp Vihar, the House of Flowers, the estate of a high-caste Hindu family at the center of the novel. The eldest daughter, fourteen-year-old Alma, is preoccupied with thoughts of her upcoming marriage to a twenty-two-year-old stranger, and with the eruptions of political and social unrest which fuel the family's daily conversation. She and her five-year-old sister, Roop, lie in their bed having a conversation that reveals their naïve understanding of both marriage and the ethnic conflict which has not yet arrived on their doorstep. In the safety and comfort of their home, they blithely discuss what they've heard and what they imagine about warring factions, torture, and murder until they drift off to sleep.

With this simplistic dialogue reflecting the innocence of the children, Razak sets a bit of context that portends a devastating unraveling of family and homeland stability. It is February 1947 in Delhi, and Alma's privileged family is living on the edge of devastation as the British and Indian leaders devise a plan to divide power among Hindus and Muslims and end the three-hundred-year-old British Raj. Alma's parents, Bappu (Brahma) and Ma (Tanisi), are both university professors. They follow the news of unrest closely and discuss it openly. On their campus, the rising tensions lead to hot-tempered verbal clashes among faculty and in classrooms. That these arguments have led to the resignations of Muslim faculty is troubling to Bappu and Ma, who hold progressive views and value the diversity of perspectives on the faculty. These troubles, like the incidents they hear about that occur in the streets, have them living with the unsettling knowledge that their family, like India itself, is in the grip of something monstrous. Life in the household continues with everyone doing what they are accustomed to doing, for it seems that carrying on the familiar keeps panic at bay. The intense alertness and contained fear are palpable on each page of the first part of the book and foreshadow the occurrence of terrible events to come.

Razak's characters, the majority of whom are women, are fully dimensional, believable, and consistent with their historical moment, place and culture. Their richly detailed backstories are constructed seamlessly so that they facilitate rather than suspend or interrupt the storyline. Each character's motivations, actions, emotions, and words realistically reflect her age, caste, culture, and how each might see herself as a girl or woman of her background and station. Presenting these characters as a collective reveals a mosaic of female life in India during the period. Though Razak's focus on the ways the women expressed deep caring or utter disregard for each other across lines of difference is set in a particular time and place, it invites the reader to consider the durable power that gender- and class-based cultural conditioning wields in any place and time, even as social structures crumble. As their society slides into chaos, it becomes painfully clear that all the women of the Pushp Vihar household, Brahmin and lower caste alike, are subject to abuse. The servants Dilchain-ji and Fatima Begum are beloved and protected by all the family members except for Alma's grandmother,

Melody Razak

Daadee Ma, who strictly upholds the rules of caste and commits grievous betrayals in the name of family honor.

The novel is divided into three parts, following Alma's journey from the safe and protective home she has known all her life to a sudden and brutal end of innocence. The tension builds continuously across the three parts of the novel as the characters respond to the disturbing unfolding of events.

Part 1 of the novel introduces the quiet but apprehensive daily life of a household sharing worries about current events and preparing for Alma's marriage, which has been arranged by Daadee Ma. Her parents are reluctant to marry her off while she is still a child but agree to it hoping that being married will give Alma added protection in India's uncertain and dangerous state. Bappu and Ma anxiously lament the political decisions being made by the departing British in collaboration with Indian leaders who are at odds about how to assure fairness in the distribution of power. As Partition becomes the inevitable outcome of the fraught decision-making process, Brahma grows increasingly distraught at the idea of dividing the country. He wonders how anyone could put boundaries on the complex mixture of tribes, cultures, and languages comprising the richness that has for centuries been the very definition of India. By the end of part 1, Alma's wedding plans have fallen through, and she boards a train to leave her family and join her aunt in Bombay.

In part 2, Pushp Vihar is no longer a sanctuary, and the family is overwhelmed. Food and supplies are dwindling. They are worried about Alma as they await her arrival in Bombay, the streets full of bloody havoc and their home regularly invaded by soldiers. As Bappu ventures out into the street to secure provisions for the household, he is confronted with a reality that he has only followed in the news. His utter shock at seeing it and being in it dazes him. He loses himself momentarily, and the reader is suddenly reminded of Bappu's privilege. Razak's prose is simple, clear, and visceral in considering his moment of disorientation and in telling a truth about the world beyond him. Razak also displays an impressive ability to tell big truths through a small story. This part of the book is action-filled, describing how the family witnessed and reacted to the horrific scenes and events in the days after the partition was put in place. The feel of the narrative shifts as the pace slows somewhat in the final part of the novel as Alma's story unfolds, and the reader learns of the extreme trauma she suffers.

The chapters of *Moth* are titled with dates to indicate what is happening within the family against the backdrop of a country literally coming apart. Frightfully momentous events wreak disaster for the family and for India within a contracted period of a few months. Millions of people were uprooted from their ancestral homes, and millions were killed in the violence between ethnic and religious groups. The chapters are not dated in a straightforward, evenly distributed timeline of events, however. Instead, some chapters cover weeks or months, while others cover only one day as the story wends through and around intimate moments in family life, protests, and brutality in the streets of Delhi, times of abject fear and desolation within and beyond the family, refugee camp scenes, and Alma's long and terrifying ordeal.

The narration is rich in graphic and redolent detail throughout each part of the novel, allowing the reader to sense the bloody chaos, tumult, and sheer terror produced by the conditions in India during this time—murder in the familiar streets of the city, beatings, the disappearances and displacement of millions of people, and the savage brutality against women. This mayhem comes horrifyingly alive all through what one family learns, witnesses, feels, and experiences firsthand.

Long-listed in 2022 for the UK's prestigious Desmond Elliott Prize, *Moth* was praised highly by critics, and the *New York Times* placed the novel on its list of the best works of historical fiction of 2022. Hephzibah Anderson, reviewing *Moth* for the *Guardian*, was impressed with Razak's focus on the violence against women as both historically accurate and currently relevant. She and other reviewers further praised Razak's skill with characterization. Bethany Latham, reviewing the novel for *Booklist*, called Razak's characterization "remarkable" and gave a nod to the skill with which the author anchored the novel in its setting using sensory references. The reader can well imagine through superbly crafted description what the characters experience through the senses. A *Kirkus* reviewer referred to *Moth*'s characters as "richly drawn," mentioning that Razak had been inspired by a BBC audio series that featured firsthand accounts of Indian people who witnessed the events leading up to and following Partition.

Writing about *Moth* for *BookBrowse*, Kim Kovacs praised the characterization in the novel as "stellar" in creating memorable portrayals. Kovacs further stated that the portrayal of the tension and trauma of Partition is an admirable element of the novel. Kovacs' review, though overwhelmingly positive, did complain that some of the scenes of Alma's naïveté had no purpose and slowed the novel's pace. The same review included a warning for "sensitive readers" about the graphic violence in the novel.

A *Publishers Weekly* reviewer praised *Moth* as an unhurried, brilliant tale, evocatively set. Shrestha Saha's review for the *Telegraph Online* attributed *Moth's* cultural authenticity to Razak's extensive travel in India, during which she absorbed "language, culture and the beat of the country" that is so reliably represented in the novel. Saha offered an explanation for the novel's title by relating the author's experience of discovering that the prized pashmina scarves she had collected over years of travel in India had been eaten by moths and disintegrated in her hands when she picked them up. This falling apart reminded her of Partition and the words of Mohammed Ali Jinnah, political leader of Pakistan, who referred to his new nation as "moth-eaten," for its internal, geopolitical divisions.

Author Biography
Melody Razak is a British Iranian writer. Prior to writing her debut novel, *Moth*, she was a café owner who decided in her forties to return to college to pursue an MFA degree in creative writing at Birkbeck University. Her short stories have been published in the *Mechanics Institute Review*, *Bath Short Story Award 2019* anthology, and *Brick Lane Short Story Prize Longlist 2019* anthology.

RoAnne Elliott

Review Sources

Anderson, Hephzibah. "*Moth* by Melody Razak Review—The End of Innocence in India." Review of *Moth*, by Melody Razak. *The Guardian*, 25 July 2021, www.theguardian.com/books/2021/jul/25/moth-by-melody-razak-review-the-end-of-innocence-in-india. Accessed 15 Dec. 2022.

Kovak, Kim. "A Stunning Debut Novel about a Hindu Family's Experience before and after India's Partition." Review of *Moth*, by Melody Razak. *BookBrowse*, 21 Sept. 2022, www.bookbrowse.com//mag/reviews/index.cfm/book_number/4511/moth. Accessed 15 Dec. 2022.

Latham, Bethany. Review of *Moth*, by Melody Razak. *Booklist*, 1 July 2022, p. 27. *Literary Reference Center Plus*, search.ebscohost.com/login.aspx?direct=true&db=lkh&AN=158170127&site=lrc-plus. Accessed 24 Feb. 2023.

Review of *Moth*, by Melody Razak. *Kirkus Reviews*, 15 June 2022, n. pag. *Literary Reference Center Plus*, search.ebscohost.com/login.aspx?direct=true&db=lkh&AN=157380769&site=lrc-plus. Accessed 24 Feb. 2023.

Review of *Moth*, by Melody Razak. *Publishers Weekly*, 6 June 2022, p. 30. *Literary Reference Center Plus*, search.ebscohost.com/login.aspx?direct=true&db=lkh&AN=157247303&site=lrc-plus. Accessed 24 Feb. 2023.

Saha, Shrestha. "All about Melody Razak's Debut Novel *Moth*." Review of *Moth*, by Melody Razak. *The Telegraph Online*, 30 Dec. 2022, www.telegraphindia.com/culture/books/all-about-melody-razaks-debut-novel-moth/cid/1829824. Accessed 30 Dec. 2022.

Mother Noise

Author: Cindy House (b. ca. 1967)
Publisher: Marysue Rucci Books (New York). Illustrated. 240 pp.
Type of work: Memoir
Time: 1970s to the present
Locales: New Haven, Connecticut; Chicago, Illinois; San Francisco, California

Mother Noise is a memoir about writer and artist Cindy House's experiences with addiction as well as her life in recovery as a mother.

Principal personages
CINDY HOUSE, the author
ATLAS, her young son
DAVID SEDARIS, her writing mentor and friend, a popular essayist

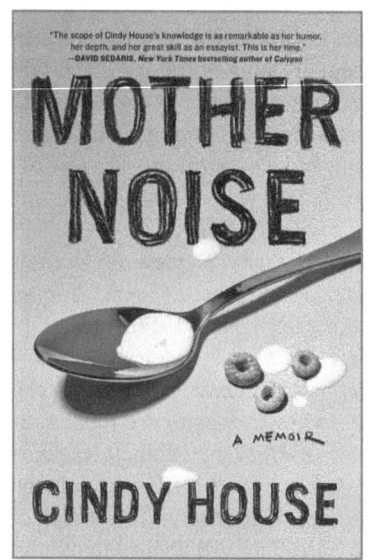

For fans of the humorous essayist David Sedaris, the name Cindy House may be a familiar one.

A former student of Sedaris's back when he was teaching writing classes in 1980s Chicago, House stayed in touch and maintained a friendship with her mentor over the years as he went from obscurity to literary superstardom. Eventually, he invited her to be the opening act of his popular book tour readings.

By reading House's debut book, *Mother Noise* (2022), it becomes clear why Sedaris believes her writing to be a worthy companion to his own. Brimming with sharp observations and raw honesty, it harkens the arrival of an important literary voice. Through its collection of essays, the memoir tells the story of House's adult life and the dual forces that have come to define it: being a mother to her son, Atlas, and recovering from heroin addiction. House alternates back and forth, writing about each of these two parts of her identity and often using their intersection as a lens to examine her present life. The end result is a poignant meditation on parenthood in recovery.

The focus on parenting in recovery is not the only reason *Mother Noise* is an important addition to the canon of literature on the subject of addiction, however. Much of what makes it so compelling stems from the fact that it is an inspirational tale. From the book's first pages, House clarifies that she is more than twenty years sober and that, after struggling with heroin addiction for seven years, she was able to get clean and slowly rebuild her life. The fact that she was able to come back after hitting her rock bottom to eventually have a happy, healthy son who is thriving and achieve her dream job is likely to give hope to readers who are former addicts and anyone else who has

Cindy House

survived a destructive life event and worries that things can never get better.

This is not to say that House ever makes recovery look easy. Throughout the memoir, it becomes clear that the emotional and physical baggage from addiction never completely disappears. In one essay, she mentions how she tried to hide the scars on her arms from some more judgmental mothers in her community. In another, she relates how she let a severe jaw pain fester for too long because she did not want to undergo any treatment or procedure that could require painkillers, possibly putting her at risk for relapsing. More than anything, however, she worried about telling nine-year-old Atlas that she was once an addict because she believed it would cause him "sorrow." In the first essay, "After the Telling," House states that she knew, in 2017, that she would have to tell him the truth about her past soon, and the question of how and when she would do so hangs over the subsequent essays, eliciting the compelling feeling in the reader that she wrote them to understand her addiction better herself so that she could explain it to him when the time was right.

The essays themselves cover a wide timeline, from House's childhood to her twenties as an addict to her forties as a mother. A large part of what makes *Mother Noise* such an interesting read is the way that House pushes the stylistic boundaries of what a memoir can be. Most of the essays are quite short and many can be categorized as works of engaging experimental nonfiction. In "Self-Storage," for example, she intersperses snippets from her old storage unit's lease and overdue notices with descriptions of the different items she was keeping in there and their significance. Because each item is a token of a specific person or memory from her past, these descriptions succeed in furthering the memoir's larger goal of providing readers with insight into who she used to be when she was abusing drugs. Meanwhile, "I'm Here to See David Sedaris" chronicles the evolution of her decades-long relationship with her mentor in reverse—beginning with House opening for a Sedaris book reading in 2019 and then working backward to the first time he ever introduced himself as her professor in 1987. In addition to offering entertaining details about what it is like to be friends with Sedaris, the piece explains how his unwavering belief in House as a writer helped her survive the darkest days of her addiction.

There are other aspects of House's writing that contribute to the memoir being a work of experimental nonfiction. For example, rather than moving in a seamless, chronological order like chapters, the essays jump around in time and can recount anecdotes that often seem out of place or random. That said, House ensures that every piece in the book ties back into its central themes of motherhood or addiction in some way. Perhaps the most stylistically unique aspect of *Mother Noise* as a memoir is its inclusion of drawings by House. Some of these are used as illustrations for the written essays while others function as their own story, or "graphic short." Tonally, these feel akin to cartoonist Alison Bechdel's graphic memoir *Fun Home* (2006).

So much of what makes *Mother Noise* engaging is House's capacity for analyzing her past with unfiltered honesty. This strength is especially evident in the essays that examine her life before sobriety—a time that she looks back on in the memoir with the intention of trying to understand why her life's trajectory unfolded in the way that it did. In "Slides," for example, she examines the broad strokes of her childhood to find clues for why she later ended up struggling with drug addiction. Having come from a "normal" family in which her parents provided food, toys, and love for her, she can only guess that she started using heroin because she suffered from crippling depression and anxiety as a young person and no longer wanted to feel anything. Later, in "A Steady Yellow Light," she tries to guess as to why she was able to recover when only "three out of ten addicts survive" and reflects on when she almost killed a pedestrian with her car because she was distracted by a bag of heroin. House posits that if she had hit the person, she would never have been able to get sober, writing, "You do something bad enough, lose your kids out of neglect, burn a house down, sell yourself for drugs, and maybe there isn't enough good left to power through the withdrawal and rebuilding."

House's point in "A Steady Yellow Light" is a poignant one but also highlights where *Mother Noise* might fall short for some readers. Throughout the memoir, House briefly mentions, in passing, several things she believed helped her survive, like Sedaris's belief in her, being institutionalized for depression, or reading Tim O'Brien's *The Things They Carried* (1990) because the book allowed her to see a world that was worse than her own. However, she does not expound much on the fact that she is a White, educated woman who came from a supportive family and how this might have contributed to her success in sobriety. In "The Roof over Our Heads," she touches on this briefly, remarking that the other residents at her rehabilitative housing called her "Princess" because she was White, had clean clothes, and a job waitressing—and that "they weren't wrong" in their assumptions. Although House would start abusing drugs again and get kicked out of that particular program, not examining how her background played into her success in achieving sobriety later is one of the few places she fails to use her trademark, painstaking honesty. It feels like a missed opportunity, especially considering that one of the memoir's best essays is "Street View," in which she does talk about the role that race and socioeconomics played in her addiction days.

In the end, however, it is difficult to fault House for not covering every aspect of her addiction and recovery. More than anything, the memoir is about her identity as Atlas's mother, and being formerly addicted to drugs just happens to be part of that identity. The book was not conceived as a series of think-pieces about the societal issues that surround drugs, but rather the story of her efforts to reckon her past with parenthood, and, when considered in this context, she succeeds brilliantly.

Although reception of *Mother Noise* was overwhelmingly positive, its experimental format was a somewhat divisive point among critics. In an otherwise positive review, the anonymous *Kirkus* reviewer stated that "the book doesn't quite add up to a satisfying whole, as some pieces are too underdeveloped to resonate." Contrarily, Manuel Betancourt wrote, in a review of the book for the *New York Times*, that "'Mother Noise' feels lovingly labored over, expertly whittled and chiseled into its current frank form." These disparate opinions make for an important point about *Mother Noise*—readers who want a beat-by-beat journey of exactly how House discovered heroin, her seven years abusing it, and the recovery process should look to other addiction memoirs. Ultimately, *Mother Noise* is a work of art, an avant-garde collection of stand-alone vignettes and drawings that have been expertly fit together. And while it does not always feel like a memoir, it still succeeds in sharing the truths that House has personally learned in her life about addiction and motherhood.

A large part of what makes *Mother Noise* such a compelling read is its dogged sense of optimism. There are many dark moments in the book—from the time House relapsed for no particular reason, to a series of abusive boyfriends, to her horrific divorce from her first husband, which led to his new wife waging psychological warfare on a young Atlas. The fact that she survived all these things to go on and maintain long-term sobriety makes her story come across as not only one of inspiring resilience but one of particular significance at a time when the opioid epidemic has continued to impact the nation. *Publishers Weekly* touched on the inspirational quality of the book in its review, concluding, "A full-throated anthem of hope, this lends light to a dark issue."

Ultimately, *Mother Noise* is an engaging, moving, and necessary book that pushes the boundaries of the memoir genre. At one point, House argues that stories about the most horrible times in people's lives are important to the survival of others—they help those in similar situations feel less alone while giving others the opportunity to spend time in someone's life worse than theirs, which can provide them with some perspective. In her final essay, House remarks that it took her years to get herself together enough to even tell her story and that, for a long time, she was afraid to tell the truth about her past; however, she writes, "If the opposite of addiction is connection, then a true story can save your life." It is not hard to imagine that the raw, beautiful storytelling of *Mother Noise* will succeed in doing this for many.

Author Biography
Cindy House is a writer of short stories and essays. *Mother Noise* is her debut book.

Emily E. Turner

Review Sources
Betancourt, Manuel. "Three Memoirs That Re-examine Challenges in Life and Identity." Review of *Mother Noise*, by Cindy House. *The New York Times*, 8 July 2022, www.nytimes.com/2022/07/08/books/review/mother-noise-my-seven-black-fathers-this-body-i-wore-cindy-house-will-jawando-diana-goetsch.html. Accessed 1 Feb. 2023.

Review of *Mother Noise*, by Cindy House. *Kirkus*, 1 Feb. 2022, www.kirkusreviews.com/book-reviews/cindy-house/mother-noise. Accessed 2 Feb. 2023.

Review of *Mother Noise*, by Cindy House. *Publishers Weekly*, 24 Feb. 2022, www.publishersweekly.com/978-1-982168-75-9. Accessed 3 Feb. 2023.

The Movement Made Us
A Father, a Son, and the Legacy of a Freedom Ride

Authors: David J. Dennis Jr. (b. 1986) with David J. Dennis Sr. (b. 1941)
Publisher: Harper (New York). 288 pp.
Type of work: Memoir
Time: 1960–64; early 2020s
Locales: United States, primarily Louisiana and Mississippi

The memoir of civil rights leader David J. Dennis Sr., written with his son, journalist David J. Dennis Jr., focuses on the elder Dennis's role in the Freedom Rides and voter registration efforts in Louisiana and Mississippi in the early 1960s. The Movement Made Us: A Father, a Son, and the Legacy of a Freedom Ride *also includes a recounting of the efforts of Dennis and his son to reach an understanding of their relationship and the impact of the father's work on that of his son.*

Principal personages
DAVID J. DENNIS SR., a grassroots activist in the civil rights movement in the early 1960s
DAVID J. DENNIS JR., his son, a journalist
JAMES BALDWIN, his friend, an author and fellow civil rights activist
MEDGAR EVERS, his friend, a fellow civil rights activist
FANNIE LOU HAMER, his friend, a fellow civil rights activist
MICKEY SCHWERNER, a White activist from New York who was killed in Mississippi
JAMES CHANEY, a Black activist from Meridian, Mississippi, who was killed in Mississippi
ANDREW GOODMAN, a White activist from New York who was killed in Mississippi

Though David J. Dennis Sr. and his son, David J. Dennis Jr., were both civil rights activists in their own time, *The Movement Made Us: A Father, a Son, and the Legacy of a Freedom Ride* (2022) largely grew out of a realization by the son that "I loved Dave Dennis. But I didn't know my dad." Born two decades after his father's work in the early 1960s, the younger Dennis grew up with only a vague idea of his father's contribution to the civil rights movement. Thus, the book works to recount David Dennis Sr.'s work as a grassroots organizer for the Congress of Racial Equality (CORE) in Mississippi and Louisiana at the height of the civil rights movement, as well as the story of a father and son struggling to understand each other.

David J. Dennis Jr.

Like soldiers, first responders, and others who have experienced traumatic events, the elder Dennis was reluctant to talk about his experiences in the early 1960s. After meeting other veterans of the civil rights movement, his son learned that his father was a hero in the fight to gain equal rights for Black Americans. Wanting to know more, he convinced his father to participate in interviews about his activities during the civil rights movement, focusing on the years 1961 to 1964, from his first involvement with the movement through the end of the Freedom Summer. David Dennis Jr., the primary author of the book, notes in the prologue that the stories are "told as my father remembers them, the blanks in his memory just as important as the details he can recall with vivid precision." While the younger Dennis admits that some minor details may not be totally accurate, and that direct quotes have been somewhat "polished," he maintains that "the stories are true to my father and felt in our lineage." The book consists of eighteen chapters in which the elder Dennis speaks in the first person about his life and work. Interspersed among these chapters are four letters from the son to his father, which explore the more personal side of their relationship and how working together on the book brought the two men closer.

David Dennis Sr. first became involved in the civil rights movement as a student at Dillard University in New Orleans in 1960. He attended a meeting of CORE simply because he was attracted to one of the women involved with the group. Although she rebuffed his romantic advances, he continued to come to the meetings, intrigued by what he learned though certain that he would never get personally involved. Over time, however, he began working on behind-the-scenes activities—preparing signs for picketers, for example, but not participating in the picketing himself. Eventually, he walked the picket lines at stores that refused to serve Black customers. This led to the first of many brushes with the police and time spent in jail.

In 1961, CORE began organizing "Freedom Rides," in which White and Black riders sat together on interstate bus rides to see whether local authorities would object, considering that the US Supreme Court had ruled such segregation was illegal in 1956. Despite that ruling, those involved in the Freedom Rides, including Dennis Sr., often faced violence from White mobs and brutality from all-White police forces. Initially, Dennis was frightened and dismayed by the violence the riders encountered, but he eventually determined that he was willing to take the risk, recalling "I knew at that moment that I was willing to welcome death with the same passion that I desired freedom." After several months of participating in various CORE protests, Dennis was made head of the organization's office in Baton Rouge, Louisiana. After six months, CORE transferred him to Jackson, Mississippi, to serve as its field secretary. Finding conditions poor in Louisiana, Dennis soon learned they were even worse in Mississippi, and he considered that in going there, he was going to war.

Over the course of his time with CORE, Dennis worked with several key leaders of the civil rights movement, including James Farmer, Martin Luther King Jr., James Baldwin, and Medgar Evers. He eventually became close friends with both Baldwin and Evers, but throughout the book, the focus is often kept on less-famous local people who regularly took great risks to advance the civil rights movement and whose stories have rarely made it into history books. Indeed, a significant strength of *The Movement Made Us* is the account it provides of "boots on the ground" workers in the civil rights movement, the risks they faced, and the tactics they used. Scholars have often argued that the history of the civil rights movement has been distorted by an overemphasis on its major leaders. Dennis himself mentions this in the book's acknowledgements: "For every Bob Moses, Medgar Evers, or Dave Dennis, there should be a woman who is just as recognized and celebrated for what she did for our freedom. If you know Dr. King, you should know Ella Baker. If you know Malcolm X, you should know Fannie Lou Hamer. If you don't, then that's a failure on all our parts."

The story of Dennis's involvement with CORE climaxes with Mississippi's Freedom Summer in 1964. That summer, many young activists traveled to Mississippi, working tirelessly to bring attention to racial inequality experienced by Black residents there. Voter registration drives took place throughout the state. Volunteers also started Freedom Schools, intended to help Black students catch up in math and reading skills and learn more about their heritage. The Mississippi Freedom Democratic Party (MFDP) was organized as well in an effort to contest for the seats of an all-White Mississippi delegation at that year's Democratic National Convention.

Because of the need for additional human resources for all these efforts, CORE decided, after vigorous debate, to invite White volunteers from the North to come to Mississippi. Dennis Jr. devotes an entire chapter to the event that ensued, as New Yorkers Mickey and Rita Schwerner, and later Adam Goodman, arrived in Jackson at Dennis Sr.'s office. The volunteers were genuinely welcomed by many of the Black workers in the movement, but many White people in Mississippi resented their presence. The book recounts the tragic fate of some of these volunteers when, in June 1964, Mickey Schwerner, Goodman, and James Chaney, a Black Mississippian, traveled to Neshoba County, Mississippi, to investigate the burning of a Black church. There, the three men were arrested for speeding, briefly jailed, and then released. However, they soon went missing, and when word reached Dennis in Jackson, he feared they had been killed. After years of investigation, it was found that the three had been murdered by a mob, with the complicity of law enforcement officials, and buried in a levee near Meridian, Mississippi. Several White people were eventually convicted of violating the civil rights of the murdered individuals, but no one was ever convicted of their murder.

Dennis, who was supposed to accompany the men to Neshoba County but was sick with bronchitis, was consumed with guilt, believing he had sent these people to their deaths. Following the murder of his close friend Medgar Evers the previous year, and the ultimate failure of the MFDP to gain serious recognition at the Democratic convention, Dennis seemed to lose heart and soon ended his work with CORE. It was not until much later in his life, in the early 1990s after the birth of Dennis Jr., that he renewed his commitment to working for equality.

In addition to the narrative of Dennis Sr.'s accomplishments in the 1960s, the book also includes the story of his complicated relationship with his son, and how they eventually grew closer by working to recall and understand the historic times the father experienced. The book is all the more powerful because of this facet of the story, but in a memoir, one might expect a broader picture of the Dennis family than is provided here. For instance, Dennis Sr. was married three times, but two of his wives, including the mother of Dennis Jr., are barely mentioned.

Both authors take a fairly radical view of what they see as a widespread and entrenched sense of White supremacy that continued to haunt the United States at the time the book was written. The younger author suggests in one of his letters that the January 6, 2021, insurrection of the US Capitol, when supporters of President Donald Trump tried to interfere with Congress's certification of the election of Joe Biden as the next president, was actually a race riot—though he gives no evidence nor expands on this observation. In a sense, this view of how poor race relations remain in twenty-first-century America may raise an ironic and likely unintended point: If there has been so little progress, then how much did the heroes of the civil rights movement in the 1960s really accomplish?

The Movement Made Us attracted more journalistic attention in news articles and interviews with the authors than in book reviews. Articles and interview transcripts included some analysis of the book, and the comments in these stories were universally positive. Several critics noted the timeliness of the book, in light of the Black Lives Matter movement of the 2020s. As the reviewer for *Kirkus* remarked, the book is "timely in an era of renewed disenfranchisement and an instructive, important addition to the literature of civil rights." Moreover, an unsigned review in *Publishers Weekly* reflected a common theme from many reviews, noting that this book "captures a remarkably intimate and vivid portrait of the human side of the civil rights movement."

Author Biography

David J. Dennis Jr. is a senior writer for *Andscape*, and his work also appeared in publications such as *The Atlantic* and the *Washington Post*. *The Root*, an online magazine focused on Black culture, named him one of the 100 Most Influential African Americans of 2020.

David J. Dennis Sr. has long been involved in the Southern Initiative Algebra Project, a nonprofit seeking to ensure quality education for children of color and other underserved groups in the South, among other organizations fighting for equal rights.

Mark S. Joy, PhD

Review Sources

Bratzler, Ahilah. Review of *The Movement Made Us: A Father, a Son, and the Legacy of a Freedom Ride*, by David Dennis Jr. with David J. Dennis Sr. *Library Journal*, 1 May 2022, www.libraryjournal.com/review/the-movement-made-us-a-father-a-son-and-the-legacy-of-a-freedom-ride-1788145. Accessed 20 Feb. 2023.

Review of *The Movement Made Us: A Father, a Son, and the Legacy of a Freedom Ride*, by David Dennis Jr. with David J. Dennis Sr. *Kirkus*, 25 Feb. 2022, www.kirkusreviews.com/book-reviews/david-j-dennis-jr/the-movement-made-us/. Accessed 5 Jan. 2023.

Review of *The Movement Made Us: A Father, a Son, and the Legacy of a Freedom Ride*, by David Dennis Jr. with David J. Dennis Sr. *Publishers Weekly*, 24 Feb. 2022, www.publishersweekly.com/9780063011427. Accessed 5 Jan. 2023.

Van Atten, Suzanne. "Book Notes: 3 New Books Examine Ongoing Struggle for Emancipation." Review of *The Movement Made Us: A Father, a Son, and the Legacy of a Freedom Ride*, by David Dennis Jr. with David J. Dennis Sr., et al. *The Atlanta Journal-Constitution*, 10 June 2022, www.ajc.com/life/arts-culture/book-notes-3-new-books-examine-the-ongoing-struggle-for-emancipation/UOI6S3XJF-5B7LLVMAVRNAF4ELI/. Accessed 20 Feb. 2023.

My Seven Black Fathers
A Young Activist's Memoir of Race, Family, and the Mentors Who Made Him Whole

Author: Will Jawando (b. 1983)
Publisher: Farrar, Straus and Giroux (New York). 240 pp.
Type of work: Memoir, current affairs, sociology
Time: 1980s–the present
Locales: Maryland; Washington, DC; Lagos, Nigeria

This inspirational memoir by attorney, civil rights activist, and local government leader Will Jawando chronicles how he navigated the pains and triumphs of life as a Black male in the United States with the help of seven Black men who mentored him over the years. His experience also sheds light on broader issues of race, family, and masculinity in society.

Principal personages

WILL JAWANDO, the author and narrator
JOSEPH JACOB, his stepfather
MR. WILLIAMS, his elementary school math teacher and mentor
JAY FLETCHER, one of his mentors, an out gay colleague of his mother
WAYNE (COACH) HOLMES, his high school football coach and choir director
DEEN SANWOOLA, one of his mentors, a Nigerian businessman
BARACK OBAMA, one of his mentors, the forty-fourth president of the United States
OLAYINKA JAWANDO, his biological father, a Nigerian immigrant
KATHY JACOB, his mother
MICHELE JAWANDO, his wife

In his debut book, *My Seven Black Fathers: A Young Activist's Memoir of Race, Family, and the Mentors Who Made Him Whole* (2022), Will Jawando combines personal reflection and research to explore what it means to be a Black male in US society. As the biracial son of a White American mother and a Nigerian father, Jawando is keenly aware that, statistically speaking, his identity came with significant obstacles due to systemic racism. These challenges were further compounded when his father left the family, threatening to make the racist stereotype of the "absent Black father" his reality. Yet, as the book's title suggests, he was able to find guidance and ultimately success in life thanks in large part to his relationships with an array of father figures, rather than just one. As he traces his dreams, aspirations, and pitfalls, Jawando invites the reader on a journey of insightful revelations and emotional highs and lows, introducing the Black men who entered his life at pivotal times and helped him navigate significant milestones while also considering more general social, economic, and political themes. In the introduction, the author explains that "*My Seven Black Fathers* is my love letter to Black men. A missive to remind Black men that your life experience can have a profound and positive impact on the lives of Black boys, notwithstanding the challenges we will endure."

Jawando's world unfolds through a balanced combination of dialogue, vivid descriptions, and astute retrospective observations. After the introduction, the book follows a chronological structure beginning with his earliest childhood memories, giving it a sometimes leisurely tempo. However, the conditions and circumstances he faces are far from easy as he comes of age in an environment rife with uncertainty, poverty, and racism. From the first pages, Jawando shows how being Black pervaded essentially every aspect of his life, including through structural inequality. Equally impactful from a young age was his fraught relationship with his father. Yet the prevailing tone is one of optimism and hope, which is apparent in Jawando's own youthful exuberance and the stabilizing presence of his mother, for example. The book's very structure also signals a theme of redemption: each chapter focuses on one of the Black men who emerged as an influential guiding figure in Jawando's life, starting with his stepfather, Joseph Jacob, and notably concluding with his birth father, Olayinka Jawando. In between are his grade school math teacher Mr. Williams; his mother's colleague Jay Fletcher; his high school coach and choir director Wayne Holmes; Deen Sanwoola, a Nigerian businessman; and President Barack Obama, each of whom is portrayed as a positive example not just for Jawando himself but also for society as a whole.

An underlying theme throughout the book is Black male perseverance in the face of adversity regardless of its origin—individual, familial, environmental, or institutional. The reader will appreciate that despite the challenges and roadblocks Jawando regularly faces, his is not a story of victimhood but of resilience. The narrative focuses not on blame but on compassion, grief, and forgiveness. Instead of shame, it emphasizes faith and healing. Jawando certainly does acknowledge the realities of living with pervasive poverty and racism and demonstrates the toil of systemic oppression using his life experiences and research. But he also illustrates the internal resources he drew upon to persist and how his fathers and others afforded him access to external resources that were meaningful in ways that changed his life trajectory. The overarching message is

Will Jawando

that while there are very real systemic problems with society, there are also concrete actions that individuals can take to at least begin to address them, to the benefit of all.

Another refreshing theme demonstrated in the book is the multidimensional complexity and depth of emotions Black men can and do experience. Jawando introduces the reader to a group of Black men with diverse experiences, feelings, and approaches to racialized gender bias. They are not flawless, but their humanity illuminates his story. Each had a significant intervention in Jawando's life, providing a template and example of how Black men have supported their communities for generations.

Unfortunately, as Jawando notes, Black men are an untapped resource all too often, partly due to overarching negative stereotypes about Black men in the dominant White society underpinned by the legacy of slavery. Decades of mass incarceration and over-policing have significantly reduced the availability of Black men to serve as mentors and role models. Jawando's story asks the reader to critically examine racist tropes of Black male identity and challenge prevailing attitudes that pigeonhole Black men into one-dimensional caricatures of absent fathers. Interestingly, despite being a civil rights activist and local government council member, Jawando does not focus *My Seven Black Fathers* on arguing for large-scale policy changes to address structural racism. Nor does he devote much attention to detailing societal reforms that might help break the grip of structural race- and class-based inequities faced by Black boys and, by extension, Black families and communities. Instead, he mainly emphasizes that by showing up in a child's life with purpose and intention, adults, related or not, can help a child navigate inequities to reach their full potential. This sentiment is expressed on the last page of the book's last chapter, where he writes, "My experience bears out that the members of a child's village don't necessarily need to know one another well or at all to effectively get the job done. How a village of acquaintances and strangers alike can raise a child is through acts, big and small, of kindness and mentorship." Still, through his personal narrative, Jawando does shine a light on racial inequities in the educational system, housing policies, and financial and economic institutions, for example. Therefore, the book holds the potential to inspire readers to advocate for racial equity through systematic change as well as individual responsibility.

The media response to *My Seven Black Fathers* was highly positive. It received a starred review from *Kirkus*, with the anonymous critic describing it as "a beautifully written and innovatively structured memoir of a biracial Black man's life journey." The *Kirkus* reviewer offered particular praise for Jawando's writing style, noting that his "talent for creating striking imagery and memorable scenes draws readers into his masterfully constructed world," and commending the way he "treats his past self with compassion without ever skirting responsibility for his mistakes." *Publishers Weekly* also gave a starred review, with the critic using terms such as "rousing," "brilliant," "vivid," and "stirring" and observing that "this effective combination of the personal and the political acts as a powerful call to action in these fraught times." Andrienne Cruz similarly highlighted the book's social commentary in a starred review for *Booklist*, calling it "a clarion call to families and communities to provide crucial support to young people, particularly young Black men." Joining the chorus of praise, the *Washington Informer* reviewer Terri Schlichenmeyer commented that Jawando compels readers to "sit up and pay attention" and suggested that "it shouldn't be a surprise if *My Seven Black Fathers* might also spur you to mentor a kid, or to somehow get involved in a child's life."

Yet another positive review came from award-winning social critic Ikhide R. Ikheloa (himself a Nigerian immigrant who became a parent in the US, like Jawando's father) in *Open Country Mag*. Ikheloa described the book as "an intimate portrait of a world at once simple and complex, drawn by a good writer with a good eye, who is also quite forgiving." Specifically, he noted that "Jawando's prose exudes quiet confidence. He is adept at immersing the reader in whatever culture he's in; you can taste it. He doesn't pander . . . no footnotes explaining too much." Consistent with other reviewers, Ikheloa recognized the memoir as "a call to action—to understand and confront the evil that is racism, the toll that it takes on everyone, the costly effects on individual, family, and community mental health."

A few critics did have a more measured take on *My Seven Black Fathers*, however. Writing for the *New York Times*, Manuel Betancourt felt that Jawando's effort to speak to broad sociological issues "makes his personal remembrances function at times, for better and for worse, as data points." Along these lines, Betancourt contended that "as a writer, Jawando can seem removed from the scenes he describes. His voice retreats into analytical abstraction at moments when he's at his most vulnerable, producing insightful yet detached lines." Nevertheless, Betancourt concluded that the book ultimately succeeds in connecting Jawando's own life to "urgent cultural conversations about present-day subjects like respectability politics and the dominant narratives of fatherless households." Indeed, readers will likely find that *My Seven Black Fathers* effectively combines memoir and social criticism, starting a conversation that both challenges and inspires.

Author Biography

An attorney, politician, and activist, William Jawando has also served as a cultural commentator and writer whose work has appeared in a variety of outlets, including the *Washington Post* and NPR. *My Seven Black Fathers* is his first book.

Valandra, MBA, MSW, PhD

Review Sources

Betancourt, Manuel. "Three Memoirs That Re-Examine Challenges in Life and Identity." *The New York Times*, 8 July 2022, www.nytimes.com/2022/07/08/books/review/mother-noise-my-seven-black-fathers-this-body-i-wore-cindy-house-will-jawando-diana-goetsch.html. Accessed 4 Dec. 2022.

Cruz, Andrienne. Review of *My Seven Black Fathers: A Young Activist's Memoir of Race, Family, and the Mentors Who Made Him Whole*, by Will Jawando. *Booklist*, 15 Mar. 2022, www.booklistonline.com/My-Seven-Black-Fathers-A-Young-Activist-s-Memoir-of-Race-Family-and-the-Mentors-Who-Made-Him-Whole-/pid=9759130. Accessed 4 Dec. 2022.

Ikheloa, Ikhide R. "*My Seven Black Fathers* by Will Jawando Review—Family, Race, & a Nigerian Son's Quest." *Open Country Mag*, 12 Sept. 2022, www.opencountrymag.com/my-seven-black-fathers-by-will-jawando-review-family-race-a-nigerian-sons-quest/. Accessed 4 Dec. 2022.

Review of *My Seven Black Fathers: A Young Activist's Memoir of Race, Family, and the Mentors Who Made Him Whole*, by Will Jawando. *Kirkus*, 1 Feb. 2022, www.kirkusreviews.com/book-reviews/will-jawando/my-seven-black-fathers/. Accessed 4 Dec. 2022.

Review of *My Seven Black Fathers: A Young Activist's Memoir of Race, Family, and the Mentors Who Made Him Whole*, by Will Jawando. *Publishers Weekly*, 7 Feb. 2022, www.publishersweekly.com/9780374604875. Accessed 4 Dec. 2022.

Schlichenmeyer, Terri. Review of *My Seven Black Fathers: A Young Activist's Memoir of Race, Family, and the Mentors Who Made Him Whole*, by Will Jawando. *The Washington Informer*, 15 June 2022, www.washingtoninformer.com/book-review-my-seven-black-fathers-a-young-activists-memoir-of-race-family-and-the-mentors-who-made-him-whole-by-will-jawando/. Accessed 4 Dec. 2022.

The Naked Don't Fear the Water
An Underground Journey with Afghan Refugees

Author: Matthieu Aikins
Publisher: Harper (New York). 336 pp.
Type of work: Autobiography, current affairs, memoir
Time: 2015–2018
Locale: Afghanistan, Turkey, Greece

In The Naked Don't Fear the Water, *the distinguished foreign correspondent Matthieu Aikins presents a compelling account of his undercover journey on the migrant trail from Afghanistan to Europe with his friend Omar, a former interpreter with the Canadian and United States armed forces in Afghanistan who hoped to escape war and poverty and make a new life in the West. Aikins book is both a tale of danger and survival and a penetrating meditation on the moral, political, and economic crisis resulting from the mass movement of people in a disordered world.*

Principal personages
MATTHIEU AIKINS, the author and a reporter who undertakes an undercover trip from Afghanistan to Europe with his friend Omar
OMAR, a former interpreter with Coalition forces in the Afghan war who decides to escape the conflict by migrating to Europe
MARYAM, Omar's mother
JAMAL, Omar's father
FARAH, Omar's sister
LAILA, the woman Omar loves
HAJJI, a smuggler
NASIM, a leader at a communal hotel in Athens

The Naked Don't Fear the Water by Matthieu Aikins explores one of the most heartrending consequences of decades of war in Afghanistan: the forced migration of refugees to places where they hope to find peace and prosperity. The Afghans are joined by people from Syria and other countries destabilized by war. Their destinations of choice are the United States, Canada, and the European Union. Unfortunately, these countries are at best ambivalent about the masses of people arriving from war-torn countries with few modern job skills and a very different religious and cultural background. The migrants compete with local labor for jobs, raise enrollment in schools and welfare systems, and, because of their numbers, instill fears in some that they are replacing the

Matthieu Aikins

existing population. This discontent ultimately sparked populist and nativist movements that have grown to be politically significant in some countries in the early twenty-first century. The problem became particularly severe in Europe, where most nations did not have a longstanding tradition of assimilating large numbers of immigrants.

Aikins is acutely conscious of the ebb and flow of attitudes towards migrants in a Europe torn between humanitarian sympathy for the victims of brutal wars and cold calculations about the economic and demographic costs of opening borders. He traces the sometimes headspinning evolution of European policy towards the desperate multitudes seeking asylum. After years of European efforts to limit the entry of large numbers of migrants, the border briefly opened in 2015 when a photograph of a three-year-old boy who drowned while his family was making the dangerous voyage from Turkey to Greece was widely disseminated in newspapers and on social media. This led to a change in public opinion, and Germany and Austria soon announced their willingness to accept large numbers of migrants. German Chancellor Angela Merkel announced that Germany possessed the economic strength to take in an indeterminate number of refugees. Crowds at train stations greeted migrants with flowers. Then the mood changed. The numbers of migrants traveling to Europe swiftly increased. An Islamic terrorist attack in Paris that killed a hundred and thirty people involved two men who had arrived as refugees. On New Year's Eve, mobs of migrant men sexually attacked hundreds of women in Cologne. Borders were once again closed, some of them fortified with barbed wire fences. Chancellor Merkel traveled to Turkey to work out a deal subsidizing Turkish help in preventing further overseas migration into Europe. The sympathy aroused by the drowned boy had evaporated. An political cartoon wondering if he would have grown up to be a sex offender reflected the hardening of European attitudes.

As Aikins notes, in the 2020s, 15 percent of the world's population lives in Europe and North America; that same amount possesses more than half of the world's wealth, leading Aikins to refer to the concept of a "citizenship premium," which measures the economic advantage a person enjoys simply by living in one of the privileged nations of the global north. The per capita income of an American is thirty times that of an Afghan. Aikins remarks that a person is likely to be ten times wealthier in Europe or America than in an disadvantaged country and asks his readers to contemplate the global inequalities that are driving the mass movements around the world. He does this very effectively by putting a human face on this phenomenon, telling the story of ordinary individuals caught up in the modern exodus from Afghanistan.

Aikins's narrative begins in Kabul during the fall of 2015, when he decides to join his friend Omar on the long and sometimes perilous journey to Europe. He had known and worked with Omar since 2009. Omar was a former interpreter with the Canadian and American military and had seen bitter combat in the heavily contested southern Afghan province of Helmand. Weary of the service, Omar switched to journalism, and partnered with Aikins as an interpreter, driver, and colleague. By 2015, Omar could see no future in war-torn Afghanistan. The occupation of a northern provincial capital by the Taliban, however brief, was an ominous sign about the direction the conflict was taking. As a former military interpreter, Omar was eligible for a Special Immigrant Visa to the United States. Unfortunately, he had not obtained the requisite paperwork from his employers while he was in service, and now it was too late.

The European Union remained an attractive option. Germany had just opened its border, raising Omar's hopes that he could make a new life there. Aikins planned to accompany Omar by posing as a fellow Afghan migrant. He could do this because he had picked up Dari, one of the languages spoken in Afghanistan, and his physiognomy as the son of a Japanese American mother and a Canadian father made him look like a Hazara, one of the ethnic subsets of the Afghan population. Love delayed Aikins's and Omar's departure. Omar had fallen in love with Laila, the daughter of his family's landlord. The situation was difficult as Omar is a Sunni Muslim while Laila's family are Shia Muslims. The economic gap between Omar's and Laila's families serves as a further complication, with Omar not measuring up to Laila's social standing. An initial marriage proposal was rejected by Laila's parents. Warned, the parents made it virtually impossible for Omar to communicate with Laila, something already difficult enough in a society that erected many barriers around marriageable young women. Omar and Laila were reduced to infrequent communications through intermediary friends. Lovelorn, Omar delayed his departure many months, hoping for a resolution of his romance with Laila, much to the frustration of Aikins, who wanted to get on with the journey and his story. Meanwhile, their trek grew more problematic as European public opinion shifted against migrants, and a failed coup in Turkey led to increased security measures at the doorstep to the continent. Omar finally decided to leave anyway, hoping to bring Laila after him once he was securely established abroad.

The heart of Aikins's book is his account of the winding and wearisome road to asylum in Europe. At times it reads like an adventure story as he and Omar travel through what is effectively hostile terrain and take a wild ride on the Aegean Sea in a motorized rubber dinghy. They deal with a succession of professional smugglers, all, by definition, criminal and sometimes extremely dangerous. Aikins is surprisingly successful in his impersonation, both because of long experience in the Middle East and because decades of war and exile have scrambled the accents of many contemporary Afghans. His narrative captures the soul-crushing alternation between brief moments of excitement and long, fretful periods of waiting. Aikins draws one line during this joint venture; he will only overtly break the law to keep them safe, so occasionally he separates from Omar, linking up later along the way.

Two extended episodes illustrate some of the larger themes that Aikins is making in his book. At one point he and Omar find themselves confined to the Moria camp for migrants on the Greek island of Lesbos. Greece is a frontline state in the migration crisis, an entry point for refugees. By the time Aikins and Omar arrive in 2016, Greece was being overwhelmed by the number of migrants crossing its borders. Aggravating the situation was a debt crisis that had gravely weakened the Greek economy. The Greeks had few resources to deal with the influx of people. The United Nations and non-governmental organizations stepped in to help, but that made little difference at Moria, where five thousand people were crammed into a camp designed for two thousand. A recent riot had led to a fire that consumed much of the housing. People were now living in tents as the weather began to change. Though migrants could leave the camp, they could not leave the island until their cases were adjudicated, a long process. Escape was the prime concern, and smuggling a big business. For Aikins, Moria becomes a symbol of the hard choices facing both migrants and the nations receiving them.

The two find a happier symbol in Athens, in a zone of the city taken over by anarchists. There, in an occupied hotel, migrants and their leftist hosts created a largely self-sufficient and self-governing community. It could not last long-term, and eventually a rightwing government would reestablish control over the area. Nevertheless, for Aikins the City Plaza hotel represents an alternative and more humane way of working with migrants.

Aikins covered the fall of Kabul to the Taliban in 2021, an event spurring even more migration, and then published this book the following year. Reviewers widely acclaimed this account of what he saw. Writing for the *New York Times*, Jessica Goudeau called *The Naked Don't Fear the Water* "A meticulously told story the world needs to hear now more than ever." Meanwhile, in a starred review, *Kirkus* called the book "riveting" and praised it for the way in which it "shines a humane spotlight" on those the author met on the migrant's trail to Europe.

Author Biography

Matthieu Aikins is a Canadian journalist who began reporting from the Middle East and Afghanistan in 2008. He is a contributing writer for the *New York Times Magazine* and a contributing editor at *Rolling Stone*. He has won the George Polk and Livingston awards, and in 2022 shared a Pulitzer Prize for reporting on a drone strike that killed innocent people in Afghanistan. *The Naked Don't Fear the Water* is his first book.

Daniel P. Murphy

Review Sources

Goudeau, Jessica. "A Journalist Went Underground as a Refugee. It Became an Act of Love." Review of *The Naked Don't Fear the Water*, by Matthieu Aikins. *The New York Times*, 15 Feb. 2022, www.nytimes.com/2022/02/15/books/review/the-naked-dont-fear-the-water-matthieu-aikins.html. Accessed 26 Oct. 2022.

Hartle, Terry W. "An Afghan Refugee Risks Everything: A Tale of Danger, Hope, Courage." Review of *The Naked Don't Fear the Water*, by Matthieu Aikins. *The Christian Science Monitor*, 14 Mar. 2022, www.csmonitor.com/Books/Book-Reviews/2022/0314/An-Afghan-refugee-risks-everything-A-tale-of-danger-hope-courage. Accessed 26 Oct. 2022.

Hayford, Elizabeth. Review of *The Naked Don't Fear the Water*, by Matthieu Aikins. *Library Journal*, Jan. 2022, pp. 69-76.

"His Brother's Record-Keeper." Review of *The Naked Don't Fear the Water*, by Matthieu Aikins. *The Economist*, 26 Feb. 2022, p. 81.

McDonald-Gibson, Charlotte. "Stories of You and Me: Things Lost and Gained in the Telling of Refugees' Tales." Review of *The Naked Don't Fear the Water*, by Matthieu Aikins. *TLS, The Times Literary Supplement*, 8 Apr. 2022, pp. 3-5.

Mondor, Colleen. Review of *The Naked Don't Fear the Water*, by Matthieu Aikins. *Booklist*, 1-15 Jan. 2022, p. 22.

Review of *The Naked Don't Fear the Water*, by Matthieu Aikins. *Kirkus Reviews*, 15 Feb. 2022, www.kirkusreviews.com/book-reviews/matthieu-aikins/naked-dont-fear-water/. Accessed 26 Oct. 2022.

Review of *The Naked Don't Fear the Water*, by Matthieu Aikins. *Publishers Weekly*, 20 Dec. 2021, pp. 87-88.

Review of *The Naked Don't Fear the Water*, by Mattieu Aikins. *The New Yorker*, 28 Mar. 2022, p. 77.

A New Name
Septology VI–VII

Author: Jon Fosse (b. 1959)
First published: *Eit nytt namn: Septologien VI–VII*, 2021, in Norway
Translated from the Norwegian by Damion Searls
Publisher: Transit Books (Oakland, CA). 208 pp.
Type of work: Novel
Time: 1960s–the present day
Locale: Norway

A New Name is the final installment of Norwegian author Jon Fosse's seven-volume Septology *series that explores ideas surrounding art, God, and the human experience.*

Principal characters

ASLE, a sixty-two-year-old widowed Norwegian painter
THE NAMESAKE, his acquaintance who is also a painter named Asle
ALES, his late wife
ÅSLEIK, his neighbor, who is a farmer
GURO, Åsleik's sister, who is hosting a Christmas dinner
ALIDA, Asle's sister, who died in childhood

In interviews, Jon Fosse has stated that his series *Septology* (2019–21) is not autobiographical. Still, it is difficult not to conflate him with *Septology*'s protagonist, Asle, who, like Fosse, is also a reclusive Norwegian artist in his sixties and a late-in-life, devout Catholic convert. At first glance, it appears that this is where the similarities between the two men end as the fictional Asle is a lonely, widowed painter of modest success while Fosse has been one of the most renowned writers in Europe since the 1980s thanks to his avant-garde novels, plays, and poems. And yet, there is so much authenticity in Asle's first-person narration that it is hard not to believe that Fosse is simply using the character as a stand-in for himself—a vessel to explore his own ideas about God, love, and the meaning of his life as an artist.

The author and his protagonist's examination of these big, existential ideas come to a head in *A New Name* (2022), the *Septology* series' superb final book that seems likely to get Fosse closer to winning the Nobel Prize for Literature that he has been an established frontrunner for. However, to appreciate everything that Fosse accomplishes in *A New Name*, it is necessary to consider it within the context of the two books that preceded it in the English translation of the series: *The Other Name* (2019) and *I*

Is Another (2020). This is because, stylistically, Fosse wrote *Septology* as one long, continuous sentence and, subsequently, *A New Name* does not work as the narrative's climax without an understanding of what events happened before it.

At first glance, the general plot of *Septology* is deceptive in that it appears to be both simple and familiar. Such familiarity is largely due to the fact that it takes place over the days leading up to Christmas and involves a flawed and lonely man grappling with the meaning of his life as he becomes increasingly aware of his own mortality. This theme and setting are well-worn Western literature tropes thanks to authors such as Charles Dickens, and yet *Septology* is not sentimental holiday storytelling but rather a work of experimental fiction that uses Christmas to amplify its exploration of God through a Catholic lens. Such religiosity is evident from its first pages, which begin with Asle attempting to finish a painting of St. Andrew's Cross and feeling dissatisfied with it as well as painting in general. Soon afterward, another painter named Asle has an accident in town and is put in critical care. As the first Asle cares for his hospitalized acquaintance's dog, Bragi, he begins reflecting on his own past and gets lost in its memories. The *Septology* narrative subsequently toggles back and forth between these flashbacks of memories and the present day, which he mostly spends with his terse neighbor Åsleik debating whether he will go to Åsleik's sister's house for Christmas.

Jon Fosse

A New Name, which comprises two of the series' seven volumes, is the series' final act and proves to be quite powerful despite having what is ostensibly a simple plot. In it, Asle makes arrangements at an art gallery for an upcoming show of his work and then finally makes the journey with Åsleik to his sister Guro's house for her famous Christmas lamb supper. On the way there, previously withheld information about his life comes to light through his conversation with Åsleik and in the form of flashbacks. Where the flashbacks from the two earlier books were mostly set in Asle's childhood and adolescence, in *A New Name* they finally reach his young adulthood to reveal one of the biggest puzzle pieces surrounding his character's identity: his relationship with his late wife, Ales. Up until this point in the series, Ales has hung like a silent shadow of grief over the narrative, which in turn created a sense of mystery and suspense around how she and Asle met and married as well as what became of them. As he crosses over the sea and relives these memories, there is a sense that he is also crossing over into a new state of being. This feeling comes more clearly into focus with the powerful scenes that unfold at Åsleik's sister's house.

Like the first two installments, *A New Name* is not easily comprehensible and, therefore, readers who want something light should probably look elsewhere. Fosse is known as the type of writer who likes to break literary conventions to ensure his readers work to understand what he is trying to say, similar to twentieth-century modernists like Samuel Beckett, whom he often cites as an inspiration. This proclivity is evidenced in *Septology*'s extremely unique literary style. Fosse's prose is luminous but spare, and his decision to write the series as one continuous sentence means that there are no periods, which creates the effect of being caught in Asle's stream of consciousness in what feels like the slow, steady pace of real time. Another unusual stylistic choice is how each volume in the series begins and ends the exact same way—opening with Asle's inner monologue about his St. Andrew's Cross painting and then many pages later closing with him saying the same prayer. These repeating scenes function as bookends to identify where act breaks might be in the otherwise uninterrupted sentence. But they also create a gentle narrative rhythm, suggesting the life of an artist is one of creating, suffering, reflecting, and trying to connect with God.

Fosse's talent for utilizing experimental fiction to explore big, existential ideas is also evident in *A New Name*'s cast. The characters that populate its pages will likely be difficult for English readers to initially differentiate because they all have Norwegian names that are spelled similarly to one another like Asle, Ales, Åsleik, and Alida. Eventually, however, it becomes clear that Fosse intended it to be confusing and that the overlap in their names suggests that all humans, despite their seeming differences, are one. This concept of all of humankind being connected in oneness is by no means a new concept, and in the hands of a lesser writer, could be offputtingly saccharine; fortunately, however, Fosse maintains a tone that feels more like Scandinavian dark realism.

Meanwhile, the presence of the other painter named Asle, who shares the protagonist's age and appearance, furthers the theme of human interconnectedness. Throughout the narrative, Fosse reveals pieces of each Asle's story in such a way that, at times, it is difficult to tell them apart or whether the protagonist's doppelganger even exists. Although it is never entirely clear what Fosse's true intention is with this character, it often feels like the doppelganger is the embodiment of Asle's "path not taken." Where Asle has been sober for many years and is a widower without children, his doppelganger is twice divorced with three estranged children and has been steadily killing himself with alcohol. And in *A New Name* it becomes clear that while Asle might have found love, sobriety, and God thanks to his late wife Ales, in the end, he is no different than the doppelganger in that he too must face death while finding significance in life. Here again, the message that the human condition is largely universal resonates.

Reception of *A New Name* was largely positive, with the book becoming a finalist for the 2022 National Book Awards in addition to being short-listed for the 2022 International Booker Prize. Still, it received somewhat limited reviews, and critics who did write about it often chose to assess *Septology* as a single book several years earlier rather than assessing each volume separately—likely because this is how Fosse intended it to be read. This is something that readers interested in *A New Name* must consider, as it technically can be read as a stand-alone novel but, in turn, it loses a lot of its meaning.

In the reviews that were published about *A New Name*, most critics agreed it was equally as good as its preceding volumes. Indeed, there is no real difference in the quality of the storytelling or prose of *A New Name* compared to *The Other Name* and *I Is Another*. Arguably the only quality that makes it even more satisfying than the two earlier books is that it offers some conclusions to all of the complex emotions, ideas, and fears that Asle has been continuously grappling with throughout the narrative. To this point, *Publishers Weekly* remarked in their review, "This haunting tale holds an intriguing puzzle at its heart: can existence only be understood as a kind of paradox? Fosse infuses the mystery with Asle's frequent paraphrasing of the German Catholic theologian Meister Eckhart . . . bringing insight to questions of love, art, and faith." Here, the review touches on how *A New Name* offers a few answers to some of the biggest questions posed in *Septology*. Early on in the series, for example, Asle wonders if his life as a painter has been futile, but then in *A New Name* he walks into Guro's house and sees dozens of his pieces hanging around it that Åsleik gifted her over the years, causing Asle to understand the significance of his work to others.

Similarly, other critics have extolled *A New Name* for the way that it brought a fascinating conclusion to Asle's questioning of the importance of religion and God. In his review for the *Financial Times*, Bryan Karetnyk wrote, "In this fine conclusion to *Septology*, the religious subtexts of the project's companion pieces at last draw into focus." Karetnyk's point alludes to one of the most beautiful ideas found in *A New Name*, about how it is here that Asle realizes that God is the light that keeps darkness from taking over the world and, therefore, his aspiration as a painter is not about achieving fame or fortune but to capture God's light for others to see as best he can.

A New Name is about many things, but ultimately the relationship between the artist and God is its most significant exploration. This does not mean that readers who are not artistic or religious cannot enjoy it, however. At its core, it is about the human condition—the universal experiences of life, love, and death. Beyond this, Fosse's writing style is so groundbreakingly powerful that it will provide readers with an extraordinary experience unlike any other. As Lola Seaton wrote in her review for the *New Statesman*, "Septology may not bring you closer to God, but you'll want to keep dwelling in the tranquil shelter Fosse has built, gratefully stupefied by the fortuitous beauty of the commingling paint."

Author Biography

Jon Fosse is a Norwegian playwright, poet, novelist, essayist, journalist, and children's book writer whose work has been translated into more than fifty languages. He is the recipient of numerous awards including the Nynorsk Literature Prize, the 2010 Ibsen Award, the 2014 European Prize for Literature, and the 2015 Nordic Council Literature Prize.

Damion Searls is an award-winning writer and translator whose translated works include those by Friedrich Nietzsche, Marcel Proust, and Robert Walser. He is the author of the short-story collection *What We Were Doing and Where We Were Going*

(2009) and the biography *The Inkblots: Hermann Rorschach, His Iconic Test, and the Power of Seeing* (2017).

Emily E. Turner

Review Sources

Karetnyk, Bryan. "A New Name by Jon Fosse—Fading of the Light." Review of *A New Name: Septology VI–VII*, by Jon Fosse. *The Financial Times*, 27 Aug. 2021, www.ft.com/content/b0aea7ef-f562-4ffc-b408-2728f73f0429. Accessed 17 Jan. 2023.

Review of *A New Name: Septology VI–VII*, by Jon Fosse. *Publishers Weekly*, 14 Dec. 2021, www.publishersweekly.com/9781945492570. Accessed 17 Jan. 2023.

Seaton, Lola. "Jon Fosse and the Art of Tedium." Review of *A New Name: Septology VI–VII*, by Jon Fosse. *The New Statesman*, 15 Jan. 2022, www.newstatesman.com/culture/books/book-of-the-day/2023/01/jon-fosse-septology-art-of-tedium. Accessed 17 Jan. 2023.

Night of the Living Rez

Author: Morgan Talty (b. 1991)
Publisher: Tin House (Portland, OR). 296 pp.
Type of work: Short fiction
Time: Twenty-first century
Locales: Penobscot Indian Island Reservation and environs, Penobscot County, Maine

Morgan Talty's first full-length work, Night of the Living Rez *(2022), collects a dozen linked stories, most published individually between 2017 and 2020, as told from the changing perspective of a young boy on the Penobscot Indian Island Reservation in Maine who seeks answers to questions about his purpose and existence.*

Principal characters
DAVID, a.k.a. Dee or D, the narrator
FELLIS, his best friend from childhood
MUMMA, his mother
PAIGE, his older sister
GRAMMY, his grandmother
FRICK, a failed medicine man

The title of Morgan Talty's debut short story collection, *Night of the Living Rez* (2022), references director George Romero's groundbreaking zombie movie, Night of the Living Dead (1968). The name carries deeper significance than a mere pun, however. Over the course of the collection, it becomes a metaphor for the existence of the characters of the work.

The central setting for each story is the Penobscot Indian Island Reservation, a real geographical area in central Maine. At less than 5,000 woodsy, swampy acres, the "rez" is a fragment of the territory the once powerful Panawahpskek (Penobscot) Nation controlled hundreds of years ago. (In a note at the end of the book, Talty explains that he uses the phonetic spelling of Penobscot words, not the Penobscot alphabet, a decision that was partially intended to increase the accessibility of the language.)

In the twenty-first century, fewer than a thousand registered members of the Penobscot Nation cluster around a village—featuring a health clinic, community building, tribal offices, and school—on Indian Island in the middle of the Penobscot River. Only since 1950 has Indian Island been connected by a bridge to the mainland, giving easy

Morgan Talty

access to the amenities (Walmart, Macy's, Burger King, Home Depot) of nearby Overtown.

Significantly, the island was formerly a sacred Penobscot burial ground. There have been sightings and earwitness reports of goog'ooks (evil spirits), who make noises in the night. A large graveyard dominates the island. Some residents even act like the walking dead, shambling mindlessly through their lives on the rez.

Talty's storytelling quickly establishes the hallmarks of life on Indian Island through the themes that color many of the short stories. In the stories, the island serves both as a prison and a sanctuary for residents: a place to escape from in search of excitement, a refuge to return to when the excitement overwhelms. For Talty's characters, day-to-day existence is stultifying, especially for the young and the old. Unemployment is rampant. Available jobs are mostly menial, paying minimum wage, and offering little opportunity for advancement. Poverty is endemic. Many households are headed by single mothers without adult males present. Depression is widespread. Hope springs eternal, only to be crushed time and again by stark reality. Residents, particularly the restless young, are desperate for emotional engagement, for adventure, for fun, for anything to break the monotony. So, they turn occasionally to unsavory activities. They plan big capers, but commit petty crimes, like theft and vandalism. They engage in substance abuse. For some, oblivion comes from alcohol: beer, wine, and cheap gin. Others add drugs for extra intoxication: marijuana, cocaine, and opioids, even if it means endless methadone maintenance treatments later.

A representative resident of the Island is a young man—called David as a youngster, Dee or D as an adolescent and adult—who narrates each story. Like author Talty, who in interviews has admitted there are autobiographical elements contained in some stories (though he does not specify where facts end and fiction begins), David grew up on the Penobscot reservation. In twelve tales that move forward and backward along a timeline spanning twenty-odd years, David/Dee interacts with a cast of recurring characters.

The stage is set at the beginning of the collection. "Burn," the shortest story, briskly introduces readers to two main characters who appear throughout *Night of the Living Rez*: Dee, the narrator, and his best friend Fellis. The story defines the territory, a Native American reservation, where youths usually wear long braids. The boys, who are in a methadone program, use local slang, like skeejins (Native Americans). "Burn" also establishes themes to be developed, with mention of goog'ooks and other elements of Penobscot life. The plot is deceptively simple: Dee, passing a frozen swamp, hears a call. He finds Fellis on the ground, looking corpse-like. But Fellis is alive: he passed out from drink and/or drugs, and when he awoke, found his hair frozen to the snow. He is helpless to free himself. What follows are Dee's attempts to free his friend, who later wishes to burn his cut hair to avoid spirits coming after him.

"In a Jar" presents a younger David and his family in a story that provides a foundation to the otherworldly thread that runs throughout each story. His mother, after separating from David's father "down south," has just moved into a house on the reservation with David and her pregnant, unmarried daughter Paige. While playing outside with his toys, David discovers under the front steps a jar "filled with hair and corn and teeth." His mother calls Frick, a medicine man, who declares the jar is a curse. To remove the curse, Frick smudges the house and everyone in it with a "giant seashell the size of a baseball glove filled with tobacco" and "sage that burned and smelled calm, like salt water." Then Frick moves into the house to become David's mother's lover. David's grandmother is also introduced, who, like Paige, often assumes a motherly role in young David's life.

Other stories fill out the community where David lives, give key details of reservation life, flesh out characters, and build upon established themes. "Get Me Some Medicine," for example, introduces Meekew, whose name means "Squirrel," a college student who deals drugs to Dee and Fellis, now in their twenties. Readers also learn about Tabitha, Dee's White, sometime girlfriend, and her apartment in Overtown. Dee has a part-time job mowing the local graveyard. He supplements his meager income by selling dead porcupines, at $20 a head, to a lady named Clara, who uses the quills to make tribal regalia. His mother tells Dee a story about the stone people who "come out and walk among us."

"Food for the Common Cold" features a scene in which eleven-year-old David uses a slingshot to shoot metal balls at a granite headstone in the cemetery. "In a Field of Stray Caterpillars" reveals that Fellis is undergoing electroconvulsive therapy (ECT). "The Blessing Tobacco" shows Grammy sinking into dementia, mistaking David for her brother Robbie, who drowned many years before David was born. "Safe Harbor" concerns David's mother making her twelfth trip in three months to the crisis stabilization unit, because "something isn't right with her brain." "Smokes Last" illustrates how David and his friends JP and Tyson entertain themselves, doing battle with sticks in the woods.

While much of Night of the Living Rez is downbeat, there are several humorous or bizarre moments to lighten the mood. "Half-Life," for instance, contains a comedic scene in which David, now twenty-eight, breaks into the house of his grandmother, recently confined to an assisted living center. He is looking for money to feed his habit of "pins," slang for Klonopin, a powerful bipolar medication. When his mother, also after money, arrives at the house unexpectedly, chaos ensues. "Earth, Speak" details a hare-brained scheme, inspired by an episode of Antiques Roadshow, to break into the tribal museum to steal and sell Indigenous artifacts. The collection's title story, "Night of the Living Rez"—in which David's mother claims Paige "believes in zombies," and which mentions another Romero zombie movie, Land of the Dead (2005)—contains a scene in which a woman uses a Super Soaker to spray innocent bystanders with her own urine.

Critics were virtually unanimous in their praise for Night of the Living Rez, which won the New England Book Award and was a finalist for Barnes & Noble and Andrew Carnegie Medal honors. Amil Niazi, writing for the New York Times, stressed how the collection teemed "with the undeniable physicality of the natural world." Niazi highlighted Talty's "incredible ability to take the seemingly disparate events of David's life and reveal how interconnected they are, how each tiny decision becomes something bigger, how the small moments click together in ways that are both heartbreaking and revelatory." The reviewer for the Maine Edge enthusiastically agreed, calling the collection "thoughtfully rendered and beautifully written stories, stopping at various points on a unique coming-of-age pathway. Each tale wrestles with large questions of identity, showing the struggle that comes with trying to maintain a connection to the past while also embracing the possibility of the future."

Reviewers also enjoyed the collection for its narrative voice. Bekah Waalkes of Ploughshares proclaimed Night of the Living Rez "the best collection I have read all year." She focused on the "haunting" voice of the narrator: "David is angry and sad, resigned and questioning, all at once. And with each decision he makes, more and more change comes. The world of Night of the Living Rez is deeply interconnected, leaving the reader to constantly wonder what each moment will set into motion." Rachel León of Fiction Writers Review mentions Talty's "singular" voice in the twelve "masterfully rendered" stories that demand "to be read, then read again."

By nearly all accounts, Night of the Living Rez embodies storytelling at its finest. Revelations unfold naturally and organically to surprise and emotionally involve readers. Talty's superb portraits of lifelike individuals—characterized by speech and action—trying to survive in a unique and hostile environment will not soon be forgotten.

Author Biography

Morgan Talty teaches in the Stonecoast MFA Program in Creative Writing and at the University of Maine. His stories have been published in such literary periodicals as Narrative, Granta, TriQuarterly, Shenandoah, and The Georgia Review.

Jack Ewing

Review Sources

Gardner, Nick Rees. "A Review of Morgan Talty's *Night of the Living Rez*." Review of *Night of the Living Rez*, by Morgan Talty. *The Adroit Journal*, 10 May 2022, theadroitjournal.org/2022/05/10/a-review-of-morgan-taltys-night-of-the-living-rez/. Accessed 26 Dec. 2022.

León, Rachel. Review of *Night of the Living Rez,* by Morgan Talty. *Fiction Writers Review*, 30 May 2022, fictionwritersreview.com/review/night-of-the-living-rez-by-morgan-talty/. Accessed 26 Dec. 2022.

Niazi, Amil. "Beer Runs, Porcupine Hunts, Jars of Teeth and Much More." Review of *Night of the Living Rez,* by Morgan Talty, *The New York Time*s, 1 July 2022, www.nytimes.com/2022/07/01/books/review/night-of-the-living-rez-morgan-talty.html. Accessed 26 Dec. 2022.

"*Night of the Living Rez* A Scintillating Short Fiction Collection." Review of *Night of the Living Rez*, by Morgan Talty. *The Maine Edge*, 6 July 2022, www.themaineedge.com/buzz/night-of-the-living-rez-a-scintillating-short-fiction-collection, Accessed 26 Dec. 2022.

Rabe, Kristen. "Starred Review: *Night of the Living Rez*, by Morgan Talty." Review of *Night of the Living Rez*, by Morgan Talty. *Foreword Reviews*, July/Aug. 2022, www.forewordreviews.com/reviews/night-of-the-living-rez/. Accessed 26 Dec. 2022.

Waalkes, Bekah. "Life and Death in Morgan Talty's *Night of the Living Rez*." Review of *Night of the Living Rez*, by Morgan Talty. *Ploughshares*, 17 Aug. 2022, blog.pshares.org/life-and-death-in-morgan-taltys-night-of-the-living-rez/. Accessed 26 Dec. 2022.

Nightcrawling

Author: Leila Mottley (b. 2002)
Publisher: Knopf (New York). 288 pp.
Type of work: Novel
Time: Present day
Locale: Oakland, California

Seventeen-year-old Kiara struggles to support herself, her brother, and the child of a neighbor. When she gets pulled into a legal case involving a group of police officers, her life is turned upside-down, forcing her to determine the true meaning of family.

Principal characters
KIARA JOHNSON, a young adult who takes care of everyone except herself
MARCUS JOHNSON, her older brother
TREVOR, her nine-year-old neighbor
ALÉ, her best friend
UNCLE TY, Kiara and Marcus's uncle, a famous rapper

Leila Mottley's 2022 novel, *Nightcrawling*, follows approximately a year in the life of Kiara Johnson, a seventeen-year-old Black girl living in Oakland, California. Though still a child herself, Kiara carries the tremendous responsibilities of her family, both the biological members and those she has added over time. The novel's central conflict is a social statement about the implications of poverty and the desperate measures Kiara goes through to survive.

One of the main themes of the novel challenges the way in which family is traditionally defined. Kiara adores her older brother, Marcus, and Marcus loves her in return, but he is incapable of putting her first at this point in his life. After taking responsibility for his younger sister after his father's death and an ensuing family tragedy, Marcus has decided that Kiara is now old enough to take care of herself, believing he deserves to do something for himself. He turns to a group of friends who encourage his selfish ambitions and drag him into illegal activities that eventually catch up to him. Meanwhile, Kiara carries the burdens of paying the rent for the apartment in which her family has lived for generations and caring for Trevor, the nine-year-old child of her drug-addicted neighbor, Dee. Though Kiara's family dynamic is troubled, her friend Alé's family is much more close-knit. Though they, too, are financially limited, Alé, her mother, and other family members live in a small apartment above a restaurant they own and run. Despite four of them sharing one bedroom, they are loving and generous with each other. This carries over into Alé's relationship with Kiara, and

Alé's own family issues interfere with the girls' friendship as she becomes angry with Kiara's survival choices, which she cannot understand.

One aspect Mottley explores in *Nightcrawling* is the responsibilities of motherhood. Kiara's mother was so in love with their father that when he died, she could not cope and ended up in prison, leaving her children without parental guidance. Out of desperation, Kiara goes to the prison to visit her mother, in hopes of finding a way to contact her uncle, who has become a famous rapper. However, her mother twists the visit, making it more about herself than her children and leaving Kiara feeling more hopeless than she had been before she went. Even after she is released from prison, she only reaches out to Kiara for selfish reasons. Another mother figure in the novel is Kiara's neighbor Dee. Dee is the mother to a sweet nine-year-old son, Trevor. However, Dee is so addicted to drugs that she is neither capable of nor interested in being a parent. As a result, Kiara, who has cared for Trevor since his birth, takes care of the boy. She gets up early in the morning to make sure he gets to school, feeds him even when she does not have enough food for herself, and takes him in when their landlord serves Dee an eviction notice. This relationship serves as the most positive thing in both Trevor's and Kiara's lives.

Leila Mottley

Because she has taken the parental role upon herself, Kiara's whole existence is based on taking care of everyone but herself. Raised rent, eviction notices, lack of food, and other issues showcase the extreme poverty these characters experience. Though she begs Marcus to find a real job to aid in the household expenses, he is unable to keep a steady position. This role becomes more poignant as Mottley furthers Kiara's responsibilities in taking care of Trevor. Without a way to pay for everything, and after being raped and then paid off following the assault, Kiara turns to sex work to bring in money.

This choice, which is not really a conscious decision for Kiara, is the catalyst of another main conflict in the novel. Mottley notes that Kiara's story is loosely based on the Celeste Guap legal case that took place in Oakland, California, in 2016. In this real-life case, a woman accused several police officers of sexually exploiting her after one of the men committed suicide, leaving a note detailing her name and other details. The novel creates a fictional version of Guap's situation when Kiara is abused by a police officer who sexually assaults her rather than arresting her. This man and several of his colleagues continue to abuse Kiara, often by gang raping her and forcing her to commit other sexual acts against her will, ultimately trafficking her among themselves and even among others outside of their group. When the scandal comes to light in the novel, Kiara contracts with Marsha, a strong female lawyer who takes the case on a pro-bono basis. Though Kiara had initially chosen sex work as a means to make enough money to support her family, she never chose to become involved with this corrupt group of men, and the publicity from the case causes her even more heartache.

This heartache is further evidence of the thematic idea of loss throughout the novel. The first loss Kiara and Marcus experience is the imprisonment of their father, a larger-than-life figure around whom their mother had based her existence. When their father dies from cancer that they cannot afford to treat, the family begins the spiral that serves as the primary impetus of the story. A tragic incident soon takes place, and their mother is incapable of dealing with it, thus leading to her imprisonment. Almost immediately, Uncle Ty, their father's brother who had been highly influential in Marcus's development, leaves Oakland, completely abandoning his niece and nephew, even after he becomes a wealthy rapper. Marcus is unable to deal with this loss, so as soon as Kiara is old enough to be more independent, he turns away from his sister to pursue his own desire to follow in his uncle's footsteps. The loss of her brother's affection and responsibility is one of the main causes of Kiara's struggle. In addition to these losses, when Alé finds out that Kiara is performing sex work, she becomes angry and does not try to understand why Kiara would choose this path, which leaves Kiara even more heartbroken. Trevor is the only light left in Kiara's life, but this relationship will be tested over time as well, and when Child Protection Services becomes involved, both Kiara and Trevor feel like their lives have imploded.

Ultimately, *Nightcrawling* is a story of poverty, desperation, and survival. Despite the darkness that surrounds the characters based on these issues, readers will find that Kiara is sympathetic. Her struggle to find happiness and love is often overwhelming, but Mottley finds a way to make Kiara's choices understandable even in the midst of personal and social conflict. Mottley also provides both sinister and lonely snapshots of villains and friends, pulling readers into the darker aspects of life in Oakland.

Though most of Kiara's life is lived in a state of desperation, there are some positive situations in the novel. Kiara's friendship with Alé is heartwarming and at some points romantic. Alé's feelings for Kiara, even when they are confused, are one of the things that keeps Kiara going. Though Marcus fails to keep his sister safe or even put her before his own desires at the time when the novel is set, Kiara remembers moments when the two were close, and she clings to those memories. Kiara's relationship with Trevor provides the most touching bond and brings laughter and joy into Kiara's otherwise desperate existence.

The reviews of the novel, for the most part, praised its language, characterizations, and social conflicts; however, there were a few less-flattering notes about the tone and relationships in the piece. Luke Gorham of the *Library Journal* stated, "It's a work of devastating social realism but cut through with a strain of pulp fiction . . . and it's executed with relentless momentum, built of purely dramatic moments and steeped in emotions that are wrung from characters as if they were wet rags," which Gorham found to create "a certain melodramatic texture." However, the reviewer for *Publishers Weekly* lauded Mottley's ability to create a "heartrending story" that "makes for a powerful testament to a Black woman's resilience." Courtney Eathorne of *Booklist* commented on the novel's characterizations and called the main character "an unforgettable dynamo," while also pointing to the social commentary that "brings critical human depth to conversations about police sexual violence." Lauren Christensen, the *New York Times* reviewer, both compliments and disparages when she concluded a note on the use of simile, writing that "beneath this gratuitous embroidery, there's a desperation—a reaching, through language, for some kind of salvation—a counterpoint to the carelessness with which the protagonist wields her body." Christensen also noted that the relationship between Kiara and Alé is "confusingly underdeveloped" and "feels unearned when it finally comes to fruition." Still, plenty of reviewers praised the novel, including Kit Fan, the *Guardian* reviewer, who stated that "*Nightcrawling* marks the dazzling arrival of a young writer with a voice and vision you won't easily get out of your head."

Author Biography

Recognition of Leila Mottley's writing career started at the young age of sixteen, when she was selected as the Oakland, California, Youth Poet Laureate in 2018. She began writing *Nightcrawling* at seventeen years old and completed it in 2020 while attending Smith College. Her debut novel was longlisted for the Booker Prize, making her the youngest author to receive this honor. She has also published poetry in the *New York Times*.

Theresa L. Stowell, PhD

Review Sources

Christensen, Lauren. "In This Sex-Trafficking Ring, the Johns Are the Oakland Police." Review of *Nightcrawling*, by Leila Mottley. *The New York Times*, 7 June 2022, www.nytimes.com/2022/06/07/books/review/nightcrawling-leila-mottley.html. Accessed 30 Jan. 2023.

Eathorne, Courtney. Review of *Nightcrawling*, by Leila Mottley. *Booklist*, vol. 118, no. 15, Apr. 2022, p. 18. *EBSCOhost*, search.ebscohost.com/login.aspx?direct=true&db=edsglr&AN=edsglr.A701067378&site=eds-live&scope=site. Accessed 27 Dec. 2022.

Fan, Kit. "*Nightcrawling* by Leila Mottley Review—A Dazzling Debut." Review of *Nightcrawling*, by Leila Mottley. *The Guardian*, 2 June 2022, www.theguardian.com/books/2022/jun/02/nightcrawling-by-leila-mottley-review-a-dazzling-debut. Accessed 30 Jan. 2023.

Gorham, Luke. Review of *Nightcrawling*, by Leila Mottley. *Library Journal*, vol. 147, no. 5, May 2022, p. 84. *EBSCOhost,* search.ebscohost.com/login.aspx?direct=true&db=lfh&AN=156688805&site=eds-live. Accessed 27 Dec. 2022.

Review of *Nightcrawling*, by Leila Mottley. *Kirkus*, 2 Mar. 2022, www.kirkusreviews.com/book-reviews/leila-mottley/nightcrawling-mottley/. Accessed 27 Dec. 2022.

Review of *Nightcrawling*, by Leila Mottley. *Publishers Weekly*, 4 Apr. 2022, www.publishersweekly.com/9780593318935. Accessed 27 Dec. 2022.

The Nineties

Author: Chuck Klosterman (b. 1972)
Publisher: Penguin Press (New York).
  384 pp.
Type of work: History, sociology
Time: The 1990s
Locale: The United States

In The Nineties, *distinguished journalist and author Chuck Klosterman presents a penetrating analysis of the last decade of the twentieth century. Mixing political and cultural commentary, he deftly analyzes a decade that, because of the digital revolution that took off in the early twenty-first century, may often seem more distant than it actually is chronologically.*

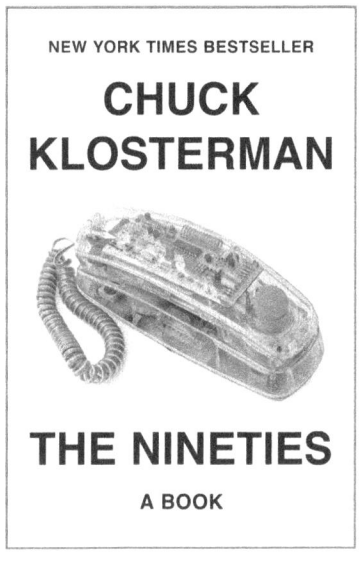

Principal personages
GEORGE H. W. BUSH, US president 1989–93
BILL CLINTON, US president 1993–2001
GEORGE W. BUSH, presidential candidate in 2000 and US president 2001–09
AL GORE, US vice president 1993–2001 and presidential candidate in 2000
ROSS PEROT, billionaire and presidential candidate in 1992 and 1996
KURT COBAIN, lead singer of the rock band Nirvana
DOUGLAS COUPLAND, author of the novel Generation X (1991)
MICHAEL JORDAN, professional basketball star
ALANIS MORISSETTE, popular singer
JERRY SEINFELD, popular comedian and star of the series *Seinfeld* (1989–98)
O. J. SIMPSON, former football star tried for the murder of his ex-wife and her friend
QUENTIN TARANTINO, popular filmmaker
OPRAH WINFREY, popular talk-show host

For over two decades, Chuck Klosterman has been an engaging and astute commentator on American popular culture. From books about his youthful taste for heavy metal to an examination of the modern understanding of human ethics, he has striven to plumb the depths of the American psyche. He has pursued this quest by immersing himself in the mass media, the modern manifestation of society's collective consciousness. Crucially, Klosterman's approach is typically nonjudgmental. As a devotee of so much that he discusses, he has freely admitted that he is not without sin when it comes to succumbing to the allure of commercially fashionable things and trends. Attempting to appreciate cultural phenomena on their own terms, he tries to avoid retrospective appraisals influenced by hindsight. This gives his work an element of freshness and immediacy missing in a more conventionally historical approach. Klosterman is a journalist, used to catching new trends, and he brings some of that spirit of wonder and excitement to a discussion of what have become memories. In other words, his modus operandi is existential; he is a master of dissecting his feelings about the cultural environment that both shaped and continues to mold his life.

In *The Nineties* (2022), Klosterman brings his formidable analytical skills to bear on a decade that simultaneously marked the end of a century and, many assumed at the time, the beginning of a new period of international peace and harmony as the Cold War came to an end. In reality, the latter was not to be. That mistake, as Klosterman notes, was only recognized in the aftermath of the terrorist attacks on September 11, 2001. He illustrates that there were plenty of warnings that the victorious conclusion of the Gulf War that ejected Saddam Hussein's Iraqi army from Kuwait had not in fact inaugurated a new world order. Most ominously, in hindsight, terrorist attacks by Islamic jihadists on the World Trade Center in 1993 and the USS *Cole* in 2000 should have raised alarms about imminent threats. Klosterman notes how, though these incidents and other global horrors of the period, including extreme weather events, were widely reported, none of this disturbed the complacency of an American public lulled into somnolence by prosperity and sensational domestic scandals. Klosterman duly covers these events, as well as traumatic moments of domestic violence and terrorism such as the fiery siege and destruction of David Koresh's compound near Waco, Texas; Timothy McVeigh's Oklahoma City bombing; and the murders by mail of Ted Kaczynski, the "Unabomber." However, all initially seemed like dark anomalies consigned to the background of most people's lives. For the generality of Americans, the nineties were a tranquil interlude between events broadly understood as "great."

Chuck Klosterman

Klosterman compellingly indicates that, bracketed by images of the fall of the Berlin Wall and the fall of the World Trade Center towers, the nineties genuinely constitute a conveniently demarcated period. It was a time that, in many ways, lived up to postmortem caricatures about grungy musicians, shows about nothing, aimless underhanded politics, and tech-driven prosperity. Klosterman focuses more on these sorts of things because this was the lived experience of so many. At the time, much of this seemed like important, or at least worthwhile, diversions to people self-consciously emerging from one epoch and moving into an indeterminate future. And, as Klosterman notes, a great deal of what was going on was indeed significant, laying the groundwork for the social and technological upheaval of the next century. During these years, everyone became aware of the internet, even if it had yet to become a major force in their lives. Amazon selling books online was still a disconcerting innovation. Mobile phones were increasingly ubiquitous, though not yet very smart, and the eventually outmoded answering machine could still play a central role in the popular sitcom *Seinfeld*. The nineties, the book effectively demonstrates, proved to be the last decade when a person could live an analog life only marginally touched by the digital.

At the same time, *The Nineties* is not a jocular catalog of ephemera. While Klosterman's book is nostalgic, his intent is very serious. He successfully recaptures elements of the decade and explores their contemporary import and continued relevance. That does not mean, however, that his work is a sustained argument, laying out a unified field theory of the nineties. Klosterman has no pretensions to being a systematic thinker. Instead, the book is best understood as an extended meditation, made up of a series of essays. Structurally, it imitates Ernest Hemingway's innovative short-story collection *In Our Time* (1925), alternating between longer chapters that address broad topics like the character of Generation X and the impact of new technologies, and shorter sections that concentrate on particularities such as the period's confusing college football championship structure or Oprah Winfrey's rise to mass media stardom. One of the benefits of such an approach and structure is that *The Nineties* can be sampled at the reader's pleasure.

While Klosterman is no revisionist and believes that the decade largely fit the stereotypical view of it, he makes a number of thought-provoking and insightful points along his way. Although politics is not a main concern for him, it proves unavoidable. He notes the remarkable fall from grace of President George H. W. Bush, who enjoyed an approval rating of 89 percent in 1991 but was then decisively defeated for reelection in 1992. The author points out that Bush certainly had problems, including a flip-flop on raising taxes that infuriated many in his GOP base, a general lack of vision for domestic policy, and a recession that was just ending in early 1992. Despite all this, he argues, Bush probably would have defeated the Democratic candidate Bill Clinton in 1992 but for the eccentric intervention of Ross Perot, a Texas billionaire with a deep distaste for the president and for deficit spending. Perot unsettled Bush with his on, off, and on again campaign and undercut the incumbent's political momentum. Here Klosterman raises a rare counterfactual case: what would have happened both to the nineties and to the larger course of American history if George H. W. Bush had served a second dignified and uneventful term? What subsequent political dramas would the country have been spared? Perot was largely forgotten by the third decade of the twenty-first century, but Klosterman intriguingly believes that he was a far more consequential figure than commonly understood. The author also wrestling with the protean figure of Bill Clinton, a pliable politician who dominated the public stage in the nineties by prudently bending with the increasingly conservative headwinds. Fully aware of the twenty-first-century #MeToo condemnation of sexual harassment, Klosterman can only cite Clinton's high poll numbers after the Monica Lewinsky scandal and acknowledge that things were different then.

Most of *The Nineties* dwells on developments in society and culture. Klosterman begins with demographics; himself a member of the Generation X that came of age in this period, he salutes it as a cohort uniquely modest about itself. In books and films,

Gen Xers often portrayed themselves as unambitious and critical of societal demands, leading to a reticence in that demographic cohort that Klosterman unironically celebrates by declaring, "Among the generations that have yet to go extinct, Generation X remains the least annoying." In discussing Kurt Cobain, the front man for the breakout alternative rock band Nirvana, Klosterman explores how he epitomized one aspect of Generation X: its discomfort with success and its trappings. Yet Klosterman also notes that the most consistently successful musical act of the decade was the country singer Garth Brooks, an artist whose drive and populism belied the contemporary image of slacker anomie.

The nineties, as Klosterman admits, were complicated. Another example comes in his examination of film and television. Computers were becoming increasingly important, but network television still dominated many people's off-hours and imaginations. Even mediocre sitcoms enjoyed many times the viewership of "prestige" television programs in the twenty-first century. Klosterman makes the interesting argument that *The Matrix* (1999) was more about the effects of television than the dangers of computers. He also highlights the cultural ramifications of VHS tapes and the neighborhood video store. Here, movie buffs were exposed to a far greater range of motion pictures than could be seen on network TV. This cinematic cornucopia fed the aesthetic of directorial auteurs like Quentin Tarantino and Kevin Smith.

Brimming with Klosterman's perceptive observations on everything from computers to the comedian Pauly Shore, *The Nineties* will absorb and delight readers. Reviewers generally praised the book, with Alana Quarles, writing for the *Library Journal*, declaring it a "fascinating exploration of Generation X from those who lived it." Alexander Moran, in a review for *Booklist*, described it as a "superb reassessment of an underappreciated decade from a stupendously gifted essayist." Klosterman's take on America's final decade of the twentieth century will likely be the starting point for anyone interested in that period for many years to come.

Author Biography

Chuck Klosterman is a journalist and best-selling author. In addition to novels, his nonfiction books have included *Sex, Drugs, and Cocoa Puffs: A Low Culture Manifesto* (2003), *I Wear the Black Hat: Grappling with Villains (Real and Imagined)* (2013), and *But What If We're Wrong? Thinking about the Present as If It Were the Past* (2016).

Daniel P. Murphy

Review Sources

Guan, Frank. "Chuck Klosterman Brings Back the Nineties." Review of *The Nineties*, by Chuck Klosterman. *The New Yorker*, 31 Jan. 2022, www.newyorker.com/magazine/2022/02/07/chuck-klosterman-brings-back-the-nineties. Accessed 10 Feb. 2023.

Jacobs, Alexandra. "Chuck Klosterman Rewinds to 'The Nineties.'" Review of *The Nineties*, by Chuck Klosterman. *The New York Times*, 1 Feb. 2022, www.nytimes.com/2022/02/01/books/review-nineties-chuck-klosterman.html. Accessed 8 Feb. 2023.

Moran, Alexander. Review of *The Nineties*, by Chuck Klosterman. *Booklist*, 1 Dec. 2021, www.booklistonline.com/The-Nineties-A-Book-/pid=9754731. Accessed 10 Feb. 2023.

Review of *The Nineties*, by Chuck Klosterman. *Kirkus*, 27 Oct. 2021, www.kirkusreviews.com/book-reviews/chuck-klosterman/the-nineties/. Accessed 8 Feb. 2023.

Review of *The Nineties*, by Chuck Klosterman. *Publishers Weekly*, 5 Oct. 2021, www.publishersweekly.com/9780735217959. Accessed 10 Feb. 2023.

Quarles, Alana. Review of *The Nineties*, by Chuck Klosterman. *Library Journal*, 1 Jan. 2022, www.libraryjournal.com/review/the-nineties-a-book-2132281. Accessed 10 Feb. 2023.

Nona the Ninth

Author: Tamsyn Muir (b. 1985)
Publisher: Tordotcom (New York). 480 pp.
Type of work: Novel
Time: Six months after the conclusion of Harrow the Ninth
Locales: New Rho; the River; the House of the Ninth; Earth

In Nona the Ninth, *the third installment in the Locked Tomb series, a young woman with amnesia navigates life in a besieged city while her companions attempt to discern her true identity.*

Principal characters

NONA, a nineteen-year-old woman who can remember only the past six months of her life
CAMILLA HECT, one of Nona's caretakers and a cavalier of the Sixth House
PALAMEDES SEXTUS, one of Nona's caretakers and a necromancer of the Sixth House; currently sharing Camilla's body
PYRRHA DVE, one of Nona's caretakers and the former cavalier of the deceased Lyctor Gideon the First, now occupying his body
THE ANGEL, a.k.a. Aim, the school's science teacher and the owner of a six-legged dog named Noodle
WE SUFFER AND WE SUFFER, leader of the Ctesiphon-1 wing of the rebel group Blood of Eden
CROWN HIM WITH MANY CROWNS THY FULL GALLANT LEGIONS HE FOUND IT IN HIM TO FORGIVE, a.k.a. Coronabeth Tridentarius, a former Lyctor candidate now working with Blood of Eden
JUDITH DEUTEROS, a Second House necromancer held prisoner by Blood of Eden
PRINCE IANTHE NABERIUS THE FIRST, a.k.a. the Saint of Awe, one of the Emperor's Lyctors
CROWN PRINCE KIRIONA GAIA, a.k.a. Gideon Nav, the resurrected former cavalier of the Ninth House and the Emperor's daughter
HARROWHARK "HARROW" NONAGESIMUS, the Reverend Daughter of the Ninth House
JOHN GAIUS, a.k.a. the Emperor Undying, the ten-thousand-year-old ruler of the Nine Houses

With the publication of *Gideon the Ninth* in 2019, writer Tamsyn Muir launched an intriguing new series that mingles the genres of fantasy and science fiction, set in

Tamsyn Muir (Courtesy Tor Publishing Group)

a spacefaring society of nine planetary Houses, each heavily reliant on necromantic magic, ruled over by a ten-thousand-year-old undying Emperor. The novel received extensive acclaim, and Muir followed with the sequel *Harrow the Ninth* (2020), which also earned much critical praise, as well as the related short stories "The Mysterious Study of Doctor Sex" (2020) and "As Yet Unsent" (2021). The Locked Tomb series, as it became known, was initially advertised as a trilogy that would conclude with a final novel titled *Alecto the Ninth*. In 2021, however, publisher Tordotcom announced that the series would now encompass four books, with a new installment, *Nona the Ninth*, to be published in 2022.

Beginning nearly six months after the events of *Harrow the Ninth*, *Nona the Ninth* differs from the two preceding novels in a number of ways, including its setting. Unlike those novels, the bulk of *Nona the Ninth* does not take place on a planet, ship, or space station with strong ties to the Nine Houses, the seemingly immortal Emperor, or the Emperor's military known as the Cohort. Rather, the novel is set primarily in a crowded city on a planet known as New Rho, which is ostensibly part of the empire but is largely indifferent to or actively hostile toward it. Occupied by both longtime residents and refugees from planets that have become unlivable, New Rho is home to multiple factions of the rebel group known as Blood of Eden, which opposes the Houses as well as the Emperor and his Lyctors—a small group of powerful necromancers who have gained near immortality by killing and absorbing the souls of their cavaliers, or warrior companions. As of the start of the novel, anti-House sentiments have grown particularly strong on New Rho. The Cohort facility on the planet is under siege, and the planet's residents have begun to kill suspected necromancers (referred to as zombies) on sight. Also concerning is the threatening blue light that has appeared in the sky, which is revealed to be the Resurrection Beast Varun the Eater—the vengeful soul of a murdered planet.

Amid the turmoil, nineteen-year-old Nona lives a relatively peaceful life focused on friendship, the members of her household, and the neighborhood dogs. Suffering from amnesia, she can remember only portions of the previous six months, and it is only in recent months that she has learned to function well enough to perform tasks such as dressing herself. Ever since she can remember, Nona has lived with Camilla Hect, a Sixth House cavalier whose body is now also home to the consciousness of her necromancer companion, Palamedes Sextus. Though Palamedes is able to take control of and speak through Camilla's body at times, Camilla and Palamedes are unable to interact directly with one another, as controlling Camilla's body in concert would cause her severe physical harm. Nona's third caretaker is the former cavalier Pyrrha Dve, whose consciousness is occupying the body of her deceased necromancer companion, who had been one of the original Lyctors.

In addition to keeping Nona safe, Camilla, Palamedes, and Pyrrha seek to discern Nona's true identity. The young woman's body is clearly that of Harrowhark "Harrow" Nonagesimus, the central character of the prior novel. However, due to the events of that book's conclusion, the others think that the consciousness within Nona may be that of Harrow, the deceased cavalier Gideon Nav, or a combination of the two. Nona's caretakers repeatedly examine her for necromantic abilities or fighting skills in the hope of determining who she is, with little success. In addition, the possibility remains that Nona is neither Harrow nor Gideon but a different entity entirely.

While Nona's caretakers maintain a complex alliance with the Blood of Eden and navigate challenging situations such as the capture and imprisonment of a group of Sixth House envoys, Nona herself remains primarily interested in the simple life she has developed over the previous months. In addition to spending time at home with her caretakers, she works as a teacher's aide at a local school. There she befriends a gang of children led by a young teenager named Hot Sauce and enjoys looking after Noodle, a six-legged dog that belongs to a science teacher known as the Angel. She also devotes much of her attention to planning a birthday party to celebrate her six months of existence, which is particularly important to Nona because her health is deteriorating. As Nona goes about her life, however, it becomes clear that the threats to her safety and that of her companions are becoming increasingly dire and that a monumental, potentially catastrophic event is approaching. The structure of the novel itself contributes to the reader's understanding of the approaching event, as each of the novel's five main sections, titled "Day One" through "Day Five," specifies the number of days remaining "until the tomb opens"—an event of obvious significance to readers familiar with the previous two Locked Tomb novels.

Nona's personal involvement in the tumultuous events taking place on New Rho becomes inevitable following the arrival of two of the Emperor's emissaries: Prince Ianthe Naberius the First, the Lyctor formerly known as Ianthe Tridentarius, who is temporarily controlling the body of deceased cavalier Naberius Tern; and the reanimated Gideon Nav, now known as Crown Prince Kiriona Gaia and identifying herself as the Emperor's daughter. Due to her amnesia and limited background knowledge, Nona's perspective on everything happening is that of an outsider, and the reader may often have a greater understanding of the conflicts at hand than she does. While this may prove frustrating for some readers, others will enjoy piecing together the puzzles presented by the narrative, drawing from both Nona's observations and the information previously revealed in the series. Nona herself is a likable character in her own right, and her childlike, innocent viewpoint makes for an intriguing contrast to the novel's more violent or grotesque elements.

In addition to chronicling Nona's experiences in the narrative present, *Nona the Ninth* is interspersed with dreamlike interludes set on the ruins of Earth following a cataclysm. There, the Emperor—also known as John Gaius—tells a listener (identified as Harrow) the story of how necromancy came to be, recounts the events leading up to the founding of the Nine Houses, and provides context for his empire's long war against the Blood of Eden rebels. This not only confirms the earlier novels' hints that the Emperor's home planet was Earth—John mentions real-world locations and references brands such as McDonald's and Coca-Cola—but also reveals the deep strains of environmental consciousness and social commentary underlying the narrative. At the same time, aspects of John's tale raise doubts about his reliability as a narrator and about his motivations, painting a fuller picture of a flawed man who is revered as a god by many in his empire.

Both those interludes and the chapters following Nona and her companions build upon the mythology of the Locked Tomb series and help drive *Nona the Ninth* toward its conclusion, which resolves several of the narrative's arcs. Yet other important characters and plot points enter the story relatively late, and the novel ends with a cliffhanger. Indeed, Muir revealed in interviews around the time of the novel's publication that *Nona the Ninth* originated as the first act of the manuscript for *Alecto the Ninth*, which at that time was intended to be the series finale. Eventually, however, Muir chose to publish *Nona the Ninth* as a separate book in order to keep the final installment from reaching an unwieldy length. Though some readers might feel impatient waiting for the conclusion to the Locked Tomb series, *Nona the Ninth* builds anticipation for the next book, raising new questions and mysteries for readers to consider in the meantime.

Reviews of *Nona the Ninth* were largely positive, with many critics identifying it as a different but worthy successor to Muir's previous acclaimed novels. The anonymous reviewer for *Kirkus* wrote that while the book "initially reads like a strange interlude from the series," it "gradually gathers speed" and ultimately "rockets to a thrilling finish." The critic for *Publishers Weekly* described the novel as "characteristically brilliant" and highlighted "Nona's lovely, simple, and occasionally silly voice" as a particular strength. In a review for *Paste*, Lacy Baugher Milas identified *Nona the Ninth* as the "most personal and human" installment in the Locked Tomb series, noting that it is "a story about life, and maybe even a little bit about hope." Most critics likewise praised the metaphors underlying the novel as well as the complexity of the narrative as a whole, though some acknowledged it could make for a somewhat difficult read. "As long as you go in without expecting fancy things like being able to understand every detail of the action in a literal and straightforward way, it will treat you right," Constance Grady wrote in a review for *Vox*.

A few reviewers were more sharply critical, however, characterizing the novel as disappointing in comparison to its predecessors. Writing for *Gizmodo*, Linda Codega described it as being "about waiting for something else to happen" and commented negatively on Nona's limited involvement in the greater plot as well as the limited role that Gideon plays in the story. Still, Codega nevertheless praised some elements, including the work's exploration of themes such as grief and sacrifice. Ultimately, *Nona the Ninth* both continues Muir's unique approach to science fiction and fantasy and adds new twists, which readers may find challenging but also rewarding.

Author Biography
Tamsyn Muir is the author of *Gideon the Ninth* (2019) and *Harrow the Ninth* (2020) as well as the novella *Princess Floralinda and the Forty-Flight Tower* (2020) and a variety of short stories.

Joy Crelin

Review Sources
Codega, Linda. "*Nona the Ninth* Is Too Much and Too Little." Review of *Nona the Ninth*, by Tamsyn Muir. *Gizmodo*, 12 Sept. 2022, gizmodo.com/nona-the-ninth-review-tamsyn-muir-locked-tomb-series-1849524213. Accessed 31 Oct. 2022.

Grady, Constance. "*Nona the Ninth* Features Dogs, Lesbians, Necromantic Battles, Increasing Levels of Catholicism." Review of *Nona the Ninth*, by Tamsyn Muir. *Vox*, 13 Sept. 2022, www.vox.com/culture/23349112/nona-the-ninth-review-tamsyn-muir-locked-tomb-series-gideon-harrow. Accessed 31 Oct. 2022.

Milas, Lacy Baugher. "*Nona the Ninth*: Tamsyn Muir's Locked Tomb Series Remains Defiantly Weird and Strangely Beautiful." Review of *Nona the Ninth*, by Tamsyn Muir. *Paste*, 13 Sept. 2022, www.pastemagazine.com/books/tamsyn-muir/nona-the-ninth-review-tamsyn-muir/. Accessed 31 Oct. 2022.

Miller, Sam J. Review of *Nona the Ninth*, by Tamsyn Muir." *Locus*, 30 Sept. 2022, locusmag.com/2022/09/sam-j-miller-reviews-nona-the-ninth-by-tamsyn-muir/. Accessed 31 Oct. 2022.

Review of *Nona the Ninth* by Tamsyn Muir. *Kirkus*, 8 July 2022, www.kirkusreviews.com/book-reviews/tamsyn-muir/nona-ninth/. Accessed 31 Oct. 2022.

Review of *Nona the Ninth* by Tamsyn Muir. *Publishers Weekly*, 9 May 2022, www.publishersweekly.com/9781250854117. Accessed 31 Oct. 2022.

Notes on an Execution

Author: Danya Kukafka (b. 1993)
Publisher: HarperCollins (New York). 306 pp.
Type of work: Novel
Time: 1973–Present day
Locale: United States

Danya Kukafka's second novel, Notes on an Execution, *traces the path of an individual as he evolves from neglected child to serial killer to Death Row inmate.*

Principal characters
ANSEL PACKER, a serial killer imprisoned on Death Row in Texas
SHAWNA BILLINGS, a guard on Death Row
LAVENDER PACKER, Ansel's mother
SAFFRON "SAFFY" SINGH, an officer with the New York State Police
JENNY FISK, Ansel's wife
HAZEL FISK, Jenny's twin sister
IZZY SANCHEZ, Angela Meyer, and Lila Maroney, teenagers who went missing in 1990

What does a person condemned to death think about on the last day of their life, as the clock ticks down toward the moment when the US judicial system has scheduled him to die? That is the simple premise of American author Danya Kukafka's suspenseful second novel, *Notes on an Execution* (2022). The answer, however, in this particular case—and perhaps in all similar cases, if related works in the popular Death Row offshoot of crime fiction, such as Stephen King's *The Green Mile* (1996) or John Grisham's *The Reckoning* (2018) are any indication—is complex, and unique.

Kukafka first came to prominence for her 2017 debut *Girl in Snow*, a thriller and murder mystery. In her second novel, Kukafka continues in the vein of mystery and crime fiction by telling the story of a condemned person sweating out his final hours before execution. He is Ansel Packer, prisoner number 999631. The media calls him "The Girly Killer" because long after his murderous spree, he was tracked down, arrested, tried, and convicted of the strangulation murders of three teenage girls who were missing for years before their remains were found. Ansel has been confined for the past seven years to a tiny cell in the Polunsky Unit (an actual facility at the time of the novel's publication, part of a maximum-security prison in West Livingston, Texas.) The novel begins twelve hours before Ansel's scheduled transfer in a heavily guarded van to the Walls Unit in nearby Huntsville, Texas, where the execution,

Danya Kukafka

viewed by selected witnesses, will take place. Readers are treated to a range of perspectives relating to Ansel's life and looming execution that draw a multifaceted portrait of Ansel as he transforms from innocent child to coldblooded murderer, and collectively suggest reasons why he turned out like he did.

Chapters told from Ansel's point of view are named based on the remaining time left in his existence, starting with the first chapter, "12 Hours," and decreasing by hours, then minutes, to the inevitability of "0," which is the novel's final chapter. Details of prison life are sprinkled throughout—the noises, the sights, the sounds, the feelings—allowing readers to vicariously share Ansel's unsettling experience.

Kukafka renders Ansel's chapters in second-person, which not only puts a psychological distance between the actor and his actions, but also attempts to elicit sympathy for someone who, under slightly different circumstances, could have become a completely different person. If Ansel, in his narration, discussed the events of his life in first-person, he would seem to be admitting his bad deeds; the use of the second-person "you" makes it seem as though someone else, an alternate Ansel, is responsible. The tone is established in the opening line, when Ansel examines his thumb and says, "You are a fingerprint."

This narrative choice subtly suggests some of Ansel's traits before they are further revealed during the course of the novel. Ansel is considered handsome. He can come across as charming, a feature Ansel shares with real-life serial killer Ted Bundy, who was executed in Florida in 1989 and is referenced in passing in the novel. Ansel is also intelligent, though is not nearly as smart as he thinks he is. While confined on Death Row, Ansel draws on his college study of philosophy to write what he refers to as the Theory, a manifesto about good, evil, and the myriad possibilities contained in every choice a human makes. He hopes the Theory will be widely distributed and published after his death.

Mostly, Ansel is capable of making people feel at ease by putting himself in their shoes, which opens them up to manipulation. This special skill adds considerable tension to the plot. During his time on Death Row, in whispered conversations and clandestine notes, Ansel has managed to win over a lonely, widowed, middle-aged female guard, Shawna Billings, and convinced Shawna that he loves her. Shawna, drugged by visions of their future life together, has been persuaded to betray her duties and try to help Ansel escape. She has snooped in the warden's office to learn the schedule for Ansel's transfer to his execution site and other key details. She has also agreed to hide her late husband's revolver beneath the van driver's seat, where Ansel can extract it with his feet; if Ansel is lucky, he will be able to use it to threaten the driver and guards in order to escape. Shawna will be eagerly waiting at her home for her would-be lover to arrive, ready with hair dye, colored contact lenses, and old clothes to replace Ansel's prison uniform.

Alternating with the tense countdown to Ansel's execution are chapters concerning other individuals—all women—who were instrumental in his development. A key contributor is his mother, Lavender Packer. Pregnant with Ansel at sixteen, she drops out of high school to move in with Ansel's father, Johnny, who inherited a rundown farm near the Canadian border in upstate New York. Lavender gives birth to Ansel in the barn in 1973. Years later, Johnny has become abusive to both Lavender and her young children; eventually, Lavender decides she has no option but to abandon them. While on the road, she secretly calls 911, pleading for her children to be rescued. Lavender winds up at a women's commune in California, where she finds peace and safety but cannot escape the guilt of deserting her children.

Another important person in Ansel's development is Saffron "Saffy" Singh, a half-Sikh preteen who grows up alongside Ansel and several other children in foster care at the home of a woman named Miss Gemma. There, Saffy becomes afraid of Ansel after she observes him killing and mutilating mice, squirrels, and other small animals. As an adult, Saffy joins the New York State Police, becomes a homicide detective, and quickly rises through the ranks to become the youngest captain in the department. In 1990, after three teenage girls—Izzy Sanchez, Angela Meyer, and Lila Maroney—go missing, Saffy investigates. She uncovers information that causes her to suspect Ansel might be responsible. She periodically stakes out his trailer and occasionally follows him. But even after a hiker discovers the girls' remains in the woods nine years after their disappearance, she cannot produce the evidence necessary to arrest and convict him.

A third important woman in Ansel's life is Hazel Fisk, the fraternal (but nearly identical) twin of Ansel's wife, Jenny Fisk. Though the twins have a longstanding rivalry—Hazel is jealous of her sister, who is more attractive and charismatic—Jenny insists she sometimes senses the emotions of her twin at a distance, a sensation she calls "the summoning." For example, Jenny claims to have felt Hazel's pain when she injured her knee. Hazel first meets Ansel when Jenny brings her fiancé home to their parents' house for Christmas. Early one morning, awakened by the barking of the family dog, Hazel sees Ansel bury something in the backyard, but thinks nothing of it at the time.

Though Ansel's crimes and death sentence are known from the outset, *Notes on an Execution* contains a number of mysteries to engage readers to the end of the novel. Why did Ansel, at age seventeen, start killing people instead of animals? How did he choose victims? Why did he apparently stop killing after murdering the three girls who went missing in 1990? If he killed in New York, why is he confined in Texas? How was he caught? Will his escape plan work? By the last page, Kukafka manages to answer all such questions.

Kukafka provides a number of memorable scenes and twists as she brings the plot toward its finale, rendering her story in memorable prose peppered with thought-provoking, epigrammatic passages. For example, Kukafka includes passages such as,

"Pity is destruction wearing a mask of sympathy." Additionally, she threads commentary on several other issues throughout the story. For example, the deleterious effects of abuse—whether physical, sexual, or emotional—provides a continuous theme. The gaps in the foster care system and the injustices perpetuated by the judicial and penal systems are also integral to the story.

Critics welcomed *Notes on an Execution* with wide praise upon its 2022 publication. Katie Kitamura, writing for the *New York Times* (25 Jan. 2022) described "the relationships between women—sisters, friends, colleagues" as "beautifully drawn, dense with detail and specificity." Kitamura also praised Kukafka for "[filling] in the lives of the women in Ansel's orbit" in an attempt to humanize those affected by Ansel's crimes. However, Kitamura also felt that Ansel "[remained] at the heart of the novel, functioning as the story's conceptual negative space," and that the story drew "propulsive power . . . from the very conventions it fail[ed] to abandon." She concluded that, in spite of this slight flaw, the novel is "nuanced, ambitious, and compelling." Rebecca Munro, writing for *Book Reporter* (4 Feb. 2022), agreed, writing, "Kukafka writes gorgeous, spellbinding prose, distilling huge, complicated themes into crystalline moments of deep, painful truths." Munro described the novel as "an emotionally resonant and grippingly taut literary thriller."

Oline H. Cogdill, writing for the *South Florida Sun Sentinel* (2 Feb. 2022), added to the acclaim, calling the novel "a masterful look at a murderer's origins and the women affected by these crimes." Suzanne Perez, writing for *KMUW Radio* in Wichita, Kansas (14 Mar. 2022), heaped on the praise, saying, "Everything about this book is propulsive and mesmerizing—an atmospheric work of literary suspense that grabs you from the start and doesn't let go." Tod Goldberg, in his four-star review for *USA Today* (23 Jan. 2022), called *Notes on an Execution* "a career-defining novel—powerful, important, intensely human, and filled with a unique examination of tragedy . . . where the reader is left with a curious emotion: hope."

Author Biography
Danya Kukafka, who began her career in the writing world as a literary agent, published her first novel, the international bestseller and critically acclaimed murder mystery, *Girl in Snow*, in 2017.

Jack Ewing

Review Sources
Cogdill, Oline H. "Book Review: Notes on an Execution Turns on the Women in Serial Killer's Orbit." South Florida Sun Sentinel, 2 Feb. 2022, www.sun-sentinel.com/entertainment/theater-and-arts/books/fl-et-notes-execution-book-review-20220202-thjmbdbfzjauvl5ahfltpckmk4-story.html. Accessed 15 Sept. 2022.
Goldberg, Tod. "Notes on an Execution Is a Different Kind of Serial Killer Story, and a Brilliant One." USA Today, 23 Jan. 2022, www.usatoday.com/story/entertainment/books/2022/01/23/danya-kukafkas-latest-different-kind-serial-killer-story/6613202001/. Accessed 15 Sept. 2022.

Kitamura, Katie. "Notes on an Execution Isn't Your Typical Serial Killer Novel." The New York Times, 25 Jan. 2022, www.nytimes.com/2022/01/25/books/review/notes-on-an-execution-danya-kukafka.html. Accessed 15 Sept. 2022.

Munro, Rebecca. Review of Notes on an Execution, by Danya Kukafka. Book Reporter, 4 Feb. 2022, www.bookreporter.com/reviews/notes-on-an-execution. Accessed 15 Sept. 2022.

Perez, Suzanne. "Notes on an Execution Explores the Psyche of a Serial Killer and the Women Who Shaped Him." KMUW Radio, 14 Mar. 2022, www.kmuw.org/podcast/book-review/2022-03-14/notes-on-an-execution-explores-the-psyche-of-a-serial-killer-and-the-women-who-shaped-him. Accessed 15 Sept. 2022.

Nothing Burns as Bright as You

Author: Ashley Woodfolk
Publisher: Versify (New York). 288 pp.
Type of work: Verse novel
Time: Present
Locale: Unknown

In her 2022 young adult novel Nothing Burns as Bright as You, *acclaimed author Ashley Woodfolk uses poetic prose to tell the story of an intense, impassioned, and troubled first love affair.*

Principal characters
You, the best friend and love interest of the narrator
THE NARRATOR, an unnamed young woman

By the time her young adult verse novel *Nothing Burns as Bright as You* was published in 2022, author Ashley Woodfolk had become a key voice in the world of young adult (YA) fiction. Her deftly written character studies focus in on the lives of young people of color, exploring the traumas, victories, challenges, and insecurities that shape young people and their relationships. In particular, she gained a reputation for writing characters that felt and sounded genuine rather than contrived or archetypical.

Woodfolk wrote her debut novel, *The Beauty That Remains* (2018), while working in marketing at a children's book publisher. In interviews, Woodfolk said she was passionate about the YA fiction she was exposed to in her youth but noticed how none of the characters ever resembled someone like her. This inspired Woodfolk's writing, which she honed through workshops and in writing short fiction, before she succeeded with her debut, which tells the story of three people coping with tragedy and loss who come together through their mutual love for one band's music. The novel won critical acclaim, became a best seller, and helped establish Woodfolk as a major new voice, while also contributing to a growing number of writers creating YA fiction featuring characters of color, queer relationships, and other story elements historically overlooked in YA fiction.

Woodfolk followed up with another best seller in 2020, *When You Were Everything*, and starting that year began releasing the *Flyy Girls* series of short novels, which center on a group of high-school girls who face profound challenges and changes as they navigate their young lives. She also contributed to several fiction anthologies, including the critically acclaimed *Blackout* (2022), in which Woodfolk joined other prominent YA writers, including Nicola Yoon and Dhonielle Clayton, for an anthology of Black teen romances.

Ashley Woodfolk

Woodfolk's sophomore novel, *When You Were Everything*, saw the author experimenting with story structure, telling the story of a friendship as it developed, while at the same time telling the story of the time after the friendship ended and the wounds of this loss. Woodfolk uses a similar device in *Nothing Burns as Bright as You*—she tells the story forward and, essentially, backward at the same time, though this time the narrative focuses on the relationship between two young Black women. The relationship transforms from friendship to romance, and from romance to toxic relationship.

As in some of Woodfolk's earlier work, one of the two main characters of *Nothing Burns as Bright as You* serves as an unnamed, first-person narrator. The other main character—the narrator's love interest, best friend, and partner in crime—is referred to only as "You." This narrative choice means that the book is essentially from the point of view of the narrator, and much of the prose contains intimate details of the narrator's angst-ridden reflections on this epic, dramatic love affair that came into her life and ended dramatically. However, by having her narrator refer to her lover in second person, Woodfolk draws the reader into the story as well, at times blurring the distinction as to whether she is referring to the character or the reader directly.

While the book is considered a novel, Woodfolk chose to write in verse, which means the book can also be read or experienced as a poetic series. Some of the verses are longer and detailed, others are sparse and short. Some describe events and interactions, providing a sense of action, while others are stray reflections and thoughts. The poetic structure affords Woodfolk an artistic freedom different from what one might employ in a standard novel. The narrator's expressions can be more overtly angst-ridden, more knowingly poetic, because the narrator is telling her own story, through her own lens. In addition, telling the story in verse means that there is less material per page and chapter, as the story is told in snippets rather than narrative scenes and acts.

The story, however interestingly it is presented, is essentially about a pair of best friends who have discovered a passionate, physical, and romantic love for one another. This relationship begins tentatively, like something from a romantic comedy; Woodfolk depicts these two young women exploring their sexuality while still uncertain of their attraction to women. This develops into a rocky, desperate passion between the narrator and her partner, and eventually escalates to an explosive breakup that leaves the characters and reader in uncertainty. This dramatic crescendo seems to be presented out of sequence, but it is actually two different, yet roughly chronological, stories that begin at different points in the characters' shared timeline. Some verses tell the story of the pair's developing romance from the beginning to the end, though

Woodfolk intersperses this narrative with verses that tell the story of the literal dumpster fire that the two women end up setting together. The interwoven verses following this segment of their relationship also progress from past to present but focus primarily on the moments in their relationship that led up to them setting this fire and the aftermath of this act of rebellious destruction.

The moment in the book where the two characters first find each other, essentially the "meet-cute" at the center of this romantic drama, takes place, readers are told, "867 Days Before the Fire." Woodfolk describes the moment when the two main characters order the "same drink" using the "same fake name," and notes how their "soft brown hands collided / like stars." By explicitly stating that this meeting took place 867 days, more than two years, before the fire, Woodfolk provides readers with a measure of the relationship's potential depth from the outset. The reader also learns, early on, about the fire that drove a wedge in their relationship, but the understanding of the incident progresses and deepens in subsequent verses, while the reader is also still learning about the young women's love for each other and seeing signs of what would eventually come for their relationship. Directly opposite the brief retelling of their first meeting, Woodfolk immediately begins to set up the event that drove them apart. Over the course of the novel, she weaves the story of their romance blooming and faltering into a close retelling of the dramatic days leading to their separation. This winding narrative ultimately draws both stories toward a shared conclusion that reveals the way that these experiences shaped their understanding of themselves and the connection they shared.

Woodfolk's verse is especially interesting when she explores the periphery of her characters' lives. In intimate fragments of conversations and pillow talk, Woodfolk's narrator reflects on the cultural strains and stresses unique to Black women, the push and pull of sexuality and societal pressure, and the appeal and revulsion of eighties teen romance films, whose lack of diversity affected the way that people interact with art and culture. These poetic asides broaden the cultural context of the novel, deepen reader's feeling for its characters, and also provide much of what makes the romance seem genuine.

While Woodfolk is writing for younger audiences, she does not shy away from depicting her teenage characters in a more realistic manner. The narrator and her lover have sex, fantasize, smoke marijuana, and swear. This realism separates Woodfolk's work from young adult fiction that has been sanitized to avoid causing controversy. Woodfolk's narrator's thoughts can be impressively poetic but also reflect the more familiar and casual ways that young people think and talk to one another.

Woodfolk's depiction of the relationship between her two young characters is another way in which the book echoes the complexities of modern life and love. Though these young lovers are intimate with each other—for example, kissing and touching each other and sharing a bed—it is made clear that neither partner explicitly defined the relationship or labeled the other as their girlfriend. They are shown as best friends and more, existing with one another in a state of chaotic ambiguity that captures the uncertainty, fear, and anxiety of young love. Fitting the novel's LGBTQ+ themes,

Woodfolk also uses the uncertainty of this relationship to explore the challenges for those conflicted in their expressions of sexuality.

The dissolution of this relationship hinges on the fire, an act of youthful, destructive rebellion, or perhaps even anarchism. The fire also symbolizes the differences between the two women that initially draw them to one another and later push them apart. From the beginning, Woodfolk's narrator explains that she and her lover are opposites, a familiar trope in the romance genre. The narrator explains that she, in contrast to her partner, wanted to set a flood instead of a fire at their school, feeling that a flood would cause less damage, raise fewer questions, and could be more easily explained as an accident rather than a criminal act. In a vivid passage, Woodfolk uses poetic language to describe the characters' opposing natures:

> And this
> is a perfect metaphor
> for us:
> Fire and water. Flames and frost.
> Hot and cold, burning and freezing.
> Opposites.

Indeed, the attraction and repulsion of dynamic opposites is a repeated theme in the book, appearing again and again in many different ways. Readers are invited to consider whether the characters' opposing natures dooms their relationship from the start or whether this dynamism makes their connection worth fighting for and preserving. Though the entire book is told from the narrator's singular point of view, with her lover presented as a distant, near-mythological figure whom the narrator both fears and reveres, the story nevertheless manages to present two different and unique perspectives on a shared love that drives the story and draws the reader into seeing where this explosive relationship ends up.

Fire is the other major poetic theme of the book—there are vivid descriptions of the literal fire at the center of the story, as well as the language the narrator uses to describe her passion, anger, and fear. Fire becomes a metaphor for the intensity of the narrator's attraction to her partner but also serves as a metaphor for the emotional risk of intimacy. Passages throughout expose the narrator's fear that she will inevitably be "burned" because she has dared to risk losing everything by loving her friend.

Nothing Burns as Bright as You received mostly positive reviews from critics upon its release. A reviewer for *Kirkus* called the book a "beautiful, emotionally charged novel," and a reviewer for *Publishers Weekly* called it a "fast-moving novel" that "captures the unbalanced experience of an all-consuming love." Kayla Fontaine, writing for the *School Library Journal*, was even more effusive, calling the book "a masterfully crafted love letter to tumultuous, young, queer love and its lessons," adding that "even the blank space on the page helps to carry this piece to its full potential." While reviews were generally positive, some readers and reviewers found the narrative structure confusing or at least challenging, while others found that the choice to write the book in verse left out narrative details that might have deepened the story. As a result, though *Nothing Burns as Bright as You* might not be considered an entry-level work in the YA genre, it is a worthy read for those interested in works that deviate from familiar formulas.

Author Biography
Ashley Woodfolk has worked as a marketing professional and writer. After publishing her 2018 debut novel, *The Beauty That Remains*, Woodfolk continued writing in the young adult genre. Her other works include *When You Were Everything* (2020) and *Nothing Burns as Bright as You* (2022).

Micah Issitt

Review Sources
Fontaine, Kayla. Review of *Nothing Burns as Bright as You*, by Ashley Woodfolk. *School Library Journal*, Apr. 2022, www.slj.com/review/nothing-burns-as-bright-as-you. Accessed 14 Feb. 2023.
Review of *Nothing Burns as Bright as You*, by Ashley Woodfolk. *Kirkus*, 5 Apr. 2022, www.kirkusreviews.com/book-reviews/ashley-woodfolk/nothing-burns-as-bright-as-you/. Accessed 14 Feb. 2023.
Review of *Nothing Burns as Bright as You*, by Ashley Woodfolk. *Publishers Weekly*, 24 Feb. 2022, www.publishersweekly.com/9780358655350. Accessed 14 Feb. 2023.
Review of *Nothing Burns as Bright as You*, by Ashley Woodfolk. *Slanted Spines*, 15 Apr. 2022, slantedspines.com/2022/04/15/nothing-burns-as-bright-as-you-a-book-review/. Accessed 14 Feb. 2023.

Nothing More to Tell

Author: Karen M. McManus
Publisher: Delacorte Press (New York). 368 pp.
Type of work: Novel
Time: 2022
Locale: Massachusetts

In Nothing More to Tell, *Karen M. McManus presents an engaging murder mystery aimed at a young adult audience. Returning to her old prep school after an absence of almost four years, student journalist Brynn Gallagher begins investigating the murder of a popular teacher that was never satisfactorily resolved; her efforts threaten to expose old secrets and lead to danger and romance.*

Principal characters

BRYNN GALLAGHER, an aspiring journalist who begins exploring the murder of William Larkin, her eighth grade English teacher
TRIPP TALBOT, a former friend of hers who was one of the three students who found Mr. Larkin's body
SHANE DELGADO, a wealthy and popular athlete who was one of the three students who found Mr. Larkin's body
CHARLOTTE HOLBROOK, a wealthy and popular social leader at school, Shane's girlfriend, and one of the three students who found Mr. Larkin's body
NICK GALLAGHER, Brynn's uncle
ELLIE GALLAGHER, Brynn's fourteen-year-old sister
CARLY DIAZ, host of the cable true-crime show "Motive" who hires Brynn as an intern
REGINA YOUNG, Tripp's employer and friend
LISA MARIE TALBOT, Tripp's mother who abandoned him and his father

Karen M. McManus has thrived as a writer for the lucrative young adult market. Her specialty is young adult mystery thrillers. She first made her mark with *One of Us Is Lying* (2017), which demonstrated her skill at constructing a satisfying murder whodunnit with teen protagonists. The novel was also a smashing commercial success, spending 130 weeks on the New York Times Best Sellers list. Since then, McManus has written a pair of series follow-ups to her debut effort as well as several stand-alone novels, of which *Nothing More to Tell* (2022) is the latest. This corpus of work has set McManus on the road to becoming the Agatha Christie of the teen set.

Writing young adult novels is not for the faint of heart. In an age of heightened political passions and sensitivities, educators, librarians, parents, and the young readers themselves have high expectations about point of view and representation. There is enormous pressure to highlight diversity and inclusion in young adult novels. Several of the reviewers of *Nothing More to Tell* made a point of noting that the core quartet of characters in the book is White. Satisfying progressive expectations while writing a murder mystery can be especially challenging. The mystery novel as a genre is fundamentally "conservative." As renowned mystery novelist P. D. James once wrote, "What the detective story is about is not murder but the restoration of order." There are, and have been, all sorts of detectives in mystery novels over the years, of both sexes, with differing sexual orientations, aged from young to old, engaged in various occupations, and inhabiting the full range of time periods; however, for all that the ethos of the classic mystery novel has never been revolutionary. As James made clear, it involves the healing of a rupture caused by an unnatural death, and a more or less successful effort to put Humpty Dumpty back together again. Whatever the sentiments of the author or the characters in such a story, solving a murder, very often by agents of established authority or those who act in effect as their proxies, is rarely an act of social transformation. In the closed world of a mystery novel, the killer is more of an agent of change than the detective.

Karen M. McManus

So McManus offers no formal innovations with this novel; instead, she bows to the conventions of the time in ancillary details. Her book reads the way a conventional television teen drama looks, as a group of ethnically assorted and mostly affluent young people wrestle with crime and relationships. The traditional mystery novel stereotypically took place in an English country house amid a crowd of aristocrats and their dependents as suspects. McManus maintains an upper-class perspective. Her book and characters exhibit the worldview of the contemporary secular monied elite, the sort of folks who draw their information from the *New York Times* and NPR, liberal in social views and politics but keeping a close eye on developments on Wall Street and the markets. McManus's heroine is Brynn Gallagher, who, after a three-year stay in the Chicago area, finds herself back in her old hometown of Sturgis, Massachusetts, and once again attending Saint Ambrose, a prestigious private school. Her father is a research scientist and her mother is an award-winning illustrator of children's books. Though Brynn was a scholarship student when she first left Saint Ambrose in eighth grade, that is not the case as she returns to finish her senior year in high school. Thanks to her father's success, money is no longer an issue. She finds herself classified with the tuition-paying "elites" rather than the financially assisted "dregs." The plot soon has her associating with some of the wealthier students in her class. Brynn's classmate Tripp Talbot, who provides a contrasting first-person point of view in the novel, is a scholarship student from a working-class and financially unstable family. Nevertheless, his good looks and rich friends place him among the "elites." Tripp also makes it clear that he has internalized the values of his haute bourgeoisie associates.

Notwithstanding its name, religion plays no part in Saint Ambrose's curriculum. Nor does religion figure in Brynn's or her friends' lives. When her little sister decides to dress up like Madonna for an eighties-themed dance, she asks Brynn if she has any crosses or rosaries; Brynn has none to offer. The only religious person in the book is a working-class character who espouses a vaguely asserted form of fundamentalist Christianity; given the ideological dynamic at work in the novel, he is a bigot and a sexist. Indeed, in this novel the less-affluent characters are generally problematic. Many behave deplorably, like Tripp's gold-digging birth mother. The men cling to their guns and two draw them on Brynn and Tripp as they conduct their investigations. The fictional town of Sturgis is described as ramshackle and run-down, and as the novel's characters admit, it is an incongruous setting for an institution like Saint Ambrose. Among some of the townsfolk, resentment of the upper-crust students runs deep. At school, Brynn is hazed by a loudly obnoxious scholarship student. As one of her privileged friends matter-of-factly explains, the standards for grants have been relaxed, leading to "a lot more local kids in the Upper School who are not quite as academically inclined." A particularly unpleasant example is the Saint Ambrose groundskeeper, who proves to be uncooperative during an interview. He is unrepentantly impertinent, makes fun of the rich kids' names, and wears a ragged "Live Free or Die" baseball cap. Brynn is out of place among such characters and would be more at home detecting in the manor house, where crime is reserved for the genteel.

Such opinions as are expressed by the characters in *Nothing More to Tell* fall safely into what was once termed the "politically correct." Though the four key players in the book are White, they are largely surrounded by racially, ethnically, and sexually diverse supporting characters. Brynn's classmates include people of East Asian and South Asian ancestry. Her employer is Hispanic. She has gay friends both in Chicago and Sturgis; her fourteen-year-old sister is attracted to the same sex. Tripp's boss at the bakery where he works is a wise and caring Black American woman. She is a stock type seen many times before, preternaturally warm and motherly, while also the voice of reason and morality.

No one reading McManus's book will be surprised at her variegated cast of characters. She has done what is expected and easily meets the current market exigencies of a young adult novel. In this regard, she is in no way original. Where McManus truly stands out is in her skill at weaving a compelling mystery. She knows how to construct a plot, provide plenty of clues, and keep the reader guessing right up to the last few pages. She builds suspense artfully, ends with a crescendo of excitement, and does not cheat on the solution to the mystery; the reader has a fighting chance to figure out who the real murderer is. With the puzzle at the heart of *Nothing More to Tell*, McManus demonstrates that she belongs in the top rank in her branch of mass-market fiction.

At the beginning of the story, Brynn is literally experiencing a winter of discontent. In the middle of her senior year in high school, her father's professional success has led to a move from the exciting environs of Chicago to the enforced small-town doldrums of Sturgis. At the same time, she believes that an undeserved embarrassment with her school paper in Chicago threatens her prospects to get into Northwestern University's journalism program. Brynn makes a bid to retrieve her reportorial dreams by persuading Carly Diaz, the host of a Boston-based true crime TV show, to take her on as an unpaid intern. Brynn impresses Carly by raising questions about the murder of her eighth-grade English teacher, William Larkin, who was found dead in a wood behind Saint Ambrose. The Sturgis police blamed the killing on a drifter who disappeared the same day. This pat solution to the crime does not satisfy Brynn, who proposes to dig deeper into the events surrounding Larkin's death. Admiring Brynn's enterprise, Carly awards her an internship and assigns her to the Larkin case. This sets in motion the events of the novel. Brynn's investigation takes her into the orbit of the eighth-grade classmates who discovered Mr. Larkin's body, the wealthy and popular Shane Delgado and Charlotte Holbrook, now a couple, and Tripp, formerly a friend but who had publicly humiliated her shortly before the murder. Brynn is a determined and resourceful detective, very much in the tradition of Nancy Drew, or, as an interlocutor observes, Veronica Mars. The only spunkier character is her younger sister Ellie, who also proves to be a formidable investigator and, arguably, deserving of a spin-off novel. Tripp is a worthy foil and source of romantic interest, with enough moodiness and closely guarded secrets to qualify him as an updated and teenaged Mr. Rochester. None of the characters exhibit anything approaching Dostoyevskian depth, but McManus is spinning a mystery, not a meditation on the human condition.

Reviewers praised *Nothing More to Tell* overall, with Rebekah J. Buchanan, writing for *School Library Journal*, describing it as a "win for mystery and suspense fans," and the anonymous *Kirkus* critic calling it an "edge-of-your-seat page-turner; the strongest yet from a master of the genre." Such praise is well deserved. McManus's latest novel is an absorbing and stimulating whodunit that will engage reader's sympathies and exercise their brain cells. Fans of McManus and those new to her work could ask for nothing more.

Author Biography
Karen M. McManus is a best-selling author of young adult thrillers. Her works include the *One of Us Is Lying* series and stand-alone novels like *Two Can Keep a Secret* (2019), *The Cousins* (2020), and *You'll Be the Death of Me* (2021).

Daniel P. Murphy

Review Sources
Buchanan, Rebekah J. Review of *Nothing More to Tell*, by Karen M. McManus. *School Library Journal*, 1 Sept. 2022, www.slj.com/review/nothing-more-to-tell. Accessed 27 Feb. 2023.
Reagan, Maggie. Review of *Nothing More to Tell*, by Karen M. McManus. *Booklist*, 1 Aug. 2022, p. 51. *Literary Reference Center Plus*, search.ebscohost.com/login.aspx?direct=true&db=lkh&AN=158462033&site=lrc-plus. Accessed 27 Feb. 2023.

Review of *Nothing More to Tell*, by Karen M. McManus. *Kirkus*, 10 May 2022, www.kirkusreviews.com/book-reviews/karen-m-mcmanus/nothing-more-to-tell/. Accessed 27 Jan. 2023.

Review of *Nothing More to Tell*, by Karen M. McManus. *Publishers Weekly*, 14 July 2022, www.publishersweekly.com/9780593175903. Accessed 27 Jan. 2023.

Now Is Not the Time to Panic

Author: Kevin Wilson (b. 1978)
Publisher: Ecco (New York). 256 pp.
Type of work: Novel
Time: 1996 and 2017
Locale: Coalfield, Tennessee

Set in the sleepy southern town of Coalfield, Tennessee, Now Is Not the Time to Panic *is a coming-of-age story, told from the perspective of teenager Frances (Frankie) Budge as she experiences a life-altering summer in which she and her friend Zeke's seemingly insignificant creation sends the whole town of Coalfield, and beyond, spiraling into unimaginable territory.*

Principal characters
FRANCES "FRANKIE" BUDGE, the novel's protagonist and narrator who is an aspiring writer
ZEKE, her teenage friend/boyfriend, an aspiring artist
CARRIE NEAL, her mom
THE TRIPLETS (ANDREW, Brian, and Charlie), her older brothers
HOBART, Carrie's boyfriend, a newspaper reporter
CYDNEY HUDSON BROWN, Zeke's mom
AARON, her husband in 2017
JUNIE, her daughter in 2017
MR. AVERY, her neighbor, an artist
MAZZY BROWER, an art critic and reporter trying to interview her as an adult in 2017

Now Is Not the Time to Panic (2022), the critically acclaimed writer Kevin Wilson's fourth novel, is a witty and endearing coming-of-age story that is told primarily from the perspective of sixteen-year-old Frankie Budge, a misfit aspiring writer living in a small Tennessee town. The novel opens in 2017 with an adult Frankie answering the phone to Mazzy Brower, an art critic writing a piece about the Coalfield Panic of 1996. At first assuming she is a telemarketer, Frankie is about to hang up when Mazzy says the words that send Frankie into a spiral of emotions: "The edge is a shantytown filled with gold seekers. We are fugitives, and the law is skinny with hunger for us."

From this point, the reader is transported to a summer day in 1996 on which sixteen-year-old Frankie is at the public pool passively observing the chaotic scene transpiring before her as a mob of boys fights over a greased watermelon. This is the moment she meets the boy she will never forget, Zeke, a "skinny and twitchy" teen from Memphis

Kevin Wilson

who is staying with his grandmother in Coalfield for the summer. Frankie is curious about this new boy, who in many ways is as awkward as she is, an outsider standing unnoticed at the fringes of daily life.

The youngest of four siblings born to a single mother, Carrie, Frankie is a loner with no real friends to speak of. Her estranged father has moved on to another town with a new wife and a new daughter, also named Frances. Throughout the novel, Frankie speculates about this "other Frances," who has clearly replaced her in her father's affections. Her three older brothers are triplets, who are themselves a force of nature, constantly creating chaos and all manners of mischief in their wake. The extreme "togetherness" of the triplets, almost to the point of a hive mind, emphasizes how much of an outsider Frankie is even in her own family.

Zeke is also the product of a troubled marriage, his father still living at the family home in Memphis, while his deeply depressed mom, Cydney, a former musical prodigy, takes him back to her hometown of Coalfield while she contemplates a divorce. Looking for a distraction from his mother's trance-like state and his grandmother's obsession with game shows, he soon begins hanging out (and making out) with Frankie, and the two bond over their shared artistic pursuits—her writing and his drawing. He suggests the two join forces to "make art," as Frankie quips, "like art was cookies or microwave popcorn." Finding an old forgotten copy machine in Frankie's garage, stolen by her brothers and long assumed to be broken, the machine comes to life again when Zeke is able to fix what amounts to be a simple paper jam. Using the machine, the two create multiple copies of a cryptic poster illustrated by Zeke and scrawled with Frankie's words, "The edge is a shantytown filled with gold seekers. We are fugitives, and the law is skinny with hunger for us." The words begin to take on a life of their own and become an obsession for Frankie who eats, sleeps, and breathes them, but she is not the only one.

As the two teenagers plaster the town of Coalfield with posters, the public, at first barely registering their enigmatic presence, suddenly runs wild with speculation fueled by a made-up story in which "the fugitives" are blamed for the kidnapping and drugging of two teens who were, in reality, out all night getting high at an abandoned house. From that point, all manners of conspiracy, satanic panic, deaths, and injuries ensue. The police ban publicly accessible copy machines around town and eventually close off the town to outsiders. A vigilante group decides to "protect" the town but ends up injuring and killing innocent citizens in their zest for justice. Even Hobart, boyfriend of Frankie's mom and newspaper writer, gets in on the act, creating tantalizing headlines and fueling speculation of a more sinister side to the mysterious posters. The panic eventually spreads beyond Coalfield, making national headlines and appearing on true-crime dramas with Frankie's enigmatic phrase scrawled on T-shirts and bumper stickers.

Through all of this, Frankie and Zeke stay silent, with Zeke's anxiety on the rise as more chaos ensues. He wants to stop, but Frankie cannot bear the thought of abandoning their mutual creation. Her taste for both her creative expression as well as the companionship Zeke provides are just too much. She has been alone too long and, now she and Zeke share a bond that no one else will ever be able to understand. The final straw occurs when Frankie and Zeke take a trip to Memphis, Zeke's hometown, and after a day enjoying the city and continuing to put up posters, the duo finds themselves at Zeke's family home. In an act of defiance, they put a poster in the mailbox only to be confronted by Zeke's father and a young woman with whom he is clearly having an affair. After a few moments of dawning horror and awkwardness, Zeke's father realizes that it is his son who is responsible for the now infamous "troublesome street art" as the media calls it. The two argue, and Zeke physically attacks his father. Frankie and Zeke rush from the scene, filled with raw emotion over all they have been through. In his frenzied state, Zeke kisses Frankie and tries to convince her to have sex with him, but she turns him down, not wanting to mar the bond they have already created. Ashamed, Zeke apologizes, and the two return to Coalfield only to find that in their absence a local teen has been shot and killed by a gun-toting gang of men thinking he is responsible for the posters.

As the novel continues, a now adult Frankie is forced to face this past that she has kept buried. She has become a famous writer, eventually publishing the "Evil Nancy Drew" novel that she had been working on that very summer when she met Zeke. She is married with a child. As her secret is threatened, Frankie confesses to her family. She also reflects on how her relationship with Zeke ended and searches him out, meeting with the boy she cannot forget for the first time since that summer and reconnecting again through art.

Wilson does a remarkable job of painting a picture of a sleepy town from the eyes of an awkward teenage girl, inspired by his own small-town roots and experiences as a young adult growing up in the 1990s. Wilson explained in an interview with NPR that Frankie's iconic phrase was actually a real quote made up by a college friend named Eric, who later moved to LA to pursue acting. "The minute he said it, it just kind of exploded in my brain. And I've held on to it ever since," Wilson explained. When Eric passed away unexpectedly during the pandemic, Wilson stated, "I felt like all I really had left was my memories of him. But then I realized I had this book, that I could write my way toward something with these fictional characters, that it was now their story. And that was freeing, in a way." Wilson's own Tourette's diagnosis as an adult also gave him a particular insight into the power of art, saying that writing "was the thing that saved" him.

The novel was met largely with praise from critics. *Kirkus Reviews* called the novel "a warm, witty two-hander that sidesteps the clichés of art school and indie film and treats its free spirits with respect" as it "focuses on the wonderful, terrible, transformative power of art." Sloane Crosley for the *New York Times* remarked on the movie-like feel of the novel, similar in sentiment to other coming-of-age plots like *Adventureland* (2009) or *Stand by Me* (1986), while also speculating on the authenticity of Frankie's adult voice, which sounds nearly identical to that of her teenage self. In an article for the *Atlantic*, Stephanie Hayes wrote that characters are "haunted but not bound" by negative past experiences and that Wilson successfully outwits the "trauma-plot-trap."

Now Is Not the Time to Panic, like many coming-of-age stories, encompasses overarching themes of friendship, first love, sentimentality, and adventure, but it is also more than that. The interesting thing about Frankie as a character is that she is the most unlikely person to have created such chaos. In her life, she is used to the antics of her brothers who are practically feral in the way they behave. By comparison, Frankie goes through life almost unnoticed. Zeke also flies under the radar as he is not even a resident of Coalfield and nearly invisible to all but Frankie. And yet, Frankie and Zeke strike the town of Coalfield with their art without even realizing the extent of their power, until they cause such a ripple effect that a simple art project born out of boredom in a messy garage becomes a force of nature.

Author Biography

Kevin Wilson is an associate professor of English at the University of the South in Tennessee. In addition to his three previous novels, *The Family Fang* (2011), *Perfect Little World* (2017), and *Nothing to See Here* (2019), he also wrote two collections, *Tunneling to the Center of the Earth* (2009), and *Baby You're Gonna Be Mine* (2018). He is a recipient of an Alex Award from the American Library Association and a Shirley Jackson award.

Aimee Bear

Review Sources

Crosley, Sloane. "In This Novel, Teenage Artists Spawn a Deadly Moral Panic." Review of *Now Is Not the Time to Panic*, by Kevin Wilson. *The New York Times*, 7 Nov. 2022, www.nytimes.com/2022/11/07/books/review/kevin-wilson-now-is-not-the-time-to-panic.html. Accessed 15 Jan. 2023.

Hayes, Stephanie. "A Novel That Will Make You Laugh and Then Punch You in the Gut." Review of *Now Is Not the Time to Panic*, by Kevin Wilson. *The Atlantic*, 2 Dec. 2022, www.theatlantic.com/books/archive/2022/12/kevin-wilson-now-is-not-the-time-to-panic-book-review/672324/. Accessed 15 Jan. 2023.

Review of *Now Is Not the Time to Panic*, by Kevin Wilson. *Kirkus Reviews*, 17 Aug. 2022, www.kirkusreviews.com/book-reviews/kevin-wilson/now-is-not-the-time-to-panic/. Accessed 20 Jan. 2023.

The Ogress and the Orphans

Author: Kelly Barnhill (b. 1973)
Publisher: Algonquin Young Readers (Chapel Hill, NC). 400 pp.
Type of work: Novel
Time: Sometime in the past
Locale: Stone-in-the-Glen

The town of Stone-in-the-Glen was once a beautiful and happy place, but after the library and several other buildings burned down, the people fell into despair. A group of orphan children and a friendly ogress, however, remain hopeful and loving, eventually showing the townspeople that being a good neighbor can make a change for everyone.

Principal characters

THE OGRESS, a lonely but loveable ogress woman who lives on the edge of town
MATRON, an elderly woman, guardian of the Orphan House
MYRON, Matron's husband, guardian of the Orphan House
ANTHEA, the oldest of the orphans, inventive and intelligent
BARTLEBY, the second-oldest child, philosophical and argumentative
CASS, Bartleby's sister, quiet, hardworking, and compassionate
THE MAYOR, a famous dragon slayer who leads the town; tricky, greedy, and suspicious

The Ogress and the Orphans (2022) is Kelly Barnhill's fifth children's novel. Best known for her fantasy children's books, this novel follows Barnhill's Newbery Medal–winning book *The Girl Who Drank the Moon* (2016). Sharing many fantasy elements with her previous works, *The Ogress and the Orphans* is especially notable for its narrative style, characterization, and thematic ideas.

Reminiscent of Lemony Snicket in the popular *Series of Unfortunate Events* books, the first-person narrator of *The Ogress and the Orphans* is a side character who seems personally involved in the action, who has observed it firsthand, and who has an opinion about both action and characters. This opinion is shared through commentary directed at the reader in a clear breach of the fourth wall of writing. The storyteller begins the tale by directing the reader to "Pay Attention." The speaker then briefly describes the protagonists of the story: an ogress, who is "not who you might think she is," and a family of orphans, who were "good children . . . studious and hardworking and kind." The narrator also specifically notes, "And they loved one another dearly, ever so much more than they loved themselves." The second chapter introduces the villain, starting

Kelly Barnhill (Courtesy Workman Publishing Company)

by telling readers, "This is also a story about a dragon. I do not like to talk about him much. I don't even like to think about him." Though the narrator does not reveal their identity until late in the novel, Barnhill drops foreshadowing hints throughout the story that adept readers will enjoy gathering in an attempt to figure it out for themselves.

The narrative layout of the novel is, occasionally, disjointed, asking readers to carefully follow the events. The first four chapters are short, quickly introducing the situation and the main characters in two to five pages. The chapters that follow shift between the characters, sometimes providing glimpses of the characters' personalities and situations and sometimes providing plot movement. Occasionally, the narrator flashes readers to an earlier time in the life of the characters or town. Despite this movement between characters and events, the story flows in a way that easily leads readers through the plot sequence.

The characters in the novel are fairly simple and straightforward, with each character demonstrating a specific set of traits that, for the most part, do not change. The ogress is "careful and considerate." She has chosen to live on the outskirts of a small town that has fallen on hard times. Though she is lonely, she does not venture into town or meet the citizens in person until late in the story. Instead, she lives a peaceful life in a crooked house with a murder of crows, a small herd of sheep, and a blind dog for company. Generous to a fault, the ogress spends her time growing a garden and preparing home-baked treats for the people of the town, delivering the gifts in the middle of the night when no one is awake to identify their benefactor. The orphans are more socially active, if nothing else because there are fifteen of them in the Orphan House, a safe haven for children who have lost their parents. The orphans consist of Anthea, a thirteen-year-old girl who considers herself the leader of the other children; Bartleby, a self-proclaimed philosopher; Cassandra, "who preferred Cass," an introspective and helpful girl; Elijah, the storyteller of the group; Dierdre, the artist; twins Fortunate and Gratitude, the entertainers; the younger children, Hiram, Iggy, Justina, Kye, Lily, and Maude; and the babies, Nanette and Orpheus. Matron and Myron, an elderly couple, are the caretakers of the Orphan House. Like the ogress, the orphans and their guardians live a peaceful life, caring for each other. The final character of note is the Mayor, a self-proclaimed dragon slayer who appeared in Stone-in-the-Glen just before its downfall. The Mayor glitters in the sunlight and holds a strange thrall over the people of the town; every time he speaks, they fall into "a state of adulation and static joy." However, when his shine begins to fade and the people stop looking to him to solve their problems, he begins to lose power.

Two other characters appear almost as background figures in the story: the stone and the dragon. The stone is a foundational rock in the center of town. Historically a place where people gathered, once the Mayor took over the direction of the town the stone was covered with junk and ignored. The dragon, like the Mayor, is antagonistic, with the narrator hinting of his influence in the damage to the town, starting with the burning of the library.

This consistency in characters enhances the conflicts and thematic ideas stressed throughout the story. Since readers know what to expect of each character, it is not surprising to find a pairing of characters in the ongoing conflicts of the novel. For instance, both the ogress and the members of the Orphan House are kind and generous, so when a character versus society conflict arises, readers are not surprised when the ogress takes precautions to protect the children. When the townspeople (with the mayor's encouragement) begin to believe the ogress is the cause of their problems, it is not unexpected that the children would find a way to protect her. Further, it is not surprising that the Mayor's selfish greed is the root of the town's problems or that townspeople who had once been generous and loving neighbors could return to their roots.

Additionally, the animals in the story also have their own personalities. Cats, crows, a blind dog, and sheep often provide humor to lighten the dark tone of the community. A murder of crows and a group of sheep live with and protect the ogress. A blind old dog gives her comfort and companionship. A herd of cats lives with and loves the orphans. Another herd of cats roams on the Mayor's property, hissing a warning message the townspeople too often ignore.

The question of who a neighbor is becomes one of the central thematic ideas of the novel. The ogress, who has been anonymously delivering homegrown and handmade food to the people in town, is clearly a good neighbor. The butcher, who angrily denies assistance to the Orphan House and encourages discord against the ogress, is clearly a bad neighbor. When one of the children disappears, the town must decide whether they will come together or react with anger and fear, thus establishing another aspect of what it means to be a neighbor. Two citizens, the cobbler and his wife, take the lead in returning the town to its glorious past when, after learning of the depth of the Orphan House's poverty, they step in and organize the other townsfolk to make a difference, thus showing that there are still good people in Stone-in-the-Glen.

The magic of books is another central thematic idea. Before the library burned, Stone-in-the-Glen was a lovely town. People gathered together and took care of each other. After the loss of the library, additional calamities hit the town, other fires, floods, and a general attitude of despair changed the once idyllic place into a dreary, distrusting, and depressing locale. Though the library building lies smoldering next to the Orphan House, the books themselves have not disappeared. One citizen rescued as many books as he could while the building burned. The saved books form a new library, which magically grows and rearranges itself, within the walls of the Orphan House. These books lead to enjoyment, education, and thoughtfulness for all who are exposed. Later in the novel, the ogress and the children begin to make their own books, distributing them throughout the town, beginning a revolution that will bring the town back to life.

Review sources provide a variety of notes about the novel. The *Publishers Weekly* review lauded the narration as well as the "ambitious, fantastical sociopolitical allegory that asks keen questions about the nature of time, the import of community care, and what makes a neighbor." In a review of the novel for the *Horn Book Magazine*, Sarah Ellis also lauded the "folksy, discursive first-person narrator." Julia Smith, for *Booklist*, noted similar trends, praising "Barnhill's gift for storytelling" and her ability to "cloak modern lessons and timeless ideas that readers will do well to take to heart, no matter their age." Smith further regarded the book as "being a response to the current loss of kindness and neighborly values in American society." In addition, the *Kirkus* writer pointed toward the "realistic empathy" and "fantastical elements" as positives. Though the majority of review comments were positive, several critics pointed out the lack of diversity in the novel, with *Publishers Weekly* stating that the characters were "cued-white" and *Kirkus* remarking, "Main human characters read as White." Despite such critiques, *The Ogress and the Orphans* was a finalist for the 2022 National Book Award for Young People's Literature.

Author Biography

Kelly Barnhill is a self-proclaimed storyteller who has written five children's novels, a novella, and numerous adult pieces of varied genres. In addition to winning the Newbery Award for her 2017 novel *The Girl Who Drank the Moon*, she has won awards such as the World Fantasy Award and the Parents Choice Gold Award.

Theresa L. Stowell, PhD

Review Sources

Ellis, Sarah. Review of *The Ogress and The Orphans*, by Kelly Barnhill. *Horn Book Magazine*, vol. 98, no. 2, Mar./Apr. 2022, p. 66. *Literary Reference Center Plus*, search.ebscohost.com/login.aspx?direct=true&db=lkh&AN=155326888&site=lrc-plus. Accessed 8 Feb. 2023.

Review of *The Ogress and The Orphans*, by Kelly Barnhill. *Kirkus*, 24 Dec. 2022, www.kirkusreviews.com/book-reviews/kelly-barnhill/the-ogress-and-the-orphans/. Accessed 8 Feb. 2023.

Review of *The Ogress and The Orphans*, by Kelly Barnhill. *Publishers Weekly*, 23 Nov. 2022, www.publishersweekly.com/978-1-64375-074-3. Accessed 8 Feb. 2023.

Smith, Julia. Review of *The Ogress and The Orphans*, by Kelly Barnhill. *Booklist*, vol. 118, no. 11, 2022, p. 55. *Literary Reference Center Plus*, search.ebscohost.com/login.aspx?direct=true&db=lkh&AN=154968382&site=lrc-plus. Accessed 8 Feb. 2023.

Olga Dies Dreaming

Author: Xochitl Gonzalez
Publisher: Flatiron Books (New York). 373 pp.
Type of work: Novel
Time: 1990–2025
Locales: New York and Puerto Rico

Debut novelist Xochitl Gonzalez's first book follows two Puerto Rican siblings living in New York as they weigh their personal lives against their larger family and social obligations.

Principal characters
OLGA ACEVEDO, a wedding planner living in New York
PEDRO "PRIETO" ACEVEDO, her brother, a United States Congressman
BLANCA, their mother, a Puerto Rican revolutionary
MATTEO JONES, a realtor and Olga's love interest
RICHARD "DICK" EICKENBORN III, a wealthy businessman
REGGIE REYES, a music mogul, entrepreneur, and activist
MABEL, Olga's cousin

Despite the novel being her full-length literary debut, Xochitl Gonzalez's *Olga Dies Dreaming* (2022) is a highly assured look at the lives of a pair of Puerto Rican siblings living in New York City. Drawing on her own experiences growing up in Brooklyn, New York, as the daughter of a Puerto Rican mother and a Mexican American father, Gonzalez brings to vivid life the stories of Olga Acevedo, a successful but dissatisfied wedding planner, and her brother, Prieto, a United States Congressman with a few secrets that he is hiding. Moving back and forth between the perspectives of these two characters, Gonzalez explores their efforts to live a satisfying and worthwhile life, balancing personal happiness with their desire to act responsibly in the larger world.

At the beginning of the novel, Olga is thirty-nine and questioning her path in life. She is a successful wedding planner who works with many high-end clients, but she lacks personal connections in her life. She is also haunted by the sense that her professional life is a waste of her intelligence and talents; she worries that she is little more than a "maid" who helps wealthy people spend lots of money. This sense is exacerbated by the fact that Olga is Puerto Rican and most of her clients are White, which makes Olga feel that she is feeding into stereotypes about people of color acting as servants of White people. She begins to find her career "tedious and stupid." Early in the book, however, she meets Matteo Jones, a biracial realtor. Olga and Matteo soon

Xochitl Gonzalez

make a romantic connection that brings new possibilities in her life.

Meanwhile, Olga's brother, Prieto, is juggling his desire to do good with his need to cover up personal secrets. A forty-five-year-old US Congressman, Prieto presents himself as a champion both of his family's home of Puerto Rico and the largely Latino neighborhood of Sunset Park, Brooklyn, where he grew up and was later elected to represent in Congress. Sunset Park is a rapidly gentrifying neighborhood that is seeing a lot of development from outside real estate interests, which has resulted in rising rents that threaten to displace its longtime residents.

Prieto's concerns are personal as well as political. He is a closeted gay man who worries that he may have contracted AIDS. Additionally, Prieto is being blackmailed by a pair of powerful developers who also have real estate interests in Puerto Rico. Because Prieto feels that the exposure of his sexuality would ruin his chances of reelection, he agrees to support all of the developers' projects in Sunset Park. At the beginning of the book, Prieto also agrees to cancel an oversight hearing that he had scheduled for PROMESA (Puerto Rico Oversight, Management and Economic Stability Act), the highly controversial law that appointed a board to restructure Puerto Rico's debt. When he cancels the hearing, he faces heavy criticism from his constituents.

Hanging over the lives of both siblings is the example of their mother, Blanca. When Olga and Prieto were children, Blanca left the family to pursue a revolutionary life in Latin America and advocate for a number of causes, including Puerto Rican independence. Although she has not seen her children since she left the US, Blanca writes her children regular letters, which Gonzalez intersperses between chapters to help fill in a wider picture of the Acevedo family. With Blanca gone and their father struggling with drug addiction and dying of an AIDS-related illness, the children are raised by their grandmother and their vibrant extended family in Sunset Park. Nonetheless, the influence of Blanca continues to haunt both siblings into their adult life as they, by turns, try to simultaneously live up to her example and define their lives in opposition to her.

One of Gonzalez's most significant achievements in her novel is to explore the intersection of the personal and the political. Both Olga and, more explicitly, Prieto, are concerned with the larger world. For Olga, her career was partially chosen as a response to her mother's path. Since her mother rejected materialism, Olga's job is, in a sense, dedicated to the perpetuation of materialism. Nonetheless, she is invested in the larger world, taking a strong interest in her community and in her ancestral home of Puerto Rico, and she senses that what she does for work is not sustainable. This is especially true when she is given her own reality show in which she plans weddings for Midwestern couples. While on the show, Olga is forced to play up Latina stereotypes. With the release of this show, Olga has, in a material sense, achieved what she sees as being the American Dream, but as she pursues her personal goals, she comes to realize the hollowness of this dream and, with the help of Matteo, begins to imagine a different life.

For Prieto, the political side of his life is far more explicit due to his work as a congressman. However, Gonzalez shrewdly portrays Prieto's political goals as both being the direct result of his personal life and as being undermined by his personal life. Prieto's very choice to go into public service is both a continuation of his mother's mission and a rejection of it. While he sees his role as a politician as being a champion of both the people of Sunset Park and the Puerto Rican community as a whole, he also becomes part of the very establishment that his mother has explicitly rejected. As Prieto soon finds, electoral politics is filled with corruption. Additionally, because of the efforts he must take to hide his sexuality, he is not able to remain above this corruption and ends up voting in ways that he knows will hurt his constituents. Over the course of the book, Prieto comes to rethink his life and look for a way he can be less compromised as both a person and as a politician.

Olga Dies Dreaming deals with many contemporary political issues, including gentrification and Puerto Rican–US relations, but it succeeds largely because it remains focused on the human level of the story. Whether she is writing from the close third-person point of view of Olga or of Prieto, Gonzalez takes the reader into her characters' thoughts in ways that make them feel like fully realized humans. Similarly, she fills in her scenes with vivid details and sharply rendered observations. For example, during the opening scene, Olga explains the difference between the napkins used at her wealthy clients' weddings and the napkins used at her less wealthy clients' weddings. Although this may seem at first to be a superficial topic of discussion, it actually plays out as a deft sociological observation; not only is it interesting in its specificity, but this scene also establishes the book's concerns with the larger differences between people with money and people without. The sections that focus on Prieto are not always as confident or as closely observed as the Olga sections, but Gonzalez still does a strong job in bringing to life the grueling dilemmas that defines his life.

As the book's plot accelerates in its second half, culminating in the various characters' response to Hurricane Maria as it devastates Puerto Rico in 2017, Gonzalez's political concerns come more to the fore. She frequently has characters give explicit voice to what seem to be her opinions on the relationship between the US and Puerto Rico. These characters feel that the US has established a colonial relationship to Puerto Rico which impoverishes the people of the island while enriching mainland business interests. This especially seems to be the case in the wake of Hurricane Maria; at this point, the novel's businessman characters plot ways to exploit Puerto Rico in the wake of tragedy.

While these sections could come across as a bit didactic to some readers, they are powerfully voiced and remain grounded in the believable motivations of the novel's characters. Because Gonzalez patiently and carefully develops her characters over the course of the novel, she is able to turn later in the book to both more extravagant plot twists and more explicit political content without straining her credibility. In fact, her control of her material throughout the book is what allows her to balance so many strands and succeed with such an ambitious project. In *Olga Dies Dreaming*, the political is always grounded in the personal and the whole book rests on a solid foundation of character and carefully-observed detail.

Olga Dies Dreaming met with almost universal acclaim upon its publication in early 2022. While Lucy Popescu, writing for the *Guardian*, called the book a "deeply satisfying and nuanced novel," the *Washington Post*'s Ron Charles marveled that a novel could "contend so powerfully and so delightfully with such a vast web of personal, cultural, political, and even international imperatives."

Critics were especially impressed by the ways in which Gonzalez combined the personal and the political, mixing her more casual storytelling with larger concerns. "What's most impressive about *Olga Dies Dreaming*," wrote Charles, "is the way Gonzalez stretches the seams of the rom-com genre to accommodate her complex analysis of racial politics." Similarly, Popescu praised Gonzalez for "cloak[ing] her polemic in page-turning prose," creating a highly readable literary experience that is always concerned with issues of great global import.

Nonetheless, some critics did find fault with how the more explicit political statements sometimes got in the way of the story. For example, Maggie Shipstead, writing for the *New York Times*, felt that the "lectures . . . along with frequent detours into backstory, sometimes feel like a frustrating countercurrent to the momentum of the book's present, ongoing plot." She felt that the novel was "most affecting and most alive" when it "turns its attention to storytelling." Still, Shipstead came away overall impressed by the novel, both by Gonzalez's narrative abilities and its focus on the theme of liberation.

When a writer publishes a first novel, the reader never knows quite what to expect. Many first novels feel uncertain or not fully realized. Luckily, this is not the case with *Olga Goes Dreaming*, as Xochitl Gonzalez delivers a confident, fully-assured novel that heralds the arrival of a bold new talent.

Author Biography

Xochitl Gonzalez was born and raised in Brooklyn, New York. She worked as a consultant, an entrepreneur, and a wedding planner before pursuing a career in writing. She earned her master of fine arts (MFA) degree in creative writing from the Iowa Writer's Workshop in 2021. *Olga Dies Dreaming* is her first novel.

Andrew Schenker

Review Sources

Charles, Ron. "Say 'I Do' to Xochitl Gonzalez's *Olga Dies Dreaming*." *The Washington Post*, 4 Jan. 2022, www.washingtonpost.com/books/2022/01/04/olga-dies-dreaming-xochitl-gonzalez-book-review/. Accessed on 27 Oct. 2022.

Gonzalez, Xochitl. "Xochitl Gonzalez: Life Is but an American Dream." Interview by Carole V. Bell. *BookPage*, Jan. 2022, www.bookpage.com/interviews/life-is-but-an-american-dream/. Accessed on 27 Oct. 2022.

Popescu, Lucy. "*Olga Dies Dreaming* by Xochitl Gonzalez Review – Nuanced Novel of Family, Race, and Politics." *The Guardian*, 9 Jan. 2022, www.theguardian.com/books/2022/jan/09/olga-dies-dreaming-by-xochitl-gonzalez-review-nuanced-novel-of-family-race-and-politics. Accessed 27 Oct. 2022.

Shipstead. "The Daughter of a Revolutionary Becomes a Wedding Planner. Drama Ensues." Review of *Olga Dies Dreaming*, by Xochitl Gonzalez. *The New York Times*, 10 Jan. 2022, www.nytimes.com/2022/01/10/books/review/olga-dies-dreaming-xochitl-gonzalez.html. Accessed 27 Oct. 2022.

Otherlands
A Journey through Earth's Extinct Worlds

Author: Thomas Halliday (b. 1989)
Publisher: Random House (New York). Illustrated. 416 pp.
Type of work: Natural history, science
Time: 550 million years ago–the present
Locale: Earth

In Otherlands: A Journey through Earth's Extinct Worlds, *paleobiologist Thomas Halliday takes readers back in time, exploring the often-unrecognizable environments of long-past eras and the creatures that thrived within them.*

When thinking about our planet's distant past, many people likely imagine a world that is for the most part indistinguishable from contemporary Earth, one that is perhaps inhabited by different animals and plants but that maintains familiar habitats and contours. This, however, could not be further from the truth. In fact, over the course of hundreds of millions of years, Earth has experienced numerous distinct eras of geological and environmental change that shaped and reshaped the planet's surface and its inhabitants. From rising sea levels to spreading glaciers to shifting continents, such changes dramatically altered the planet as a whole, ensuring that disparate geologic periods separated by hundreds of millions of years, such as the Ediacaran and the Jurassic, for example, might appear to be two different worlds entirely. Such distinct environments form the focus of *Otherlands: A Journey through Earth's Extinct Worlds* (2022), the debut book by Thomas Halliday. A paleobiologist by training and a winner of the prose division of the 2018 Hugh Miller Writing Competition (an event dedicated to the geodiversity of Scotland), Halliday is well suited for the project, possessing both the scientific knowledge and engaging authorial voice needed to transport readers back in time to the varied "lands" of ancient Earth. In doing so, Halliday not only creates a strong addition to the field of natural history but also reveals how that history can help scientists of the twenty-first century understand ongoing environmental changes in the contemporary world—and understand the consequences of letting such changes proceed unchecked.

Following an introduction in which Halliday explains the purpose of his work and the reasons for its unique structure, *Otherlands* begins its journey through time at a point twenty thousand years before the book's publication, arriving at a site in what is now Alaska during the Pleistocene epoch. Though far in the past, this world remains a relatively familiar one. The area under discussion is a northern plain inhabited by animals such as wild horses, mammoths, and the immense bear *Arctodus simus*, all animals with recognizable counterparts in the twenty-first-century world. Human beings have already arrived in what is now North America, and changes to the global climate are threatening vulnerable animal populations, particularly as environmental changes such as rising sea levels increasingly limit their ability to migrate to more suitable locations. As this first chapter reveals, environmental change will be a constant throughout this journey into the past. Halliday repeatedly calls the reader's attention to the commonalities between the changes taking place in the past and the changes occurring in the reader's own world, characterizing the past as a source of valuable information to use when considering the future throughout the text.

Thomas Halliday

With each of the subsequent chapters, Halliday transports the reader farther into the past, moving backward through each epoch of the Neogene and Paleogene periods—the Pliocene, Miocene, Oligocene, Eocene, and Paleocene—before proceeding on to the Cretaceous, Jurassic, Triassic, Permian, Carboniferous, Devonian, Silurian, Ordovician, Cambrian, and Ediacaran periods. As *Otherlands*'s journey through time and space progresses, the once-familiar world becomes far more foreign, particularly in terms of its geography. Each chapter focuses on one specific place at a particular point in time, and Halliday explains clearly where that place correlates to in the modern world. Due to changes in the locations of landmasses over time, however, the sites in question are not always located where one might expect them to be on the planet. A site that in the twenty-first century is located in Soom, South Africa, for instance, was located on the supercontinent Gondwana 444 million years ago, during the Ordovician period. To aid the reader's comprehension of the changes that the planet underwent over the course of the more than five hundred million years covered by *Otherlands*, each of the book's chapters is accompanied by a map that depicts the relevant area at the time Halliday is discussing, calling attention to the changing sizes and locations of landmasses such as Gondwana, Laurentia, and Pangaea.

The animals living in the worlds Halliday depicts also become increasingly unfamiliar as the chapters progress, although they are initially quite recognizable. The wild horses of Pleistocene Alaska are not the same horses that would live in the North America of the twenty-first century, as horses would eventually become extinct on that continent and not reappear until they were reintroduced alongside European colonization, but they nevertheless represent a recognizable analogue to animals the readers themselves may have encountered during their lives. Older creatures such as the deer-like Miocene animal *Hoplitomeryx matthei* likewise bear certain resemblances to animals of modern times, despite flourishing more than five million years ago. However, they also display some striking differences—including, in the case of *H. matthei*, features such as saber teeth—and these tend to become more pronounced the further back in time the book explores.

Portions of *Otherlands* dealing with the far more distant past do, at times, also feature animals of which many readers will likely be aware, such as various dinosaurs of the Triassic, Jurassic, and Cretaceous periods as well as the famed arthropods known as trilobites, which first emerged during the Cambrian but endured through multiple geologic periods. But Halliday notes many lesser-known and stranger species as well. He particularly emphasizes the biological diversity of Earth's many worlds and calls attention to the factors that contributed to such diversity, including the effects of isolation from the rest of the world on the evolution of animal populations and the diversity emerging from the so-called Cambrian explosion, which saw the proliferation of a wide variety of trilobites, crustaceans, worms, and other lifeforms in regions then located underwater. Notably, in addition to Halliday's own vivid descriptions of animals, plants, and landscapes, *Otherlands* is interspersed with art by science illustrator Beth Zaiken that visualizes a number of the lifeforms under discussion, including the Jurassic pterosaur *Rhamphorhynchus muensteri*, the Carboniferous scale tree *Lepidodendron*, and the Cambrian worm *Omnidens amplus*.

While Halliday writes about these "extinct worlds" with authority, he does not shy away from calling attention to the ongoing and incomplete nature of research into early life on Earth and the limitations that scientists face in investigating such periods. For instance, he writes that the fact "that practically all our information about life comes only from death"—that is, from the fossilized remains of deceased animals and plants—is "the crucial paradox at the heart of palaeontology." Fossils depict a lifeform as it was after its death and thus cannot reflect that being's behavior during life. As Halliday explains, trace fossils such as fossilized footprints can give insights about behavior, but these traces cannot always be easily linked to a particular animal. Similarly, he notes that lifeforms with hard parts such as shells were commonly preserved, while soft body parts were not. Halliday reveals that the Cambrian explosion, with its sudden increase in animals, "is in part an illusion" caused by the evolution of new, hard body parts during that period, which meant that fossils from the Cambrian would simply be preserved more easily than fossils from earlier periods in Earth's history.

The issues inherent to the study of the fossil record are particularly relevant to the final period featured in the book, the Ediacaran, which saw the proliferation of multicellular life in the sea 550 million years ago. Halliday notes that prior to the 1950s, fossils dating from the Ediacaran period were presumed to be from the Cambrian period, as scientists did not believe that visible fossils existed from any period earlier than the Cambrian. However, this understanding changed following the discovery of undoubtedly Ediacaran fossils in several locations. Fittingly, Halliday leaves space for further revelations in his field, noting that the scientific "perception of this world is incomplete."

Having led the reader many millions of years into the past over the course of *Otherlands*, Halliday concludes his work with an epilogue in which he returns to his own era. Reflecting on humanity's spread throughout the planet and influence on it, he turns his attention to the contemporary problem of global climate change and the lessons that can be learned from the environmental changes of the past, which include sobering illustrations of the far-ranging and heavily detrimental effects that rising carbon dioxide levels can have on wildlife populations. In addition, he writes that while humanity possesses the technology to weather many such changes, the means to survive climate change are not distributed equally among the world's population, and those who will be harmed most by climate change are those who contribute the least to it. Yet despite the severity of the problem, Halliday cautions against pessimism, arguing that "success and failure is not a binary choice" in this particular context. He likewise touches on promising discoveries of the twenty-first century, including the revelations that certain bacteria and fungi may be capable of breaking down plastics and thus reducing the effects of plastic waste on the environment. Ultimately, however, Halliday stresses the importance of "enter[ing] into a more mutualistic relationship with our global environments," an undertaking that can be aided with insights gleaned from studying Earth's past.

Otherlands received highly positive reviews prior to and following its publication. In a representative review, the anonymous critic for *Publishers Weekly* characterized the book as a "fascinating" and "show-stopping work" that "deserves wide readership." The book also garnered substantial praise from the reviewer for *Kirkus*, who noted that Halliday "write[s] with clarity" and described *Otherlands* as "a bracing pleasure for Earth-science buffs and readers interested in diving into deep history." Many reviews commented approvingly on the work's structure and focus on specific locations and moments in time. Writing for the *Scotsman*, Stuart Kelly described the book's structure as "elegant," while Gege Li, in a review for *NewScientist*, characterized the travelogue-like approach to history as the work's "most distinctive feature." Both critics additionally praised Halliday's detailed approach to describing the environments and creatures of the distant past: Li wrote that Halliday is "appropriately lavish in his depiction of the variety and resilience of life, without compromising on scientific accuracy," while Kelly took note of the author's use of "precise detail that enlivens and estranges the reader." Meanwhile, writing for the Associated Press, Amancai Biraben praised Halliday's "vivid writing style" as well as *Otherlands*'s "intricate analysis of our planet's interconnected past." Indeed, the connections Halliday forges between the past and present, particularly regarding the problem of climate change, earned praise from several critics. The book's selection of illustrations was also widely commended, although critics such as Kelly suggested that including even more would have been a welcome addition.

Author Biography
Thomas Halliday is a paleobiologist based in England. *Otherlands* is his first book.

Joy Crelin

Review Sources

Biraben, Amancai. "Review: Journey to the Origins of the Earth." Review of *Otherlands: A Journey through Earth's Extinct Worlds*, by Thomas Halliday. Associated Press, 2 Feb. 2022, apnews.com/article/entertainment-arts-and-entertainment-book-reviews-14bb03b2168da92057bf749ce53dbc94. Accessed 31 Jan. 2023.

"Briefly Noted." Review of *Otherlands: A Journey through Earth's Extinct Worlds*, by Thomas Halliday, et al. *The New Yorker*, 28 Mar. 2022, www.newyorker.com/magazine/2022/04/04/lucky-breaks-chilean-poet-otherlands-and-aurelia-aurelia. Accessed 31 Jan. 2023.

Kelly, Stuart. "Book Review: *Otherlands: A World in the Making*, by Thomas Halliday." *The Scotsman*, 9 Feb. 2022, www.scotsman.com/arts-and-culture/books/book-review-otherlands-a-world-in-the-making-by-thomas-halliday-3560251. Accessed 31 Jan. 2023.

Li, Gege. "*Otherlands* Review: A Fascinating Journey through Earth's History." Review of *Otherlands: A Journey through Earth's Extinct Worlds*, by Thomas Halliday. *NewScientist*, 19 Jan. 2022, www.newscientist.com/article/mg25333700-600-otherlands-review-a-fascinating-journey-through-earths-history/. Accessed 31 Jan. 2023.

Review of *Otherlands: A Journey through Earth's Extinct Worlds*, by Thomas Halliday. *Kirkus*, 11 Jan. 2022, www.kirkusreviews.com/book-reviews/thomas-halliday/otherlands/. Accessed 31 Jan. 2023.

Review of *Otherlands: A Journey through Earth's Extinct Worlds*, by Thomas Halliday. *Publishers Weekly*, 5 Jan. 2022, www.publishersweekly.com/9780593132883. Accessed 31 Jan. 2023.

Our Missing Hearts

Author: Celeste Ng (b. 1980)
Publisher: Penguin Press (New York). 352 pp.
Type of work: Novel
Time: Near future
Locales: Cambridge, Massachusetts; New York

Celeste Ng's third novel, Our Missing Hearts, *is a story about the power of love during crisis. As the United States begins to experience extreme political upheaval in a dystopian near-future, Bird is a shy and awkward child who must learn to live without his mother as his father turns ever more inward.*

Principal characters

BIRD, a.k.a. Noah, a shy twelve-year-old Chinese American boy who is trying to reconcile the destruction of his family following his mother's disappearance

ETHAN, his loving father who has been destroyed by the disappearance of his wife. A former linguistics professor, he now works in a local university library shelving books

MARGARET, his mother, who disappeared three years ago. A writer who published a singular volume of poetry, she has become the unlikely face of resistance to the new restrictions in US culture

SADIE, his best friend and one of the re-placed children who have been taken from their families following the introduction of PACT, which criminalizes "unpatriotic" behavior

DOMI, Margaret's closest friend whom she lived with in New York City during the Crisis; Domi comes from a wealthy family and is very involved across activist networks

Celeste Ng's *Our Missing Hearts* (2022) takes the reader to a place both eerily familiar yet slightly out of reach. It is set partly in Cambridge, Massachusetts, where twelve-year-old Bird, whose given name is Noah, and his father, Ethan, are attempting to put a life together in the near-distant future despite a tense authoritarian atmosphere in the United States and the absence of Margaret, Ethan's wife and Bird's mother. Other parts of the story unfold in New York City, with the novel blending carefully constructed characters with love-affirming plot lines. The result is a story about the lengths people go to in the hopes of preserving personal freedoms and the deepest love that feels true to the experiences of its characters. Culling from true-to-life crises and events like

Celeste Ng

child separation at the US border and the financial fallout following the COVID-19 pandemic (though COVID-19 itself does not exist in this book), *Our Missing Hearts* examines how many small moments can eventually lead to a sharp shift in culture that embraces fear rather than love.

The novel's opening finds Bird still reeling from the sudden and seemingly inexplicable departure of his mother three years earlier. At twelve, he has trouble making friends and is often teased at school by his classmates. At home, he lives with his father, who has essentially been worn down to a husk of a human following his wife's disappearance and the rise of the intense authoritarian and xenophobic culture that has taken over the United States. Part of what has created this atmosphere was the passage of the Preserving American Culture and Traditions act, colloquially known as PACT, which has been used to imprison people who question the government as well as the act itself. PACT has also been used to separate children from their parents if they are deemed to be unpatriotic or even sympathetic to unpatriotic ideas or efforts. In particular, Chinese Americans, as well as others of Asian descent mistaken to be Chinese American, have been the targets of PACT, blamed for interfering with the international market and causing its implosion, leading to a global financial crisis. As a result, this group is often the target of racism and violence that is vividly captured throughout the novel.

Margaret, a poet whose parents had immigrated from China, is now a fugitive because of PACT. Her poem "All Our Missing Hearts" was adopted by the resistance and has become a battle cry, showing up on signs at protests and as graffiti on buildings. The missing hearts in question are those children who have been taken from their families and are now unable to be traced. Meanwhile, librarians have taken up the cause of helping those children, building an intricate network of contacts and notes across the country in the hopes that at least some children will be able to be reunited with their families someday. Bird uses this network—after receiving a mysterious letter in the mail that he is sure is from his mother—to attempt to track her down, relying on a fairy tale she once told him about a boy who drew cats on the wall and her collection of poems for clues, though he finds his most important clue in an unlikely place pulled from his happier childhood memories.

Our Missing Hearts first follows Bird's point of view, as he grapples with daily life and attempts to stay out of trouble but follow his heart, nonetheless. Later in the novel, the reader hears Margaret's story from her own point of view, as the book becomes a story within a story. Most effective is Bird's voice. His youthfulness becomes an asset as Ng sets up the world Bird must make it through. His fear is frequently undercut by curiosity in situations involving the police—at one point there is an incident while he and his father are eating dinner in the school cafeteria and Bird cannot seem to look away from the police filling the street outside despite his father's urging to keep his head down—and during other moments, like when he receives the note from his mother in the city. While he understands the repercussions of pursuing more information about her, his boyish innocence will not allow him to turn away. When he sets off on his quest to find his mother in New York, his anxiousness about leaving his home of Cambridge for the first time in his young life is believable, as are his first moments in New York upon arrival. Margaret's voice does not feel quite as believable, however, due in part to Ng's own writing style. The overworked similes that frequently show up in her prose feel more natural in the mind of a child, but when they are applied to Margaret, who is fiercely intelligent and independent, the reader is to believe, they feel clichéd and flat. However, the bond between the two characters is what carries the novel.

Much of the novel's middle section is spent describing what happened during the Crisis, and it is through these moments that the reader gets to know Margaret and what she has experienced since leaving the family. An undergrad in college during the early days of the Crisis, Margaret saw her life change in ways she had never expected during those years. However, these moments also give the reader some insight into who Margaret is and how she came to be the woman she is since leaving the family. Rich details about living in New York City in a cramped apartment with other young people during the Crisis and about her early days of meeting and then falling in love with Ethan are some of the more interesting moments of her story.

The character of Sadie is particularly interesting and endearing. A fierce thirteen-year-old girl, Sadie is seemingly unbreakable despite a system that aims to do just that—break her. She has long lost track of her parents—wonders if they are still out there, in fact—but does not let that get in the way of her believing there is a future. She is a great foil to Bird's timidity, often encouraging him to be brave in the face of threat. Sadie is also seamlessly used to illustrate how PACT has impacted the lives of both children and adults. Her backstory, which reveals why she was taken from her home, shows the reader just how extreme efforts are to contain any sort of transgressive thought or action within this version of the US. Bird's own brushes with authority, too, are powerful moments that further reveal what people are meant to deal with and how constricted their lives have become as a result.

Our Missing Hearts was widely well received by critics, though it did receive mixed reviews from the *Chicago Review of Books* and some other outlets. Reviewing the book for the *New York Times*, Stephen King wrote, "The gears in this story for the most part mesh very well. And Bird is a brave and believable character, who gives us a relatable portal into a world that seems more like our own every day." For the *Washington Post*, Diana Abu-Jaber wrote, "*Our Missing Hearts* is at its core a parable about the wages of fear, how it can lead to bigotry, racism and institutionalized hatred. Painted with broad strokes, it's also reminiscent of works like *The Old Man and the Sea* —with its elevated, mythic quality—and it can seem a little message-driven at times." Though noting that the book is a worthwhile read overall and a continuation of Ng's impressive oeuvre, Malavika Praseed, writing for the *Chicago Review of Books*, did find some fault with the overly ambitious coverage of issues undertaken, arguing that they cannot be satisfactorily dealt with in the scope of the novel while also focusing on Bird's relationship with his mother. Most reviewers agreed that it is, regardless, an engaging, well-written, and compelling narrative. It is a chillingly recognizable, significant story about what can happen when violence and fear are met with apathy.

Author Biography
Celest Ng is the best-selling author of the novels *Everything I Never Told You* (2014), *Little Fires Everywhere* (2017), and *Our Missing Hearts* (2022). Her stories and essays have been published in a variety of outlets, and *Little Fires Everywhere* was adapted for a 2020 Hulu miniseries.

Melynda Fuller

Review Sources
Abu-Jaber, Diana. "In Celeste Ng's 'Our Missing Hearts,' a Boy Fights for Freedom." Review of *Our Missing Hearts*, by Celeste Ng. *The Washington Post*, 28 Sept. 2022, www.washingtonpost.com/books/2022/09/28/celeste-ng-our-missing-hearts/. Accessed 25 Nov. 2022.

Đinh, Thúy. "Celeste Ng Makes the Case for Art as a Weapon against Oppression in Her New Novel." Review of *Our Missing Hearts*, by Celeste Ng. *NPR*, 7 Oct. 2022, www.npr.org/2022/10/07/1127451738/celeste-ng-our-missing-hearts-review. Accessed 25 Nov. 2022.

Grady, Constance. "Celeste Ng is Back with a Dark Parable of America's History of Child Removal." Review of *Our Missing Hearts*, by Celeste Ng. *Vox*, 6 Oct. 2022, www.vox.com/23387768/our-missing-hearts-celeste-ng-review. Accessed 25 Nov. 2022.

King, Stephen. "Celeste Ng's Dystopia Is Uncomfortably Close to Reality." Review of *Our Missing Hearts*, by Celeste Ng. *The New York Times*, 22 Sept. 2022, www.nytimes.com/2022/09/22/books/review/celeste-ng-our-missing-hearts.html. Accessed 25 Nov. 2022.

Patrick, Bethanne. "Review: 'Little Fires Everywhere' Author Celeste Ng Ventures Boldly into the Dark Future." Review of *Our Missing Hearts*, by Celeste Ng. *Los Angeles Times*, 3 Oct. 2022, www.latimes.com/entertainment-arts/books/story/2022-10-03/celeste-ng-ventures-into-the-future-our-missing-hearts-review. Accessed 25 Nov. 2022.

Praseed, Malavika. "Stretching the Boundaries of American Political Reality in 'Our Missing Hearts.'" Review of *Our Missing Hearts*, by Celeste Ng. *Chicago Review of Books*, 5 Oct. 2022, chireviewofbooks.com/2022/10/05/review-our-missing-hearts/. Accessed 25 Nov. 2022.

Properties of Thirst

Author: Marianne Wiggins (b. 1947)
Publisher: Simon & Schuster (New York). 544 pp.
Type of work: Novel
Time: 1940s
Locale: Owens Valley, California

Award-winning author and Pulitzer Prize finalist Marianne Wiggins writes about World War II, the Los Angeles water wars, and Japanese internment in her 2022 novel Properties of Thirst.

Principal characters
ROCKWELL "ROCKY" RHODES, the Rhodes family patriarch, a rancher and son of a railroad magnate
LOU, his wife, who dies of polio
CAS, his twin sister
SUNNY, his daughter, a self-trained chef
STRYKER, his son and Sunny's twin, a sailor lost at Pearl Harbor
SCHIFF, a Jewish lawyer with the Interior Department, manager of the Manzanar internment camp

Marianne Wiggins's sweeping historical novel *Properties of Thirst* (2022) is arranged into eleven sections, each defining one of the so-called "properties of thirst" named in the book's title. Among those properties are "recognition," "truth," "memory," and "the thwarting of desire." Thirst is an all-too-familiar concept to the Rhodes family at the heart of Wiggins's World War II–era saga. Family patriarch Rocky, the son of a railroad magnate, escaped his controlling industrialist father to make a new life for himself and his beloved wife, Lou, in Owens Valley, California. The couple builds a ranch and calls it Three Chairs, after a quote from Henry David Thoreau, whose ideals and writing Rocky admires so much he has committed much of it to memory. Lou gives birth to twins, Sunny and Stryker, but the family's happiness is short-lived. After Lou dies of polio, Rocky's own twin sister, the austere Cas, moves in—but beyond that, Rocky, still calcified in his grief, has no real desire for company.

As Rocky thirsts for his wife, the growing city of Los Angeles thirsts for water. Rocky makes reference to the water wars of the early 1900s, when city officials in Los Angeles and ranchers in Owens Valley vied for water rights in a violent conflict. The water wars were ended by presidential executive order; Teddy Roosevelt ordered the water be diverted to the city, declaring the "needs of the many outweigh the needs of the few" and leading to major challenges for Owens Valley farmers and ranchers

Marianne Wiggins

like Rocky. But there is a larger conflict on the horizon. When the novel opens, the Pearl Harbor Naval Base in Hawaii has just been bombed by Japanese warplanes. It is an event that hits far too close to home, even for the reclusive Rhodes. Stryker, stationed in Honolulu, is believed to be dead. Meanwhile, the government is intruding on Rocky's land, again, not for water this time but to build an internment camp for Japanese Americans.

Author Wiggins was near completion of *Properties of Thirst* when she suffered a massive stroke in 2016. Her daughter, photographer Lara Porzak, helped her complete the novel for publication in 2022. Wiggins is best known for her 2003 novel, *Evidence of Things Unseen*, which was a finalist for the National Book Award and the Pulitzer Prize. That novel, also an ambitious historical saga, is a domestic love story and a tragedy that explores the science behind the atom bomb that ended World War I. *Properties of Thirst*, which is also, at its heart, a love story, is similar in its angle and scope. Rooted in the lives of the Rhodes family members, it probes the complexities of history, if not science. Thirst is a malleable concept in the book, but most importantly, thirst implies want, and want implies lack. The characters yearn for lost people and lives they might have led, but Wiggins has said she was compelled to write the book after discovering the "lost" history of Japanese internment, specifically Manzanar, the camp where the story is set.

After the attack on Pearl Harbor in December 1941, President Franklin D. Roosevelt issued an executive order that led people of Japanese descent, including American citizens, to be removed from their homes and detained in internment camps. For many years, this aspect of the war was carefully omitted from the larger historical narrative. Japanese internment, a horrific echo of Jewish concentration camps in Europe, complicates the accepted narrative of the war, revealing how the self-proclaimed moral victors committed atrocities of their own. The characters in *Properties of Thirst* are uncomfortable with the internment policy but do not resist it. This ambivalence extends to Schiff, a young Jewish lawyer who has been hired by the US Department of the Interior to construct and manage Manzanar. Schiff is too busy acquiring materials to house and feed thousands of people to worry about complicity or moral obligation. (He is not too busy, though, to spend long hours trying to win Sunny's affection.) When the camp opens and the detainees come to be processed, moral quandaries become harder to avoid, though they are usurped by concerns both large and small. The camp needs toilet paper, and the men are requesting a later curfew. Meanwhile, there is toxic dust, an unwelcome outcome of the decision to divert the water of Owens Valley to Los Angeles. The dust likely made Lou, Rocky's wife, fatally ill, and now scientists want to study its effect on the detainees.

Surprisingly, given all of these moving parts, a good amount of the book is about food. Lou, who was French Canadian, was a masterful chef, and Sunny has the talent to follow in her mother's footsteps. Sunny is self-trained, piecing together what she can learn from Cas, the Indigenous women on the ranch, and her mother's cryptic recipe cards, none of which seem to contain any actual recipes. One of the cards, for "rainbow hash," says, "Discard fish heads. (Trouts' eyes will follow you around the room.)" Another: "SALT is lightning in the BLOOD. Salt is the only ROCK we eat." Many of the cards are written in French, an additional hurdle, and Sunny has spent years, armed with her meager French and her own growing culinary knowledge, trying to decipher them. Sunny attacks the recipes with the urgency of a wartime code breaker. She is driven by the idea that understanding them will lead her to understand her mother, whom she barely knew. As Wiggins writes of Sunny, "She likened reading through her mother's cards to reading an anthology of silences, the lost history of a soul."

Food is, obviously, an important symbol in *Properties of Thirst*. At one point, Schiff observes, "Show me what you eat and I'll tell you who you are." Meals are described in sumptuous detail, passages that are particularly striking alongside the meager rations afforded the detainees at Manzanar. Recollections—"sense memories"—of what characters ate and when convey the strong emotions that the Rhodes family struggle to express in words. Early on, Sunny tells Schiff a story about how Rocky took her and Stryker, just five years old, on a camping trip soon after Lou's death. The entire passage is suffused in that grief, but Sunny also describes her initial fear of the dark forest and how Rocky told them to bury fresh eggs in the ash surrounding their campfire before going to sleep. In the morning, Sunny's fear—of the forest, of life without her mother—was transformed upon uncovering the still-warm eggs. She recalls eating it, smoky and thick like custard, her voice heavy with emotion. "My whole life: I. Have never. Tasted anything. As perfect as that egg," she says.

Descriptions of food and eating are where Wiggins's prose most shines, but these long passages, including a lengthy flashback to Sunny's first European vacation, can slow the plot. Wiggins's asides are beautiful, but there are so many that the effect can be overwhelming. *Properties of Thirst* is a massive saga that is, counterintuitively, also presented in granular detail. The writing is superb but also dense, making it easy to lose sight of the larger story. This unwieldiness might have led Fran Hawthorne of the *New York Journal of Books* to note in her largely positive review, "Indeed, even at 544 pages, this novel is too thin for all the themes and subplots that it tries to tackle." But Hawthorne's review, one of the more thorough, also praised Wiggins's attention to each character's idiosyncratic mode of speech, comparing her to Russian novelist Fyodor Dostoyevsky. "The voices are all Dostoevskian in their run-on intensity, though they can have their quirks," she wrote. "Schiff frequently breaks up his sentences with parenthetical asides; Rocky favors lots of terse, one-line paragraphs, often beginning with an em-dash." Meanwhile, a reviewer for *Publishers Weekly* noted Wiggins's obvious delight in playing with words in the text. "Wiggins's wordplay is stellar, as when the properties of a souffle become metaphor for the emotions of those about to eat it," the anonymous reviewer wrote, offering the quote, "Sunny folded one thing—the inflated egg whites—into the other, le fond—with the greatest care, aware of both their fragile properties."

Other critics also offered enthusiastic praise for *Properties of Thirst*. Sally Bissell of *Library Journal* noted the book's "visceral sense of time and place." Indeed, Wiggins is adept at transporting the reader to 1940s California, evoking its smells, sights, and tastes. She also captures the era's profound uncertainty, none of the characters knowing, of course, what horrors the war might bring. Hawthorne and others noted the book's guiding theme, as expressed by numerous characters, including Rocky in the opening line of the novel: "You can't save what you don't love." This applies to Rocky and his fierce defense of Owens Valley, but the theme is ultimately more intimate in scope. As Hawthorne wrote, "The important thirst isn't for water, however. It's for connection." In a starred review for *Kirkus*, the reviewer, like Hawthorne, was disappointed by the conclusion—which is somewhat excusable given the author's medical emergency prior to finishing the novel—but went on to describe the book as "majestic," observing, "Wiggins' interwoven plotlines . . . and colorful characters are entrancing and as cinematic as the real-life Westerns that were filmed in the valley in which the book is primarily set. But what makes the novel soar is the way Wiggins can evoke landscapes both interior and exterior, especially the expansive valley that has come to exemplify America's best qualities—and its worst."

Author Biography

Marianne Wiggins is the award-winning author of novels and short stories, including *John Dollar* (1989), *Eveless Eden* (1995), and *The Shadow Catcher* (2007). Her 2003 novel, *Evidence of Things Unseen*, was a finalist for the National Book Award and the Pulitzer Prize. *Properties of Thirst* (2022) is her eighth novel.

Molly Hagan

Review Sources

Bissell, Sally. Review of *Properties of Thirst*, by Marianne Wiggins. *Library Journal*, 1 July 2022, www.libraryjournal.com/review/properties-of-thirst-2152321. Accessed 13 Feb. 2023.

"Briefly Noted." Review of *Properties of Thirst*, by Marianne Wiggins, et al. *The New Yorker*, 31 Oct. 2022, www.newyorker.com/magazine/2022/11/07/the-other-side-of-prospect-the-beloved-vision-the-hero-of-this-book-and-properties-of-thirst. Accessed 13 Feb. 2023.

Hawthorne, Fran. Review of *Properties of Thirst*, by Marianne Wiggins. *New York Journal of Books*, www.nyjournalofbooks.com/book-review/properties-thirst. Accessed 13 Feb. 2023.

Review of *Properties of Thirst*, by Marianne Wiggins. *Kirkus*, 22 June 2022, www.kirkusreviews.com/book-reviews/marianne-wiggins/properties-thirst/. Accessed 13 Feb. 2023.

Review of *Properties of Thirst*, by Marianne Wiggins. *Publishers Weekly*, 2 June 2022, www.publishersweekly.com/9781416571261. Accessed 13 Feb. 2023.

The Rabbit Hutch

Author: Tess Gunty (b. ca. 1982)
Publisher: Alfred A. Knopf (New York). 352 pp.
Type of work: Novel
Time: Present day
Locale: Vacca Vale, Indiana

Tess Gunty's debut novel, The Rabbit Hutch, *offers a wide-ranging and highly assured look at the lives of a handful of characters living in a declining Midwestern city.*

Principal characters
BLANDINE WATKINS, an eighteen-year-old woman living in Vacca Vale, Indiana
JAMES YAGER, her former music teacher
JACK, Malik, and Todd, her roommates
MOSES ROBERT BLITZ, the middle-aged son of famous actress Elsie Blitz
JOAN KOWALSKI, Blandine's neighbor

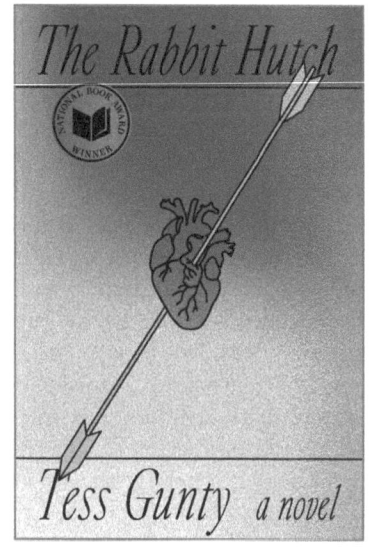

Tess Gunty's 2022 debut novel, *The Rabbit Hutch*, examines the lives of a handful of characters living in the fictional city of Vacca Vale, Indiana. Drawing on her own experience of growing up in South Bend, Indiana, Gunty creates a polyphonic work that brings to life these characters' sense of quiet desperation and their yearning for some sort of spiritual release. Mixing brutality and tenderness, the grittily realistic and the surreal, Gunty paints an engrossing portrait of spiritual emptiness and the violence that results from these feelings of hopelessness.

The city where the book takes place, Vacca Vale, is a former industrial town that has fallen on hard times. Ranked first on *Newsweek*'s list of "Top Ten Dying American Cities," it is a place that has never been the same since its chief employer, the Zorn automobile company, closed decades earlier. While Vacca Vale is a fictional city, it recalls a number of real-life towns and cities in the Rust Belt, a region encompassing parts of the Midwestern and Northeastern United States. During the last decades of the twentieth century, many cities and towns in the Rust Belt began to suffer from the side effects of deindustrialization, including high unemployment, shrinking populations, and general economic decline. Many of these communities never recovered from their chief industries leaving town and the general loss of manufacturing jobs in the US. In interviews, Gunty noted how this trend affected her hometown of South Bend, and cited places hit even harder by deindustrialization, such as Flint, Michigan, and Youngstown, Ohio, as the inspirations for Vacca Vale. Against this backdrop, Gunty establishes that her characters' lives will not be easy and that they are yearning

Tess Gunty

for something more fulfilling than their current circumstances can offer.

Much like Vacca Vale itself, the building where many of the main characters live is both run-down and reminiscent of more optimistic intentions. Known officially as the La Lapinière Affordable Housing Complex, it is universally referred to by its residents by the far less glamorous English translation of its name, the Rabbit Hutch. The apartment building, which used to be a Zorn factory, was intended to offer its residents a dignified home. In reality it is a poorly designed building with paper-thin walls and its residents are a cast of unhappy characters. This setting perfectly suits the themes of the novel, because it recalls a more hopeful past and because its name suggests a dehumanizing setting in which the residents are trapped in their lives.

Chief among the residents of the Rabbit Hutch is an eighteen-year-old woman named Blandine Watkins. On the book's opening page, Blandine "exits her body," and the third-person narrator explains that "she has spent most of her life wishing for this to happen." The narrator suggests that Blandine exiting her body is something out of an ancient mystical tradition, as well as the result of some violence being inflicted on her at the moment. In the book's opening section, which is only three paragraphs long, Gunty provides the reader with a startling and intriguing series of images but little explanation. Although she does not spell out what exactly it means for Blandine to leave her body, she establishes the book's embrace of mysticism alongside its everyday realism. She also establishes this scene as the book's climax. After the opening, the novel flashes back and moves slowly forward toward the moment that Blandine experiences violence and leaves her body, which Gunty only returns to and clarifies at the end of the book.

Blandine is a highly intelligent and thoughtful young woman who is obsessed with the writings and ideas of Christian mystics from the Middle Ages. She works at a coffee shop but seems born for larger things. She is prone to giving long speeches and dabbles in minor acts of sabotage against the developers who are trying to "revitalize" Vacca Vale by destroying her favorite park. Notably, Blandine is a graduate of the foster care system and lives with three male roommates who are also former foster children. In a lengthy chapter that occurs about a third of the way through the book, Gunty fills in Blandine's backstory by revealing that she was a promising high school student with a bright future until she dropped out of school following a sexual relationship with her teacher, James Yager.

The book's other central character is Moses Robert Blitz, the middle-aged son of star actress Elsie Blitz. At the beginning of the novel, Elsie dies, leaving Moses to process the resentment he feels about her neglectful parenting. This death inadvertently triggers the narrative momentum of the book when a series of events causes Moses to come to Vacca Vale, a city he has never visited before, to extract a bizarre form of revenge on Joan Kowalski, one of the residents of the Rabbit Hutch. Although Blandine and Moses are the book's main characters, Gunty provides readers with little glimpses of the lives of the building's other residents in several chapters throughout the book. The result is a rich echoing of the lives of these main characters, expanding the scope of the novel to show a wide-range of dissatisfied people trying to live their lives as best they can. At the book's climax, these separate narrative threads all converge on Blandine's apartment.

Gunty's novel is a very ambitious work that includes not only a wide range of characters, but also a variety of themes and literary techniques. While Blandine's spiritual journey lies at the center of the book, Gunty gives due space to the emotional awakenings of other characters in the novel. In particular, she dives into the transformation of Joan Kowalski, an introverted, forty-year-old woman whose return to a more engaged life begins with a chance encounter with Blandine at the laundromat. The book also widens its scope to touch on topics such as the gentrification and revitalization of cities, the failures of the foster care system, and the pitfalls of growing up amidst Hollywood glamor. Not all of these threads are equally successful. For example, the passages about the development of Vacca Vale feel a little too superficial to reach their full potential. Nonetheless, these passages remain interesting and still manage to add to the richness of the book.

Stylistically, Gunty is highly ambitious, with largely dazzling results. Most sections are written in third-person. In these passages, Gunty's prose ranges from a more straightforward narration to passages filled with ornate descriptive language. In addition to these sections with third-person narration, Gunty includes a series of sections narrated in the first person by Jack, one of Blandine's roommates. In addition to using different types of narration, Gunty also incorporates some unique storytelling techniques, including fictional newspaper stories about Vacca Vale, online comment sections, and even a series of woodblock prints created by her artist brother, Nicholas Gunty. The result is a narrative mosaic that allows the reader to see the book's characters from multiple angles and gain a wider perspective on their lives.

Ultimately, Gunty's book is about the violence that people inflict on each other. As one of the novel's minor characters puts it, "The plot of contemporary life . . . is about everyone punishing each other for things they didn't do." This violence is especially present for the book's women. Even before the book's climax, Gunty makes clear the everyday physical threats that Blandine faces; for example, in one scene, she walks to the park and must deflect the attentions of several aggressive men. However, alongside this constant threat of violence is the possibility of some sort of spiritual release. For Blandine, this release is tied up with her constant reading of the works of Christian mystics. The concepts of violence and release come together in the climax, at which point pain and pleasure, as well as bodily damage and spiritual release, become indistinguishable. It is a remarkable moment of synthesis and one that brings Gunty's novel to a startling yet satisfying close.

Although *The Rabbit Hutch* was Gunty's first novel, it received a significant amount of attention and accolade in the literary world, and ultimately won the prestigious National Book Award for Fiction in 2022. Typical of the critical reception was Leah Greenblatt's review for the *New York Times*, in which she called the book "dense, prismatic, and often mesmerizing . . . a novel of impressive scope and specificity." Greenblatt particularly praised Gunty's ability to "press her thumb on the frailty and absurdity of being a person in the world." Other critics had similar praise to offer. Sam Sacks, writing for the *Wall Street Journal*, singled out the book's "unnerving vision and conviction" and called it the most promising first novel he had read in 2022. *The Boston Globe*'s Clea Simon was even more effusive in her assessment. She called the book "transcendent" as well as "compelling and startingly beautiful."

Nonetheless, a number of critics had some minor reservations. Sacks was less enthusiastic about the lengthy chapter detailing Blandine's relationship with her teacher, while Greenblatt felt that the book's larger ambitions occasionally worked against it. According to Greenblatt, the book "falters mostly when it works too hard to wedge its storytelling into some broader notion of Big Ideas." Despite these quibbles, most critics were highly impressed by the novel and it was listed as one of the best books of the year by numerous publications. One of the more assured and confident literary debuts in recent years, *The Rabbit Hutch* establishes Gunty as not only a talented and ambitious novelist, but one who is able to successfully balance a number of different thematic and stylistic elements and weave them together into an impressive whole.

Author Biography

Tess Gunty has had her writing published in outlets such as the *Los Angeles Review of Books* and the *Iowa Review*. The National Book Award–winning *The Rabbit Hutch* is her first novel.

Andrew Schenker

Review Sources

Ditum, Sarah. Review of *The Rabbit Hutch*, by Tess Gunty. *The Guardian*, 3 Aug. 2022, www.theguardian.com/books/2022/aug/03/the-rabbit-hutch-by-tess-gunty-review-a-riveting-debut-about-love-and-cruelty. Accessed 13 Dec. 2022.

Greenblatt, Leah. "One Apartment Building, Many Lives." Review of *The Rabbit Hutch*, by Tess Gunty. *The New York Times*, 2 Aug. 2022, www.nytimes.com/2022/08/02/books/review/tess-gunty-rabbit-hutch.html. Accessed 13 Dec. 2022.

Price, Emily. "*The Rabbit Hutch* Is a Frenetic Debut about Alienation." Review of *The Rabbit Hutch*, by Tess Gunty. *Paste Magazine,* 15 Aug. 2022, www.pastemagazine.com/books/tess-gunty/the-rabbit-hutch-review-tess-gunty/. Accessed 13 Dec. 2022.

Sacks, Sam. Review of *The Rabbit Hutch*, by Tess Gunty. *The Wall Street Journal*, 5 Aug. 2022, www.wsj.com/articles/fiction-reviews-novels-the-rabbit-hutch-by-tess-gunty-11659710617. Accessed 13 Dec. 2022.

Simon, Clea. "Transcending the Mundane in 'The Rabbit Hutch.'" Review of *The Rabbit Hutch*, by Tess Gunty. *The Boston Globe*, 25 Aug. 2022, www.bostonglobe.com/2022/08/25/arts/transcending-mundane/. Accessed 20 Jan. 2023.

Red Paint
The Ancestral Autobiography of a Coast Salish Punk

Author: Sasha taqʷšəblu LaPointe (b. 1984)
Publisher: Counterpoint (New York).
  240 pp.
Type of work: Memoir
Time: Mid-1800s–present day
Locale: Washington State

Interweaving personal life experiences with ancestral history, Coast Salish writer and artist Sasha taqʷšəblu LaPointe explores loss, healing, and the enduring spirit across generations of women in her memoir, Red Paint. *The author also probes the wounds of her ancestors, exploring the intergenerational burdens of trauma and the path toward healing.*

Principal personages
SASHA TAQʷŠƏBLU LAPOINTE, the author, a Coast Salish woman
BRANDON, her husband, a punk rock musician
RICHARD, her teenage boyfriend and close friend
VIOLET TAQʷŠƏBLU HILBERT, her great-grandmother, an important storyteller and preserver of the Lushootseed language
COMPTIA KOHOLOWISH, her ancestor whose family died of smallpox in the nineteenth century

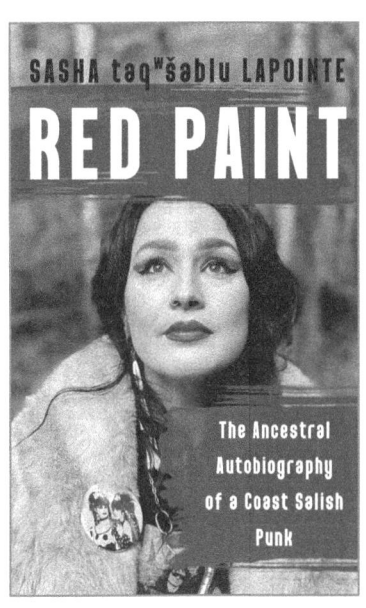

Red Paint: The Ancestral Autobiography of a Coast Salish Punk (2022) opens with the words of Violet taqʷšəblu Hilbert, the author's great-grandmother, presented in a paired translation of English and Lushootseed, one of the traditional languages of the Coast Salish Indians: "you have to learn how to be like the cedar, / how to be flexible and pliable / and you yourself will not break." These words enable Sasha taqʷšəblu LaPointe to bring together the threads of her memoir: ancestral wisdom, trauma, and healing. LaPointe is a Coast Salish tribal member, from the Nooksack and Upper Skagit tribes. Having been raised on a reservation in Washington State, she lived her life in the region of her ancestral homelands. Yet the reservation is a temporary home, serving as a reminder of the homelessness and structural disempowerment faced by Indigenous peoples throughout history. The history, violence, and oppression of settler-colonialism and US imperialism permeate *Red Paint*, but this pulsing background of pain is not the driver of the book. Instead, LaPointe wishes to convey the strength of her ancestors' healing spirit. The memoir is to a great degree a reflection of LaPointe's journey to discover this legacy of healing and the Indigenous wisdom held in the female line of her family—and to use those resources to set her own life on a more stable, healing path.

This is not a straightforward memoir, but rather an "ancestral autobiography," as the book's subtitle states. LaPointe writes "there is a way that memory lives in our bodies, imprints us with feeling." These embodied memories are not solely the imprints of the author's own experiences, but also those of her ancestors. For LaPointe, and for her maternal ancestors whose stories she explores, severe trauma is built into body memory. Over the course of the book, LaPointe recounts and reckons with being raped at age ten by a trusted elder. She offers flashes into subsequent assaults endured during her teenage years when she frequently ran away from home, seeking community and escape among other troubled teens in the local punk music scene. Later, in the portion of her life concurrent with the memoir's narrative, LaPointe experiences a late miscarriage, which she describes in graphic physical and emotional terms. LaPointe wonders, though she cannot fully affirm, how her personal traumas might echo those of her ancestors.

Sasha LaPointe

As the memoir unfolds, she digs deeper into her own memories, while also seeking to know more about the women who came before her. In one powerful scene, LaPointe bathes herself in the Skagit River and finds herself cleansed by its waters, then later learns of tribal and family wisdom telling of a healing location on the river, just near where she entered. She traces the story of Comptia Koholowish, a distant Chinook ancestor who lost her entire family and village to smallpox when European settlers arrived in Washington State in the nineteenth century. At age twenty, Koholowish married one of the traders who settled in the area but she lived alone in a small cabin behind her husband's large house. LaPointe travels to Koholowish's home and finds the small building in the rear still standing. She further locates a historical marker at the site recognizing the main house as one "built by Captain Johnson, a sea captain." Koholowish's story, however, is not remembered on the marker, and the one reference to her on the signage is inaccurate.

In tracing her female ancestry and their individual stories of trauma and resilience, LaPointe is responding to the cutting words of Brandon, her husband, who in a turning point in their relationship exclaims: "You're not well. It's like all the women in your family, your mom, your grandma, you all have the same thing, you're all sick. You need help." His comment may, in fact, have been well-intentioned—LaPointe was experiencing significant post-traumatic stress disorder during that period, including blackouts, punishing anxiety, and other symptoms. But for LaPointe, this comment becomes a rallying cry. Ultimately, she reframes her husband's comment and her conceptual response to it in the form of a poem with which the book concludes. LaPointe reads the poem while touring with a punk band, wearing the red paint that her ancestors had worn, a symbol of their role as medicine workers in their community. At the beginning of the memoir, LaPointe had requested her mother's permission to finally be granted the honor of wearing this red paint. Now, at its conclusion, the reader learns of her mother's affirmation, and the paint serves as LaPointe's "own ritual of healing." The act is significant and redolent with symbolism. "When I wore the red paint it was for the wounds we carried in our bodies, through generations," writes LaPointe. "It was for the grief of losing our land, our bodies, our language, and our children . . . to remind me of where I came from."

The concept of home and the landscape of the Pacific Northwest also play a vivid role in LaPointe's memoir. Although she has lived most of her life in the same region as these ancestral homelands, LaPointe presents her own life, and that of all the generations since settler-colonialism, as characterized by homelessness. As her marriage disintegrates, this theme rises to the forefront, but it is a familiar autobiographical theme for LaPointe stretching back to her young childhood. When LaPointe inherits land after the death of her grandmother, she sells the marshy reservation tract back to the tribe and uses the funds to buy elsewhere. She hopes her new home will make her grounded and able to build a strong foundation with her unborn child, but soon thereafter the miscarriage derails these plans. Still, this new home and its plot of land offer the promise of something more secure and enduring—and a more permanent reclaiming of land and ownership than the reservation would have offered. The repeating motif of homelessness is offset by powerful descriptions of nature that are worked throughout the book. Coastline, river, and mountain trails all tie LaPointe to her ancestor's secure connection with the landscape in the years before settler-colonialism. As Ellen Wayland-Smith wrote in her review in the *Los Angeles Review of Books*, "the natural beauty of her surroundings . . . form more than just the story's backdrop," referring to LaPointe's continued appreciation of the natural world and reliance on it to help preserve her own mental health. "The Skagit River, in particular, becomes a crucial character in helping LaPointe navigate her way back from the seductive shores of the spirit world, into which she is tempted to disappear."

Much of *Red Paint* centers on LaPointe's romantic relationships—specifically with Brandon and another former boyfriend from her teenage years named Richard. Both of these men are White, and Brandon also comes from a much more secure financial background. Across the course of the book, Brandon and LaPointe marry, but almost immediately become estranged. During their estrangement, LaPointe rekindles her friendship with Richard and, though they are not sexually intimate, their emotional attachment is deep. LaPointe's separation from Brandon is triggered by a betrayal related to their finances and their planned honeymoon. But the strain in their relationship had started earlier, as LaPointe began to work on her autobiographical writing and to dig deeply into her past sexual traumas as part of her graduate work at the Institute of American Indian Arts. That work brought up psychological wounds and many repressed memories that she had not previously shared with Brandon. LaPointe spirals deep into depression, along with some level of substance abuse, and experiences numerous physical crises. Eventually, LaPointe finds deep reserves of ancestral strength and begins to heal—which, as she notes, is a different and more intentional process than "self-medicating." By then, however, her marriage is over.

LaPointe touches on the complexities of interracial relationships, and the particular inherited weight of race and injustice on her relationship with Brandon, but she does not mine as deeply into this aspect of her personal life as might be desirable, given the themes that rise to the forefront of this memoir. LaPointe herself is biracial and in this memoir she largely sets aside any deep discussion of her White ancestry, focusing instead on the Indigenous women (rather than the White men) in her ancestral past. This decision is deeply tied to her journey of healing and self-discovery, but perhaps sidesteps some of the complexities of heritage and identity that her life story might reveal. Despite that minor criticism, reviews of *Red Paint* were largely positive and praised the author's ability to cover such intense topics so thoroughly. "The author deftly navigates multiple timelines, weaving in and out of family history, personal narrative, and a host of other tangential topics," wrote the reviewer for *Kirkus Reviews*, for instance.

Thus, *Red Paint* is the story of one woman and her Indigenous maternal ancestors. Through this lens, LaPointe speaks of ancestry, but also of her own complex, contemporary identity. Rejecting the labels of "resilience" and "survival," she also seeks to cast off "the names white people had given us." Instead, she offers other possible labels for herself: "Call me a writer. Call me a riot grrrl. Call me Coast Salish or poet. . . . Call me anything other than survivor. I am so many more things than brave." Indeed, because much of the memoir is focused on LaPointe's efforts to reconnect with her ancestral stories and with the repressed corners of her own life, this passage toward the end of the book is an important reminder of what *Red Paint* might offer a general reader. LaPointe is a tribal member *and* a contemporary woman in the United States *and* a professional writer seeking to find her voice. Her account in *Red Paint* offers a road map of what it might take on an individual level to work through and confront the violent heritage of colonialism. It is also, ultimately, an embrace of the diverse heritage and cultural currents of contemporary life—and a call to move forward, forging a new path of healing.

Author Biography

Sasha taqʷšəblu LaPointe is a poet, punk performer, and essayist. She holds a master's degree in creative nonfiction and poetry from the Institute of American Indian Arts in Santa Fe. *Red Paint* is her first book. Her writing has appeared in numerous publications, including *Indian Country Today*, the *Yellow Medicine Review*, the *Portland Review*, and the *Rumpus*.

Julia A. Sienkewicz, PhD

Review Sources

Alcalá, Kathleen. Review of *Red Paint: The Ancestral Autobiography of a Coast Salish Punk*, by Sasha taqʷšəblu Lapointe. *Raven Chronicles Press*, 21 Sept. 2022, www.ravenchronicles.org/book-reviews/kathleen-alcala-reviews-red-paint-by-sasha-lapointe. Accessed 4 Dec. 2022.

Gresham, Lisa. Review of *Red Paint: The Ancestral Autobiography of a Coast Salish Punk*, by Sasha taqʷšəblu Lapointe. *Cascadia Daily News*, 12 Apr. 2022, www.cascadiadaily.com/news/2022/apr/12/review-red-paint-by-sasha-lapointe/. Accessed 4 Dec. 2022.

Review of *Red Paint: The Ancestral Autobiography of a Coast Salish Punk*, by Sasha taqʷšəblu Lapointe. *Kirkus Reviews*, 24 Dec. 2021, www.kirkusreviews.com/book-reviews/sasha-lapointe/red-paint-ancestral/. Accessed 4 Jan. 2023.

Wayland-Smith, Ellen. "The Missing: On Sasha LaPointe's 'Red Paint: The Ancestral Autobiography of a Coast Salish Punk.'" Review of *Red Paint: The Ancestral Autobiography of a Coast Salish Punk*, by Sasha taqʷšəblu Lapointe. *Los Angeles Review of Books*, 10 June 2022, lareviewofbooks.org/article/the-missing-on-sasha-lapointes-red-paint-the-ancestral-autobiography-of-a-coast-salish-punk/. Accessed 4 Dec. 2022.

Rise
A Pop History of Asian America from the Nineties to Now

Authors: Jeff Yang (b. 1968), Phil Yu (b. 1978), and Philip Wang (b. 1984)
Publisher: Mariner Books (Boston). 496 pp. Illustrated.
Type of work: Graphic nonfiction, miscellaneous, history

Rise *brings together a wide range of contributors and draws on a number of different genres to tell the story of Asian America and its culture over the last thirty years.*

Rise: A Pop History of Asian America from the Nineties to Now is a diverse and inspiring compendium of Asian American life and culture from the past three decades. Compiled and written by Jeff Yang, Phil Yu, and Philip Wang, three prominent Asian American creatives, the book also features contributions from over eighty additional participants. Approaching Asian American life from a dizzying variety of perspectives, the material that makes up the book includes essays, lists, short comics, interviews, roundtable discussions, charts, timelines, and many more genres. Taken together, they reveal Asian American pop culture to be exciting, diverse, and in many ways surprising.

The idea for the book came about in 2020 during the early days of the COVID-19 pandemic, when the United States was still in a period of quarantine. As the book's introduction, which consists of an illustrated comic depicting the genesis of the project, explains, the authors each felt that Asian American culture had been progressing steadily over the past few decades and that Asians were finally getting much more visibility in entertainment and the arts. With the pandemic, not only did that momentum stall, but a wave of racist attacks on Asian people plunged the Asian American community into a moment of crisis. As Jeff Yang explains in the opening comic, these events "reminded us how quickly successes can be erased and progress can disappear." To combat these negative trends, they decided to put together a book that would highlight the work of Asian Americans over the last thirty years—both mainstream and overlooked—as well as the positive and negative experiences of the community that led to these works.

Because *Rise* covers thirty years of culture, the authors decided to arrange the book by decades, with the 1990s, 2000s, and 2010s each getting a section of their own. There is also an introductory section labeled "Before," which provides extensive background on Asian American life before 1990, and a final section, "Beyond," which looks towards the future. Each chapter begins with an in-depth introductory essay and, because each of the three authors came of age in a different decade, they are responsible for that section's

Jeff Yang

essay. Jeff Yang, a long-time journalist and writer, handles the 1990s as well as the introductory essay for "Before," while prominent blogger Phil Yu writes the essay for the 2000s, and multimedia producer Philip Wang takes on the 2010s. All three writers collaborate on the introduction for the "Beyond" section. These introductory essays are the heart of the book, with each writer not only summarizing the major trends and events in Asian American life during the decade in question, but telling their own stories as creators against that backdrop. The result in each case is a shrewd blending of the personal with the wider culture, as the authors bring to life both the ways that they were shaped by their unique culture and how they in turn shaped that culture.

The concept of Asian America, as Jeff Yang explains in the introduction to "Beyond," is somewhat nebulous and really only dates back to 1968. Although people from Asia have immigrated to the United States since at least the nineteenth century, and possibly much earlier, before the 1960s, the different Asian communities never thought of themselves as a whole. They considered themselves to be Chinese or Filipino or Korean, but not Asian. This began to change, when in 1968, students in Berkeley, California, formed a group called the Asian-American Political Alliance, inspired by the African American, Native American, and Chicano movements of the time. Not only did they coin the term "Asian American," but they brought together diverse communities to achieve positive change. As Yang writes, this "represent[ed] the first time Asians had embraced a sense of common identity for *ourselves*, by *choice*, and the discovery of a budding power in that choice." Although the concept of Asian America has remained somewhat amorphous since then, both in terms of who qualifies as Asian American on the census and how members of individual communities see themselves in the larger picture, the idea of a common cause among these communities had taken root and would continue to develop over the years. As Yang concludes, "the term 'Asian American' originated as a way to make sure that we'd be seen and heard in a crowd . . . but it also set us on the path toward controlling our own narrative."

Although the purpose of *Rise*, as Yang and the other writers make clear in their essays, is a serious one, there is also plenty of room for fun in the book. This is above all, a highly visual project, a gorgeous object with dozens of sharply drawn comics; generous illustrations, hand-drawn, painted, and photographed; and an attractive layout that ensures that each time the reader turns the page, something fresh will await them. The visual diversity on the book's pages mirrors the diversity of the Asian American experience as depicted in *Rise*, a conjunction made clear on the book's cover which consists of small hand-drawn illustrations of the faces of dozens of different notable Asian Americans from a wide variety of fields.

The book contains several running features that are present in each of the book's sections. These include "The Asian American Playlist," in which, for each decade, Filipino American DJ Richie "Traktivist" Menchavez provides a brief overview of the period's most notable songs by Asian Americans, and "The Asian American Yearbook," where Jeff Yang creates a faux-yearbook spread, highlighting each decade's most notable Asian Americans with high school-style superlatives like "best dressed" and "homecoming king and queen." Some of these running features take on more serious notes, highlighting problems affecting the Asian American community, such as a running segment where the writers discuss the most prominent examples of "yellowface" in each decade's movies and TV shows, in which White actors play Asian and Asian American characters. In all, these recurring segments give the book continuity and a tight structure while allowing the reader to see all the ways that things have changed—or have stayed the same—in Asian American culture and communities over the years.

Apart from the recurring segments, each section is full of numerous other enlightening features. Perhaps the most valuable of these are the roundtable discussions that are featured prominently in the book and which cover a variety of subjects, from bhangra dance to Asian American representation in film. Two of these roundtables in particular, though, are of special interest and speak to the need for intersectionality. The first is a discussion of the Los Angeles Riots of 1992, which exacerbated the tense relationship between African Americans and the city's Korean community, and the second is a more general discussion of African American/Asian relations and is found in the book's final section, "Beyond." These two sections recount the difficulties these communities have had relating to each other, the ways that they have been pitted against each other by outside interests, and the ultimate importance of coming together in a united cause. As television producer Monica Macer, who is both Black and Korean, puts it in the second roundtable, "there's just a divide-and-conquer mentality in our society. . . . We're constantly encouraged to fight each other, as opposed to banding together. . . . If we join together, we can outnumber everyone else."

Although *Rise* did not receive a large number of reviews, those that it did receive were uniformly positive. The book earned star reviews from *Publisher's Weekly*, *Kirkus Reviews*, and *Library Journal*. John Rodzvilla, the reviewer for *Library Journal*, called the book, "a remarkable collection of stories from Asian Americans: a mix of essays, interviews, comics, playlists, and more," and praised the book's nuanced approach, deeming it "an essential read." Similarly, *Kirkus Reviews* found the project to be "a hip, entertaining book, as imaginative in its presentation and stories as the generation it portrays." *Publishers Weekly* called *Rise* a "celebration of Asian American culture" that "illustrate[s] the obstacles Asian Americans have come up against and brilliantly juxtapose[s] them with stories of how those barriers have been thwarted."

By focusing on the smaller moments of Asian American culture as well as the more prominent breakthroughs like *The Joy Luck Club*, *Fresh Off the Boat*, and *Crazy Rich Asians*, Jeff Yang, Phil Yu, and Philip Wang ensure that the story of Asian America's rise to prominence is told thoroughly and with great richness. By drawing on so many different and appealing genres Yang, Yu, and Wang ensure that the reader will remain enthralled as they explore, in the authors' own words, "how much [the Asian American] community has accomplished in the past three decades, and how big, complex, nuanced and diverse it really is."

Author Biographies
Jeff Yang is a journalist and writer who has worked for *The Wall Street Journal* and the *San Francisco Chronicle*. He has written several books and was the publisher of the groundbreaking Asian American publication, *A. Magazine*.

Phil Yu is a writer and consultant best known for creating and running the blog *Angry Asian Man*. He has worked for the Center for Asian American Media and joined the board for the nonprofit media arts organization Visual Communications in 2010.

Philip Wang is a filmmaker and, along with Wesley Chan and Ted Fu, cofounder of the media collective Wong Fu Productions. His video work has earned more than 3 million subscribers and half a billion views on YouTube.

Andrew Schenker

Review Sources
Review of *Rise: A Pop History of Asian America from the Nineties to Now*, by Jeff Yang, Phil Yu, and Philip Wang. *Kirkus Reviews*, 12 Oct. 2021, www.kirkusreviews.com/book-reviews/jeff-yang/rise-pop-history/. Accessed 11 Jan. 2023.

Review of *Rise: A Pop History of Asian America from the Nineties to Now*, Jeff Yang, Phil Yu, and Philip Wang. *Publisher's Weekly*, 21 Sept. 2021, www.publishersweekly.com/9780358508090. Accessed 11 Jan. 2023.

Rodzvilla, John. Review of *Rise: A Pop History of Asian America from the Nineties to Now*, by Jeff Yang, Phil Yu, and Philip Wang. *Library Journal*, 1 Jan. 2022, www.libraryjournal.com/review/rise-a-pop-history-of-asian-america-from-the-nineties-to-now-2129014. Accessed 11 Jan. 2023.

River of the Gods
Genius, Courage, and Betrayal in the Search for the Source of the Nile

Author: Candice Millard (b. ca. 1967)
Publisher: Doubleday (New York). 368 pp.
Type of work: History, biography
Time: Largely 1850s–60s
Locales: East Africa, the Middle East, London

Writer Candice Millard presents a compelling account of the turbulent relationship between explorers Richard Francis Burton and John Hanning Speke in their nineteenth-century quest to locate the source of the Nile River.

Principal personages
RICHARD FRANCIS BURTON, a British explorer
JOHN HANNING SPEKE, a British explorer
SIDI MUBARAK BOMBAY, a formerly enslaved African guide for British explorations
ISABEL ARUNDELL BURTON, wife of Richard Burton
JAMES AUGUSTUS GRANT, a British explorer
CHRISTOPHER PALMER RIGBY, a British diplomat
ATKINS HAMERTON, a British diplomat
RODERICK IMPEY MURCHISON, president of the Royal Geographic Society
LAURENCE OLIPHANT, a British diplomat and author

Western histories of the nineteenth-century frequently describe the period as a continued era of exploration. Fueled by ambition to become the first to chart the many blank spaces on their world maps, many Europeans set out to discover lost cities, ancient kingdoms, and spectacular geographic features in far-away and largely unknown regions in the Americas, Asia, and, especially, Africa. The latter continent was then thought to be a place of great danger, but for those who could bring home its secrets, map its terrain, and open up new fields for Christian evangelization, the chance to achieve notoriety (and perhaps riches) made the challenges worth the risk. By the middle of the century, Richard Francis Burton was one of the most famous adventurer-explorers, known to thousands who read accounts of his travels in books and articles he turned out with great alacrity and lionized by a periodical press eager to trumpet Great Britain's conquests of the unknown corners of the world. In 1855, fresh from successes in penetrating the forbidden Muslim cities of Mecca and Harar, Burton mounted an expedition to settle a question that had vexed European societies for centuries: Where did the Nile River begin?

Candice Millard

Candice Millard's *River of the Gods: Genius, Courage, and Betrayal in the Search for the Source of the Nile* (2022) chronicles that journey and several others undertaken by Burton and his one-time companion and subordinate John Hanning Speke in the 1850s and 1860s. More than a mere travelogue, Millard's book exposes the personalities of these two ambitious, proud, and fearless men whose zeal for adventure and the accompanying fame and fortune it might bring led them first to travel as uncomfortable allies and later to become bitter rivals. Millard concentrates on the expeditions Burton and Speke undertook in East Africa during the 1850s. On their first journey together, a trek into Somaliland, Burton took along Speke because Speke possessed skills Burton needed, even though their relationship was often strained. Both were wounded in an attack by locals; although Speke received eleven wounds and almost lost his life, Burton accused him of acting cowardly during the skirmish. When the expedition ended, Burton collected Speke's notebooks and would later publish much of the information in his own account of the expedition, giving Speke no credit. Speke never forgot or forgave what he considered personal and professional affronts.

Despite the testy nature of their association, when Burton received support from the Royal Geographic Society (RGS) in 1855 to mount an expedition to locate the source of the Nile, he chose Speke as his second in command. Their already stormy relationship became even more strained during the three years over which the journey was organized and carried out. Burton had found an ally in Atkins Hamerton, the British consul on the island of Zanzibar, the jumping-off point for many treks into East Africa and the Middle East. When Burton returned to Zanzibar to assemble a party for his inland journey in search of the headwaters of the Nile, Hamerton made promises to supplement the meager stipend Burton had received from the RGS with funds from the government. Hamerton died shortly after Burton and Speke departed for the interior, however, and the new consul, Christopher Rigby, refused to honor his predecessor's commitments. Furthermore, Rigby, who did not like Burton, became friends with Speke, setting up additional complications for Burton both during and after the expedition.

The venture that began in 1856 and ended in 1859 did not really prove anything. Burton, convinced that the headwaters of the Nile lay at the northern end of Lake Tanganyika, led his party to the lake's southern shore. Unfortunately, illness prevented him from traveling further, so he could not confirm for himself that a river at the northern edge of the lake was actually the headwaters of the Nile. While Burton lay recuperating at Lake Tanganyika, Speke went off with a smaller party and traveled northeast to Lake Nyanza. At the southern shore of that lake, he heard stories of a great river issuing from the lake's northernmost point, leading him to believe he had found the true source of the Nile. On their return to London, Burton and Speke argued over the claim to have successfully located the river's headwaters.

Since neither had seen the site they claimed as the origin of Africa's longest river, the RGS, at the urging of President Roderick Murchison, sponsored a new expedition to settle rival claims. This time, Speke was in command, with James Augustus Grant as his deputy; Burton was not a member of the party. Speke was successful, claiming upon his return that he had been the first person to see the great falls that pour out of Lake Nyanza—which he had promptly renamed Lake Victoria, to honor the British queen. To confirm his claim, Speke returned to England by traveling from the headwaters down the Nile into Egypt. He claimed in a letter sent to Murchison in 1863, "the Nile is settled." The squabbling between Burton and Speke did not stop, however. The two men, now bitter rivals for fame and financial support, continued arguing until Speke's untimely death in 1864. Burton, an accomplished linguist, spent the rest of his life in minor consular posts, working on translations of several important Middle Eastern texts.

Like many who write about nineteenth-century figures, Millard is aided in her research by the mass of printed materials left behind by these figures. Burton was a prolific author, and his wife, Isabel, also published several books. Speke, Grant, and Rigby each brought out accounts of their exploits in the region, as did several others with whom the principals in Millard's study had dealings. However, not all of these accounts are entirely trustworthy, and one of Millard's principal tasks as a modern-day chronicler is to sift through these documents and the dozens of books and articles published later to get at a version of the truth that represents accurately the available facts.

Naturally, the facts are subject to interpretation, and in her assessment of the feud between Burton and Speke, Millard does take sides. She paints Burton as a besieged if flawed victim, and Speke as a vain, vindictive rival unable to share the spotlight with anyone—and certainly not with the man whom he felt was constantly eclipsing him in the public eye. The feud between Speke and Burton was also kept alive by others, including Rigby, and actively encouraged by Speke's friend Laurence Oliphant. An aristocrat like Speke and his close friend, Oliphant held a long-standing grudge against Burton, who, in advising the British high command during the Crimean War on a plan for relief of the Turkish garrison at Kars, seemed to have ignored Oliphant's earlier writings on the subject. Oliphant's resentment lingered, and his constant encouragement of Speke's natural inclination to belittle others as a means of bolstering his own achievements kept the two explorers at odds for nearly a decade.

As noted by several reviewers, Millard's account of these expeditions is informed by a twenty-first-century sensibility to the myopia and arrogance of European exploration in the nineteenth century. The euphoria that explorers felt over their "discoveries" is subtly placed in context. Speke may have been the first European to see the spot where the waters of Lake Nyanza spill over the Ripon Falls (so named by Speke to honor a former president of the RGS) to form the headwaters of the White Nile. However, as Millard points out repeatedly, the Englishmen of whom she writes traveled through a land well known to Arab traders—and enslavers—who had, for hundreds of years, been exploiting the people and natural resources on the continent. Additionally, adventurers like Burton and Speke could only undertake their journey with the aid of dozens, sometimes hundreds, of African guides, porters, cooks, and others who both literally and metaphorically "carried the water" for their European employers. Many did so at the behest of local leaders whom Burton and Speke coopted for support. The promise of good pay was a strong motivating factor for many of the people whose daily work allowed the expeditions to move forward. Others among this nameless group had no choice about their participation: in Africa, slavery was then a common practice, carried out by others Africans as well as foreigners.

The importance of the Indigenous population to the success of these journeys of exploration is highlighted in Millard's portrait of the guide Sidi Mubarak Bombay. An African who had been captured and enslaved in childhood and taken to India, by the 1850s Bombay had returned to Africa following the death of his enslaver and become a knowledgeable guide available for hire to those wishing to penetrate the interior of the continent. Burton hired him for the trek to Lake Tanganyika, and Speke took him on to guide his party to Lake Nyanza. Indefatigable in his work habits and loyal to the men whom he agreed to guide, Bombay emerges as perhaps the most admirable character in Millard's account.

While the principal subjects of Millard's account are men, she is able to highlight the status of European women by chronicling the at-home exploits of a woman interesting in her own right: Isabel Arundell, who in 1861 became Burton's wife. Millard's account of Isabel's fascination with, and eventually marriage to, the older Burton is a study of determination coupled with what seems to have been willing acceptance of Victorian society's notions of marriage in a period when the doctrine of separate spheres declared that a woman's proper role in society was to stay at and run the home. With her imagination fired by reading of Burton's exploits, Isabel was only too ready to fall in love with the man at their first meeting. For a decade, she held firm to her belief that she would marry him, facing down strong objections from her family, particularly her mother. Millard makes it clear that Isabel saw herself as Burton's helpmate, someone in whom he could trust implicitly to provide a home where his will would be unchallenged. Some twenty-first-century readers may find Isabel's acquiescence to conventional gender norms of behavior unsettling or even unhealthy, but for her time, Millard argues, she was as adventuresome as most women were able to be.

The ironies of European exploration of Africa chronicled in Millard's fast-paced, critically praised account, are brought home in her epilogue: In 2006, British explorer Neil McGrigor reported that his party had found the *real* source of the Nile, the headwaters of the Kagera River, which originates in Rwanda and feeds into Lake Nyanza. In the end, Millard suggests, neither Burton nor Speke were right. Their adventures, however, provide insight into the mindset of European explorers who were willing to risk life and limb in the pursuit of knowledge—and the notoriety that came with being the first to report on the people and places hitherto unknown to Europeans hungry to map and master the world.

Author Biography
Candice Millard, a former writer and editor for *National Geographic*, is also the author of the acclaimed books *The River of Doubt* (2005), *Destiny of the Republic* (2011), and *Hero of the Empire* (2016). In 2017 she was recognized for her achievements in biography by the Biographers International Organization.

Laurence W. Mazzeno

Review Sources
Dolnick, Edward. "Exploration at the Edge of Disaster." Review of *River of the Gods: Genius, Courage, and Betrayal in the Search for the Source of the Nile*, by Candice Millard. *The New York Times*, 15 May 2022, www.nytimes.com/2022/05/15/books/review/river-of-the-gods-candice-millard.html. Accessed 7 Nov. 2022.

Krist, Gary. "They Found the Source of the Nile—and Became Lifelong Enemies." Review of *River of the Gods: Genius, Courage, and Betrayal in the Search for the Source of the Nile*, by Candice Millard. *The Washington Post*, 27 May 2022, www.washingtonpost.com/outlook/2022/05/27/they-found-source-of-nile-became-lifelong-enemies/. Accessed 7 Nov. 2022.

Schneider, Howard. "*River of the Gods* Review: In Search of the Source of the Nile." Review of *River of the Gods: Genius, Courage, and Betrayal in the Search for the Source of the Nile*, by Candice Millard. *The Wall Street Journal*, 6 May 2022, www.wsj.com/articles/river-of-the-gods-book-review-in-search-of-the-source-of-the-nile-11651849253. Accessed 7 Nov. 2022.

Swearingen, Jim. "Candice Millard Takes Us on a Pulse-Racing Search for the Source of the Nile River." Review of *River of the Gods: Genius, Courage, and Betrayal in the Search for the Source of the Nile*, by Candice Millard. *The National Book Review*, 19 May 2022, www.thenationalbookreview.com//features/2022/5/19/review-candice-millard-takes-us-on-a-pulse-racing-search-for-the-source-of-the-nile-river/. Accessed 7 Nov. 2022.

Rogues
True Stories of Grifters, Killers, Rebels and Crooks

Author: Patrick Radden Keefe (b. 1976)
Publisher: Doubleday (New York). 368 pp.
Type of work: Essays
Time: The twentieth and twenty-first centuries
Locales: The United States, the Netherlands, the Middle East, Mexico, Switzerland, Spain, Guinea, Vietnam

Veteran journalist Patrick Radden Keefe's Rogues: True Stories of Grifters, Killers, Rebels and Crooks *gathers together twelve memorable long-form nonfiction pieces originally published in the New Yorker exploring people's motivations, behavior, and morality in a variety of situations, including criminal ones.*

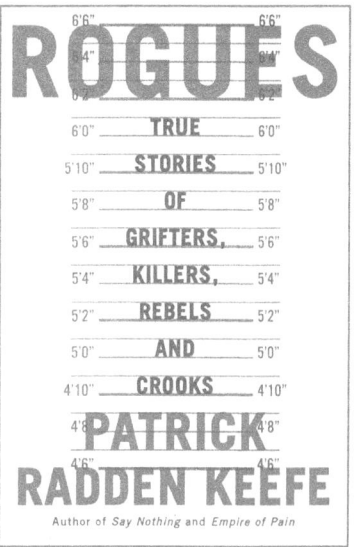

Principal personages

HARDY RODENSTOCK, a.k.a. Meinhard Goerke, a German wine collector
WILLEM "WIM" HOLLEEDER, a.k.a. the Nose, a Dutch mobster
KEN DORNSTEIN, the brother of one of the victims of the 1988 explosion of Pan Am Flight 103
MATHEW MARTOMA, a hedge-fund portfolio manager who worked for SAC Capital Advisors and was involved in an insider trading scandal
AMY BISHOP, a mass murderer
JOAQUÍN GUZMÁN LOERA, a.k.a. El Chapo, leader of the Sinaloa cartel in Mexico
MARK BURNETT, a television producer
HERVÉ FALCIANI, a staff member of HSBC's private Swiss bank
MONZER AL-KASSAR, a prominent arms dealer
JUDY CLARKE, a defense lawyer who has represented several clients facing the death penalty
BENY STEINMETZ, owner of a mining company
ANTHONY BOURDAIN, a celebrity chef, television presenter, and world traveler

In the preface to *Rogues: True Stories of Grifters, Killers, Rebels and Crooks* (2022), renowned investigative reporter Patrick Radden Keefe refers to his "abiding preoccupations: crime and corruption, secrets and lies, the permeable membrane separating licit and illicit worlds, the bonds of family, the power of denial." Indeed, the journalist's previous nonfiction books, covering investigative subjects spanning the globe, confirm such proclivities. Chatter: Dispatches from the Secret World of Global Eavesdropping

(2005) explores governmental surveillance activities that invade privacy and ride roughshod over citizens' rights. The Snakehead: An Epic Tale of the Chinatown Underworld and the American Dream (2009) casts light on the vicious battle between law enforcement and organized crime in New York City's Chinatown. Say Nothing: A True Story of Murder and Memory in Northern Ireland (2018) examines the brutal killing of a woman in Northern Ireland during the violent sectarian Troubles. Empire of Pain: The Secret History of the Sackler Dynasty (2021) takes aim at the wealthy Sackler family, which built its fortune on the promotion of a powerful and addictive drug, OxyContin, largely responsible for America's ongoing opioid crisis.

Patrick Radden Keefe

Rogues highlights the author's writing interests by presenting a dozen of his pieces that originally appeared in the New Yorker between 2007 and 2019. Like Keefe's books, his long-form articles are meticulously researched, well organized, and written in a clear, clean style that builds a what-will-happen-next suspense as new information is layered on, giving the complicated subjects he takes on shape and definition. Every contribution is capable of immersing a reader in a gripping, authoritative, scrupulously fact-checked story. At the same time, the articles are loosely but thought-provokingly linked by a common purpose: each demonstrates a creative application of situational ethics. Unlike his books, the articles are short enough to be read in an hour or less, providing intellectual engagement during a commuter ride or a lunch break.

Most of the articles, Keefe intriguingly explains upfront, are what the magazine trade calls "writearounds," or articles about subjects who, for one reason or another, refuse to be interviewed. This modern reluctance to be recorded requires the author to seek out the subject's friends, family, and associates—plus experts to opine about aspects of the issue at hand—to create a fully rounded portrait of the individual(s) under scrutiny. Further offering valuable insight into his investigative and writing processes that reaffirms the quality of his work, he divulges that producing a finished article often consumes most of a year in research, travel, and writing, with time apportioned according to need. The stories span a wide range in geography, time periods, and subject matter. They cover a colorful assortment of dictionary-definition rogues who largely fit into one or more of four broad, sometimes overlapping categories: grifters (con artists, swindlers, defrauders), killers (both those who commit murder and those who arrange killings), rebels (those who oppose authority or defy norms), and crooks (criminals and lawbreakers). Rogues provides several detailed but engaging examples of each type, and every article has been briefly updated with new information about the subject since publication.

The first, and earliest-published, article in Rogues illustrates Keefe's modus operandi of latching onto cases that present intriguing ambiguities. The author spotlights the primary issue by interviewing those with some connection to the (usually absent) main figure in the controversy. "The Jefferson Bottles" (2007) is one of several studies in grifting. Another is "Winning" (2019), which tells how producer Mark Burnett cast Donald Trump in the role of a successful businessman in the TV series *The Apprentice*, thereby changing the course of American political history. "The Jefferson Bottles" goes back, in part, to 1985, when a bottle of rare wine, an irresistible trophy for wealthy collectors, came up for auction at Christie's in London, England. The wine was allegedly of a prime eighteenth-century vintage, part of a cache from several renowned chateau vineyards supposedly found behind a bricked-up wall in the cellar of a building in Paris, France. Bottles were inscribed "Th.J," suggesting they had been the property of US president Thomas Jefferson, a known lover of fine French wines who had served as American minister to France beginning in 1785.

The wine bottles were authenticated by recognized experts, and a single bottle was subsequently purchased for more than $150,000, the most expensive wine ever sold at the time. The sale created a frenzy among other serious and well-heeled collectors eager to have their own Jefferson wine to display in their climate-controlled cellars. Prominent among the wine-obsessed was Bill Koch, multimillionaire brother of industrialists Charles and David Koch. Also, a collector of fine art and Western antiques, Koch spent half a million dollars buying four "Jefferson bottles" at auction.

The sudden escalation in prices of rare wine, however, had spawned a vigorous counterfeiting industry, particularly in the United States and in Asia. Over time, the Jefferson bottles became suspect. They had been offered by German collector Hardy Rodenstock, whose real name turned out to be Meinhard Goerke. After testing, though ultimately inconclusive, one of his bottles was suspected of consisting of adulterated wine. There were also questions about the marks on the bottles, which were concluded to have been made with tools that did not exist in the eighteenth century. While "Rodenstock" refused to be interviewed, Koch, his hired investigators, and others in the wine business were, despite their chagrin at being duped, willing to talk with Keefe after questions arose about the authenticity of the bottles. The article is bolstered with relevant discussions of wine counterfeiting techniques and methods of detecting fakes.

Several articles in *Rogues* deal with less genteel crimes. "Crime Family" (2018), for example, focuses on the nefarious activities of Dutch mobster Wim "the Nose" Holleeder. A multiple murderer considered "a huggable criminal" in Amsterdam, in this article Wim can be viewed through the eyes of some he has hurt or menaced, like his sister, Astrid, who betrayed him to the law and lived in hiding to avoid Wim's revenge. "The Hunt for El Chapo" (2014) likewise portrays a major narcotics trafficker with "a Zorro-like reputation" for foiling the law, despite being responsible for directly or indirectly causing scores of particularly violent deaths. "The Avenger" (2015), meanwhile, concerns the hunt, as carried out by the brother of a victim, for the perpetrator behind the 1988 Flight 103 bombing over Lockerbie, Scotland. "A Loaded Gun" (2013) dramatizes and delves into the motivations behind the 2010 murders of several colleagues by Professor Amy Bishop at the University of Alabama in

Huntsville. Other pieces involve more subtle crimes: financial scandals ("The Empire of Edge," 2014), dark banking secrets ("Swiss Bank Heist," 2016), and efforts to wrest control of a huge natural resource in Africa ("Buried Secrets," 2013). *Rogues* concludes with "Journeyman" (2017), an in-depth examination, containing in-person visits with, famous rebel chef and television personality Anthony Bourdain.

Reception of *Rogues*, as with all of Keefe's best-selling books up to that point, was largely positive. Rachel Newcomb, writing for the *Washington Post*, enthusiastically called the book "a fast-paced and frequently suspenseful read" and its author "a virtuoso storyteller" who "leaves the overwhelming impression" that "justice in our violent, turbulent world is fragile and elusive." Likewise, reviewing *Rogues* for *Bookreporter*, Cindy Burnett mentioned how Keefe "ferrets out the most intriguing stories about people behaving badly, writing about their exploits so effectively it is hard to put down his books and articles." The reviewer pointed especially to the author's "attention to detail, word choice and narrative," which "brings his writing to life in a way that few writers can pull off." In a review for *The Observer*, Abhrajyoti Chakraborty praised the book overall but did include a few negative comments, mostly centered on the author's style. Chakraborty, while admiring "a preternaturally attentive reporter at work," argued that Keefe's essay on Bourdain is a "weak link." Though he highlighted Keefe's ability to "paint complicated portraits of victims and vigilantes alike," Chakraborty also noted that the journalist tended to include descriptions he considered to be "formulaic flourishes" of long-form journalism.

The individual articles in *Rogues* will undoubtedly elicit a range of different responses. Some stories may be too visceral for certain readers, while other stories may be too cerebral. But separately or collectively, Keefe's long-form pieces will compel readers to rethink assumptions and reconsider their own attitudes toward concepts such as morality.

Author Biography

A staff writer at the *New Yorker* since 2006, Patrick Radden Keefe published his first book, Chatter: Dispatches from the Secret World of Global Eavesdropping, in 2005. He won the National Magazine Award for Feature Writing in 2014, and the National Book Critics Circle Award in 2019.

Jack Ewing

Review Sources

Burnett, Cindy. Review of Rogues: True Stories of Grifters, Killers, Rebels and Crooks, by Patrick Radden Keefe. Bookreporter, 1 July 2022, www.bookreporter.com/reviews/rogues-true-stories-of-grifters-killers-rebels-and-crooks. Accessed 6 Dec. 2022.

Chakraborty, Abhrajyoti. "Rogues by Patrick Radden Keefe Review—a Preternaturally Attentive Reporter at Work." Review of Rogues: True Stories of Grifters, Killers, Rebels and Crooks, by Patrick Radden Keefe. The Observer, Guardian News and

Media, 19 June 2022, www.theguardian.com/books/2022/jun/19/rogues-by-patrick-radden-keefe-review-a-preternaturally-attentive-reporter-at-work. Accessed 6 Dec. 2022.

Newcomb, Rachel. "Tales of Complicated Rogues—from the Lovable to the Murderous." Review of Rogues: True Stories of Grifters, Killers, Rebels and Crooks, by Patrick Radden Keefe. The Washington Post, 8 July 2022, www.washingtonpost.com/outlook/2022/07/08/tales-complicated-rogues-lovable-murderous/. Accessed 6 Dec. 2022.

Nolan, Tom. "'Rogues' Review: Tales of Crime and Rascality." Review of Rogues: True Stories of Grifters, Killers, Rebels and Crooks, by Patrick Radden Keefe. The Wall Street Journal, 21 June 2022, www.wsj.com/articles/rogues-review-tales-of-crime-and-rascality-11655848224. Accessed 6 Dec. 2022.

Schaub, Michael. "'Rogues' Showcases Patrick Radden Keefe's Preternatural Gift for Reading People." Review of *Rogues: True Stories of Grifter, Killers, Rebels and Crooks*, by Patrick Radden Keefe. *NPR*, 27 June 2022, www.npr.org/2022/06/27/1107254895/rogues-showcases-patrick-radden-keefes-preternatural-gift-for-reading-people. Accessed 6 Dec. 2022.

The School for Good Mothers

Author: Jessamine Chan
Publisher: Simon & Schuster/Marysue Rucci Books (New York). 336 pp.
Type of work: Novel
Time: Near future
Locale: Philadelphia, Pennsylvania

Jessamine Chan's debut novel, The School for Good Mothers, *imagines a world in which negligent mothers are forced to attend a prison-like school in hopes of winning back their children. Drawing on real-world policies, Chan's impressive and devastating dystopian satire offers a glimpse of a near-future dominated by incarceration, surveillance, and perpetual punishment.*

Principal characters

FRIDA, a second-generation Chinese American mother who is ordered to attend a special parenting school after leaving her eighteen-month-old daughter home alone
HARRIET, her daughter
GUST, her ex-husband, Harriet's father
SUSANNA, Gust's girlfriend
RENEE, her lawyer
EMMANUELLE, her doll; a robotic surrogate child provided by the school to help Frida learn to be a "good" mother

It was just "one very bad day," Frida Liu, the frazzled mother and protagonist of Jessamine Chan's debut, *The School for Good Mothers* (2022), tells readers. On that day, Frida—overworked, underfed, and sleepless—made the reckless decision to leave her eighteen-month-old daughter Harriet alone in her bouncy chair so she could drive to get a cup of coffee. But the ten-minute errand stretches to two hours, and by the time Frida is driving home, she receives a call from Child Protective Services. A neighbor heard Harriet crying and called the police, setting in motion the machinery of the state. Frida cannot simply apologize and take her daughter home. Harriet must be examined for signs of abuse; Frida must be questioned and her custody temporarily suspended. Harriet is whisked away to live with her father, Gust ("Like the wind," one reviewer wrote), and his girlfriend Susanna, the young and gratingly self-righteous Pilates instructor for whom he left Frida when she was pregnant. Frida, meanwhile, becomes a guinea pig for a new, court-mandated program built to assess if she is fit to be Harriet's mother at all. Drawing on real-world policies regarding women and children, Chan's impressive and devastating dystopian satire offers a glimpse of a near-future

Jessamine Chan (Courtesy Simon & Schuster)

dominated by surveillance, incarceration, and the belief that perpetual punishment is a social good.

In interviews about *The School for Good Mothers*, Chan has cited the influence of Rachel Aviv's 2013 *New Yorker* article "Where Is Your Mother?" The article follows a woman whose story is remarkably similar to that of the fictional Frida. The woman, computer consultant Niveen Ismail, lost custody of her young son after leaving him home alone, telling authorities that she had thought his father would be there to watch him. The child showed no signs of physical abuse and seemed to be happy with his mother. Yet social workers and judges found fault in the dirty dishes in Niveen's sink; her quiet demeanor, which seemed "shifty"; and the fact that she was an immigrant, and guarded about her history. One social worker said that there was "a great deal of mystery about the mother's circumstances." Based on a litany of such inferences, Niveen was deemed negligent, and unfit to parent her child. Niveen's story is significant in the context of Chan's book. While *The School for Good Mothers* is a work of speculative fiction—some have compared it to the Margaret Atwood 1985 classic *The Handmaid's Tale*—Niveen demonstrates the surprising depth to which the story is rooted in real-life policies and mores. Chan was struck by the overwhelming number of stories like Niveen's, the fact that such tragic stories of child loss rarely make the news, and how much power social workers and judges can have over a family's life.

As with Niveen, every aspect of Frida's life and history, every object in her home and her every word and gesture are scrutinized and found suspicious, even sinister. The clutter in her house, her stained shirt—"This is how you showed up to work?" a police officer asks. When Frida finally consults her lawyer, Renee, she tells her that the state is implementing a new program geared toward "transparency and accountability, something about data collection." When Frida asks why she had not heard about it, Renee is blunt. "You probably didn't pay attention, because it didn't apply to you," she says. "Why would you? You were just living your life." The new program involves several months of intensive surveillance. Cameras are installed in every room of her house, except the bathroom. Her phone is tapped to monitor calls, text messages, and internet searches. Her movements are harvested and analyzed by psychologists. The psychologists are troubled by what they see: no visitors, an increase in non-work-related calls. Her facial expressions, they say, "suggested feelings of resentment and anger, a stunning lack of remorse, a tendency toward self-pity." The court orders that Frida must attend a new, year-long rehabilitative program, the school alluded to in the book's title.

Frida is not like most of the mothers at the school, located in the buildings of a liberal arts college outside the city that has since been closed—a detail suggestive of the character of the book's alternate reality. Most mothers are young and poor; many are Black or Latina. Frida is nearly forty, and while she is financially struggling, she enjoys the cushion of her family's upper-middle class wealth. Her parents, both Chinese immigrants, are retired economics professors. She is however, one of, if not the only, Asian mother at the school. The school is run by no-nonsense social workers, all of them women. They wear pink lab coats, a sharp detail suggestive of weaponized femininity, and punishment with a benign façade. The pink lab coat women will fix their students, instilling them with the maternal instincts they have been judged to lack. The pink lab coat women insist that the mother always introduce themselves by stating their crime—negligence, abandonment, etc.—and force them to repeat the mantra: "I am a bad mother, but I am learning to be good." And later: "I am a narcissist. I am a danger to my child."

All of this is horrifying and surreal, but then Chan deploys her most stunning dystopian element. On the first day of class, each mother is paired with a "doll"—an artificially intelligent robot of the same sex, age, and ethnicity as their real-life child. The dolls look and feel stunningly human, and can think and communicate as a real child would; they can cry and feel pain. They are also built with a chip that harvests data from the mothers, which the school will analyze, and can be calibrated to fit the lesson plan, programmed to be fussy, get sick—they can vomit, or express "body curiosity," accordingly. An awkward blue knob on their back secures a cavity containing the pungent "blue goo" that powers them. The mothers must name their dolls; Frida names hers Emmanuelle. Altogether, the mothers and dolls make for a compellingly discordant cast of characters. Chan has a real feel for each individual and is perceptive of the ways in which they might bond to or repel one another. Outside of class, while the dolls are plugged in and "sleeping," their frozen faces a mask of confusion and terror, the mothers make and break friendships and allegiances. Race and class differences and constant surveillance lend their interactions, both intimate and guarded, the feel of how people might relate to each other in prison.

In fact, the school is a prison, making *The School for Good Mothers* both a commentary on the social policing of mothers but also the concept of incarceration. The school describes itself as rehabilitative, yet the mothers' progress is always weighed against their original crime—the one thing that the mothers will never be able to change. Hitting one's daily quota of sufficiently authentic "motherese," the term the school uses to describe the high-pitched, enthusiastic patter parents use with their children, will not negate the fact that Frida once left Harriet home alone. Many reviewers noted how maddening it felt to inhabit this position, one familiar to so many incarcerated people. "There is no winning in rehab, only endless ways to lose," Molly Young wrote for the *New York Times*. "On kitchen duty, Frida is berated for inefficiently quartering grapes and wielding her knife with a 'hostile grip.'" During the handful of times Frida is allowed to speak to her daughter on the phone, she must follow a rigid set of rules and impossible standards of perfection. She is only allowed to say, "I love you," once to Harriet, but is criticized for insufficient warmth. When she gives voice to her feelings, she is accused of smothering—too much love, or "coddling," being a subset of abuse, according to the school. There is a partner school for fathers, but its rules are significantly more lax. "Chan poses a grim question," Young wrote: "What happens to a person when she has no way to beat an intolerable system and no way to escape it?"

The School for Good Mothers was a New York Times Best Seller and received starred reviews from both *Publishers Weekly* and *Kirkus*, and was selected for the *Today Show*'s Read with Jenna Book Club, offering it a significant boost in readership. Reviewers praised the way Chan's clipped prose created a pervasive sense of unease. Kate Knibbs, who reviewed the book for *Wired*, wrote that she consumed the book in a single evening, though she periodically felt compelled to set it down and perform chores. "This book is a horror story so potent it will fill even the most diligent parent with an itchy impulse to panic-clean, to straighten up, to act like someone's watching," she wrote. Rebecca Shapiro, for *Columbia Magazine* published by Columbia University, wrote that Chan "takes these all-too-common fears and spins them into the stuff of absolute nightmares. The result is a satire so perfectly executed, so incisive and uncomfortable, that it ought to come with a trigger warning." Shapiro and Knibbs also praised the complexity of Frida's character. It was, frankly, pretty reckless of Frida to leave her eighteen-month-old child home alone, they concede. For this and other reasons, Knibbs wrote, Frida "is not always the easiest person to sympathize with, which is, of course, the point. Frida's flaws ask us to confront how easy it is to turn our noses up at a mom who sometimes gives in to her worst impulses, even if she is genuinely loving."

Author Biography

A former reviews editor at *Publishers Weekly*, Jessamine Chan's short fiction has appeared in *Tin House* and *Epoch* and her essays have been published in *Bon Appetit, Elle, and The Millions*. *The School for Good Mothers* is her first novel.

Molly Hagan

Review Sources

Knibbs, Kate. "Dystopia Is All Too Plausible in *The School for Good Mothers*." Review of *The School for Good Mothers*, by Jessamine Chan. *Wired*, 24 Jan. 2022, www.wired.com/story/school-for-good-mothers-dystopian-reality/. Accessed 30 Dec. 2022.

Review of *The School for Good Mothers*, by Jessamine Chan. *Kirkus*, 27 Oct. 2021, www.kirkusreviews.com/book-reviews/jessamine-chan/the-school-for-good-mothers/. Accessed 30 Dec. 2022.

Review of *The School for Good Mothers*, by Jessamine Chan. *Publishers Weekly*, 9 Sept. 2021, www.publishersweekly.com/9781982156121. Accessed 30 Dec. 2022.

Shapiro, Rebecca. Review of *The School for Good Mothers*, by Jessamine Chan. *Columbia Magazine*, Spring/Summer 2022, magazine.columbia.edu/article/review-school-good-mothers. Accessed 30 Dec. 2022.

Young, Molly. "A Chilling Debut Novel Puts Mothers under Surveillance and into Parenting Rehab." Review of *The School for Good Mothers*, by Jessamine Chan. *The New York Times*, 11 Jan. 2022, www.nytimes.com/2022/01/11/books/review-school-for-good-mothers-jessamine-chan.html. Accessed 30 Dec. 2022.

Sea of Tranquility

Author: Emily St. John Mandel (b. 1979)
Publisher: Alfred A. Knopf (New York). 272 pp.
Type of work: Novel
Time: 1912, 2020, 2203, 2401
Locales: Earth, the moon

Emily St. John Mandel's sixth novel, Sea of Tranquility, *combines elements from metafiction and speculative fiction to provide fresh twists on familiar time-travel tropes.*

Principal characters

GASPERY-JACQUES ROBERTS, a time traveler from the twenty-fifth century
ZOEY, his older sister, a physicist and investigator for the Time Institute
EDWIN "EDDIE" ST. JOHN ANDREW, a twentieth-century scion of a prominent British family
PAUL JAMES SMITH, a twenty-first century experimental composer and video artist
VINCENT ALKAITIS NÉE SMITH, Paul's sister
MIRELLA KESSLER, Vincent's friend
OLIVE LLEWELLYN, a twenty-third century novelist
TALIA ANDERSON, a former classmate of Gaspery's

Emily St. John Mandel's novel *Sea of Tranquility* (2022) opens on an appropriately tranquil note. It is 1912, and Edwin St. John Andrew is sailing across the Atlantic Ocean on a vessel bound from England to Canada. A descendant of William the Conqueror, eighteen-year-old Edwin made disparaging remarks in public about British colonialism and has been banished in disgrace, ironically to a former British colony. Edwin, though he has aspirations of becoming a gentleman farmer, will never inherit the family earldom and estate (both will eventually go to his oldest brother). Thus, he is relegated to the status of a "remittance man": an emigrant who depends on regular allowances from home. Landing in Halifax, Nova Scotia, Edwin connects with old school chums living in Canada to travel west, eventually arriving in Victoria, British Columbia. He boats along Vancouver Island, landing at the settlement of Caiette, where he takes lodging at a boardinghouse. While exploring the nearby thick forest one day, he encounters a man named Roberts, who claims to be a priest. Shortly afterward, Edwin walks into the shade of a spreading maple tree, where he experiences what he considers a supernatural event. He hallucinates a series of sounds, including violin music, crowd noises, and a whooshing sound. He wakes up disoriented on the beach.

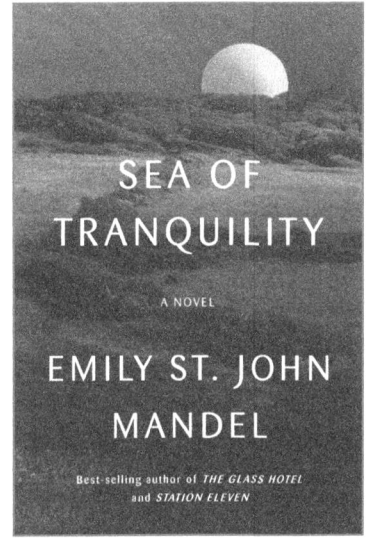

In part 2, "Mirella and Vincent," the action leaps forward to 2020. The plot of the novel, and the author's intentions, begin to take shape. The second section features several characters—Mirella Kessler, Vincent Alkaitis, Paul Smith—from Mandel's previous novel, The Glass Hotel (2020), which is partially set at Caiette, a real place. Significant events from the prior novel are highlighted in a brief recap, necessary to understand the action in Sea of Tranquility: Vincent was married to investment broker Jonathan Alkaitis, who was convicted of fraud, and while out on bail fled abroad to escape incarceration; Mirella, who, as a child, witnessed a double homicide in Ohio, was married to Faisal, who killed himself after being financially ruined in Jonathan's Ponzi scheme. In Sea of Tranquility, Mirella, hoping to track down her friend Vincent, attends a concert in which Paul has composed music to accompany a strange video shot in a Canadian forest by his sister. After the concert, Mirella talks to Paul, who tells her his sister is dead, drowned in a container ship accident. Also present, waiting to talk to Paul, is a man named Gaspery Roberts, who, to Mirella, resembles the alleged murderer she saw in Ohio years before.

Emily St. John Mandel

The third part, "Last Book Tour on Earth," flashes forward almost two hundred years to 2203. The focus is now on novelist Olive Llewellyn (a fictional creation representing author Mandel as she might exist in the future) and her publicist, Aretta. A resident of domed Colony Two on the moon, along with her husband and young daughter, Olive is on an extended global signing and lecture tour of Earth to promote a new edition of her novel Marienbad. The novel concerns a pandemic (this references Mandel's fourth novel, Station Eleven [2014]). Marienbad's main character is named Gaspery-Jacques, who bears a tattoo reading "We knew it was coming." On the last stop on the tour, as rumors spread of a new viral outbreak in the South Pacific, Olive meets a journalist named Gaspery-Jacques Roberts who asks her about a scene in the novel where a character hears violin music and other strange noises at the Oklahoma City Airship Terminal.

Part 4, titled "Bad Chickens," is set in the year 2401 and provides the final necessary link that helps explain what has gone before and anticipates what is still to come. Here, the reader follows the fortunes of Gaspery, a hotel detective at Moon Colony One, and his older sister Zoey, an investigator for a secretive government entity called the Time Institute, which controls the only known working time machine. Wanting to lend meaning to his inconsequential life, Gaspery convinces his sister to take him on as a time-traveling investigator trainee. His five-year training program, which requires considerable research into the time periods he will visit, is centered around the principle that time travelers, regardless of their sympathies, cannot interfere with events as they occur, such as moving individuals out of harm's way. Doing so could alter the timeline of history in unforeseeable ways. Those who are caught violating this rule risk creative punishment: they will be stranded in a past era, essentially lost in time with no way back to where they belong. When his training is complete, Zoey sends Gaspery to investigate an anomaly in the past, characterized by the phenomena experienced by Edwin in part 1, whereby "moments from different centuries are bleeding into one another." His mission is to visit key points in times past to track down and interview principal figures involved in those moments. His goal is to find the cause of the anomaly then correct it so history is not adversely affected and the future can unfold as expected.

Sea of Tranquility is cleverly constructed and grandly paced, and Mandel explores the traditional time-travel trope in which small actions can cause great disruptions in the continuum of time. There is also a related, suspenseful subtheme to consider: the theory that humans are living not in a real universe but are merely avatars in a supercomputer simulation. The author has an uncanny ability to transmit large amounts of information in few words. She does not spend considerable time describing futuristic settings but uses small, suggestive scenes that allow the imagination of readers to fill in blanks. Colony Two on the moon, for example, is presented as a 150-square-kilometer city "of white stone, spired towers, tree-lined streets and small parks," all situated under a dome, where artificial lighting mimics Earth's sky. Other technological advancements or societal changes—the Republic of Texas, the Atlantic Republic, the domed city-state of Los Angeles, hovercraft and airships, interactive holograms, giant agricultural robots, the Far Colonies on Titan—are similarly sketched, as though they already exist and should be familiar.

There is subtle humor, especially when the author, through her near-doppelgänger Olive, slyly references highlights and lowlights of her career, such as the inane questions interviewers often ask, or the assumptions people make. For example, a seatmate on an airship asks what Olive does. She replies that she writes books. "For children?" he asks. Olive's lectures about Marienbad deal with illness. Her talks encompass information about past pandemics, including the Antonine Plague in the Roman Empire and an eighteenth-century smallpox outbreak on Vancouver Island, and foreshadow a possible new pandemic. Olive's main thrust is that illness frightens humans because it is chaotic and random.

The language of Sea of Tranquility is particularly praiseworthy: simple, with memorable lines that resonate, lifting the novel above genre, elevating it to the level of art. One character, for instance, notes, "When you lose someone, it's easy to see patterns that aren't there." Another declares, "Bureaucracy exists to protect itself." Gaspery maintains, "A life lived in a simulation is still a life."

Critical reception of Sea of Tranquility was overwhelmingly positive. Laird Hunt, in a review of the novel for the New York Times, concluded that "Mandel offers one of her finest novels and one of her most satisfying forays into the arena of speculative fiction yet." Ron Charles, writing for the Washington Post, called attention to the author's "facility with a range of tones and historical periods" and alluded to her "impish blend of wit and dread." Oprah Daily's Stacey D'Erasmo pointed to one of the author's particular strengths: "Mandel's world-building in *Sea of Tranquility* is fluid, believable, and only as detailed as it needs to be." The reviewer also highlighted Mandel's ability to engage the reader: "As the book doubles back on itself, inviting us to read and rethink every page, it also, ever so charmingly, invites us to rethink what our choices might be in similar circumstances, and why."

The most negative remarks came from Lily Zhou of the *Stanford Daily*. While acknowledging *Sea of Tranquility*'s scope and complexity and ambitions, Zhou was "ultimately disappointed by its worldbuilding and character arcs," and complained that the characters "lie somewhere between fully fleshed-out people and archetypes: they are given just enough interiority to pass as adequately sympathetic characters, but can't be considered to have any real depth." While this is a somewhat valid claim, it must be remembered that *Sea of Tranquility*, though a stand-alone novel, frequently references Mandel's earlier work, featuring more fully drawn characters that reappear as relative snapshots in the later novel. This fact should not only encourage readers of *Sea of Tranquility* to visit or revisit *Station Eleven* and *The Glass Hotel*, but also to anticipate Emily St. John's next novel.

Author Biography

A writer for online magazine *The Millions*, best-selling author Emily St. John Mandel published her first novel, *Last Night in Montreal*, in 2009. *Station Eleven* (2014) was a finalist for the National Book Award and the PEN/Faulkner Award; she has been nominated for numerous other honors.

Jack Ewing

Review Sources

Charles, Ron. "Emily St. John Mandel's Sea of Tranquility Is a Mind-Bending Novel." The Washington Post, 12 Apr. 2022, www.washingtonpost.com/books/2022/04/12/emily-st-john-mandel-sea-of-tranquility-book-review/. Accessed 6 Sept. 2022.

D'Erasmo, Stacey. "Station Eleven Author Emily St. John Mandel Heads to Outer Space aboard a Dazzling New Novel." Review of Sea of Tranquility, by Emily St. John Mandel. Oprah Daily, 16 May 2022, www.oprahdaily.com/entertainment/books/a39995112/sea-of-tranquility-emily-st-john-mandel/. Accessed 6 Sept. 2022.

Hunt, Laird. "A Dazzling New Foray into Speculative Fiction from Emily St. John Mandel." Review of Sea of Tranquility, by Emily St. John Mandel. The New York Times, 30 Mar. 2022, www.nytimes.com/2022/03/30/books/review/sea-of-tranquility-emily-st-john-mandel.html. Accessed 6 Sept. 2022.

Nguyen, Sophia. "Emily St. John Mandel's Neatly Designed Worlds." Review of Sea of Tranquility, by Emily St. John Mandel. The Nation, 11 Apr. 2022, www.thenation.com/article/culture/sea-tranquility-emily-mandel/. Accessed 6 Sept. 2022.

Zhou, Lily. "Emily St. John Mandel's Sea of Tranquility Is an Overly Simplistic Exploration of Nihilism." The Stanford Daily, 24 May 2022, stanforddaily.com/2022/05/24/emily-st-john-mandels-sea-of-tranquility-is-an-overly-simplistic-exploration-of-nihilism/. Accessed 6 Sept. 2022.

Seeking Fortune Elsewhere

Author: Sindya Bhanoo
Publisher: Catapult (New York). 240 pp.
Type of work: Short fiction
Time: Present day
Locales: Georgia, Pennsylvania, Washington, South India

Seeking Fortune Elsewhere *is the debut short story-collection from journalist Sindya Bhanoo. Centered largely around characters who are of South Indian descent, the stories touch on topics ranging from aging to parenthood to the strains and rewards of living in a new country while also keeping an eye on the past.*

Principal characters
KAMALA, the US-based daughter of an elderly widow living in South India
CHAND, a college professor whose relationship with his students becomes strained
GAURI, a middle-aged divorced woman returning to the town where her daughters were raised for her youngest daughter's wedding
NEELA, a high school senior who is having trouble accepting her father, a national religious figure and speaker

Sindya Bhanoo's debut short story-collection, *Seeking Fortune Elsewhere* (2022), explores themes that include how families remain connected across generations, changing cultural norms, and the immigrant experience—specifically, that of South Indian immigrants who have left their families in India to pursue careers in the United States. Bhanoo, a seasoned journalist who has worked for the *New York Times* and the *Washington Post*, turns her analytical eye toward the ways in which people struggle to build or maintain a life and how that struggle is what unites everyone. In a series of stories that take place across India and the United States, *Seeking Fortune Elsewhere* is as concerned with what gets left behind or forgotten as it is interested in the shiny new lives of many of its characters. Told in sharp, clear prose, the stories found within this collection are united by themes of loneliness, confusion, familial longing, and nostalgia.

One of *Seeking Fortune Elsewhere*'s greatest strengths is its sensitively developed characters. The stories' cast of characters span generations, from those living out their teenage years, like high school senior Neela in "His Holiness," to those entering their later years, like the elderly narrator of the collection opener, "Malliga Homes," and the soon-to-retire couple in "No. 16 Model House Road." Along with this assortment of characters, the collection offers glimpses of life in a wide variety of locations, including South India; Spokane, Washington; and Pittsburgh, Pennsylvania. The sometimes-mundane atmospheres of these lesser-celebrated American cities serve to reinforce the experiences of their characters, offering a quieter place to support the smaller moments of their lives. In "His Holiness" and the collection closer, "Three Trips," which both take place in and around Pittsburgh, characters spend time at the mall, local coffee shops, and other everyday locations. "Malliga Homes" and "No. 16 Model House Road" feature older empty nesters adjusting to a changing culture and striving to relate to children who are living in a modern world that sometimes feels unfamiliar. Though the stories in *Seeking Fortune Elsewhere* are not connected, the themes that move each story's character through are what unite them.

Sindya Bhanoo

As a writer, Bhanoo understands loneliness, whether that loneliness takes the form of feeling out of place, feeling left behind, or feeling like one no longer has a place with those to whom they were once closest. The theme of loneliness is especially evident in the collection's first story, "Malliga Homes," which received a prestigious O. Henry Prize for short fiction upon its publication. The narrator of the story is a recent widow whose daughter, Kamala, has insisted she move to a retirement facility in Tamil Nadu in South India. Kamala, though, lives far away in the United States and has begun visiting her mother less and less frequently, leaving the narrator increasingly sad and lonely. The elderly woman longs for the past, when children were less likely to move far away from their Indian parents "to seek their fortunes elsewhere"—that phrase thus lending itself to the collection's title.

Loneliness is also explored in "Buddymoon." In this story, the reader is introduced to the character of Gauri, a middle-aged woman whose husband divorced her when their two daughters were young. In an effort to make their daughters' lives continue to feel as normal as possible, Gauri relinquishes custody to her husband, lets him keep their house, and moves into a small studio across town in Pullman, a suburb of Seattle. But this plan backfires, creating a deep divide between Gauri and her children, with her eldest daughter, Sahana, holding the deepest resentment. At the wedding of her youngest daughter, Anita, Gauri finds herself adrift. Her husband has found someone new who accompanies him to the wedding, and her daughters have absorbed none of the cultural traditions Gauri finds familiar. A pair of earrings is ultimately what brings this divide into clearest focus: Anita has chosen a modern, red dress for her wedding ceremony, and her father has bought her a new necklace to wear with it. Gauri offers a pair of her favorite pearl earrings, to which Sahana quickly replies that they will not match. Anita quietly agrees to wear them instead.

Like other stories in the collection, "Buddymoon" relies on flashbacks to build the characters' relationships, and the careful construction of Anita and Sahana's childhoods positioned against the struggles Gauri faces as a single, divorced mother creates a beautiful tension for the story. A similar tension shows up in "A Life in America." Chand, a beloved college professor who has created close ties with his Indian students through the years, considering himself a surrogate parent of sorts to those young people who have found themselves newly abroad, is now being questioned about those relationships. Former students have accused him of making them work without compensation, through chores such as housesitting, yard work, or loading the dishwasher at a party. The reader sees Chand's side of the story: how he considered the students like family and did not think he was overstepping any boundaries by asking them to do such work. A careful tension with a fellow professor with whom Chand has often been at odds adds a deeper element to the story, and Chand wonders if his students are being manipulated. Like "Buddymoon," "A Life in America" relies on flashbacks to build this tension for the reader, and to great effect.

"His Holiness" is one of a couple of stories that focus on the experience of a young person who is caught between two cultures: her immigrant parents and her American youth. Protagonist Neela is a high school senior who is not living up to her Indian parents' expectations: she smokes, performs poorly on her SATs, and is friends with a boy named Colin of whom they do not approve. However, Neela is dealing with her own family issues. Her father, who used to be a college professor, has taken on a calling as a religious figure, traveling around the country and speaking at community centers, often to audiences of scruffy White people with an interest in Hinduism. Bhanoo sets up the tension first between Neela and her mother. Neela's father is often on the road, touring, leaving the rest of the family at home alone. Bhanoo does an excellent job of setting up Neela's struggles as a teenager, and the difficulty and resentment she feels toward her father, before even introducing her father in the story. The result is a surprisingly sympathetic portrait of them both. Like so many of the other stories found in this collection, "His Holiness" is interested in how misunderstandings drive people further apart or, sometimes, bring them closer together, and how everyone is ultimately hoping to connect and be understood by those they love. "His Holiness" does this on two levels: by focusing on Neela's teenagerhood and by establishing the differences between daughter and parents.

Seeking Fortune Elsewhere was widely praised upon publication. For the *New York Times*, Samantha Hunt noted that Bhanoo's characters are "outsiders twice" and applauded the writer's broad view and tightly observed focus, writing, "These stories rattle and shake with the heartache of separation, rendering palpable the magnitude of small decisions in our less-than-small world." In a starred review, the critic for *Kirkus* likewise stated, "These are psychologically astute stories—and also riveting. By carefully withholding key details, Bhanoo transforms human drama into mystery." *Seeking Fortune Elsewhere* also received starred reviews from *Publishers Weekly* and *Booklist*, with the *Booklist* reviewer noting that "Bhanoo's piercing stories further augment the growing shelves of spectacular first short story collections by women of color." The *Harvard Review* also hailed the collection, with critic Rajpreet Heir stating, "As a collection, *Seeking Fortune Elsewhere* achieves a level of poignancy most writers can only dream of. . . . Through her adept storytelling, we see just how complex the immigrant experience can be and how asserting one's individuality can grant characters a way out of the past—or lead them back to it."

The world that Bhanoo creates across eight short stories is impressive, and the fact that this is her debut marks the start of a promising literary career sprung from a successful run as a journalist. Taking in each of the isolated lives of the characters within *Seeking Fortune Elsewhere* is an act of empathy, sure to enrich readers and impact the way they see the world around them. No life is too small, or too big, for the minute complexities that make up a modern human experience.

Author Biography

Sindya Bhanoo's short stories have appeared in literary journals including *Granta*, *New England Review*, and *Glimmer Train*. Her debut short-story collection, *Seeking Fortune Elsewhere*, was long-listed for the 2023 American Library Association's Carnegie Medal and received the 2022 New American Voices Award. Bhanoo, a longtime newspaper reporter, was a Knight-Wallace Reporting Fellow at the University of Michigan.

Melynda Fuller

Review Sources

Felicelli, Anita. "Homegoing." Review of *Seeking Fortune Elsewhere*, by Sindya Bhanoo. *Alta*, 7 Mar. 2022, www.altaonline.com/books/fiction/a39263731/sindya-bhanoo-seeking-fortune-elsewhere-book-review/. Accessed 20 Dec. 2022.

Heir, Rajpreet. Review of *Seeking Fortune Elsewhere*, by Sindya Bhanoo. *Harvard Review*, 7 June 2022, harvardreview.org/book-review/seeking-fortune-elsewhere/. Accessed 20 Dec. 2022.

Hong, Terry. Review of *Seeking Fortune Elsewhere*, by Sindya Bhanoo. *Booklist*, 1 Jan. 2022, www.booklistonline.com/Seeking-Fortune-Elsewhere/pid=9756268. Accessed 20 Dec. 2022.

Hunt, Samantha. "Lifestyles of the Rich, Damaged and Totally Despicable." Review of *Seeking Fortune Elsewhere*, by Sindya Bhanoo, et al. *The New York Times*, 25 Mar. 2022, www.nytimes.com/2022/03/25/books/review/new-short-story-collections.html. Accessed 19 Jan. 2023.

Review of *Seeking Fortune Elsewhere*, by Sindya Bhanoo. *Kirkus*, 15 Dec. 2021, www.kirkusreviews.com/book-reviews/sindya-bhanoo/seeking-fortune-elsewhere/. Accessed 20 Dec. 2022.

Review of *Seeking Fortune Elsewhere*, by Sindya Bhanoo. *Publishers Weekly*, 12 Nov. 2021, www.publishersweekly.com/978-1-64622-087-8. Accessed 20 Dec. 2022.

Serious Face

Author: Jon Mooallem
Publisher: Random House (New York). 320 pp.
Type of work: Essays
Time: 2010s and 2020s
Locales: Spain, United States, United Kingdom

Writer Jon Mooallem's first book of essays collects twelve of his pieces previously published in the New York Times Magazine, *as well as one newly written essay, that explore a variety of offbeat subjects with curiosity and empathy.*

Jon Mooallem is a writer and journalist whose long-form essays feature regularly in the *New York Times Magazine*. Mooallem has always been interested in the natural world and humans' interactions with their larger environment, and this theme has been reflected in much of his work. His first book, *Wild Ones: A Sometimes Dismaying, Weirdly Reassuring Story About Looking at People Looking at Animals in America* (2013) is a wide-ranging look at Americans' relationship with nature, both past and present. He followed that up with *This Is Chance!: The Great Alaska Earthquake, Genie Chance, and the Shattered City She Held Together* (2020), a look at the 1964 earthquake that nearly destroyed Anchorage, Alaska, and the efforts of the local citizens to rebuild their community.

In his *New York Times Magazine* essays—twelve of which are collected in *Serious Face* (2022)—Mooallem continues to explore humankind's interactions with nature. The essays, published between 2012 and 2021, cover such topics as California wildfires; an escaped monkey-at-large in Tampa, Florida; and the Cloud Appreciation Society. Hanging over all these essays is the threat of climate change, which he acknowledges as changing society's relationship with nature in a way that is increasingly dangerous. But his interests are wide-ranging, and his essays also cover a variety of topics unrelated to nature. Whether tagging along with two men who help recently released prisoners adapt to outside life or agonizing about how to write about filmmaker Charlie Kaufman, Mooallem's essays are evidence of an ongoing curiosity about all aspects of living in the contemporary world.

In the introduction to *Serious Face*, Mooallem attempts to find a common thread that links all the essays in his book. Tempted to say that his selection of topics is "all utterly random," he instead remembers a line from a poem that reads "Why are we not better than we are?" In Mooallem's grappling with humanity, this question can be asked of the subject of almost every one of his essays, including Mooallem himself.

Whether it is the scam artist of the essay "Birdman," or humanity as a whole in its inability to prevent climate change, the book illustrates the weaknesses of humankind. Mooallem is not out to point fingers, however; instead, he realizes that humanity is flawed and that, in many cases, people are doing the best that they can, even if their best is often not good enough.

Mooallem is a journalist who writes with a light touch. The typical essay in *Serious Face* begins with an intriguing hook that plunges the reader right into the unusual situation that will be the topic of the piece. For example, the book's first essay, "A House at the End of the World," is a profile of B. J. Miller, a palliative care doctor who lost three of his limbs and nearly died in a freak accident while in college and who is now working to transform the way in which the terminally ill are cared for. The essay begins with a sentence that draws the reader immediately in: "First, the backstory, because, B. J. Miller has found, the backstory is unavoidable when you are missing three limbs." After Mooallem narrates the accident that led to Miller's losing three limbs, he jumps forward to the present, explaining how Mooallem took over the pioneering Zen Hospice Project in San Francisco and cared for a dying acquaintance of his named Randy Sloan.

Jon Mooallem

Throughout the essay, Mooallem mixes crisply narrated backstory with sharply observed details and interviews with his subjects to create a panoramic view of his topic. Although his role as observer means much of the essay is devoted to recording what he sees and hears, he does occasionally turn reflective, offering his own insights to the reader. In reflecting on the Zen Hospice Project's mission, which aims to rethink how to best care for a dying person, he struggles to come to terms with his own emotions. Feeling that he may have misunderstood the project's mission altogether, he reflects that the mission is "about wresting death from the one-size-fits-all approach of hospitals, but it's also about puncturing a competing impulse, the one I was scuffling with now: our need for death to be a hyper-transcendent experience." For Mooallem, as for many people, the idea that a person's final moments should be full of mysterious revelations is a natural one, but as Miller makes Mooallem see, this is not necessarily how things happen or even how they should happen.

In addition to these glimpses into Mooallem's own psyche, the writer also appears more directly in a few of the essays. Among the best essays in the book is the one titled "This is My Serious Face," which is the only piece not previously published in the *New York Times Magazine*. In this first-person essay, a couple of Mooallem's friends spot a photograph of a legendary bullfighter while eating at a restaurant in Spain. Finding the matador to bear a striking resemblance to Mooallem, they send him a picture of the photograph. This leads Mooallem to research the matador, who turns out to be one of the most celebrated bullfighters in Spanish history, a man named Manolete who dominated the sport in the 1940s before being killed by a bull in 1947. Manolete was known for both his reserved, non-flashy style of bullfighting and for being physically unattractive. "Manolete was ugly," Mooallem writes. "He was *remarkably* ugly—by which I mean, people could stop remarking about how ugly he was."

Because Mooallem looks just like Manolete, this inevitably leads the writer to reflect on his own appearance. Mooallem's face is noticeably crooked, but the physical defect was not the result of any accident—it simply grew that way over time. If Manolete's brand of ugliness projects a gloomy, melancholy aspect, then Mooallem feels that his face must do the same. This leads him to larger reflections about his identity. Rejecting others' suggestions that he have plastic surgery, he uses the question of physical appearance to ponder what it says about his inner self. Does his exterior self reflect his inner self, he wonders, and what exactly is this inner self? "Surely all of us," he writes, "have felt ourselves in conflict with some deeper and more essential self: addled by insecurity or shame about who we are, or exhausted by our restless attempts to change it." The problem, as he sees it, is that a person can never be sure what their real "essential" self is, and so they always remain in conflict with themselves. For him, this is an inevitable part of being human, and, although it can be considered a weakness, it is part of what defines the species.

Although "This is My Serious Face" looks mostly inward, most of the essays in the book face outward instead, reflecting on the interactions of humankind with the larger planet. The most gripping of these essays is called "We Have Fire Everywhere." This essay offers a harrowing account of the Camp Fire, the deadliest wildfire in California history, which in 2018 destroyed the town of Paradise and nearby communities in the foothills of the Sierra Nevada mountains. The essay follows the experience of Paradise resident Tamra Fisher as she tries to escape the fire in her car. Mooallem's narration is straightforward and not embellished by rhetorical flourishes. This allows the story to take center stage; its harrowing details are more than enough to carry it.

To paint a larger picture of the wildfire, though, Mooallem interviews several other people who were involved, including members of the crew who were responsible for taming the conflagration. He also intercuts background information about California's ecology and its history of wildfires. Thus, although Tamra's story is at the center of the essay, Mooallem expands his purview and offers a devastating portrait of environmental collapse, while always keeping the human element at the forefront. Offering a vision of the destructiveness that climate change has visited on the earth—and will undoubtedly continue to inflict—he ends the essay with an assessment of the Camp Fire's impact. Striking a pessimistic tone, he notes that the 3.6 million metric tons of greenhouse gases that the fire released were enough to cancel out a year's worth of California's anti-climate change policies. Summing up the ongoing environmental impact of California's wildfires, he concludes his essay with a brief and powerful question-and-answer. "How did it end?" he asks about the natural disaster before concluding: "It hasn't. It won't."

Although *Serious Face* was not widely reviewed, it received highly positive press from every outlet that covered it. In a starred review, the anonymous *Publishers*

Weekly reviewer noted that "Mooallem has a real knack for evoking places, people, and emotions," and praised the author for putting "a human face on larger issues such as climate change and conservation." Writing for *Booklist*, reviewer Amanda ReCupido called *Serious Face* "an intellectually moving collection" and noted that "readers will laugh and tear up as Mooallem makes us care about his subjects and feel better off for knowing their stories." In a similar vein, the reviewer for *Kirkus Reviews* called the book "a winning, captivating, engrossing collection," while referring to Mooallem as a "master essayist." In particular, "We Have Fire Everywhere" was singled out for praise, with the reviewer writing that "the author's narrative prowess is on full display" in this "powerful, tragic essay."

Although most of the essays in *Serious Face* were previously published in the *New York Times Magazine*, having them together in one volume allows the reader to experience the full scope of Mooallem's investigations. For readers who have not previously encountered these essays, *Serious Face* will serve as a powerful introduction to one of the most consistently engaging essayists writing during the 2020s, and one whose curiosity and empathy bring to life a wide swath of humanity.

Author Biography

Jon Mooallem is a staff writer for the *New York Times* and the author of three nonfiction books. His first book, *Wild Ones*, was named a New York Times Notable Book and a New Yorker Best Book of the Year. Mooallem is also a writer-at-large for *Pop-Up Magazine* and a contributor to various podcasts.

Andrew Schenker

Review Sources

Cary, Alice. Review of *Serious Face*, by Jon Mooallem. *BookPage*, June 2022, www.bookpage.com/reviews/serious-face-jon-mooallem-book-review/. Accessed 23 Nov 2022.

ReCupido, Amanda. Review of *Serious Face*, by Jon Mooallem. *Booklist*, 1 May 2022, booklistonline.com/Serious-Face/pid=9762546. Accessed 23 Nov 2022.

Review of *Serious Face*, by Jon Mooallem. *Kirkus Reviews*, 8 Mar. 2022, www.kirkusreviews.com/book-reviews/jon-mooallem/serious-face/. Accessed 23 Nov 2022.

Review of *Serious Face*, by Jon Mooallem. *Publishers Weekly*, 27 Jan. 2022, www.publishersweekly.com/978-0-52550-994-3. Accessed 23 Nov 2022.

Vognar, Chris. "Jon Mooallem's Essays Are Like Nutritious Candy." Review of *Serious Face*, by Jon Mooallem. *Washington Examiner*, 7 July 2022, www.washingtonexaminer.com/opinion/jon-mooallems-essays-are-like-nutritious-candy. Accessed 30 Dec. 2022.

Seven Empty Houses

Author: Samanta Schweblin (b. 1978)
Publisher: Riverhead Books (New York). 208 pp.
First published: *Siete casas vacías*, 2015, in Spain
Translated from the Spanish by Megan McDowell
Type of work: Short fiction
Time: Present day
Locales: Spain, Argentina

Seven Empty Houses by Samanta Schweblin explores themes of loneliness, love, and isolation through the guise of seven houses and apartments. Drawing on both familial intimacy that strains those closest to each other and the relentless passing of time, this collection understands that sometimes strangeness is what breaks a person, but sometimes a stranger is the one to save us.

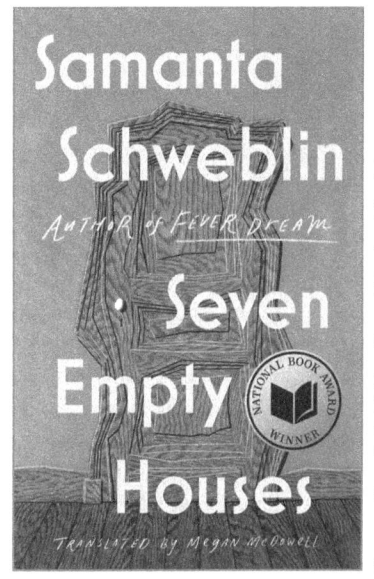

Principal characters

UNNAMED NARRATOR, a daughter seemingly in her late teens to early twenties who accompanies her mentally ill mother on drives to look at other people's houses
MARGA, wife of the unnamed narrator of "My Parents and My Children" who is chastising him because of his unruly parents
MR. WEIMER, a next door neighbor who often comes to collect his dead son's clothes after his wife throws them out the window
LOLA, an older woman with heart trouble who is rapidly sinking into dementia

Samanta Schweblin's short story collection *Seven Empty Houses* centers on several separate houses and apartments to explore how the emptiness people carry inside of them can lead to neglect, pain, and conflict. Employing an array of narrative structures that makes for a satisfying variation between stories, the collection also boasts an interesting cast of characters ranging from the very young—a pair of girls, one of whom is often pushed aside for her drama-attracting younger sister—to the very old—a couple who are in the final years of their lives, attempting to sort their possessions and complicated feelings about both a new set of neighbors and a long-dead son. Dead children feature throughout the collection, with their most prominent impact being the extreme loneliness they impart on their parents, but Schweblin also connects feelings of loss and melancholy to items, whether a keepsake from a long-dead parent or a box of office supplies marked for charity. Schweblin's stylistically simple prose allows the places and people in her stories to fully capture the reader's attention, creating a ripple effect through the series of unconnected tales that allows each story's atmosphere to build upon the last. City streets feel more alive following the claustrophobia of a cluttered apartment; the chaos of a newly occupied house is juxtaposed against the stability of a decades' worth of living.

Each story's setting in *Seven Empty Houses* starts wide, out in the world, before collapsing in on the intimacy of an apartment being organized, only to once again retread that road to public life. Opener "None of That" finds a mother and daughter driving around a wealthy neighborhood together, only to become stuck in the mud in front of one of the larger mansions, while "My Parents and My Children" offers a snapshot in the day of a separated couple meeting up so their children can spend some time with their paternal grandparents. "It Happens All the Time in This House" takes the scope of its landscape smaller, as two characters spend the story in the backyard of one of their houses. "Breath from the Depths," the centerpiece of *Seven Empty Houses*, is a sprawling story that follows the slow decline of its main character Lola. Following "Breath," the stories are a bit less focused in their theme, with "Two Square Feet" revealing an evening between a woman and her mother-in-law as one sets out to buy aspirin for the other; "An Unlucky Man" chronicling a strange encounter between a young girl and an older man in a hospital waiting room; and "Out," which finds a couple at odds with each other, inspiring a woman to slink out of her apartment still in a bathrobe with wet hair.

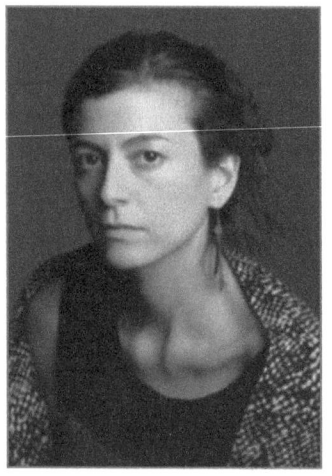

Samanta Schweblin

A common theme throughout the collection is the importance of maintaining things or objects, particularly those belonging to the now-dead. In "None of That," the mother of the mother and daughter duo, makes her way into the house of the wealthy family whose yard her car is stuck in. She locks herself in a bathroom, then the primary suite, where she urges her daughter to join her. The house, which has three living rooms, all for different purposes, causes the older woman to sob as she observes the wealth around her. When her daughter makes her way into the bedroom, she notices that her mother has taken a sugar bowl, a porcelain one she first observed on the family's coffee table, which the owner's young son told her was for decoration only. As the mother goes into another bathroom and begins to take down objects and empty drawers into the garbage, her daughter must contend with the soon-to-be-stolen sugar bowl and how to get her mother out of the house. A subsequent moment of empathy from the daughter brings the story into focus. "My Parents and My Children" continues this theme of dealing with mentally ill older parents and how their actions impact the lives of their adult children. The story's protagonist, a separated middle-aged father, has offered to let his estranged wife and two children visit his parents at their home in the suburbs near spacious estates. The catch: his parents have chosen that day to dance naked in the backyard, ahead of the children's arrival, leaving Marga, his wife, in disarray. When the children do arrive and disappear along with the narrator's parents, chaos ensues, with the police intervening. The story, much like the relationship between the narrator and Marga, feels spiraling, out of control, echoing the repeated attempts by Mr. Weimer in the following story "It Happens All the Time in This House," as he deals with his own troubled marriage following the death of their son. Themes established in "It Happens All the Time in This House" show up later on, specifically in "Breath from the Depths" and "An Unlucky Man," each of which are cast in a shadow of danger.

Schweblin's writing style has an air of mystery and fantasy, which lends itself well to these stories that are so very rooted in the ordinary. While the heart of a short story could be said to be the revelations uncovered in life's smallest moments, often readers of *Seven Empty Houses* are left to wonder if they're still rooted in reality themselves. This is most apparent in "Breath from the Depths." Lola, the reader quickly learns, is preparing for the death of herself and her husband as she slowly packs up their belongings into well-marked boxes which are stored in the garage. She has removed as much of the personal touches as she can with each package, and notices that her day-to-day life is becoming more and more empty with each box. She is prepared to die, but death never comes. Her methodical planning is pitted against her husband's active gardening, which he does with the company of a new young boy who has moved to the neighborhood. The boy sits alongside her husband on a small stool and watches as her husband tends to vegetables and other plants. But by the story's middle, Schweblin's smooth prose has backed Lola into a corner. No longer is the reader sure of what she's experiencing in the present and what might be an echo from the past. This story, like so many others in the collection, resonate, even evoke a real terror, as the reader is left to consider the fate of any human faced with the reality of aging.

Seven Empty Houses received a positive reception from critics, for the most part. In the *New York Times*, Liska Jacobs wrote, "Schweblin challenges the reader's sanity by showing her characters' — and thus our — reliance on the material world for their very survival. Our homes are an extension of us. Remove certain pieces or shift any of the parts and in essence our reality changes." She later noted that this collection was released in Spanish in 2015 to a world very different from the one we know now. She wrote, "Years before the [COVID-19] pandemic, the world didn't yet know the particular terror of being isolated at home, either alone or with friends or family." For the *Observer*, Lucy Popescu wrote, "Schweblin is good at depicting the destabilising effects of grief and absence. Occasionally a story misses the mark or is too ethereal to fully satisfy, but her fractured worlds make compelling reading." In the *Chicago Review of Books*, Gianni Washington noted the collection's interest in "missing people, objects, and pieces of themselves," and wrote, "With *Seven Empty Houses*, Samanta Schweblin urges us to confront the emotions, ideas, and personal qualities we would dearly love to ignore, or to erase outright. Willful ignorance, Schweblin argues, is no kind of solution. Certainly, not one of any permanence." Schweblin's collection was also reviewed by the *Washington Post*, *Oprah Daily*, the *Sunday Times*, in addition to receiving early reviews by *Kirkus Reviews*, which called it, "Seven compelling explorations of vacancy in another perfectly spare and atmospheric translation." *Publishers Weekly*, however, was less enthusiastic about the collection and stated, "Schweblin's stories are far more evocative than substantive… and [leave] the reader hungry for deeper imaginative leaps."

Author Biography
Samanta Schweblin is the author of the novels *Fever Dream* (2017) and *Little Eyes* (2020), as well as the short story collections *Mouthful of Birds* (2019) and *Seven Empty Houses*. An Argentine Spanish-language author, Schweblin's work has been translated in more than thirty languages and her books have been finalists and shortlisted for the International Booker Prize. *Seven Empty Houses* won the National Book Award for Translated Literature in 2022. Schweblin's stories have appeared in *The New Yorker*, *Granta*, *The Drawbridge*, *Harper's Magazine*, and *McSweeney's*. Her novel *Fever Dream* was adapted for Netflix in 2021.

Megan McDowell is an award-winning translator whose previous collaborations with Schweblin, *Mouthful of Birds* and *Little Eyes*, both received International Booker Prize nominations. McDowell was born in Richmond, Kentucky, and lives in Santiago, Chile.

Melynda Fuller

Review Sources
Cain, Hamilton. "Samanta Schweblin Infuses Dreamlike Menace into *Seven Empty Houses*." Review of *Seven Empty Houses*, by Samanta Schweblin. *Oprah Daily*, 19 Oct. 2022, oprahdaily.com/entertainment/books/a41684558/seven-empty-houses-samanta-schweblin-book-review/. Accessed 11 Jan. 2023.

Crispin, Jessa. "*Seven Empty Houses* by Samanta Schweblin Review - What's That Creaking Noise Upstairs?" Review of *Seven Empty Houses*, by Samanta Schweblin. *The Times*, 28 Oct. 2022, www.thetimes.co.uk/article/seven-empty-houses-by-samanta-schweblin-review-cvg8wvmtb. Accessed 11 Jan. 2023.

Jacobs, Liska. "Peepholes into Private Lives, Dark and Unstable." Review of *Seven Empty Houses*, by Samanta Schweblin. *The New York Times*, 14 Oct. 2022, www.nytimes.com/2022/10/14/books/review/samanta-schweblin-seven-empty-houses.html. Accessed 11 Jan. 2023.

Oldweiler, Cory. "Samanta Schweblin's *Seven Empty Houses* Will Keep Readers Guessing." Review of *Seven Empty Houses*, by Samanta Schweblin. *The Washington Post*, 14 Oct. 2022, www.washingtonpost.com/books/2022/10/18/samanta-schweblin-seven-empty-houses-review/. Accessed 11 Jan. 2023.

Popescu, Lucy. "*Seven Empty Houses* by Samanta Schweblin Review – Tales of Everyday Darkness." Review of *Seven Empty Houses*, by Samanta Schweblin. *The Guardian*, 6 Nov. 2022, www.theguardian.com/books/2022/nov/06/seven-empty-houses-by-samanta-schweblin-review-tales-of-everyday-darkness-fever-dream. Accessed 11 Jan. 2023.

Review of *Seven Empty Houses*, by Samanta Schweblin. Translated by Megan McDowell. *Kirkus Reviews*, 12 Oct. 2022, www.kirkusreviews.com/book-reviews/samanta-schweblin/seven-empty-houses/. Accessed 6 Feb. 2023.

Review of *Seven Empty Houses*, by Samanta Schweblin. Translated by Megan McDowell. *Publishers Weekly*, 21 Jul. 2022, www.publishersweekly.com/9780525541394. Accessed 6 Feb. 2023.

Washington, Gianni. "The Crushing Weight of Negative Space in *Seven Empty Houses*." Review of *Seven Empty Houses*, by Samanta Schweblin. *Chicago Review of Books*, 5 Oct. 2022, chireviewofbooks.com/2022/10/28/the-crushing-weight-of-negative-space-in-seven-empty-houses/. Accessed 11 Jan. 2023.

The Seven Moons of Maali Almeida

Author: Shehan Karunatilaka (b. 1975)
First published: *Chats with the Dead*, 2020, in India
Publisher: W. W. Norton (New York). 400 pp.
Type of work: Novel
Time: 1989
Locale: Colombo, Sri Lanka

The Seven Moons of Maali Almeida *is a ghost story set amidst the backdrop of the Sri Lankan civil war. It is the second novel by the award-winning Sri Lankan writer Shehan Karunatilaka.*

Principal characters
MAALI, a war photographer stuck between life and death
JAKI, his best friend, who posed as his girlfriend when he was alive
DD, his lover, whom he regularly cheated on
SENA, a spirit who wants to be his guide in the afterlife
DR. RANEE SRIDHARAN, another spirit who wants to guide him

In October 2022, it was announced that *The Seven Moons of Maali Almeida* (2022), by Shehan Karunatilaka, was that year's Booker Prize winner. It was a shock, as for years Western publishers had refused to buy the rights to the book, which was originally published in 2020 in India as *Chats with the Dead*, because they believed its focus on Sri Lankan politics and mythology would be too alienating to their readers. Eventually, the small British publisher Sort of Books decided that, because Karunatilaka's debut, *Chinaman: The Legend of Pradeep Mathew*, had won the 2012 Commonwealth Prize, his next novel might be a risk worth taking. Upon agreeing to Sort of Book's terms, Karunatilaka reworked *Chats with the Dead* for two years until it became *The Seven Moons of Maali Almeida*—a new version of the novel that would not only prove more accessible to foreigners but worthy of one of the most coveted awards in literature. W. W. Norton then published the book in the United States later in 2022.

Beyond being a prestigious Booker Prize winner, *The Seven Moons of Maali Almeida* is a difficult book to categorize. On the one hand, it can be described as a dark political satire about the horrors of the twenty-six-year Sri Lankan Civil War. On the other, it is a murder mystery steeped in existential fantasy. Ultimately, the novel's ability to shirk all established literary labels speaks to a larger, more defining quality about it—that it is a wholly original creation from one of the most imaginative storytellers of contemporary literature.

Shehan Karunatilaka

Such originality might not be initially evident to those browsing a quick summary of the novel. In its simplest description, *The Seven Moons of Maali Almeida* is about a ghost trying to figure out who murdered him before moving on to the next stage of the Afterlife. Here, comparisons can be made to other stories about purgatorial spirits grappling with unresolved issues like Alice Sebold's *The Lovely Bones* (2002) or the 2017 Booker Prize winner *Lincoln in the Bardo* (2017), by George Saunders. Yet, any real similarities to Sebold or Saunders are in fact quite limited, as the book's use of fantasy combined with its very specific focus on the late 1980s chapter of Sri Lankan history makes for an unprecedented reading experience.

Karunatilaka's determination to take readers on a journey unlike they have ever been on before becomes clear from the novel's first pages, when its protagonist, a photojournalist named Malinda Albert Kabalana, or "Maali," awakens to find himself in the crowded waiting room of the next spiritual dimension, or the "In Between." In the scene, Karunatilaka playfully suggests that the sight of ghosts who appear as mangled corpses are not nearly as stomach-turning as long queues, seemingly arbitrary rules, and the overall, red-taped bureaucracy that exists in the In Between and the forty-two-floor office building it operates out of. It is one of many darkly comedic moments that prevent the many horrific things that the book explores from ever feeling too depressing or disturbing.

Maali is quickly approached by two figures, both of whom he knew of when they were all living, who try to help him make the best of his time in the In Between. There is Dr. Ranee Sridharan, a former academic, who wears a white sari and has been assigned to him by the In Between to be his helper, a fairy godmother–like figure. She informs him that he has "seven moons," or a week, to make peace with his life's sins before walking into The Light. Then there is Sena, a garbage bag–clad ghoul who used to work for the Communist Party and claims that Maali does not have to walk into the Light at all but should stay in the In Between where he can get vengeance on those who wronged him in Life. The two diametrically opposed figures represent one of the book's larger themes of grappling with bad events from the past and whether they should be forgotten or dug up and confronted. Upon learning that he was murdered, Maali decides that he will try to figure out who killed him so he can keep his friends safe from his killer within seven moons—if he does not go into The Light by the deadline, he will be trapped in the In Between forever as a ghoul or demon.

As Maali navigates his new existence as a spirit, Karunatilaka's brilliance for worldbuilding shines through. While in the In Between, Maali can travel anywhere that he has been to before in Life. Although the living cannot see or hear him, with the exception of the rare soothsayer, he can watch them. And now that he is dead, Maali sees that ghosts are everywhere in the city of Colombo; they appear how they died, meaning that there are a lot of children with snapped necks, singed women, and massacre victims. The omnipresence of their gory imagery become a stark reminder of the horrific violence that was happening in 1989 Sri Lanka, where the book is set.

Indeed, Karunatilaka's use of spirits, ghouls, demons, and other monsters throughout *The Seven Moons of Maali Almeida* often comes across as an allegory for the real-life horror story that was the Sri Lankan Civil War. To help contextualize this historical setting, early in the novel Karunatilaka has Maali refer to a "cheat sheet" that he once gave an American journalist. A list of all the different factions in the conflict, it reveals that among the Sri Lankans themselves there are the Liberation Tigers of Tamil Eelam (LTTE), who want their own sovereign state, and the Janatha Vimukthi Peramuna (JVP), communists who are trying to overturn the country's capitalist government. Then, there are the outsiders in Sri Lanka who are also adding to the conflict's chaos, like the UN, CIA, and the Indian Peace Keeping Force.

While the cheat sheet does help, it quickly becomes clear that the most important thing to understand about all of these different groups is that each is so devoted to its own respective cause that it will kill anyone who stands in their way—including its own people. This is even true of groups that ostensibly exist to maintain order like the Indian Peace Keeping Force, which will burn down entire villages in the name of "peace." Meanwhile, the government is no better, with its corrupt ministers and military leaders as well as its "special task force" that kidnaps and tortures anyone it suspects is associated with LTTE or JVP. For readers who do not know anything about the Sri Lankan war, it is quite shocking to learn about how prevalent the violence was.

Amidst all of this blood-soaked chaos is Maali, who, when he was alive, had no particular allegiance and would sell photos of the war's atrocities to anyone who paid him enough while keeping some of the more damning photos in a secret box underneath his bed. He soon believes that these photos must be what his killer was after, as their images could have taken down some very powerful people and governments. In turn, much of the novel's plot revolves around the photos and trying to direct his living friends Jaki and DD to their whereabouts.

In addition to its original plot, worldbuilding, humor, and insight into the Sri Lankan Civil War, much of what makes *The Seven Moons of Maali Almeida* work is its characters. Maali proves to be an interesting protagonist, especially considering that, when he was alive, he lived as a gay man during the height of the AIDS crisis when homophobia was still widespread in Sri Lanka and, although he was not out in public, in private he was unapologetic about his love for sleeping with men. Meanwhile, in his career as a photojournalist, he was one of the few brave enough to go to the frontlines and capture images of horrific truths. Karunatilaka ensures that he is not just a flawless gay hero, however. Maali also used to spend his nights drinking and gambling his money away at seedy casinos and could be superficial, dishonest, and selfish with the people who loved him most, including his boyfriend DD and his best friend Jaki, whom he pretended to be in a relationship with.

Maali might not be an especially likeable character, but he remains one who is easy to root for thanks to his charm and humor. And while his treatment of Jaki and DD when he was alive was often dishonest and disloyal, his love for them in death becomes one of the book's most compelling throughlines. This is amplified by the fact that Jaki and DD are also well-crafted LGBTQ characters whose own strengths and shortcomings make them enjoyable to follow as they try to solve Maali's murder back in the world of the living.

Thanks to an excellent cast of characters, a murder mystery plot, and a wild imagination, *The Seven Moons of Maali Almeida* will likely be enjoyed by a wide range of readers. Most reviews about the novel were overwhelmingly positive, with many praising how Karunatilaka's deft storytelling skills successfully shine a light on a historical atrocity that many have tried to forget. To this point, *Kirkus* concluded that the novel is "a manic, witty, artfully imagined tale of speaking truth to power." Additionally, many other critics praised the uniqueness of the novel's writing style, defined by the second-person "you" perspective of Maali's narration and the highly descriptive literary style of the prose. To this point, Tomiwa Owolade wrote in his review for the *Guardian*, "Another compelling feature is the vivid use of similes: one man's battered body is described as having ribs caved in 'like a broken coconut.'"

Not everyone felt that the novel was a complete success, however. In his review for the *New York Times*, Randy Boyagoda argued, "Maali is perhaps a little too perfect a guide for liberal Western readers: a self-deprecating, salty-tongued, godless gay brown mensch killed because he is a man as committed to satisfying his gambling habit and libido as he is to transcending sectarian furies while chronicling their consequences." It is important to note here that Boyagoda himself is of Sri Lankan descent and is likely more capable of spotting the amendments that Karunatilaka made in the original version of the novel so that it would resonate with Western readers. While the character of Maali may not be an accurate representation of what a Sri Lankan photojournalist was like during the 1980s, an argument can be made that whatever embellishments Karunatilaka has given him ultimately serve the story well.

Many have compared *The Seven Moons of Maali Almeida* to Salman Rushdie's *Midnight's Children* (1981) and Mikhail Bulgakov's *The Master and Margarita* (1967), and it is true that, like these books, the novel does use magical realism and satire to make political commentary. Despite these similarities, however, Karunatilaka's novel still proves to be a unique reading experience—the kind that is difficult to forget.

Author Biography
A Sri Lankan writer, Shehan Karunatilaka made his authorial debut with the 2012 Commonwealth Prize–winning novel *Chinaman: The Legend of Pradeep Mathew* (2010). In 2022, he won the Booker Prize for *The Seven Moons of Maali Almeida* (2022).

Emily E. Turner

Review Sources

Boyagoda, Randy. "The Hero of This Novel Is Dead. He'd Like to Find Out Why." Review of *The Seven Moons of Maali Almeida*, by Shehan Karunatilaka. *The New York Times*, 28 Oct. 2022, www.nytimes.com/2022/10/28/books/review/shehan-karunatilaka-seven-moons-maali-almeida.html. Accessed 1 Feb. 2023.

Charles, Ron. "*The Seven Moons of Maali Almeida* Is a Booker-Winning Ghost Story." Review of *The Seven Moons of Maali Almeida*, by Shehan Karunatilaka. *The Washington Post*, 1 Nov. 2022, www.washingtonpost.com/books/2022/11/01/booker-prize-winner-seven-moons-of-maali-almeida/. Accessed 23 Feb. 2023.

Owolade, Tomiwa. "Life after Death in Sri Lanka." Review of *The Seven Moons of Maali Almeida*, by Shehan Karunatilaka. *The Guardian*, 9 Aug. 2022, www.theguardian.com/books/2022/aug/09/the-seven-moons-of-maali-almeida-by-shehan-karunatilaka-review-life-after-death-in-sri-lanka. Accessed 2 Feb. 2023.

Review of *The Seven Moons of Maali Almeida*, by Shehan Karunatilaka. *Kirkus*, 16 Nov. 2022, www.kirkusreviews.com/book-reviews/shehan-karunatilaka/the-seven-moons-of-maali-almeida/. Accessed 1 Feb. 2023.

Shy
The Alarmingly Outspoken Memoirs of Mary Rodgers

Authors: Mary Rodgers (1931–2014) and Jesse Green (b. 1958)
Publisher: Farrar, Straus and Giroux (New York). Illustrated. 480 pp.
Type of work: Memoir
Time: 1931–2014
Locales: New York City, Los Angeles

In this exceptionally candid memoir, noted composer, author, and philanthropist Mary Rodgers offers insight into her own remarkable life as well as a wealth of juicy details about the many famous people she knew. Her incisively witty recollections, bolstered by extensive notes from coauthor Jesse Green, provide a unique view of the world of twentieth-century American musical theater.

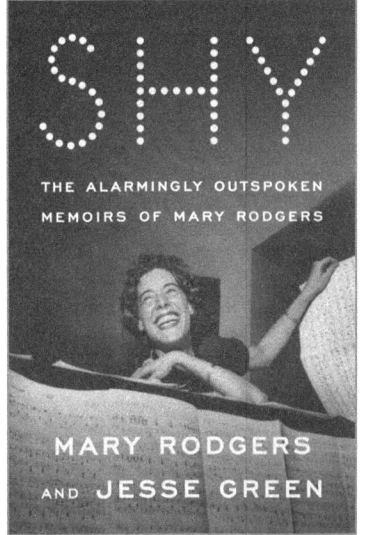

Principal personages

MARY RODGERS, the author, a composer and writer
RICHARD RODGERS, her father, one of the most famous composers in the history of musical theater
DOROTHY RODGERS, her mother
STEPHEN SONDHEIM, her close friend, himself a famed musical theater composer
JULIAN B. BEATY JR., her first husband, with whom she had three children
HENRY GUETTEL, her second husband, with whom she had three sons
ADAM GUETTEL, her son, an acclaimed composer
HAL PRINCE, her friend and one-time romantic interest, a prominent theater director and producer
OSCAR HAMMERSTEIN, one of Richard Rodgers's most celebrated collaborators
LORENZ HART, another of Richard Rodgers's artistic partners

Many fans of musical theater are likely aware of Mary Rodgers, who died in 2014 at the age of eighty-three. A composer best known for the hit comedy *Once Upon a Mattress* (1959), she is perhaps even more famous as the daughter of one of the best-known Broadway composers of all time, Richard Rodgers, and also the mother of another acclaimed composer, Adam Guettel. Others may recognize Rodgers as the author of the enduringly popular children's novel *Freaky Friday* (1972), which has been adapted for film several times. Yet even those familiar with the broad strokes of Rodgers's life will surely find the aptly titled *Shy: The Alarmingly Outspoken Memoirs of Mary Rodgers* (2022) an eye-opening read. This defiantly forthright and witty book

Mary Rodgers
Courtesy Farrar, Straus and Giroux

provides plenty of intimate history and gleefully scandalous gossip among its take-no-prisoners recollections, painting a vivid portrait of life among the twentieth-century artistic elite. The result is a work that is highly worthwhile for not only dedicated fans of musical theater but also anyone more generally interested in candid personal narratives.

Shy stands out for its interesting format. It centers Rodgers's wry commentary—which jumps back and forth across her life in an almost stream-of-consciousness manner—but also provides contextual information from coauthor Jesse Green in the form of copious footnotes. A journalist and theater critic, Green struck up a friendship with Rodgers and was eventually enlisted to help her put together a memoir. He interviewed her extensively during the several years before her death, typing out and organizing everything she had to say—most of which is presented here with apparently little alteration. Rather than interrupting Rodgers's narrative to explain various references, Green annotates her recollections. These notes balance Rodgers's often cutting frankness with a more measured factual tone, but they also frequently contain humor of their own. The effect is that readers hear Green's distinctive voice alongside Rodgers's, in a kind of complementary dialog or collaboration.

While the book does not unfold in a totally straightforward chronological fashion, it does effectively convey the arc of Rodgers's life. One of the main threads is her description of what it was like to live, in many ways, in the shadow of her father. Richard Rodgers, after all, wrote the music for such landmark works as *Oklahoma!*, *Carousel*, *South Pacific*, *The King and I*, and *The Sound of Music* (in partnership with Oscar Hammerstein) and won essentially every major award in the entertainment industry. Drilled in music instruction from a young age, Mary Rodgers followed in her father's footsteps as a composer of popular tunes. But while she had some notable successes, particularly with *Once Upon a Mattress* (which helped make Carol Burnett a major star) and 1966's *The Mad Show* (built on the satirical *Mad Magazine*), she soon recognized that she did not have quite the same level of songwriting genius. She had several flops or projects that were never produced, and as her career progressed she had a harder and harder time finding work as a composer. However, Rodgers is not bitter about the fact that she never matched her father's output, assessing his legacy and her own work in the same blunt manner she uses throughout. She also acknowledges that her successful pivot to writing books for children and young adults, most notably *Freaky Friday*, was both an effort to carve out a creative space of her own and a practical career decision.

Rodgers also often worked behind the scenes as well, maintaining many connections to the music and theater communities. She had a significant role in producing conductor and composer Leonard Bernstein's long-running series of *Young People's Concerts* with the New York Philharmonic, which was broadcast on CBS from 1958–1972, for example. She later served for years as chair of the board of directors of the famous Juilliard School of Music, in addition to holding positions on various other boards for prominent prep schools and colleges. Her status as the daughter of Richard Rodgers, along with her own varied talents, gave her entrée into a broad society of American creative artists, especially in New York City but also in Hollywood and elsewhere. One of the main appeals of *Shy* is the way Rodgers delivers anecdotes about many familiar (and also many unfamiliar) names. She enjoyed many of the people she met but does not hesitate to drop dirt—and plenty of it—on numerous others. Even the people she admired (such as Bernstein) often come in for snarky criticism, and the people she despised, such as the playwright Arthur Lorents, take a real beating in the pages of this no-holds-barred book. Some of the figures who make prominent appearances include the director and producer Hal Prince, whom she dated seriously; the popular actor Mary Martin; the genuinely appealing Carol Burnett (one of the few people not skewered here); her father's early collaborator Lorenz Hart; the somewhat hapless "Ockie" Hammerstein (whose virtues she praises but whose faults she freely recounts), and the acid-tongued author Larry Kramer. Practically anyone who was anybody or did anything even halfway significant in American musical theater in the latter half of the twentieth century is remembered here, sometimes fondly but always candidly.

Jesse Green

Of special note is Rodgers's discussion of her relationship with famed composer Stephen Sondheim. She met him when they were both very young, and the two quickly became fast friends. She enjoyed his wit, his intelligence, and his looks and soon developed an enduring crush on him. For his part, Sondheim also seemed to deeply cherish their connection, though, being gay, he did not reciprocate the romantic attraction. Despite that barrier, they even briefly tried to live together in a kind of awkward trial marriage. Rodgers characterizes Sondheim as the true love of her life, and he gets the distinction of being one of the relatively few people in this book whom she almost never criticizes. Nevertheless, the level of personal detail she reveals about him is as unreserved as ever—indeed, some reviewers have speculated that *Shy* was deliberately withheld from publication until after Sondheim died, lest he dispute any of its claims.

While Sondheim may have been Rodgers's ideal life partner, she turned elsewhere for romance, and she details all those relationships as well. On several occasions she was again attracted to gay men; notably, her first husband, Julian B. Beaty Jr., eventually came out as gay (he was also physically abusive, and they divorced in 1957). She also had numerous affairs, and she remains upfront, recounting which of her various partners were good in bed and which were not. Rodgers takes a softer tone in discussing her second marriage, to Henry Guettel, which endured for many decades and seems to have been genuinely happy for both partners in various ways.

Similarly, Rodgers speaks glowingly of her experience as a mother, having had three children with Beaty and three with Guettel. She notes that she always loved being pregnant and raising kids, and, according to her account, she seems to have been a successful, if somewhat unconventional, parent. Some particular attention goes to her son Adam, who became a highly acclaimed composer in his own right. She also maintains her candor even when talking about the grief of losing one of her children to an illness.

This kind of affection between parents and children was unfortunately not a feature of Rodgers's relationship with her own father (often referred to as Dick Rodgers or "Daddy") and mother (Dorothy Belle Feiner Rodgers, or "Mummy"), which is a major recurring theme throughout the memoir. Indeed, Rodgers turns her harshest criticism to her parents. Dick Rodgers is seen, through his daughter's eyes, as a cold, distant, hypercritical father with little time or affection for his family. Though she has respect for his musical genius, she portrays him as a work-obsessed, skirt-chasing drunk who became increasingly depressed as his talent began to drain away. Her mother, however, seems even worse. "Mummy" is presented as a cold, judgmental, self-important, and hyper-opinionated prima donna (whose friends ironically called her "La Perfecta"), and a terrible parent who either ignored her daughters or interfered overbearingly in their lives. According to Rodgers, her parents told her from a very early age that they loved her but did not like her (although she thinks that toward the end of her mother's life Dorothy actually liked her but did not love her). Her father often criticized her weight and appearance, among other supposed flaws, while her vain and haughty mother never wanted to play with her kids because doing so might mess up her carefully pressed clothes. It is clear that this emotional trauma was a powerful force in Rodgers's life. Nevertheless, she does show an ability to consider her family's dynamics from a broader perspective at times. For example, in an especially memorable episode, she indicates that "Daddy" despised "Mummy" almost as much as she did. She also relates how her parents were supportive in certain ways, such as bailing her and her second husband out of a major debt.

The considerable focus on Rodgers's unsparing portrayal of her parents, as well as her many other stinging critiques of those around her, may make *Shy* a somewhat depressing or difficult read for some. However, for many other readers the dry humor will shine through. Rodgers is also never hesitant to mention her own foibles and shortcomings as she sees them, so the book reads more like a truly open, honest recollection rather than a bitter attack or act of vengeance. Whether one appreciates her blunt style is ultimately a matter of preference, but there is no denying that this is a memorable book with a clear voice.

Critical reception to *Shy* was very strong, with many reviewers noting that the book was highly anticipated for its tell-all approach covering many famous figures. It received starred reviews in both *Publishers Weekly* and *Kirkus*, with the critic for the latter concluding that it "deserves to become a classic of music theater lore." Writing for the *Washington Post*, Wendy Smith praised "Rodgers's sense of humor, clever way with words, and refusal to indulge in self-pity." Daniel Okrent had a similarly positive take in a review for the *New York Times*, noting that "the book is pure pleasure—except when it's jaw-droppingly shocking." He also commended "Green's many illuminating footnotes, which enrich the pages of *Shy* like butter on a steak." For fans of musical theater or even general readers, Rodgers and Green have succeeded in producing a riveting account of an important chapter in American cultural life.

Author Biography

Mary Rodgers is best known for composing the music for the hit play *Once Upon a Mattress* (1959) and writing the best-selling children's novel *Freaky Friday* (1972), which she also adapted for the 1976 film version. She was also a prominent philanthropist and served on the boards of various educational institutions.

Jesse Green is an author and journalist who served as theater critic for the magazine *New York* from 2013 to 2017 before becoming chief theater critic for the *New York Times*. His publications include the novel *O Beautiful* (1990) and the memoir *The Velveteen Father: An Unexpected Journey to Parenthood* (1999).

Robert C. Evans, PhD

Review Sources

Allen, Brooke. "'Shy' Review: A Broadway Princess with a Song of Her Own." Review of *Shy: The Alarmingly Outspoken Memoirs of Mary Rodgers*, by Mary Rodgers and Jesse Green. *The Wall Street Journal*, 2 Sept. 2022, www.wsj.com/articles/shy-book-review-mary-rodgers-a-broadway-princess-with-a-song-of-her-own-11662131400. Accessed 30 Nov. 2022.

Okrent, Daniel. "Broadway Baby: The Astonishing Autobiography of Mary Rodgers." Review of *Shy: The Alarmingly Outspoken Memoirs of Mary Rodgers*, by Mary Rodgers and Jesse Green. *The New York Times*, 5 Aug. 2022, www.nytimes.com/2022/08/05/books/review/shy-mary-rodgers.html. Accessed 30 Nov. 2022.

Review of *Shy: The Alarmingly Outspoken Memoirs of Mary Rodgers*, by Mary Rodgers and Jesse Green. *Kirkus*, 19 May 2022, www.kirkusreviews.com/book-reviews/mary-rodgers/shy-rodgers/. Accessed 21 Feb. 2023.

Review of *Shy: The Alarmingly Outspoken Memoirs of Mary Rodgers*, by Mary Rodgers and Jesse Green. *Publishers Weekly*, 6 May 2022, www.publishersweekly.com/9780374298623. Accessed 21 Feb. 2023.

Smith, Wendy. "Mary Rodgers's Memoir Weighs in on Her Famous Dad and Stephen Sondheim." Review of *Shy: The Alarmingly Outspoken Memoirs of Mary Rodgers*, by Mary Rodgers and Jesse Green. *The Washington Post*, 11 Aug. 2022, www.washingtonpost.com/books/2022/08/11/mary-rodgers-memoir-sondheim-review. Accessed 30 Nov. 2022.

Siren Queen

Author: Nghi Vo (b. 1981)
Publisher: Tordotcom (New York). 288 pp.
Type of work: Novel
Time: 1920s to the 1960s
Locales: Los Angeles and San Francisco, California

Seamlessly blending fantasy and reality, Siren Queen *presents a unique take on the golden age of Hollywood, focusing on a Chinese American actor who stops at nothing to become an immortal silver screen star.*

Principal characters
LULI WEI, a Chinese American actor
GRETA NILSSON, a Swedish actor
EMMALINE SAUVIGNON, an American starlet
OBERLIN WOLFE, a powerful studio mogul
HARRY LONG, an aging former silent film star
JACKO DEWALT, a film director
TARA LUBOWSKI, an androgynous screenwriter

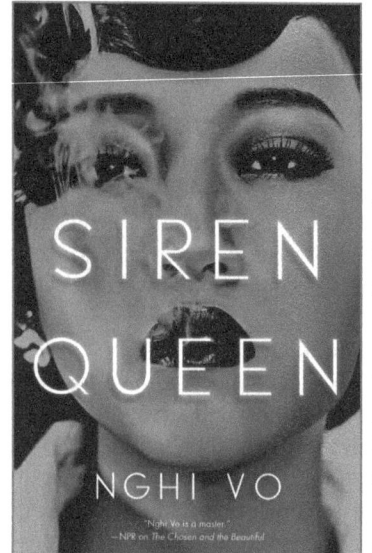

The period from the late 1920s to the early 1930s was a unique, and in many ways magical, time in cinematic history. Not only was there a momentous transition from silent films to "talkies," it was also the last gasp of an unregulated Hollywood, as scandals and moral panic led to growing calls for strict censorship of motion pictures from government officials and religious groups across the country. Fearing the impact that a patchwork of state-level regulations would have, the film industry decided to proactively introduce its own code of rules and guidelines that would prevent filmmakers from including any subject matter seen as morally inappropriate or controversial. In 1930, the Motion Picture Producers and Distributors of America, the trade association representing the major film studios, introduced the so-called Hays Code to dictate what content was allowed on screen. However, the code was technically voluntary and proved difficult to enforce, leading many filmmakers to push its boundaries or ignore it all together with provocative works that reflected the looser social attitudes of the time and satiated an American public looking for an escape from the harsh realities of the Great Depression. This lasted until 1934, when the Hays Code began to be more strictly enforced through an approval system overseen by the Production Code Administration.

This celebrated era of filmmaking, known as pre-Code Hollywood, forms the backdrop of Nghi Vo's historical fantasy novel *Siren Queen* (2022). The book centers

Siren Queen / VO

Nghi Vo (Courtesy Tom Doherty Associates)

around Luli Wei, a Chinese American actor who embarks on a dogged and uncompromising quest to become a star of the silver screen. Similar to Nathanael West's classic novel *The Day of the Locust* (1939), *Siren Queen* features all made-up characters, using Hollywood only as a framework for a fully imagined world. Yet while Vo makes no mention of any real-life movie stars or directors, she does offer up unabashedly frank depictions of sex, violence, and power, which very much runs in line with pre-Code tropes—and provides a sharp element of social commentary from a twenty-first century perspective. Meanwhile, Vo also adds another layer of interest: in addition to movie magic, the world of the novel includes actual magic, which underlies the very structure of the film studio system. This version of Hollywood is equal parts dreams and nightmares, where monsters are very real and would-be movie stars literally sell their souls in the name of everlasting glory.

Luli—which, significantly, is not her real name—narrates her story from the future, looking back on her life and her career in three acts (followed by an epilogue). Readers first encounter her as a young girl growing up in the Hungarian Hill neighborhood of Los Angeles. Along with her younger sister, she works in her parents' modest Chinese laundry, which sometimes caters to glamorous Tinseltown stars. The potential of those stars' fame and immortality holds much allure for young Luli, whose life is changed after she sees her first film, *Romeo and Juliet*, at a new nickelodeon (movie theater) next to her family's laundry. To pay for admission, she cuts off an inch of her hair, and it is not long before she starts selling off more to see other films, "feeding myself on dreams in black and silver, and then much, much later, miraculously and magnificently, in color."

Luli's dreams become reality when one day in 1932, at age twelve, she accidentally wanders onto her first film set. She lands a one-line role as a beggar in a film starring Maya Vos Santé, an exotically beautiful Mexican actor whose rise to fame has been shrouded in myth and rumor. Santé only makes a one-off appearance but is one of the many examples of otherness that Vo celebrates throughout her novel—that of an outsider making it, or at least trying to make it, in an inherently corrupt, misogynistic, and xenophobic Hollywood film industry. Embodying that industry is predatory director Jacko Dewalt, who, after taking a liking to Luli, recruits her for more bit parts. Luli quickly becomes a regular on Jacko's sets, but after toiling on studio backlots for several years, she devises a plan to satisfy her unquenchable desire for stardom, eventually blackmailing Jacko into orchestrating a meeting with the extremely powerful studio head Oberlin Wolfe.

Like many scenes in *Siren Queen*, Luli's tête-à-tête with Wolfe is surreal and rife with metaphor, as Vo blurs the line between fantasy and reality. Tall and handsome with "sharp and slightly alien" features, Wolfe, living up to his surname, inspects, circles, and lunges at Luli, appearing at times as a shape-shifting monster. Luli manages to both reject his advances and pass her impromptu audition with confident ease. She agrees to a three-year, $250 per week studio contract but refuses to take on the usual stereotypical roles for Asian women, asserting to Wolfe, "No maids, no funny talking, no fainting flowers." She does not escape the meeting totally unscathed, however. In a moment of desperate self-preservation she uses her sister's name—Luli—as her own, a theft that will long haunt her. Names wield enormous influence in Vo's Hollywood, it turns out, so much so that both cast and crew members use pseudonyms to avoid the arcane control of the studios. Luli is not one to be controlled, however, and opts to carve her own path to stardom.

After signing her contract, which marks the end of the novel's first act, Luli moves into dorms on the Wolfe Studios lot and goes through the wringer of weekly dance, voice, and acting lessons. Because she resists being typecast, roles come slowly for her. From androgynous messenger girls to high-kicking cabaret dancers to drunken nightclub flirts, Luli gradually earns her way "a bit of silver at a time." During this period she falls in with a fringe community of Hollywood players, including her roommate, Greta Nilsson, an earthy Swedish actor who was reportedly born with a cow's tail and abducted from her mountain village by a studio scout, and Emmaline Sauvignon, a Minnesota-bred starlet with whom she has a heated love affair. Presenting a diverse set of characters, Vo effectively engages with sexuality, gender, race, and other issues of identity throughout, acknowledging the attitudes and obstacles of the era and championing acceptance but never letting the social commentary distract from characterization and story. The forbidden romance between Luli and Emmaline is kept under close wraps by the studio, which manufactures another relationship for Emmaline with an up-and-coming male star to protect her ingenue status. Luli, too, knows she must play the game to avoid being swallowed up and spit out by the system, but her stubborn fight for acceptance as a queer, Chinese American outsider grounds Vo's magical flourishes firmly in reality.

Vo also expertly introduces the more fantastical elements, working them seamlessly into the narrative without overexplaining. For example, much of Luli's networking occurs at ritual Friday night fires held on the Wolfe Studios lot. There, actors and directors strike deals and seize lovers while trying to avoid a sinister stalking phantom known as the Wild Hunt. This is where Luli first meets Emmaline and becomes privy to the darker forces ruling Hollywood, ones involving human sacrifice, monsters, and Faustian contracts etched in blood. Here, Vo dazzles with her fantastical worldbuilding and hypnotic prose, as Luli and friends wander off and get lost in shadowy labyrinthine corners amid grotesque courtyards.

Luli finally wins acceptance after being cast, ironically, as a slithering Atlantean monster known as the Siren Queen in a hit film series that instantly catapults her to stardom—which inevitably comes with its own pitfalls. Most of the novel's second and third acts follow Luli as she navigates her newfound fame through the Hollywood maelstrom. She finds a mentor and friend in costar Harry Long, an aging but still dapper former silent-film star, and artistic champions in Scottie and Whalen Mannheim, the series' sibling directors. Her relationship with Emmaline, however, fizzles, eventually giving way to another romance with screenwriter Tara Lubowski, who works under a male pseudonym to disguise her gender. All the while, Luli continues to maintain her fierce independent streak, but does so under the watchful eye of Harvey Rose, Wolfe's menacing right-hand man.

Throughout the novel, the magic of movies reigns supreme, and Vo fittingly concludes Luli's story with a bravura film-like set piece: the long-delayed and tumultuous filming of the eponymous *Siren Queen*, the seventh and final installment of the highly successful series. Luli fights to cement her place as an immortal Hollywood legend with a wildly risqué closing scene that would please the most discriminating of pre-Code aficionados. Meanwhile, raging fires, mysterious disappearances, erotic trysts, sudden unwelcome professional reunions, and more welcome family reconciliations fill out the thrilling conclusion. Ultimately, the novel's fantastical and surreal elements are just supporting parts in a transcendent human story, as Luli's sheer force of will and determination come to the foreground.

Critical reception to *Siren Queen* was very positive. Many reviewers agreed that it was a beguiling follow-up to Vo's award-winning debut novel *The Chosen and the Beautiful* (2021), which strikingly reimagines F. Scott Fitzgerald's seminal masterpiece *The Great Gatsby* (1925) through the perspective of another strong-willed, queer, Asian female protagonist. Though Vo's seamless melding of fantasy and reality may pose a challenge to readers looking for a more straightforward narrative, those willing to go along for the ride will likely find much to enjoy. As the critic for *Publishers Weekly* wrote, *Siren Queen* convincingly secures Vo "as a force to be reckoned with in speculative fiction." In a review for *Locus*, Gary K. Wolfe offered a similar assessment, praising the work's "memorable characterization," "elegant style," and "vividly detailed sense of place," while declaring Luli to be "one of the more appealing fantasy heroes in recent years."

Fantasy hero status notwithstanding, Luli is also fascinating when considered in a more realistic historical context. Cinephiles will notice undeniable parallels to the groundbreaking real-life Chinese American actor Anna May Wong, who similarly overcame racial discrimination and typecasting to forge an internationally recognized film career. Some of Wong's most classic films, such as *Daughter of the Dragon* (1931) and *Shanghai Express* (1932), were released during the pre-Code Hollywood era, which Vo researched closely when writing *Siren Queen*. This meticulous historical research is apparent in other elements of the novel as well. Vo noted that she read a number of biographies on other popular stars from that era, such as Greta Garbo and Ramon Navarro, who directly inspired the characters of Greta Nilsson and Harry Long, respectively. There are also compelling passages describing era-accurate film sets, equipment, and costume pieces, which will surely be of interest to film buffs as well as general readers.

Of course, while *Siren Queen* gives an interesting glimpse at pre-Code Hollywood, it is also easy to interpret its social commentary in a more contemporary sense. Indeed, in her acknowledgements, Vo states that she started writing the novel in the summer of 2017, right as the #MeToo movement against sexual misconduct generated much attention in Hollywood. Readers might draw parallels between Oberlin Wolfe and real-life predators like the former Hollywood mogul and convicted rapist Harvey Weinstein, for example. This grounding in realities of the film industry that persist into the twenty-first century makes tough, no-nonsense protagonist Luli all the more memorable as something beyond the typical fantasy hero. Her resistance to and conquest of overpowering men and exploitative system they control, as a outsider living fully on her own terms, helps make *Siren Queen* not just a page-turner but also a complex, thought-provoking read.

Author Biography
Nghi Vo is an author known for both short and long fiction. Her fantasy novella *The Empress of Salt and Fortune* (2020) won both a Crawford Award and a Hugo Award, and her best-selling debut novel, *The Chosen and the Beautiful* (2021), was a Locus Award finalist.

Chris Cullen

Review Sources
Cohen-Perez, Stephanie. Review of *Siren Queen*, by Nghi Vo. *BookPage*, May 2022, www.bookpage.com/reviews/siren-queen-review/. Accessed 3 Oct. 2022.
Harris, Marlene. Review of *Siren Queen*, by Nghi Vo. *Library Journal*, 1 Apr. 2022, www.libraryjournal.com/review/siren-queen-2140543. Accessed 3 Oct. 2022.
Kingsbury, Margaret. "17 Amazing Fantasy and Science Fiction Novels out This Spring." Review of *Siren Queen*, by Nghi Vo, et al. *BuzzFeed News*, 1 Apr. 2022, www.buzzfeednews.com/article/margaretkingsbury/new-science-fiction-and-fantasy-recommendations-spring. Accessed 3 Oct. 2022.
Rapa, Patrick. "The Best New Books to Read in May." Review of *Siren Queen*, by Nghi Vo, et al. *Philadelphia Inquirer*, 27 Apr. 2022, www.inquirer.com/arts/books/may-2022-new-books-20220427.html. Accessed 3 Oct. 2022.
Review of *Siren Queen*, by Nghi Vo. *Publishers Weekly*, 20 Dec. 2021, www.publishersweekly.com/9781250788832. Accessed 3 Oct. 2022.
Von Essen, Leah. Review of *Siren Queen*, by Nghi Vo. *Booklist*, 1 Apr. 2022, www.booklistonline.com/Siren-Queen-/pid=9757404. Accessed 3 Oct. 2022.
Wolfe, Gary K. Review of *Siren Queen*, by Nghi Vo. *Locus*, 19 June 2022, locusmag.com/2022/06/gary-k-wolfe-reviews-siren-queen-by-nghi-vo/. Accessed 3 Oct. 2022.

Small World

Author: Jonathan Evison (b. 1968)
Publisher: Dutton (New York). 480 pp.
Type of work: Novel
Time: 1851–2020
Locales: New York City; Chicago; Portland and McMinnville, Oregon; San Francisco, Red Bluff, and Shasta City, California; various other locales across the United States

Spanning 170 years of American history, this epic and ambitious novel tracks the intersection of four modern families and their nineteenth-century ancestors as they struggle to find hope, meaning, and purpose in a rapidly changing world.

Principal characters

WALTER BERGEN, a senior Amtrak train operator
NORA BERGEN, an Irish immigrant, Walter's nineteenth-century ancestor
FINN BERGEN, Nora's fraternal twin brother
JENNY CHEN, an Amtrak corporate consultant
WU CHEN, a Chinese immigrant, Jenny's nineteenth-century ancestor
BRIANNA FLOWERS, a Black single mother
MALIK FLOWERS, Brianna's seventeen-year-old son
OTHELLO/GEORGE FLOWERS, Brianna and Malik's nineteenth-century ancestor
LAILA TULLY, a waitress of American Indian descent
LUYU TULLY, Laila's Miwok ancestor

The American dream is defined differently for individual people, but most would agree that the pursuit of it represents an overriding sense of hope and optimism for the future. Whether it be landing a better job, making more money, becoming a homeowner, having kids, or simply finding an inner place of calm shielded from the madness of everyday life, people—irrespective of age, race, class, and gender—often like to believe that their best days are still ahead of them. And it is this belief that continually drives people, lured in by the promise of boundless possibility, to become the best version of themselves. These types of individuals abound in award-winning author Jonathan Evison's ambitious seventh novel, *Small World* (2022), which follows the lives of four modern families and their nineteenth-century forebears over 170 years of American nation-building. Similar to his 2011 novel, *West of Here*, Evison tells his story from numerous points of view, with chapters alternating between storylines from different time periods—specifically, the present-day and the mid-nineteenth century—to create

Jonathan Evison

Courtesy Penguin Publishing Group

a sweeping panorama of American individualism, diversity, and interconnectedness.

Small World centers around the premise of a train accident in 2019, and on a larger scale, is set against the backdrop of US railroad expansion in the 1850s and 1860s, which crystallized with the completion of the country's first transcontinental railroad in 1869. Powerful symbols of modernity and technological progress, railroads and trains forever revolutionized the way Americans traveled, bringing them closer together faster than ever before. They spurred development beyond coastal cities, though at considerable human and environmental cost. In both a literal and figurative sense, they created a smaller world. Through his characters and their intersecting lives and experiences, Evison tackles the question of whether a "small world" is a good or bad thing, and by novel's end, readers will likely arrive at an answer that lies somewhere in between, an answer that highlights all the glorious imperfections of the great American experiment.

Many of those imperfections, of course, take shape in the very human beings who make up that experiment. The novel opens with a prime example: a train accident caused by human error. The culprit behind the accident is Walter Bergen, a sixty-three-year-old senior Amtrak train operator who, after being forced into early retirement due to corporate cutbacks, finds himself working the final run of a distinguished three-decade-long career, a trip from Portland, Oregon, to Seattle, Washington. For Walter, who hails from a long line of railroad workers, the trip is bittersweet, as he fears leaving the familiar for the unknown, embodied by a rapidly changing world that has become foreign to him. He muses about his wife Annie's plans for him, his daughter Wendy's upcoming marriage, and his own current place in the world—which, according to his daughter, is not a very relevant one ("According to Wendy it was time for Walter and the rest of the old white guys to step aside and get out of the way"). The train accident itself is introduced in brief and somewhat vague terms, with the details of what happened and what ensues slowly revealed throughout the rest of the novel. The incident serves above all as a framework for Evison to fold in the stories of the train's passengers, their ancestors, and of how, due to various circumstances, they all arrived together at that fateful moment. As one passenger tells his griping young son early on, "It's about the journey, pal."

For the Bergen family, that journey is an epic and tumultuous one that begins on the Atlantic Ocean in 1851. Walter is a descendant of the fraternal twins Nora and Finn Bergen, who sail with their mother, Alma, from Cork, Ireland, to the United States in hopes of passing through the "Golden Door" to a better life, one free from hunger, poverty, and disease. Their struggles only continue, however, after they arrive in New

York, where, after failing to locate their cousins, they are taken in by a kind Irish immigrant woman and her father. Eventually, the Bergens make their way west to Chicago, but when Alma dies, Nora and Finn become orphaned and, eventually, devastatingly separated. Driven by dreams of reuniting, the twins make their own separate ways in the world, with Finn ultimately migrating westward to work on the first transcontinental railroad, "one of those intrepid and criminally underpaid souls who drove spikes halfway across the prairie and blasted through the mountains all the way to Promontory Point for that historic joining of the Union and Central Pacific lines."

Meanwhile, the family stories of several of the passengers on Walter's train also emerge, with relatively short chapters jumping back and forth between the narratives. Jenny Chen is a mid-thirties corporate consultant for Amtrak who, ironically, supervised the buyouts that led to Walter's early retirement. She is a descendant of Wu Chen, a Chinese immigrant who travels to America during the California Gold Rush. As one of the pioneering "forty-niners," Chen makes a small fortune in gold, but not without enduring violence and tragedy. A fortuitous set of circumstances helps Wu Chen make his way to San Francisco, where he marries a grocer's daughter and launches a highly successful grocery chain. Generations later, Jenny inherits her ancestor's enterprising spirit, earning a "healthy six-figure income" in her corporate role, enough to ensure an affluent life for her family of four. With a loving stay-at-home husband, Todd Murphy, two endearing young sons, Winston and Tyler, and a generally comfortable existence, Jenny seems to have it all—but she is miserable and deeply unfulfilled. "I don't have time to think about what really matters to me, I'm too busy trying to maintain our outsized life," Jenny explains to her husband at one point. "It's like I'm on a hamster wheel most of the time."

It is this feeling that something is missing in her life that prompts Jenny to move with her family from San Francisco to Todd's hometown of McMinnville, Oregon, which is how they all end up taking an Amtrak train trip to Seattle. Through the Chen-Murphys, with their hyphenated surname, diverse immigrant origins, and rags-to-riches success story, Evison depicts the quintessential modern American family. They are, on the surface, an embodiment of the American dream, but as Jenny and her husband, who himself ponders how he "ended up on the sidelines of his own life," demonstrate, that dream is not all it is chalked up to be. Accruing wealth at the expense of others, living in an exorbitantly priced and overcrowded city, and eating dinner in front of the television most nights with children glued to their smartphones creates instead a portrait of familial disillusionment and isolation. Their experience is far removed from the proud cultural traditions Jenny holds dear and the core American values and liberating "wide-open spaces" Todd was raised on in rural Oregon.

Hope nonetheless reigns supreme in *Small World*, and it is the ceaseless striving for a better and more fulfilling quality of life that propels the characters forward, even in the face of unspeakable hardship and adversity. Rounding out the novel's central cast are the Flowers and Tully families, whose ancestral histories mirror less the American dream than the American nightmare. In 2019, Brianna Flowers, a hard-working but cash-strapped Black single mother, finds herself traveling on the same train as the Chen-Murphys, but unlike them, it is not for pleasure. She has taken out a payday loan to send her seventeen-year-old son, Malik, a talented six-foot-nine basketball star, to an event in Seattle in the hope that he can draw the attention of college recruiters. Brianna and Malik are the descendants of an enslaved man called Othello, who in the 1850s escapes captivity in Chicago, renames himself George Flowers, finds love with a free kitchen maid named Cora, and tries to take charge of his life under the ever-present specter of slavery. Malik is riding on aspirations of a professional basketball career, which would bring life-changing riches and effectively break the chains of generational struggle and poverty. Brianna, whose family mantra growing up was "expect the worst," knows that, despite his talent, Malik's chances of fulfilling those aspirations are slim. Still, she does her best to provide him with the best possible life. "Chances were, nobody would ever hand Malik ten million dollars," Brianna muses. "But was that any reason not to let him dream?"

Also soldiering on in life is fellow train passenger Laila Tully, a down-on-her-luck waitress from Red Bluff, California. She, too, has dreams, but on a smaller scale: leaving her abusive boyfriend and dead-end hometown. Thanks to a compassionate colleague she has secured the funds necessary to flee California, which is how she finds herself on the Amtrak train. Meanwhile, her ancestral story is shown through the character Luyu Tully, a Miwok woman in the 1850s who is also uprooted and in search of a new beginning. Raised by a family of Methodists after her parents are murdered, Luyu longs for a "freedom she'd only ever heard about, the freedom the whites had stolen from her people." She eventually marries an American Indian man named John Tully, and they venture across northern California as homesteaders in search of a life away from racial discrimination, injustice, and oppression.

Issues of identity, especially race and economic class, both link and divide each of the main characters in *Small World*. For example, Evison effectively juxtaposes the tribulations of the wealthy Chen-Murphys with the harsher struggles faced by Brianna and Laila, whose hand-to-mouth financial struggles reveal some of the grittier and more uncomfortable truths of American life. "Sitting at the little table in the kitchen, she figured the numbers one more time, knowing in advance her calculations were futile," he writes about Brianna, giving readers a palpable sense of poverty. The legacy of racism and cultural oppression is also a prominent theme throughout the book. By the time all the characters' lives intersect on the train for the novel's suspenseful and satisfying finish, however, they find themselves on the same level playing field in the all-too-human battle of life versus death.

In writing *Small World*, Evison admittedly set out to write a "Great American Novel," and in the eyes of many critics, he succeeded in that quest. Exemplifying this sentiment was Bill Kelly in a review for *Booklist*, who declared the book a "masterpiece" in which "each character displays the fierce fortitude and stubborn resilience that define the American spirit." According to Kelly, "Evison eloquently shows that perhaps the most authentically American ideal is the ongoing, blended palette of stories." Similarly, writing for *Vol. 1 Brooklyn*, Ian Maloney opined that the novel "reads like Evison's best work, to date," describing it as "a timeless American story, with vivid well-rounded characters, who have a lot to tell us about the world we live in today as well as the one we've inherited from the past." The book received a starred review from *Kirkus* and was included on recommended book lists from several outlets, among other enthusiastic praise.

Not all reviewers, however, were as laudatory. Notably, in a review for the *Washington Post*, Charles Arrowsmith felt that Evison too often takes on a "sententious, editorial register" that distracts from the storytelling, while the "prose is often marred by hackneyed phrases." Although Arrowsmith commended Evison's "weighty ideas and worthy commentary on oppression and racism," he argued that "the book's moral simplicity rather leaches it of urgency and vigor." Still, for many readers *Small World* will prove a worthwhile, if imperfect, look at important issues from the perspectives of engagingly imperfect characters. Taken as a whole, it is an immersive and entertaining experience, one filled with transporting imagery, timeless themes, and a kaleidoscope of three-dimensional humanity that captures the best of the American spirit.

Author Biography

Jonathan Evison is an award-winning and best-selling author known in particular for his novels, including *All About Lulu* (2008), *West of Here* (2011), *The Revised Fundamentals of Caregiving* (2012), and *Lawn Boy* (2018).

Chris Cullen

Review Sources

Arrowsmith, Charles. "Jonathan Evison's *Small World* Feels Like a Big Statement about America." Review of *Small World*, by Jonathan Evison. *The Washington Post*, 21 Jan. 2022, www.washingtonpost.com/books/2022/01/21/jonathan-evison-small-world-book/. Accessed 19 Jan. 2023.

Kelly, Bill. Review of *Small World*, by Jonathan Evison. *Booklist*, 1 Nov. 2021, www.booklistonline.com/Small-World-/pid=9753265. Accessed 19 Jan. 2023.

Maloney, Ian. "Generations, Wrecks, and the Great American Novel: A Review of Jonathan Evison's *Small World*." *Vol. 1 Brooklyn*, 22 Apr. 2022, vol1brooklyn.com/2022/04/22/generations-wrecks-and-the-great-american-novel-a-review-of-jonathan-evisons-small-world/. Accessed 19 Jan. 2023.

Nesbit, TaraShea. "A Fateful Train Ride Connects Eras and Cultures in This Novel." Review of *Small World*, by Jonathan Evison. *The New York Times*, 11 Jan. 2022, www.nytimes.com/2022/01/11/books/review/jonathan-evison-small-world.html. Accessed 19 Jan. 2023.

Review of *Small World*, by Jonathan Evison. *Kirkus*, 29 Sept. 2021, www.kirkusreviews.com/book-reviews/colleen-hoover/reminders-of-him-hoover/. Accessed 19 Jan. 2023.

Review of *Small World*, by Jonathan Evison. *Publishers Weekly*, 26 Oct. 2021, www.publishersweekly.com/9780593184127. Accessed 19 Jan. 2023.

Venters, Amberlee. Review of *Small World*, by Jonathan Evison. *Open Letter Review*, 16 Jan. 2022, openlettersreview.com/posts/small-world-by-jonathan-evison. Accessed 19 Jan. 2023.

Solito

Author: Javier Zamora (b. 1990)
Publisher: Hogarth (New York City). 400 pp.
Type of work: Memoir
Time: Twenty-first century
Locales: El Salvador, Guatemala, Mexico, the United States

In the memoir Solito, *award-winning author Javier Zamora chronicles his journey from El Salvador to the United States as an unaccompanied nine-year-old.*

Principal personages
JAVIER, the narrator, a nine-year-old Salvadoran boy who journeys to the United States alone
ABUELITA NELI, his grandmother
GRANDPA CHEPE, his grandfather
TÍA MALI, his aunt
TÍA LUPE, his aunt
MOM, his mother
DAD, his father
DON DAGO, a coyote who takes his parents to the United States
PATRICIA, a woman who takes care of him as they travel
CARLA, Patricia's daughter and his playmate as they travel
CHINO, a man who takes care of him as they travel

Solito (2022) is not for the faint of heart, nor is it a story about heroes and villains. In his complex and nuanced best-selling memoir, author Javier Zamora brilliantly captures the voice of his nine-year-old self to tell a harrowing story about his experience journeying across three countries and through desert terrain with a group of strangers led by coyotes (a term for those who escort undocumented immigrants across the southern border of the United States) to be reunited with his parents in Arizona. His nine-week journey is, at once, captivating and horrifying, which makes it harder and harder with each turn of events to stop reading and catch a breath. Zamora details his experiences with exquisite, painstaking descriptions that engage the reader's senses, imagination, and worst fears. With every unexpected adversity or setback he faces along the way, it is difficult to comprehend that he completes the journey successfully, despite the book serving as concrete evidence. The language of the book seamlessly and accessibly flows between Spanish, English, and Spanglish with a smoothness that

Javier Zamora (photo courtesy Random House Publishing Group)

enlivens and anchors. It gives the reader an up-close and personal seat on Zamora's journey.

Solito is also a story about the humanity of those affected by the circumstances of civil war and an imperialistic global community that breeds corruption and exploitation where survival is ensured by any means necessary. As Zamora's work suggests, the consequences of survival in this system include unavoidable trauma and suffering. While not picture-perfect, his home environment provides young Zamora with some sense of safety, security, and love, especially from his grandmother and aunties. He is an intelligent child and was rewarded for his academic skills at an early age. Zamora depicts his life in the tiny village of La Herradura, El Salvador, as materially poor yet wealthy beyond measure in regard to the deep and nurturing interpersonal relationships he has with his family and friends. It is the strength of his family bonds and friendships that sustain him, along with the tangible assistance of a few significant adults, Patricia and Chino, who help him survive the treacherous journey to Arizona.

Throughout the book, Zamora reminds the reader of his childlike innocence, which acts as a temporary balm of emotional relief from the ongoing hardship he faces once his grandfather leaves him in the hands of strangers to make the trip. This is often achieved through Zamora's imagination as he pulls characters from his toys and scenes from the television programs he watched at home into his reality as if he is on a journey with superheroes and he is one of them. At other times, he demonstrates this through his internal dialogue in response to trying to understand adult expressions, the English language, and profanity, for example. Zamora also experiences age-appropriate challenges with body modesty, talking about and seeing adult genitals, and realizing that he likes Carla, the immigrant girl he meets on the trip. The ways Zamora depicts the personality of his nine-year-old self are effective in their timing and tone. Strangely, at times, his portrayal also provides the reader with some comic relief from an otherwise heartbreaking experience. Zamora also offers masterfully detailed descriptions of the many immigrants and coyotes he meets along the way, reflecting personalities, attitudes, beliefs, and behaviors using particular descriptors and dialogue to provide a complex, nuanced narrative of the human and geographical terrain he had to navigate as a child constantly.

After nine grueling weeks, his journey finally ends, but Zamora does not give his readers a fairy-tale ending. Instead, the reader is left with a glimpse of the distress his parents felt, not knowing where he was during most of his trek and seeing him for the first time in a condition of filth and bodily stench unfit for human habitat. The reader is also left with the haunting reality that, likely, many of the people who made the trek with him did not survive. He writes, "I never found out what happened to Chele, or to any of the countless others who were with me. I fear they died in the Sonoran Desert." Zamora dedicated the book to the immigrants who helped him cross the desert as well as those he never saw again.

Solito received a largely positive response from critics. In a starred review, the anonymous reviewer for *Publishers Weekly* called it "an immensely moving story of desperation and hardship" that Zamora "transforms . . . into a stirring portrait of the power of human connection." The *Publishers Weekly* reviewer recognized Zamora's command of engaging readers in describing "a two-month nightmare pocked with seedy characters, days spent locked in various hideouts . . . and a never-ending stream of promises shattered." Similarly, the starred anonymous review from *Kirkus* described it as a "beautifully wrought work that renders the migrant experience into a vivid, immediately accessible portrayal." The *Kirkus* reviewer marveled at how Zamora "meticulously re-creates his tense, traumatic journey, creating a page-turning narrative that reads like fiction." Writing for NPR, Gabino Iglesias praised *Solito*, describing it as "an incredibly detailed chronicle" and "the kind of narrative that manages to bring a huge [immigration] debate down to a very personal space, bridging the gap between the unique and the universal in ways that make both look like one and the same." Iglesias also complimented "Zamora's voice, sense of humor, and heart," noting that these features "make [*Solito*] a standout story about survival and the pursuit of the American Dream." Lastly, referencing his own "obsession with the use of Spanish and Spanglish" in his writing, Iglesias observed that "Zamora treads the interstitial space between languages with grace, humor, and style."

Reviewing for *Latinx in Publishing*, Allison Argueta-Claros also celebrated Zamora, noting, "His detailed descriptions and observations are both honest and zany . . . his meticulous reporting of dates and events, and his attention to the smells and textures associated with his time in the desert are all notable." Argueta-Claros recognized *Solito* not only as a book about migration but "an ode to the family [Javier] found in the strangers that accompanied him, Chino, Patricia, and Carla." She also asserted that the book offers a counter-story to the construct of "unaccompanied minors" politicized through media coverage and "forces you to move past the legalistic term through impeccable detail, rendering the grueling 3,000-mile journey in the most visceral of emotions." Argueta-Claros concluded her review by describing the book as "a must-read" that lets "us in on the reality of migration."

The *Washington Post* reviewer, Steven V. Roberts, recognized *Solito* as more than an immigration story; "It is a coming-of-age tale about a 9-year-old whose journey toward maturity—another mythic land—was compressed into one season." Consistent with other reviews, Roberts noted that "Zamora writes with economy and eloquence, and his narrative connects the reader directly to the tastes and terrors, smells and stresses of life on the run from the law." Despite his otherwise positive review, Roberts also offered some criticism and stated that "this compelling story has some minor flaws. It's too long, and it contains many Spanish phrases that are never translated." Roberts warned that "some readers who don't know the language may not fully grasp the tone and texture of the narrative." He also believed that Zamora owes his readers an explanation of "how this book came about," and noted that "[Zamora] was 9 when the story occurred, so presumably he didn't take notes, and 23 years later he has produced an exceptionally detailed account." Finally, Roberts questioned, "Is this really a memoir? Or is it more like a novel, inspired by real events but leavened by imagination?" Still, Roberts ended his review on a positive note by recognizing *Solito* as "a valuable book" as it "puts a human face, a child's face, on all those anonymous immigrants we only see on the news as pawns in a political game."

New York Times reviewer Karla Cornejo Villavicencio joined the chorus of other reviewers in noting that "Zamora writes in such a way that you never forget that this harrowing journey is being experienced by a child." She observed that assuming a child's perspective takes a "popular terrain for novelists and beat reporters" and makes "the subject [of the southern border] feel fresh with a shift of perspective." Villavicencio praised the way Zamora conveys the innocence of a child "describing his surroundings with plainness, presenting his survival without bluster," and contrasting simple things like learning to use the toilet and washing his undergarments with the challenges of facing "uniformed men with machine guns, smugglers, [and] Border Patrol." She also recognized the "limitations to experiencing this journey from a child's point of view. One is that children don't know why things are happening." Nevertheless, Villavicencio acknowledged *Solito* as "an important, beautiful work," and stated that "his account reads like a reporter's notebook; everything is described meticulously so that it can be remembered. Zamora writes like someone who cannot afford to forget." It is doubtful that readers will forget this remarkable journey either.

Author Biography

Javier Zamora is an award-winning poet and author. He has held a Stegner Fellowship from Stanford University, a Radcliffe Fellowship from Harvard, and fellowships from the National Endowment for the Arts and the Poetry Foundation.

Valandra, MBA, MSW, PhD

Review Sources

Argueta-Claros, Allison. Review of *Solito*, by Javier Zamora. *Latinx in Publishing*, 17 Nov. 2022, latinxinpublishing.com/blog/2022/11/17/solito-javier-zamora-review. Accessed 31 Jan. 2023.

Iglesias, Gabino. "*Solito* Is a Personal Story of Immigration That Sheds Light on the Universal." Review of *Solito*, by Javier Zamora. *NPR*, 29 Sept. 2022, www.npr.org/2022/09/29/1125275405/javier-zamora-solito-is-a-personal-story-of-immigration-that-is-also-universal. Accessed 23 Jan. 2023.

Review of *Solito*, by Javier Zamora. *Kirkus*, 6 Sept. 2022, www.kirkusreviews.com/book-reviews/javier-zamora/solito-zamora/. Accessed 23 Jan. 2023.

Review of *Solito*, by Javier Zamora. *Publishers Weekly*, 9 May 2022, www.publishersweekly.com/9780593498064. Accessed 23 Jan. 2023.

Roberts, Steven. "A Migrant Child's Long Journey to Gringolandia." Review of *Solito*, by Javier Zamora. *The Washington Post*, 22 Sept. 2022, www.washingtonpost.com/books/2022/09/22/migrant-childs-long-journey-gringolandia/. Accessed 23 Jan. 2023.

Villavicencio, Karla Cornejo. "The Harrowing Migration Story of One 9-Year-old Child." Review of *Solito*, by Javier Zamora. *The New York Times*, 8 Sept. 2022, www.nytimes.com/2022/09/08/books/review/solito-javier-zamora.html. Accessed 23 Jan. 2023.

The Song of the Cell
An Exploration of Medicine and the New Human

Author: Siddhartha Mukherjee (b. 1970)
Publisher: Scribner (New York). 496 pp.
Type of work: History of science, medicine, science
Time: 1600s–the present day
Locales: North America, Europe, Asia

The Song of the Cell, by Pulitzer Prize-winner Siddhartha Mukherjee, explores the past, present, and future of cellular biology and its implications for one day eradicating cancer and other diseases.

Principal personages

RUDOLF VIRCHOW, a German physician-scientist who pioneered modern cellular biology
EMILY WHITEHEAD, the first person to have their T cells successfully weaponized against cancer
LOUISE BROWN, the first person to be born from the in-vitro fertilization (IVF) process
ANTONIE VAN LEEUWENHOEK, a Dutch cloth merchant who identified cells as animalcules
ROBERT HOOKE, an English polymath also credited with discovering cells
SAM P., Mukherjee's friend, a sports journalist who died from melanoma

Over the course of his career, author and physician Siddhartha Mukherjee has been many things. In addition to being an oncologist who specializes in hematology and immunology, he worked as a cancer researcher, a professor at Columbia University, the founder of several biotech companies, and a jazz musician. As a public figure, he developed a reputation as one of the most important voices on the state of medicine and disease in the twenty-first century through both the brilliance of his work as a physician and scientist and his expertise as a writer.

The Indian American doctor first became a literary sensation with *The Emperor of All Maladies: A Biography of Cancer* (2010). Written in the style of a thriller, the book chronicles the evolution of cancer treatment throughout human history. This work came to define Mukherjee as a science writer, both as one worthy of the Pulitzer Prize, which was awarded to him in 2011, and as one who understood how to blend fact, narrative, and memoir to make esoteric topics more accessible. This authorial tendency resurfaced in Mukherjee's 2016 New York Times Best Seller, *The Gene: An Intimate*

Siddhartha Mukherjee (Courtesy Scribner)

History, which sought to decipher the "code of life." Indeed, Mukherjee's distinctive approach to science writing is also apparent in his 2022 work, *The Song of the Cell: An Exploration of Medicine and the New Human.*

Continuing Mukherjee's tradition of creating primers on the world's smallest yet most powerful biological forces, *The Song of the Cell* takes a comprehensive look at cellular science and its implications for modern medicine. It is a fascinating read that puts every facet of Mukherjee's polymathic resume to use, particularly his experience as a professor. Like his previous books, *The Song of the Cell* seeks to provide readers with a foundational understanding of a scientific topic that could otherwise be intimidating. It succeeds in this goal, largely thanks to Mukherjee's impressive ability to relay complex information to others without ever dumbing it down.

Meanwhile, the book's organization has the feeling of a well-developed syllabus in that its chapters steadily build upon one another, which ensures that readers are equipped with the knowledge necessary to understand what comes next. Although the book is not fully chronological like *The Emperor of All Maladies*, it borrows aspects of this narrative framework. Specifically, Mukherjee breaks the book down into different sections, each of which revolve primarily around its own mini-chronology. In other words, he explains each chapter's topic by recounting how specific scientific breakthroughs in history contributed to contemporary understanding of that topic. This approach allows readers' knowledge of the cell to evolve alongside the knowledge of the scientists whose discoveries are being recounted on the page.

Although *The Song of the Cell* is quite dense in the amount of information that Mukherjee includes on every page, its scope of topics remains reasonable. Throughout the book, readers are sent on a journey that begins with seventeenth-century figures such as Dutch cloth merchant Antonie van Leeuwenhoek and English scholar Robert Hooke, who were among the first to ever see individual cells up close under the lenses of their primitive microscopes. Mukherjee progresses through the centuries to a number of other individuals, including Rudolf Virchow, a nineteenth-century pioneer of cellular biology, who built upon their predecessors' understandings of what the cell was to identify its role in disease. The book also tackles biological concepts, including cell anatomy, how cells enable physiological processes like immunity and reproduction, and what happens when cells malfunction. While these scientific overviews are heavy on information, Mukherjee's descriptions of them ultimately read more like an examination of the fundamentals anchored by a handful of themes.

Chief among these themes is the powerful idea that in order to understand life, one must first understand how its "simplest unit" works. Here, the word "simplest" almost feels like a misnomer because although the cell is the fundamental building block of life, it is by no means simple. As Mukherjee demonstrates repeatedly throughout *The Song of the Cell*, even during the first decades of the twenty-first century, scientists still did not understand major aspects of cellular biology. Such gaps in cellular knowledge become painfully clear in the book's section on the COVID-19 pandemic—a viral event that killed millions of people in the early 2020s for immunological reasons that the medical community did not have the cellular knowledge to stop. Drawing on the earlier writings of Virchow, Mukherjee argues that human beings are "citizenships of cells" or the sum of their cellular parts. Until scientists understand "the song of the cell," or how cells signal each other to coordinate their interconnected actions that together sustain human life, it will be impossible to eradicate illness.

The fact that Mukherjee is quick to point out how much more there is to learn about cellular biology to advance the state of medicine might make *The Song of the Cell* sound discouraging. However, the author's approach is better described as evenhanded; as much as Mukherjee discusses scientific failures, setbacks, and the challenges of treating disease, he pays just as much attention to the many incredible scientific breakthroughs that promise a better future in human health. For example, after concluding a story about his friend Sam P., who died of melanoma despite getting the most advanced form of cancer treatments, Mukherjee relays how one of his postdoctoral students had begun using cells genetically altered with jellyfish proteins to build new cartilage in joints—a glimmer of hope in the quest to cure arthritis. Glimmers of hope might not seem like much, but thanks to the future-focused perspective that Mukherjee has forged both as a researcher and biotech entrepreneur, their power still resonates.

The many scientific breakthroughs described throughout *The Song of the Cell* serve the narrative in other important ways. For one, these stories make for an engaging read. For example, it is fascinating to learn about how the treatment for diabetes came from the findings of scientists who, in 1922, extracted insulin from a dead dog's pancreas. Additionally, these stories of scientific breakthroughs help illustrate whatever cellular function Mukherjee is explaining. For instance, the role that T cells play in the human body and cancer becomes clear when Mukherjee relays the story of Emily Whitehead, who as a child became the first patient to have her T cells extracted, genetically modified, and weaponized against the leukemia that was killing her. Similarly, the story of how in-vitro fertilization (IVF) was developed and used to create the world's first "test tube baby," Louise Joy Brown, in 1978, enhances Mukherjee's explanation of cellular reproduction.

Storytelling is ultimately a large part of what makes *The Song of the Cell* work on multiple levels. As a science writer, Mukherjee understands that in order for readers to grasp complex information, he must package it in an emotionally charged narrative focused on real people. As such, he populates the book with anecdotes about his experiences as a doctor and researcher. Mukherjee recounts the patients whose cases still haunt him; these cases help personalize different diseases to communicate the urgency of finding cures for such "cellular catastrophes" and dysfunction. Additionally, Mukherjee's moments of wonder, such as the first time he ever saw a cell through a microscope, are contagious. His respect for some of the figures he describes, such as Virchow, as both scientists and people also shines through.

Upon its release in 2022, many critics lauded *The Song of the Cell* as one of the year's most notable books. A reviewer for *Kirkus* called the book "a luminous journey into cellular biology." Many critics highlighted the quality of Mukherjee's prose, which they felt helped the author transform potentially dry topics into nearly poetic descriptions. In her review for the *Washington Post*, Siri Hustvedt touched on how the book's resonant prose successfully brought complex topics into focus, and singled out the author's "lucid sentences dense with metaphors as pedagogical tools." Hustvedt alluded to how the confluence of Mukherjee's many identities as a scientist, teacher, and writer came together in an enjoyable, harmonious way, evident from his playful metaphors: "the cell as 'spacecraft;' the cell's nucleus as 'command center;' . . . and MHC class 1 molecules on a cell's surface as 'two open halves of a hotdog bun.'"

However, not all reviews had unilateral praise for *The Song of the Cell*. In her review for the *New York Times*, Jennifer Szalai complimented the book's "cellular" organization, but noted how "the overall effect can feel sprawling—like a city that allowed developers to keep building lovely houses while doing little to contain them." Szalai's description of the book as "sprawling" feels valid—at times, keeping up with the incredible expanse and speed of Mukherjee's mind as he constantly pivots to make connections between everything from different historical events, pathologies, functions, people, and cultures can be overwhelming and dilute the clarity of the lessons that he aims to teach. Still, readers who are willing to relax and tag along with Mukherjee's constantly evolving thought process will likely find themselves on an entertaining ride. Indeed, at the end of the day, *The Song of the Cell* is not so much a textbook as it is a work of extremely literary nonfiction.

In this way, *The Song of the Cell* lives up to the standards Mukherjee set for himself with his previous books—something that a critic for *Publishers Weekly* concluded in their review, which described the work as "another winner from Mukherjee." While readers looking for a book similar to the thriller style of *The Emperor of All Maladies* might be disappointed, *The Song of the Cell* does exactly what it sets out to do by providing an entertaining, educational look at cellular biology and its importance given that all disease is cellular dysfunction. Readers will come away with an understanding of the science's history, its current state, and what its future might hold for human health. In the process, they will gain a new understanding of the nature of scientific discovery and how breakthroughs are born from countless failures. For those who are hopeful for cures to various illnesses, Mukherjee comforts them with reminders of the importance of patience and resilience.

Author Biography

Siddhartha Mukherjee, PhD is a cancer physician, researcher, writer, and entrepreneur. A former Rhodes scholar, he is the author of a number of books, including the Pulitzer Prize-winning *The Emperor of All Maladies: A Biography of Cancer* (2010) and *The Gene: An Intimate History* (2016).

Emily E. Turner

Review Sources

Hustvedt, Siri. "Siddhartha Mukherjee Considers the Cell, and the Future of Humans." Review of *The Song of the Cell: An Exploration of Medicine and the New Human*, by Siddhartha Mukherjee. *The Washington Post*, 24 Oct. 2022, www.washingtonpost.com/books/2022/10/24/siddhartha-mukherjee-cell-book-review/. Accessed 12 Feb. 2023.

Review of *The Song of the Cell: An Exploration of Medicine and the New Human*, by Siddhartha Mukherjee. *Kirkus Reviews*, 25 June 2022, www.kirkusreviews.com/book-reviews/siddhartha-mukherjee/the-song-of-the-cell/. Accessed 12 Feb. 2023.

Review of *The Song of the Cell: An Exploration of Medicine and the New Human*, by Siddhartha Mukherjee. *Publishers Weekly*, 9 Aug. 2022, www.publishersweekly.com/9781982117351. Accessed 12 Feb. 2023.

Szalai, Jennifer. "Siddhartha Mukherjee Finds Medical Mystery—and Metaphor—in the Tiny Cell." Review of *The Song of the Cell: An Exploration of Medicine and the New Human*, by Siddhartha Mukherjee. *The New York Times*, 24 Oct. 2022, www.nytimes.com/2022/10/24/books/review/the-song-of-the-cell-siddhartha-mukherjee.html. Accessed 12 Feb. 2023.

South to America
A Journey below the Mason-Dixon to Understand the Soul of a Nation

Author: Imani Perry (b. 1972)
Publisher: Ecco (New York). 432 pp.
Type of work: History, memoir, travel
Time: Seventeenth century–the present
Locale: American South

Imani Perry's National Book Award–winning work South to America: A Journey below the Mason-Dixon to Understand the Soul of a Nation, *combines cultural criticism, travelogue, and memoir to present a sociopolitical history of the Southern United States.*

Principal personages
SHIELDS GREEN, the "Emperor of New York," a Black man who was executed in 1859 after helping lead John Brown's raid on Harper's Ferry
ZORA NEALE HURSTON, author and anthropologist who wrote several travelogues and cultural histories of Black life in the American South and Caribbean
GEORGE FLOYD, security guard and former rapper whose murder inspired a global racial justice movement in 2020

In the introduction to her sprawling 2022 nonfiction work *South to America: A Journey below the Mason-Dixon to Understand the Soul of a Nation*, award-winning author and historian Imani Perry describes the French quadrille, an intricate dance for four couples that was brought to New Orleans, Louisiana, in the nineteenth century. For Perry, the dance is a metaphor. "At certain moments, all dancers take the same steps. Other times they pivot and turn against each other," she writes. "Train your eyes on *one* duo," she advises. "You'll get lost if you try to look everywhere at once." In this context, the history of the American South is not a straightforward series of events but rather a complex, ever-shifting association of people, places, and cultures. For example, Louisiana was shaped by its former French rulers, just as Florida was shaped by Spanish colonialism, the legacy of slavery, and generations of immigration from the Caribbean, Latin America, and other parts of the world. Both states are also part of the larger cultural web of the South, the quadrille itself. It is best to keep the quadrille in mind when reading Perry's book, an impressionistic cultural history and travelogue that examines regions as culturally far-flung as Harper's Ferry, West Virginia, and Havana, Cuba.

Perry, who was born to activist parents in Birmingham, Alabama, uses examples such as these to emphasize the diversity and cultural depth of the American South, a

Imani Perry
Courtesy HarperCollins Publishers

region often dismissed or blamed for the original sins of the United States, namely the nation's White supremacy and racism. Perry, who travels from Maryland and West Virginia to Cuba and the Caribbean over the course of the book, makes a case that the soul of the US, for good and ill, resides in the South. "Paying attention to the South," she writes, "allows us to understand much more about our nation, and about how our people, land, and commerce work in relation to one another, often cruelly, and about how our tastes and ways flow from our habits."

South to America won the National Book Award for Nonfiction in 2022, Perry's most prestigious accolade up to that point in her career. Perry, who has also worked as a professor of African American studies at Princeton University, has long explored issues of race, history, and American culture in her work. For example, her book *Looking for Lorraine* (2018) focuses on the radical, queer Black playwright Lorraine Hansberry, who is best known for her 1959 play *A Raisin in the Sun*. Perry has also written about the Black National Anthem, the poetics of hip hop, and racial justice activism. Her view of the South is rooted in her own upbringing, as well as her deep engagement with Black arts and cultural history, past and present. Her thesis for *South to America* is clear. "Race is at the heart of the South," Perry writes, "and at the heart of the nation."

The book's broad scope can be overwhelming; Perry touches on hundreds of figures and institutions, and only a scant handful of them reappear. She does this knowingly, stalwart in her refusal to make a singular point about the "soul of a nation" she references in the title. This is not a definitive history, she writes. It is a "collection" of stories, memories, and observations, as well as "an excision, a pruning like we might do to a plant in order to extend its life." As this surprising and poetic analogy suggests, the rewards of *South to America* are in the details; in the lyricism of a dance that can evoke feeling even when it cannot be completely understood. In the book's epigraph, Perry offers a quote from the legendary Black choreographer Alvin Ailey: "The dance speaks to everyone. Otherwise it wouldn't work."

Perry's inspiration to write *South to America* came from Albert Murray's 1971 travelogue and memoir *South to a Very Old Place*. Murray, an essayist and novelist who died in 2013, was a contemporary of mid-century Black luminaries such as James Baldwin, Richard Wright, and Ralph Ellison—all of whom receive attention in *South to America*. Indeed, "Murray hovers all over Perry's volume," Carlos Lozado wrote in his review of Perry's work for the *Washington Post*, in ways both explicit and implicit. Murray was also from the South—he grew up in Mobile, Alabama, in the 1920s—and his book sought to place his own story within the larger cultural history of the South. However, Perry utilizes a more potent political lens. To outsiders, the South has become a "projection" of the country's "national sins," Perry argues, but in her view, this is "a mis-narration of American history and identity." In her review of *South to America* for the *New York Times*, award-winning novelist Tayari Jones felt the book's central thesis "[was] that race and racism are fundamental values of the South, that 'the creation of racial slavery in the colonies was a gateway to habits and dispositions that ultimately became the commonplace ways of doing things in this country.'" Jones went on to highlight how the book makes it impossible to ignore the history of the South as an "embarrassing relative" of the rest of the US, as "the South is America."

In traveling around the South for her book, Perry writes that she was "impious" in her movements. "I passed over many famous places and lingered in unusual ones," she says. One famous place in which she did linger, though, was her own hometown of Birmingham. In their professional careers, Perry's mother was a scholar and her father was an epidemiologist, but both were heavily involved in the social justice movements of the 1960s and 1970s. Fittingly, a visit from Angela Davis, the celebrated Black activist and Marxist scholar, provides the Birmingham chapter with its frame. Davis also grew up in Birmingham and knew the young girls who were killed in the bombing of the city's 16th Street Baptist Church in 1963. Birmingham, Perry writes, has become synonymous with such sites of Civil Rights–era violence, but to see the city in this context alone offers an impoverished view of a much more meaningful and complex place. For Perry, Birmingham is "more than a memorial," it is "home."

The Birmingham chapter combines Perry's own memories with historical asides, offering a taste of the book at its best. Perry writes about her grandmother, a former domestic and hospital caregiver who gave birth to twelve children and raised thirteen. Her grandmother, with love and labor, helped keep Birmingham alive, just as its first Black mayor, Richard Arrington, did from 1979 to 1999 after the collapse of the coal and steel mining industry and ensuing White flight. Perry attempts to show how the ordinary nature of their contributions in the face of oppression and adversity informed the radicalism embodied by more famous figures like Davis and imprisoned activist Richard Mafundi Lake. These people saw activism not merely as a social good but as a necessity for survival. Their work informed and was informed by revolutionaries in African nations and elsewhere around the world. "My point is that some, in the plantation South, saw the struggle not as one about inclusion in the American project," Perry writes. "They saw it as the unfinished revolution against the age of empire." Perry continues to trace the threads of empire further south, stopping in Havana and the Bahamas. These places are an intriguing and welcome inclusion, as is, to the North, her attention on West Virginia and Maryland, where both Harriet Tubman and Frederick Douglass were enslaved before escaping enslavement and becoming major figures of the abolitionist movement.

South to America generally received positive reviews, though critics expressed some frustration with the book's meandering structure. A reviewer for *Publishers Weekly* praised the book as a "rich and imaginative tour of a critical piece of America" while conceding that Perry often sacrificed "depth" for "breadth." Meanwhile, in a starred review for *Kirkus*, another reviewer described the book as a "graceful, finely crafted examination of America's racial, cultural, and political identity." A critic who reviewed the work for the *New Yorker* noted the importance of Perry's own appearances in the book, such as her descriptions of meeting strangers and an anecdote about running out of money in Cuba—a misfortune that offered Perry the opportunity to meet an unnamed American dissident just before her death. The *New Yorker* critic quoted Perry with appreciation, writing, "Perry admits to 'a bit of navel-gazing' but observes that, 'if you gaze anywhere with a critical eye, you do have to look at your own belly, too.'"

Author Biography

Imani Perry is an award-winning author and professor. Her publications include *Prophets of the Hood* (2004), *More Beautiful and More Terrible* (2011), *Looking for Lorraine* (2018), *May We Forever Stand* (2018), and *Breathe: A Letter to My Sons* (2019). Her 2022 nonfiction work *South to America* won the National Book Award for Nonfiction.

Molly Hagan

Review Sources

"Briefly Noted." Review of *South to America: A Journey below the Mason-Dixon to Understand the Soul of a Nation*, by Imani Perry, et al. *The New Yorker*, 24 Jan. 2022, www.newyorker.com/magazine/2022/01/31/south-to-america-the-uninnocent-the-stars-are-not-yet-bells-and-the-swank-hotel. Accessed 30 Nov. 2022.

Jones, Tayari. "Search for America, South of the Mason-Dixon." Review of *South to America: A Journey below the Mason-Dixon to Understand the Soul of a Nation*, by Imani Perry. *The New York Times*, 25 Jan. 2022, www.nytimes.com/2022/01/25/books/review/south-to-america-imani-perry.html. Accessed 30 Nov. 2022.

Lozado, Carlos. "An 'Exile' from the American South Finds the Nation's Soul There." Review of *South to America: A Journey below the Mason-Dixon to Understand the Soul of a Nation*, by Imani Perry. *The Washington Post*, 20 Jan. 2022, www.washingtonpost.com/outlook/2022/01/20/imani-perry-review/. Accessed 30 Nov. 2022.

Review of *South to America: A Journey below the Mason-Dixon to Understand the Soul of a Nation*, by Imani Perry. *Kirkus*, 25 Jan. 2022, www.kirkusreviews.com/book-reviews/imani-perry/south-to-america/. Accessed 30 Nov. 2022.

Review of *South to America: A Journey below the Mason-Dixon to Understand the Soul of a Nation*, by Imani Perry. *Publishers Weekly*, 5 Oct. 2021, www.publishersweekly.com/9780062977403. Accessed 30 Nov. 2022.

The Stardust Thief

Author: Chelsea Abdullah
Publisher: Orbit (New York). 480 pp.
Type of work: Novel
Time: Indefinite time in the past
Locale: Desert kingdom near the Sandsea

Loulie al-Nazari is the Midnight Merchant, known as a dealer in magical relics which she tracks with her mysterious bodyguard, Qadir. After a brief meeting with the Sultan's youngest son, she is coerced into chasing after a legendary lamp containing one of the last of the jinn kings. The ensuing journey is filled with mystery, adventure, and tragedy.

Principal characters
LOULIE AL-NAZARI, the Midnight Merchant
QADIR, her bodyguard, a jinn
PRINCE MAZEN BIN MALIK, the Sultan's youngest son
PRINCE OMAR BIN MALIK, the Sultan's oldest son, leader of the forty thieves
AISHA BINT LOUAS, one of Omar's forty thieves
AHMED BIN WALID, the Sultan-appointed guardian of the city of Dhyme

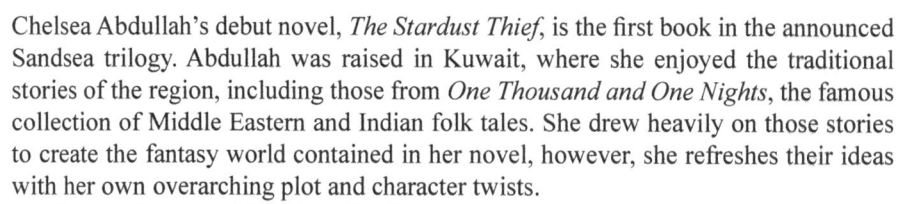

Chelsea Abdullah's debut novel, *The Stardust Thief*, is the first book in the announced Sandsea trilogy. Abdullah was raised in Kuwait, where she enjoyed the traditional stories of the region, including those from *One Thousand and One Nights*, the famous collection of Middle Eastern and Indian folk tales. She drew heavily on those stories to create the fantasy world contained in her novel, however, she refreshes their ideas with her own overarching plot and character twists.

The novel opens with "The Tale of the Jinn," a story that provides an introduction to one of the main conflicts of the novel. This tale explains that a jinn—a magical, shape-shifting spirit common in Arabic culture—had been blessed with magic by the gods in exchange for the commission to take care of the earth. However, after a time, seven jinn kings became discontented and, in a quest for more power, devastated the earth with wind and fire. This destruction left the world covered in sand, and the gods punished the jinn, leading to the disappearance of the magical creatures and opening the door for the creation of humans, non-magical beings who would not question the gods. Now, when the silver blood of the jinn is spilled, nature blooms again. The chapter, which had been narrated to Loulie by her mother, draws to a close with a caution that Loulie remember that "not all jinn are evil." This warning foreshadows a conflict that will ask Loulie to question what she had been taught and to test her mother's lesson.

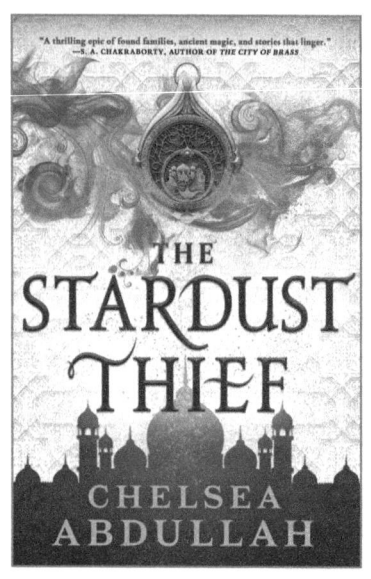

Chelsea Abdullah

After that prologue story, the novel continues with seventy chapters, alternately narrated around Loulie, Mazen, and Aisha. Loulie is the renowned Midnight Merchant, the finder of lost relics. She and her shapeshifting, jinn bodyguard, Qadir, travel the world recovering jinn treasures and selling them to the highest bidder. Prince Mazen is the youngest son of the Sultan. Mazen is so sheltered that he must sneak out of the palace by bribing guards. The artistic young man yearns for the company of others and for the stories told in the souk (marketplace) of the city of Madinne. Aisha is one of the famed forty thieves, led by Mazen's oldest brother, Omar, a cruel and selfish man who hunts jinn, killing them for the Sultan. Loulie's thirty-two chapters establish her as the main character; Mazen, dubbed the "cowardly prince" in Abdullah's description of the story, is the focus of twenty-seven chapters; Aisha, follower of Omar, claims the center spot for nine chapters. Interspersed between the chapters are tales, like the opening one, that establish the legends behind the surrounding events. These share the stories of "Amir and the Lamp," "the Queen of the Dunes," and "Shafia."

Loulie, Qadir, Mazen, and Aisha are brought together when they are sent on a quest by the Sultan. His desire for a jinn relic, a lamp which holds a jinn king, has been an obsession. Though he has sent many to search for the treasure, none have survived the Sandsea, where the lamp is rumored to have been hidden. The Midnight Merchant's arrival in the capital city gives him a reason to send yet one more person to locate the treasure, and since Loulie has sold magical items despite a ban on them, she has no choice but to take on the task. Qadir, of course, will not leave her side, so he travels with her. The Sultan orders Omar to go to protect the Sultan's interest. Omar himself does not go, however. He instead forces his youngest brother to go in his place. Mazen, desirous of adventure, allows himself to be coerced into wearing a bangle that makes him appear as Omar, while Omar wears its twin, appearing as Mazen at home in Madinne. In addition, Omar orders Aisha to join the quest to protect his interests.

The quest leads the four characters on a trip across the desert to find the dangerous Sandsea, under which the jinn kingdom had, according to legend, sunk. Along the way, they run into danger, confront dangerous jinn, fight for their lives, and struggle with their own pasts as Loulie, Mazen, and Aisha have all survived tragic situations which have been influential in the development of their own personalities. Plagued by injuries, loss of faith, and murder, the three strive to succeed in a journey that holds a different boon for each.

The stories that interrupt the narrative draw attention to the importance of storytelling itself. Influenced by *One Thousand and One Nights*, Abdullah plays with tropes most readers will at least recognize. "Amir and the Lamp" is reminiscent of "Aladdin's

Lamp," but that similarity is largely superficial. Prince Omar's forty thieves will remind readers of "Ali Baba and the Forty Thieves." Again, the author does not directly copy the plot of the original story, twisting it to fit her story, but the competition and betrayal of the brothers in the original can be identified in *The Stardust Thief*.

Within the novel, the theme of storytelling is significant to establishing several of the characters. For Mazen, the act of storytelling allows an escape from the sheltered life forced upon him by his father and brings memories of his mother, who was famous for her tales. Loulie also enjoys the escape provided by the stories. Both are influenced by the stories of Old Rhuba, an old man who draws audiences from near and far to hear his tales. Qadir also holds a wealth of stories, which are shared only when necessary. Eventually, however, Mazen and Loulie both question not only their own identities but their relationships with others when they discover that the legends they had been told as fiction were actually true history.

The truth behind the stories is just one of the secrets that are kept in the novel. Most of the characters' relationships are based on secrets, lies, and betrayals. All three of the major characters are drawn into plots that undermine their understanding of their own identities as those secrets come to light. Prince Mazen, for instance, is pulled into the adventure when he bargains with his older brother, Omar, who has found him sneaking out of the castle. Omar promises to keep Mazen's secret from their father if Mazen offers a boon of Omar's choosing; Omar sends Mazen on the quest in his place. Loulie lives in secret, identifying as the innocent Layla when she does not want to be recognized as the Midnight Merchant. Her past and her relationship with Qadir are based on lies. Furthermore, Aisha, one of Omar's thieves, finds herself beginning to question the lies and betrayal of a man she had trusted, as her cover story for the real reason she is sent on the quest starts to fall apart.

Another significant thematic idea in *The Stardust Thief* is family. Loulie comes from a tribe that was senselessly slaughtered when she was a child. Her mother had hidden the child, who was found by a mysterious stranger, Qadir. The stranger took custody of the young Loulie, raising her as if she were his own. Mazen has also lost a parent. When he was a child, he found his mother, the Sultan's third wife, murdered in her own bed. Mazen's surviving family includes his father, the Sultan, a man who is known for the murder of a series of wives; a stepbrother, Hakim; and a half-brother, Omar. Though Mazen thinks his father's rules are confining and unnecessary, the Sultan proves to love his youngest son above his siblings. Aisha also carries a heartbreaking family past filled with senseless murder. This connection allows the three to bond despite their differences, and they all discover that a found family is just as important as one into which a person is born.

Magic is another necessary element in the novel. Centered around the jinn, magic makes life both easier and harder for the characters. Helpful magic includes a coin that helps Loulie identify whether someone is telling the truth or a falsehood, and a compass that leads her to the treasures she seeks. Qadir, himself, is magical too. His shapeshifting ability, mostly from man to lizard, allows him to discover secrets of others. Mazen's bangle is the most visible of the magics for this character, but he also has a shadow magic that allows him to become invisible. Aisha, too, becomes magical after almost dying in a battle. Magic is the basis for several plot twists as well, such as when Loulie, Mazen, and Aisha are confronted with the betrayals of people they had trusted. The jinn themselves are the basis of all the magic.

The reviews of *The Stardust Thief* largely followed the opinion of the *New York Times* reviewer Amal El-Mohtar, who called Abdullah's first book "a gorgeous fantasy." She expanded further, stating, "I was especially impressed by her dexterous weaving of contemporary Arabic's cadences and vocabulary into her narration and dialogue." Other reviewers also lauded the novel's world-building as well as the writing. Judith Utz, in a review for *Booklist*, claimed, "Abdullah is a gifted storyteller, weaving together three disparate points of view in order to bring to life a rich world, rife with magic." In addition, Neal Wyatt, writing for *Library Journal*, layered onto the praise of the author's world-building, saying "Abdullah transports readers into this rich world and literary heritage by crafting characters with deep backstories; maintaining an engrossing pace; and, most impressively, layering details into the story so deftly that the veil between magic and reality slips and bends delightfully." While much of the reviews were positive, several reviews gave less positive criticism on the pacing of the novel, especially when "multiple revelations tumble over one another during a climactic battle that ends up feeling both rushed and too slow," as explained by El-Mohtar. In addition, *Kirkus Reviews* critiqued the "obvious" aspects of Omar's role in the story. Despite such comments, however, the *Kirkus* writer concluded that *The Stardust Thief* was a "marvelous plunge into a beautifully crafted adventure." Utz agreed, exclaiming it as "a beautifully crafted novel."

Author Biography

Kuwaiti American author Chelsea Abdullah has an MA in English from Duquesne University. *The Stardust Thief*, the first in The Sandsea Trilogy, is her debut novel. The second book, *The Ashfire King*, was announced in 2022.

Theresa L. Stowell, PhD

Review Sources

El-Mohtar, Amal. "Storytelling Can Be a Dangerous Game in These New Novels." *The New York Times*, 27 May 2022, www.nytimes.com/2022/05/27/books/review/new-science-fiction-fantasy.html. Accessed 6 Feb. 2023.

Review of *The Stardust Thief*, by Chelsea Abdullah. *Kirkus Reviews*, 16 Mar. 2022, www.kirkusreviews.com/book-reviews/chelsea-abdullah/the-stardust-thief-volume-1-the-sandsea-trilogy-1/. Accessed 6 Feb. 2023.

Utz, Judith. Review of *The Stardust Thief*, by Chelsea Abdullah. *Booklist*, vol. 118, no. 15, Apr. 2022, p. 28. *Literary Reference Center Plus*, search.ebscohost.com/login.aspx?direct=true&db=lkh&AN=156069055&site=lrc-plus. Accessed 6 Feb. 2023.

Wyatt, Neal. Review of *The Stardust Thief*, by Chelsea Abdulla. *Library Journal*, vol. 147, no. 5, May 2022, p. 75. *Literary Reference Center Plus*, search.ebscohost.com/login.aspx?direct=true&db=lkh&AN=156688772&site=lrc-plus. Accessed 10 Feb. 2023.

Stay True

Author: Hua Hsu (b. 1977)
Publisher: Doubleday (New York). 208 pp.
Type of work: Memoir
Time: 1980s–early 2000s
Locales: Cupertino, Berkeley, and San Diego, California; Taiwan

In his debut memoir, Stay True, *Hua Hsu recounts the unlikely friendship he struck up with Ken, a gregarious, confident young man who seemed his polar opposite, while they were attending the University of California, Berkeley, in 1990s California. When tragedy struck, Hsu turned to writing to excavate his grief.*

Principal personages

HUA HSU, the author, a son of Taiwanese immigrants who became a writer working for the *New Yorker*
KEN, a charismatic Japanese American whom he met at Berkeley; a frat boy who exuded confidence
PARAAG, his freshman-year roommate and friend from high school
DAVE, another of his freshman-year roommates and friend from high school
GWEN, a girl who was part of a larger friend group at Berkeley
MIRA, his girlfriend his junior year
ANTHONY, his roommate after he moved off campus his sophomore year; also part of a larger friend circle

Hua Hsu, a writer for the *New Yorker*, has been haunted by the loss of his close friend Ken since he was in college in the 1990s, when Ken was killed in a carjacking that turned deadly. Hsu first began to take notes on his thoughts and feelings following the tragic event ahead of his senior year at the University of California's Berkeley campus. The author had long planned to put these musings and reflections to use in a memoir that would eulogize his lost friend while also capturing the culture of 1990s Berkeley, turning focus to the politics, music, art, literature, and zine culture that permeated his life as well as the lives of his close-knit group of friends. To Hsu, and so many others, those four years spent as an undergraduate meant more than learning a set of skills or obtaining a degree to carry one into the first years of a career. Rather, college was a time for a person to consider who they wanted to be in the larger world, to take stock of values and interests, and to learn from those who were doing the same around them. Thus, *Stay True* (2022), the title taken from an inside joke between Hsu and Ken that

Hua Hsu

neither could ultimately remember the origin of, is a chronicle of Ken's untimely death but also a time capsule rich with historical details that place the reader front and center in California's 1990s youth culture.

Stay True begins with Hsu reminiscing about the long drives he and Ken—whom Hsu hated when they first met—would take during college, whether that be a drive into San Francisco for a quick meal, an overnight road trip, or a late-night meander where the two would listen to music and talk. Music, Hsu subtly but effectively wants the reader to know, is at the heart of his connection to others, and his friendship with Ken seemed rather unlikely because of this. While Hsu was into independent rock like Pavement, Ken's taste was more mainstream, leading him toward bands like Pearl Jam and Dave Matthews Band. Hsu recalls the careful mixes he put together for these drives, when other friends like Sammi and Paraag joined them, Hsu testing the sophistication of his friends all along. But he reminds the reader that this was all a part of youth, part of growing up: testing one's taste against those whom they deemed their closest companions. And it is through this focus on authenticity that Hsu later has to question how his sense of it compared to Ken's after all.

Before fully diving into his story of youthful focus and unexpected violence, though, Hsu wants the reader to know who he is and where he comes from. Born in Illinois, Hsu and his family moved around the US, with stops in Texas and other places, before settling into Cupertino, California, when he was nine. It was in Cupertino that Hsu began to develop his identity, noticing the records his father bought and played obsessively in their house and listening to his parents' stories about their early days in the United States as newly immigrated students. Then his father left for Taiwan, where he could work more authentically at an executive level. Father and son conversed via a fax machine, with Hsu offering up many of their conversations to the reader in poignant snippets that show his father trying to parent from afar, doing his best to be a moral guide in his young son's life. Hsu demonstrates a relationship between a son and parents that was supportive, without the pressures felt by many young people. He began to be interested in music, like his father, at a young age, scouring record store bins and hoping to be the first to discover a band—the most prominent case of which was Nirvana. Further, Hsu tells the reader about his love of thrifting clothes and making zines, all in an attempt to connect with other like-minded young people in the pre-internet days of teen culture. Hsu's details about growing up as a teenager in 1990s California are carefully put together to create a world from which the author can launch into his college years effectively and believably.

Stay True is told loosely in two sections (though the book is not formally broken up that way): before and after Ken. When Hsu arrived at Berkeley, he is careful to remind the reader, he was still into undiscovered bands and his taste in culture was, he believed, more sophisticated and more authentic than those around him. This attitude comes across effectively in his narration, allowing him the hubris of an eighteen-year-old while he reflects from his adulthood. Hsu describes the cramped triple he and his high school friends Paraag and Dave shared; the types of parties they went to, despite the fact that Hsu was, initially, against drinking and partaking in any other substances; and the classes he and his friends enrolled in. Most effective are Hsu's descriptions of late nights spent with friends—whether that involved hanging out with his friend Sammi, who helped him put together his zines from time to time, or infiltrating right-wing chatrooms on the early internet with his roommates. The shadowy closeness shared by those in college learning how to establish their identities is compellingly palpable through Hsu's writing. When he relates how he and Ken began to hang out one-on-one, the reader can comprehend their friendship as believable because of this effect. Hsu tells the reader that Ken was Japanese American and therefore part of a culture that other Asian Americans often aspire to, believing that there is an effortlessness to their assimilation into White culture. He also describes him as a preppy dresser—often clad in Nikes and Polo shirts with the collar popped up. He intimates that he judged Ken for his style, but the reader can sense an element of envy underneath it, too. Held against Ken and his ability to capture the attention of a room full of people or talk to women, Hsu's social floundering allows for a moment of important examination.

Though the memoir does an excellent job of capturing those heady college days, Hsu does struggle in successfully describing figures that resonate after Ken's death. Scenes from the funeral and Ken's parents' house feel important and well depicted, but the writing lacks the emotion one might expect around such a monumental moment. Despite this flaw, *Stay True* carries its message through to its last pages, showing, and perhaps reminding, the reader how everyone remains a work in progress.

Hsu's memoir was largely well received by critics as an ultimately affecting work, earning plaudits from outlets like the *New York Times*, the *Washington Post*, the *Wall Street Journal*, and the *San Francisco Chronicle*'s *Datebook*. A best-seller, the memoir was shortlisted for the National Book Critics Circle Award for Autobiography. For the *New York Review of Books*, Lucy Sante commented favorably on the vast reach of the book's subjects, writing, "A meditative essay on friendship weaves through Hua Hsu's memoir, which is also about youth, Asian identity, zines, time, education, California, mixtapes, and more." Noting the transportive power of the author's personal but relatable and thought-provoking narration for the *Brooklyn Rail*, Elizabeth Lothian wrote: "Hsu delicately captures the urgency and intimacy of adolescent friendships. Through his prose you are pulled back to your own coming-of-age years. Yes, you remember, you too were always eager for something to happen, hands deep in your pockets, trying to figure out where to go next." Using descriptors such as "wrenching" and "richly detailed," Marc Weingarten, writing for the *Wall Street Journal*, echoed this common critical sentiment, stating, "'Stay True' is a nuanced and beautiful evocation of young adulthood in all its sloppy, exuberant glory." While critics generally agreed that the book is a successful tribute to the power of friendship, Charles Arrowsmith, in a review for the *Washington Post*, added that Hsu writes with "devastating emotional precision, questioning the possibility of meaning in tragedy and the value of the stories we tell while attempting to find it."

Author Biography
A professor of literature at Bard College beginning in 2022, Hua Hsu taught at Vassar College and also serves as a staff writer for the *New Yorker*. His first book, *A Floating Chinaman: Fantasy and Failure across the Pacific*, was published in 2016, and his work has also been featured in outlets such as the *Atlantic* and the *Wire*.

Melynda Fuller

Review Sources
Arrowsmith, Charles. "Hua Hsu's 'Stay True' Questions the Meaning of a Senseless Tragedy." Review of *Stay True*, by Hua Hsu. *The Washington Post*, 4 Oct. 2022, www.washingtonpost.com/books/2022/10/04/stay-true-memoir-hua-hsu/. Accessed 21 Feb. 2023.
Lothian, Elizabeth. Review of *Stay True*, by Hua Hsu. *The Brooklyn Rail*, Oct. 2022, brooklynrail.org/2022/10/books/Hua-Hsus-Stay-True-A-Memoir. Accessed 9 Feb. 2023.
Sante, Lucy. "Models for Being." Review of *Stay True*, by Hua Hsu. *The New York Review of Books*, 24 Nov. 2022, www.nybooks.com/articles/2022/11/24/models-for-being-stay-true-hua-hsu/. Accessed 9 Feb. 2023.
Sullivan, James. "Review: In Moving Memoir, New Yorker Writer Answers Loss with Wondrous Writing." Review of *Stay True*, by Hua Hsu. *Datebook*, 19 Sept. 2022, datebook.sfchronicle.com/books/review-in-moving-memoir-new-yorker-writer-answers-loss-with-wondrous-writing. Accessed 9 Feb. 2023.
Szalai, Jennifer. "A Formative Friendship Cut Short by Tragedy." Review of *Stay True*, by Hua Hsu. *The New York Times*, 25 Sept. 2022, www.nytimes.com/2022/09/25/books/review/stay-true-hua-hsu.html. Accessed 9 Feb. 2023.
Weingarten, Marc. "'Stay True' Review: Finding Themselves Together." Review of *Stay True*, by Hua Hsu. *The Wall Street Journal*, 7 Oct. 2022, www.wsj.com/articles/stay-true-book-review-memoir-finding-themselves-together-11665151100. Accessed 21 Feb. 2023.

Stories from the Tenants Downstairs

Author: Sidik Fofana
Publisher: Scribner (New York). pp. 224
Type of work: Short fiction
Time: Present day
Locale: Harlem, New York City

Stories from the Tenants Downstairs is a collection of interconnected short stories that explore gentrification, class struggle, and aspiration. It is the debut book from American author Sidik Fofana.

Principal characters

MIMI, a young mother trying to make rent
SWAN, the father of Mimi's child
VERONA DALLAS, a public school paraprofessional
MR. BRODERICK, a White teacher who went to Harvard University
DARIUS "DARY" KITE, a gay man and aspiring hairdresser
KANDESE BRISTOL-WALLACE, a teenage girl dealing with a personal tragedy
QUANNEISHA "NEISHA" MILES, a former gymnast trying to help the tenants at Banneker Terrace
KAY, a woman with whom Neisha has a complicated history

Stories from the Tenants Downstairs (2022), author Sidik Fofana's excellent debut, is a testament to his talent for capturing people from all walks of life—something he attributes to working as a New York City public school educator. "You're with the children of bus drivers and home health aides and landscapers and corrections officers," Fofana explained in an August 2022 *Literary Hub* interview with Jane Ciabattari. "And these are kids who are brilliant, just instinctively brilliant, who haven't fully developed a sense of inhibition and say the most wonderful revealing things about themselves."

Indeed, so much of what makes the eight stories of *Stories from the Tenants Downstairs* compelling is the realism that surrounds its characters as they grapple with the kind of everyday problems that are mundane yet still powerful enough to determine the fate of people's lives. Put more simply, this is a book about making rent and the challenge of keeping a roof over one's head in the United States. It proves to be a compelling theme, one that Fofana establishes through the book's setting of a low-income apartment building called Banneker Terrace in Harlem, which has recently been threatened by gentrification. A character in its own right, with dimly lit hallways and trash chutes that smell like rotten milk, Banneker Terrace embodies the losing side of class struggle.

Sidik Fofana

Because Fofana is a dexterous writer, his examination of class struggle is never heavy handed but rather carefully woven into the tapestry of each character's story. If there is any place where the theme feels more directly spelled out, it is in the book's first short story, "Rent Manual," which follows the tenant in apartment 14D, Mimi, as she scrapes together the $350 needed for her rent, dollar by dollar. Fofana ensures that all of his characters are never one-dimensional martyrs but people struggling against both systemic forces and their own personal shortcomings; Mimi is no exception to this rule. A single mother, she is unquestionably not paid enough as a waitress or self-employed hairdresser to survive, but she also has a tendency to spend her wages on luxury items that she cannot afford under the belief that each of these purchases will be her last irresponsible one. In turn, she owes five months of back rent and is facing eviction.

Most of the book's other characters are like Mimi in that they might have flaws, or difficult personalities, or engage in behavior that some consider immoral. Still, it is impossible not to root for these characters, thanks to Fofana's ability to create empathy for marginalized people simply by letting their humanity shine through. One of the most effective ways that he accomplishes this is by having every short story function as a portal into a different character's life. More specifically, Fofana gives each story a unique perspective, literary style, and language that aligns to the specific character it follows in order to transport readers into their worldview. Just as Mimi's story is written from a second-person point of view in the vernacular of a young Black American woman from Harlem, the story "lite feet" is written as a letter from the twelve-year-old Najee Bailey, whose misspellings reflect an underfunded education.

Fofana's decision to give each short story a completely different literary style also succeeds in communicating one of the book's most poignant messages—that poor and working-class people of color are not a monolith but are instead real human beings with individual hopes, dreams, challenges, and shortcomings. The story "Camaraderie," for example, is about Darius, or "Dary," from 12H—a gay man who is an obsessive fan of a popstar named Katrez and is being pressured by his friends into doing sex work. Meanwhile, "Tumble" follows Apt. 21J's Quanneisha B. Miles, who is grappling with complex feelings about her past as an "almost" Olympic gymnast as she volunteers to protect Banneker tenants from getting kicked out. There is also Swan in 6B, the father of Mimi's child, whose friend has just gotten out of jail, and Mr. Murray in 2E, who just wants to play chess with passersby. Fofana manages to bring all of these characters to life with such a sense of authenticity that it is difficult to imagine that they are not real people.

Often, Fofana's talent for authenticity ends up being heartbreaking, especially when it comes to the stories that are centered on children. One of the collection's most affecting narrative journeys follows a girl named Kandese Bristol-Wallace. First introduced as a background character who gets expelled from the middle school that the protagonist of another story works at, Kandese takes the spotlight in "The Young Entrepreneurs of Miss Bristol's Front Porch." In this story, Fofana challenges whatever readers might have believed about Kandese before to show a completely different side of her; he allows her resilience and creativity to shine through as she organizes a candy-selling business with her friends. The business becomes so successful that Kandese writes to a local television station with the hope that the business might get featured.

The way that Fofana has secondary and tertiary characters from one story become the protagonists in another, and vice versa, provides some amusing narrative Easter eggs. More than that, however, it amplifies the fact that these characters belong to a community. If there is one thing readers will walk away with about this community, it is that they all aspire for better lives. Just as Kandese dreams of being a successful entrepreneur celebrated on television, Mimi wants a house in the wealthy community of Westchester, while Darius has plans to open a salon that does not just nurture people's hair but their souls as well. The fact that these characters' dreams might come across as impossible to most readers is a testament to how successful Fofana is at capturing the enduring myth of the American Dream. It is a message most prominent in what is arguably one of the collection's finest stories, "Ms. Dallas," which centers on Verona Dallas, a Black paraprofessional whose job is to assist in a young, White, Harvard-educated teacher's classroom. At one point in the story, the teacher, Mr. Broderick, is trying to "help" his students by telling them that they are poor and must try to pull themselves up by their bootstraps. At first, readers will likely find the teacher's actions cringeworthy, but then it becomes disturbingly clear that Broderick, like many Americans, believes that anyone can make it in the US if they work hard enough. As Fofana's characters demonstrate through their futile efforts to push back against all the odds that are stacked against them, this is often not true.

Reception of *Stories from the Tenants Downstairs* was overwhelmingly positive upon its publication in 2022. Most critics praised the strength of Fofana's writing and the importance of his message. A reviewer for *Kirkus* called Fofana "a potentially significant voice in African American fiction" and praised how the collection "give[s] faces, voices, and meaning to lives otherwise neglected or marginalized." Meanwhile, other critics focused on how well Fofana's writing conveys each character's unique voice and worldview. Don J. Rath touched on this in his review for the *Southern Review of Books*, in which he wrote, "At the root of Fofana's robust characterization is his use of language." Indeed, most readers will discover that language is the beating heart of *Stories from the Tenants Downstairs* and that Fofana, a hip-hop aficionado who writes the book's introduction in rap verse, knows how to wield specific words, pacing, and rhythm to maximum effect.

Although much of the book's writing is poetic and even beautiful in its careful construction, the way that characters speak, think, and act could be uncomfortable to some readers. For example, throughout the book, several engage in illegal activities while others use the n-word and other profanities. Yet one of the primary reasons *Stories from the Tenants Downstairs* works so well is because Fofana does not shy away from harsh realities or try to make anything more palatable for readers who are outsiders to the world of Banneker Terrace. To this point, a critic for *Publishers Weekly* praised the collection's "engrossing and gritty stories of tenuous living in a gentrifying America," and praised Fofana for "deliver[ing] the hardy, profane, violent, and passionate narration in Black English Vernacular, and [finding] the humanity in all his characters as they struggle to get by." Here, the reviewer touched on the fact that the book is not one for those who are looking for escapism and happy endings.

It is important to note that while it is not always an easy read, *Stories from the Tenants Downstairs* is also not depressing. As Hephzibah Anderson wrote in her review for the *Guardian*, "Fofana's triumph is in allowing these people to burst from the page as individuals who may perhaps be fated, but who are also gloriously flawed, funny and bold, rather than being mere victims of their social challenges." Anderson's argument here captures exactly what makes the book work so well. In the hands of a lesser writer, many of these characters' lives would feel unilaterally tragic, but Fofana shows that life is more complex than that. While many of his characters, like Najee and Kandese, endure tragedies and hardship, most of them try to make the best of their situations while aspiring for something better. At one point in "The Rent Manual," Mimi wonders why everyone only focuses on the bad things that happen at Banneker Terrace and not the good things, namely the summer cookouts that the tenants have. Although Fofana's focus is primarily on the systemic injustices and personal challenges that affect this marginalized community, he still takes time to depict the figurative cookouts. Through funny moments and a plot point lurking in the background of some stories about a few tenants organizing to fight against the greedy landlords who are trying to push them out, Fofana makes it clear that no matter how bad things get, there is always a glimmer of hope.

Author Biography

A 2018 fellow for the Center for Fiction, Sidik Fofana's work has been published in *Sewanee Review* and *Granta*. His debut short-story collection, *Stories from the Tenants Downstairs*, was published in 2022. He has worked as a New York City public school educator.

Emily E. Turner

Review Sources

Anderson, Hephzibah. "Bold, Funny and Gloriously Flawed Voices of New York." Review of *Stories from the Tenants Downstairs*, by Sidik Fofana. *The Guardian*, 29 Jan. 2023, www.theguardian.com/books/2023/jan/29/stories-from-the-tenants-downstairs-by-sidik-fofana-review-bold-funny-and-gloriously-flawed-voices-of-new-york. Accessed 6 Feb. 2023.

Cassara, Joseph. "Family, Home and Heartbreak in Three Debuts." Review of *Stories from the Tenants Downstairs*, by Sidik Fofana, et al. *The New York Times*, 16 Aug. 2022, www.nytimes.com/2022/08/16/books/review/stories-from-the-tenants-downstairs-calling-for-a-blanket-dance-sirens-and-muses-sidik-fofana-oscar-hokeah-antonia-angress.html. Accessed 10 Feb. 2023.

Rath, Don J. "The Raw Humanity of Real-Life Stories." Review of *Stories from the Tenants Downstairs*, by Sidik Fofana. *Southern Review of Books*, 30 Aug. 2022, southernreviewofbooks.com/2022/08/30/stories-from-the-tenant-downstairs-sidik-fofana-review. Accessed 6 Feb. 2023.

Review of *Stories from the Tenants Downstairs*, by Sidik Fofana. *Kirkus*, 8 June 2022, www.kirkusreviews.com/book-reviews/sidik-fofana/stories-from-the-tenants-downstairs. Accessed 6 Feb. 2023.

Review of *Stories from the Tenants Downstairs*, by Sidik Fofana. *Publishers Weekly*, 31 May 2022, www.publishersweekly.com/9781982145811. Accessed 6 Feb. 2023.

The Summer of Bitter and Sweet

Author: Jen Ferguson (b. 1985)
Publisher: Heartdrum (New York). 384 pp.
Type of work: Novel
Time: Present day
Locale: Alberta Prairies near Edmonton, Canada

The young adult novel The Summer of Bitter and Sweet *tells the story of a Métis teenager named Lou whose last summer before leaving for college does not turn out as she had planned. After an old friend returns to the area, she begins to recognize not only how much she has changed but the extent to which her life has been based on lies. Author Jen Ferguson explores themes of family, friendship, sexuality, and trauma throughout the book.*

Principal characters

LOUISA "LOU" NORQUAY, a Métis teen who just graduated from high school
LOUISA, her mother
KING NATHAN, her love interest and former friend
WYATT, her ex-boyfriend
FLORENCE, her best friend
TYLER, her former best friend
DOM, her uncle who co-owns an ice cream shack
PETER ENGLAND, her biological father

Though Jen Ferguson has been recognized for her writing prior to *The Summer of Bitter and Sweet* (2022), this is the author's debut work for young adult readers. In addition to this novel, Ferguson published the adult novel *Border Markers* in 2016. Her writing has also included a significant number of short stories, poems, and essays. Academically, she has contributed to a book on the writing craft and another on the pedagogy of writing.

The novel opens with the dedication "To all the angry girls; to the Indigenous girls carrying worlds on their shoulders; girls who ride or die for each other; the girls still in the process of becoming—." Ferguson follows the dedication with a personal note, where she acknowledges the challenges many teens face and, with humor and compassion, lets readers know they are worthy of love and healing. Ferguson foreshadows the complications in the story by concluding with the comment: "Your health, happiness, safety, and well-being matter more than reading this book. If you're not ready now,

Jen Ferguson

that's okay." These notes encapsulate the main themes developed throughout the novel, preparing readers for the fact that this will not always be an easy read.

Organized into thirty-five chapters, dated June 12 through September 4, the story follows Lou, an eighteen-year-old Métis living on the Canadian prairie, who is graduating from high school and planning to head to college in the fall. Each chapter begins with the description of a color and the flavor profile that goes with that color as it relates to the ice cream that Lou's family sells at their seasonal business, an ice cream shack called Michif Creamery. For instance, the first chapter begins with "RED," noting "When the season opens at the Michif Creamery, we start with reds. They contrast loudly, wake us up, as spring announces itself with what seem like impossible buds on trees."

Lou's summer starts with the opening of the Creamery. On the first day, readers are introduced to Lou's mother, Louisa; her uncles Dom (the genius behind the ice cream itself) and Maurice; and her best friend, Florence. There is mention of Lou's boyfriend, Wyatt, who is a no-show for helping. The base personalities of the characters are quickly established in this first chapter, with added depth as the novel develops.

The novel quickly moves into developing its often difficult themes, one of which is teen sexuality. Two days after opening the Creamery, Lou sits on the porch of her family home waiting for her boyfriend to pick her up for a date. She is unsettled, thinking about the number of times they have kissed and dreading the fact that Wyatt will want to increase that number. Despite the fact that he is late and inconsiderate of Lou as a person, he expects her to pleasure him, something that sickens her. Though she breaks up with him before the date even has a chance to begin, this evening sets the tone for Lou's relationship with her own sexuality that troubles her throughout the story.

Lou's confusion over her sexuality is partially based on the teenage experience of her mother, which led to Lou's conception. At sixteen, her mother was raped at a party by a local White boy from a wealthy family. This situation becomes one that is repeated throughout the book, as Indigenous girls drink too much alcohol and White boys take advantage of them. For Lou personally, the experience leads her to question why she does not feel any interest in sex itself. Though she feels attraction toward her friend King Nathan, she does not feel a desire to take their relationship any further. This introduces a discussion of other sexual identities that fall under the LGBTQ umbrella, including bisexuality, demisexuality, and asexuality. Lou ultimately identifies as demisexual, a term used to describe someone who only experiences sexual attraction in very specific situations, which complicates her emotional attachments—in her heart she wants to be with King, but in her mind, she cannot stop thinking about how the idea of physical intimacy disgusts her.

Because Lou was conceived as a result of the rape of her teen mother, family is complicated in the novel. Lou and her mother spent the early years of her life moving from place to place, running from something only the elder Louisa could truly understand. As the novel begins, they have lived in a house shared with Louisa's brothers for several years, so Lou has finally established some roots and friendships. In many ways, Louisa is a pillar of strength, caring for her daughter no matter what it takes, but she is also flawed, covering her own needs behind walls that hide her from the eyes of those who know what happened to her. During the summer the story takes place, Louisa leaves to travel the powwow circuit selling hand-beaded items. Lou knows her mother needs this time, but the girl still feels abandoned by the one consistent presence in her life. Lou's uncles, Dom and Maurice, continue to be a physical presence, but her relationships with them are complicated by their own concerns.

The most problematic familial relationship appears when Lou's biological father, Peter England, is released from prison and begins pursuing her in a threatening way. Peter encroaches on his daughter's personal space by leaving letters hidden in her belongings or with her friends. The letters are seemingly innocent, but when Lou refuses to acknowledge Peter, they become more sinister, threatening her family's home and business.

Friendships are an added thematic idea in the novel with which teen readers especially will connect. Florence, Lou's best friend, is a bipolar White girl whose manic personality leaves Lou acting as a guardian more than a friend at times. King is a young man with whom Lou was friends several years earlier but abruptly left town without saying goodbye. When he returns, Lou is both excited and frustrated with the attraction she feels. Elise, the White girl with whom Lou's ex-boyfriend, Wyatt, begins dating after he and Lou break up, becomes a surprising ally, and Tyler, another Indigenous teen with whom Lou was formerly close, stands up when Lou needs her.

Tied up in the theme of friendship is one of secrecy, as Lou comes to recognize that the lies and secrets upon which she has been living must be cleared up if she wants to move forward. A major lie that she has perpetuated is that of her Indigenous identity. Physically pale and blue-eyed, Lou had been passing as White since first returning to her uncles' home, but living with others in the Indigenous community, she begins to acknowledge and appreciate her Métis roots. However, the lies she has told have damaged her friendships and, sometimes, her friends themselves. For instance, foreshadowing throughout the story hint at illegal activity that Lou and Tyler had been involved in that had more far-reaching consequences than they considered at the time. Her father's return from prison is another secret that affects Lou's family as both she and her uncles hide his presence from Louisa, who is stronger than any of them expect and who has been keeping secrets of her own.

In addition to these issues, Ferguson addresses the racism that runs rampant in the Canadian prairies. This is exemplified in Lou's desire to pass as White for a time in her early teens. When she claims her Métis identity, she begins to recognize the dangers to which Indigenous women, like her mother, are exposed. Her Métis friend Tyler is also a generational victim of racism, her mother having been murdered by a White man. King, who is of Jamaican heritage, has been victimized as well, and his mother, who struggled with drugs, was raped by a White man and lost her daughter to child services; King's father, a respected local veterinarian is even questioned after a local fire. In another instance, Lou attends a party with King and Florence, where Tyler's younger sister, Cami, is attacked by a group of White boys and Lou herself is injured in an attempt to protect the younger girl.

Indeed, the bitter aspects of Lou's summer sometimes overwhelm the story, but there are moments of sweetness to give readers a break from the heavier issues. For instance, Lou and King agree to go out on three dates. During one date planned by King, the teens travel throughout the province competing in a radio competition to send selfies with large statues scattered over several hundred miles. Their adventure is filled with moments of joy and fun, helping to lighten the tone of the narrative. Lou's friendships add another positive note, and Dom's ridiculous ice cream flavors provide a touch of humor.

The reviews of the novel commented on a variety of issues. The *Publishers Weekly* review, for instance, noted the thematic development of the "sweetly complex debut" and its "well-wrought, complicated characterizations and prose that sings with poetry." The *School Library Journal's* verdict was just as complimentary, stating, "The honesty and complexity of this book make it a gripping read." *Booklist*'s reviewer also commended the novel's thematic issues and characterization, calling Lou "complex, smart, and honest, and a narrator readers will trust, love, and learn from as she works to repair friendships and gain security for her treasured family." *Kirkus Reviews* claimed Ferguson's handling of sensitive thematic issues was handled "with nuance and care." As the author is Canadian, and the novel is set in Canada, it feels important to include a critique from *CM: Canadian Review of Materials*. Reviewer Lindsey Baird praised the author's opening note as providing "beautiful content warnings," further noting that "readers begin the novel surrounded with grace and vulnerability, in a move that . . . would benefit many books that tackle tough subjects for teenagers." Baird also called the characters "complex and lovable." The plot, on the other hand, was not favored by this reviewer, who argued that "the number of secrets being kept from the reader sometimes contorted the plot." Overall, however, the novel is one to be appreciated and celebrated. As the reviewer for *Kirkus* proclaimed, *The Summer of Bitter and Sweet* is "heart-rending and healing; a winning blend that will leave readers satisfied."

Author Biography

The Summer of Bitter and Sweet is Jen Ferguson's first young adult novel. In addition to her own writing, Ferguson teaches writing at Coe College. The author, like her character in this novel, is proudly Métis and Canadian.

Theresa L. Stowell, PhD

Review Sources

Baird, Lindsey. Review of *The Summer of Bitter and Sweet*, by Jen Ferguson. *CM: Canadian Review of Materials*, vol. 28, no. 40, June 2022, p. 11. *Academic Search Ultimate*, search.ebscohost.com/login.aspx?direct=true&db=asn&AN=157572756. Accessed 30 Jan. 2023.

Fredriksen, Jeanne. Review of *The Summer of Bitter and Sweet*, by Jen Ferguson. *Booklist*, vol. 118, no. 17, May 2022, p. 41. *Education Research Complete*, search.ebscohost.com/login.aspx?direct=true&db=ehh&AN=156574327. Accessed 30 Jan. 2023.

Montgomery, Nicholl Denice. Review of *The Summer of Bitter and Sweet*, by Jen Ferguson. *Horn Book Magazine*, vol. 98, no. 3, May 2022, pp. 143–44. *Literary Reference Center*, search.ebscohost.com/login.aspx?direct=true&db=lfh&AN=156491408. Accessed 30 Jan. 2023.

Saarinen, Tamara. Review of *The Summer of Bitter and Sweet*, by Jen Ferguson. *School Library Journal*, vol. 68, no. 9, Sept. 2022, pp. 113–14. *Literary Reference Center*, search.ebscohost.com/login.aspx?direct=true&db=lfh&AN=158662140. Accessed 30 Jan. 2023.

Review of *The Summer of Bitter and Sweet*, by Jen Ferguson. *Kirkus Reviews*, 2 Mar. 2022, www.kirkusreviews.com/book-reviews/jen-ferguson/the-summer-of-bitter-and-sweet/. Accessed 8 Feb. 2023.

Review of *The Summer of Bitter and Sweet*, by Jen Ferguson. *Publishers Weekly*, 7 Apr. 2022, www.publishersweekly.com/9780063086166. Accessed 30 Jan. 2023.

Swim Team

Author: Johnnie Christmas
Publisher: HarperAlley (New York).
  256 pp.
Type of work: Graphic novel
Time: Present day
Locale: Florida

Swim Team, a middle-grade graphic novel from illustrator Johnnie Christmas, follows a young girl named Bree as she faces her fear of swimming and learns to build lasting friendships. The book also explores the history of racism and segregation that continues to shape access to the sport of swimming.

Principal characters

BREE, a middle-schooler who has just moved to Florida from Brooklyn
RALPH, her overextended but loving father
CLARA, her new friend, a teammate on the swim team
KEISHA, her teammate, a transfer from Holyoke Prep
MS. ETTA, her neighbor, a former champion swimmer

Swim Team (2022), a middle-grade graphic novel by comic book author and illustrator Johnnie Christmas, begins with an explanation of a theory called the butterfly effect. The idea behind it, single dad Ralph tells his young daughter, Bree, is that a butterfly can flap its wings in one place, and in doing so cause a ripple effect that influences the weather across the globe. Or, to put it more succinctly, as Ralph does: "It's a PROCESS that explains how little changes can have a BIG effect." Christmas's book, about a young girl moving to a new place, evokes the butterfly effect in ways that will resonate with young readers and adults alike. Forced to take a swimming class at school, Bree embarks on a journey of learning and friendship that will change the course of her life, and perhaps inform the future of her new school. Meanwhile, through the backstory of Bree's neighbor Ms. Etta, Christmas illustrates the profound generational consequences of racist policies from the early 1900s barring Black people from beaches and local swimming pools.

In interviews, Christmas has said that like Bree, he did not learn to swim as a young child, and after nearly drowning in a pool when he was five, swore off learning until he was an adult. Christmas's personal fear of the water, though, can be linked to actions taken long before he was born. During the era of racist Jim Crow laws, many beaches and pools were strictly segregated throughout the South, leaving most Black people without access to swimmable water at all. These obstacles continued even after

Swim Team / CHRISTMAS

Johnnie Christmas

Courtesy HarperCollins Publishers

race-based segregation had technically ended, as facilities were privatized and largely restricted to wealthy, White neighborhoods. Without access to places where one might learn how to swim, many Black people in the US never acquired the skill, and in turn, were unable to teach their children—the ongoing butterfly effect of institutional racism. Thus, there are generations of deprivation behind a thought expressed by Bree as a matter of fact: "Black people aren't good at swimming," she tells Ms. Etta, dejected.

Ms. Etta assures Bree that this is ridiculous. (Bree and Ms. Etta, like most of the book's characters, are Black.) Anyone can learn to swim, but kids like Bree see their not-knowing as a personal failure, not a societal one. Bree, who has just moved to Florida with her father, tells readers from the jump that she does not like pools. She sees her fear and shame around the water as an unchangeable aspect of her personality in the same way that she loves math class and complicated puzzles. She just doesn't like swimming, period. But during her first day at her new middle school, she discovers that she must take a swim class—which would be okay if she were not too embarrassed to tell her teacher that she never learned. Bombarded by negative thoughts, ("You'll be so embarrassed. They're gonna laugh at you, too.") Bree, an exemplary student, decides to skip class instead.

Thankfully, Ms. Etta, who turns out to have been a champion swimmer when she was a student at Bree's middle school years ago, is there to help. Ms. Etta teaches Bree the basics and as it turns out, the math whiz actually likes to swim after all. But there are more threads to Christmas's story. Bree's middle school—Enith Brigitha Middle School, named after the first Black woman to win an Olympic medal in swimming—is struggling financially. There is talk that they might sell the land on which the pool sits to a smoothie franchise. (The smoothies *are* really good, nearly every character observes.) But there is a chance that if the swim team wins the state championship, the school might decide to keep the pool.

Clara, Bree's new best friend, certainly hopes so. She cannot stand the cruel, snobby girls at nearby Holyoke Prep, a wealthy, private school with an elite swim team. When Bree arrives, Clara is determined to take the state title from Holyoke and save her pool. Bree eventually joins the team, too, giving Christmas the opportunity to explore joys beyond learning to swim in and of itself. Bree loves learning new techniques, like flip turns and starting off a block, but more than anything, she delights in the comradery and encouragement of her teammates both in the water and on land. Their exploits can be quite funny. When the team—plus their costume designer sidekick, Humberto—decides to go on a secret mission to scope out their rivals at Holyoke, Humberto promises to outfit them in Holyoke uniforms so they will not be recognized. He raids the theater department's closets, and the team shows up to the prep school wearing fur coats and colonial wigs. Like any sport, Christmas makes clear, swimming is not just about winning; it is about friendship, too.

Christmas links these two ideas through the concept of a relay team. Bree and three of her teammates swim an event called the individual medley relay, in which each swimmer performs a different stroke. This becomes a perfect metaphor for friendship and teamwork: each swimmer brings their own special talent in service of pursuing a larger goal. For instance, perhaps one swimmer is best suited to the technically challenging breaststroke, while another can summon the raw speed of a freestyle sprint. The format of this race also gives Christmas the opportunity to explore conflict. When Keisha, a talented swimmer from Holyoke Prep, transfers to Enith Brigitha, she must replace someone on the relay team. The remaining girls will have to learn to cooperate with their former rival if they want to win the race at the state championship.

Keisha, a character with her own vulnerabilities and insecurities, is in a larger sense a perfect complication to the burgeoning team dynamic. She is a fierce competitor, highly cognizant of the fact that swimming is still an individual sport in many ways. An athlete very well could focus exclusively on their own race in a relay-type event, and it seems that this is Keisha's plan. The girls are suspicious of this attitude, fearful that Keisha will be too self-focused at the expense of the relay team. Further, the team thinks Keisha is just biding her time until she can return to her rightful place at Holyoke, and they wonder aloud if she is actually a spy. Of course, she ultimately has some things to teach them, too. She knows how to eat healthy and train hard. With her introduction, Christmas lets the reader know that while swimming is fun, it is also hard work.

Swim Team is Christmas's first book for young readers. He is perhaps best known as an illustrator for his work on the graphic novel series Angel Catbird, a trilogy published between 2016 and 2017 written by award-winning novelist Margaret Atwood. His illustrations for *Swim Team* evoke the palette of a Florida sunset reflected off the water, the colors bright but also translucent. His rounded figures are similarly warm and pleasant, cartoon-like without being cartoonish. "Characters are drawn with warmth and personality—even villains contain multitudes," Bonnie Tsui observed in her positive review for the *New York Times*. She is perhaps referring in particular to the star of the Holyoke team, who struggles to please her tyrannical coach—another, less savory, aspect of sports that the book touches on. A reviewer for *Publishers Weekly*, meanwhile, described Christmas's drawings as "kinetic contemporary art." Other reviewers noted the way Christmas breaks with the book's style when he conveys Bree's intrusive thoughts, which ooze into the frame in amorphous grey bubbles with thick black outlines, sneaking up on her like a monstrous blob. "Sometimes NEGATIVE THOUGHTS take over," Bree explains. "And I think about the things that make me nervous or scared." Christmas effectively employs a similar style to convey the cruel laughter of the Holyoke team when they find out, at the beginning of the book, that Bree cannot swim.

A widely acclaimed best-seller, *Swim Team* was longlisted for the National Book Award for Young People's Literature in 2022 and received starred reviews from

Publishers Weekly and *Kirkus*. The latter praised the nuance with which Christmas balances history with Bree's personal journey and described the book as a "deeply smart and inspiring story." Annie Metcalf, who reviewed the book for *BookPage*, commented on the effective plot structure of *Swim Team*, noting it is shaped by "a countdown-to-competition plot." Readers know that the book is working toward the big state championship, and Christmas does an effective job of bringing together the various threads of the book within the context of this event. "While *Swim Team* includes a few minor inaccuracies that may be distracting to readers who swim competitively," Metcalf further pointed out, perhaps referring to Christmas's oddly casual interpretation of swimming competitions, "its depiction of swimming's joys and challenges is spot on." But then again, "swimming is only part of the story," Metcalf continued, and Christmas "creates an affectionate portrait of Bree and her friends, a group of kids who love their sport, long to win and get up to some funny hijinks along the way."

Author Biography
Johnnie Christmas's graphic novel *Firebug* (2018) earned him a nomination for the Joe Shuster Outstanding Cartoonist Award. He also illustrated the Angel Catbird series, written by novelist Margaret Atwood; its three graphic novels were published between 2016 and 2017.

Molly Hagan

Review Sources
Metcalf, Annie. Review of *Swim Team*, by Johnnie Christmas. *BookPage*, 11 May 2022, www.bookpage.com/reviews/swim-team-johnnie-christmas-book-review/. Accessed 16 Jan. 2023.
Mroczek-Bayci, Emily. "Heavy Medal Mock Newbery Finalist: *Swim Team* by Johnnie Christmas." Review of *Swim Team*, by Johnnie Christmas. *School Library Journal*, 5 Jan. 2023, heavymedal.slj.com/2023/01/05/heavy-medal-mock-newbery-finalist-swim-team-by-johnnie-christmas/. Accessed 16 Jan. 2023.
Review of *Swim Team*, by Johnnie Christmas. *Kirkus Reviews*, 2 Mar. 2022, www.kirkusreviews.com/book-reviews/johnnie-christmas/swim-team/. Accessed 16 Jan. 2023.
Review of *Swim Team*, by Johnnie Christmas. *Publishers Weekly*, 14 Apr. 2022, www.publishersweekly.com/9780063056763. Accessed 16 Jan. 2023.
Tsui, Bonnie. "Water Dance." Review of *Swim Team*, by Johnnie Christmas. *The New York Times*, 29 July 2022, www.nytimes.com/2022/07/29/books/review/johnnie-christmas-swim-team.html. Accessed 16 Jan. 2023.

The Swimmers

Author: Julie Otsuka (b. 1962)
Publisher: Alfred A. Knopf (New York).
  175 pp.
Type of Work: Novel
Time: Present day
Locale: United States

The Swimmers is a slim, stunning novel that meditates on the nature of aging, dementia, and identity, as well as mother-daughter relationships.

Principal characters
ALICE, an older Japanese American woman who is losing her memory
ALICE'S DAUGHTER, a middle-aged writer
COMMUNITY POOL SWIMMERS, most of them unnamed

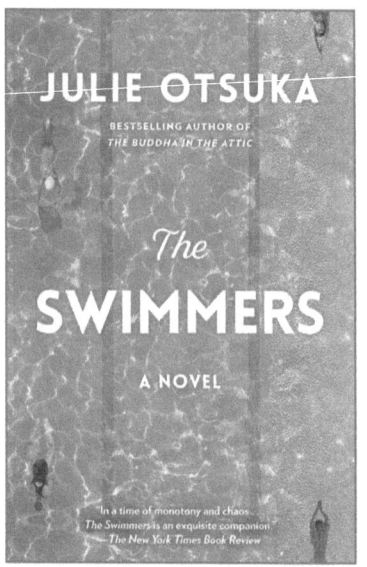

The Swimmers is a stunning meditation on the nature of aging, dementia, and identity. Julie Otsuka brings to her third novel the spare, supple prose and narrative command that illuminated her earlier books, *When the Emperor Was Divine* (2002) and *The Buddha in the Attic* (2011). *The Swimmers* explores the world of Alice, an older woman whose long-established routines and lifestyle are upended by her impending dementia. Otsuka's experiments with narrative voice and literary form cast the reader themselves into Alice's role and situation, so that reading *The Swimmers* can be a profoundly disquieting experience.

Otsuka's novel consists of three distinct sections, each of which is told in a different narrative voice and each of which focuses on a different aspect of its protagonist's worsening dementia. The first half of the book, entitled "The Underground Pool," is set at a community pool frequented by people of all backgrounds and walks of life. Otsuka's use of first-person plural narration ("we" and "us") envelops the reader, making them part of this eclectic community of swimmers. The choral quality of Otsuka's narration expresses the collective commitment of the swimmers to their shared passion. The pool serves as a powerful corrective to the "usual aboveground afflictions" of its users; in the water, they become creatures of habit and routine.

As this section progresses, a named protagonist, an older woman named Alice, gradually emerges. Otsuka's narrator addresses her directly, as if singling her out from the group:

> You wake up one day and you can't even remember your own name (It's Alice). But until that day comes you keep your eyes focused on that painted black line on the bottom

Julie Otsuka

of your lane and you do what you must: You swim on.

It is a moment that encapsulates the central conflict of this novel. For now, the pool serves as a reassuringly familiar place for Alice, one that may even help keep at bay her encroaching memory loss. Swimming, by the same token, becomes a stand-in for life as a whole. One goes through the regular routines of daily life the way a swimmer puts in their laps.

Having established the nature of the community pool and the swimmers that frequent it, Otsuka introduces into her novel an alarming conflict: a crack that appears on the pool's floor. It starts small enough that the swimmers can ignore it or wish it away by speculating that it is a trick of the eye or a harmless prank. The pool's management begins consulting a series of experts, but their efforts fail to stop the relentless expansion of the crack. The swimmers are likewise unsuccessful in their attempts to find an alternate location for continuing their hobby.

As with swimming itself, the crack in the pool becomes a symbol for something far more significant. It may be a visible manifestation of the creeping, unseen health issues that can disrupt one's life and lead to a pivotal change or loss. Much like a growing tumor, a clogging artery, or Alice's gradual loss of memory, the crack can only be wished away or ignored for so long. Eventually, the problem with the pool and the problem with Alice's mind will each become a crisis. For Alice, the two events coincide, so the closure of the pool corresponds with and perhaps precipitates her moving into an assisted care facility. She loses both the world of the swimmers and her familiar "aboveground" world.

The crack in the pool is a powerful symbol that reverberates well beyond the concerns of the swimmers or even of Alice herself. The novel's publication in 2022, in the context of the COVID-19 pandemic of the early 2020s and widespread political and social turmoil in the United States, makes it hard to imagine a reader who cannot relate to characters who experience a sudden and uncontrollable disruption in their daily lives. When the swimmers lament that, "It all went by so fast," or, "I was so happy in my lane," they are speaking to a common concern and sense of loss. Otsuka has created a powerful parable for modern times and has captured the pervasive sense of loss that the pandemic engendered in many people around the world in the early 2020s.

The novel's second section is titled "Diem Perdidi," Latin for "I have lost the day," and focuses on Alice's failing memory. At this point Otsuka pivots to third-person narration, with the narrator listing what Alice does and does not remember. This experimental and deliberately repetitive listing format produces a powerful catalogue of Alice's life. Over the course of this section, the reader learns of Alice's childhood in California, the trauma of being interned with her family and thousands of other Japanese Americans during World War II (1939–45), her doomed first love, and her eventual marriage. Alice's relationship with her daughter—a stand-in for the narrator—likewise becomes apparent in this section of the novel. Whereas Alice has lived a life that centered on her marriage, family, and routine, her daughter has carved out a very different path for herself by becoming a writer and by choosing not to have children. As Alice loses her memory and her autonomy, her daughter must grapple with the question of why she has chosen to keep such emotional distance between herself and her mother and whether she has misjudged the value of a simpler way of life.

Reading "Belavista," the third and final section of *The Swimmers*, can be a harrowing experience. This part of the book is narrated in the second person and is framed as a direct address to someone who is being admitted into an assisted living facility. Alice's dementia has reached the point where she can no longer live independently, and the reader understands why Belavista, with its structures, protocols, and constant monitoring, may be a better place for her. No longer able to follow her own routines, Alice must be in a place where those routines are set for her and where she and her peers are supervised by attendants. However, Otsuka also incorporates a subtle sense of horror, both in the setting of Belavista and the memory condition that requires Alice to move there. Otsuka's portrait of Belavista is comprehensive, touching on every aspect of how the place functions, from its financial structure to the minor details of its residents' daily routines. Otsuka's narrative strategy of addressing Alice in the second person heightens the sense of dread associated with this place; this approach casts readers in Alice's role, and it is not just a stranger, but the reader, who is losing their autonomy and independence.

Midway through this section, Otsuka shifts her focus from Alice to Alice's daughter. Seeing her mother in a diminished and dependent state prompts the daughter to reckon with the dynamics of their relationship. She is filled with a sense of regret for having kept her emotional distance. It is too late for Alice's daughter to invite Alice for a visit or to fly her off for a vacation in Paris. The daughter seems only now to gain an appreciation for the life that Alice has lost: one of simple routines, old friends, and modest undertakings. Alice's life stands in stark contrast to the independent existence her daughter has chosen for herself. Ironically, it is Alice's dementia that finally draws her daughter close. Although Alice gradually loses the ability to speak, she seems still to take comfort in and wonder at her daughter's presence by her side.

The Swimmers received overwhelmingly positive reviews from critics upon its publication in 2022. Many readers saw *The Swimmers* as speaking to the pressures and existential dread of the COVID-19 pandemic and of other challenges in contemporary US society. Maureen Corrigan, reviewing the novel for National Public Radio, praised Otsuka's book as "a slim, brilliant novel about the value and beauty of mundane routines that shape our days and identities," noting that "it could also be read as a grand parable about the crack in the world wrought by this pandemic," directly comparing the COVID-19 pandemic to the ominous crack which appears in the pool. Like many readers and reviewers, Corrigan was impressed by the "signature spare style" of Otsuka's prose, arguing that "suits her capacious vision." In her review for the *New York Times*, Rachel Khong likewise saw Otsuka's novel as a parable for the contemporary world, writing, "In a time of monotony and chaos . . . when cracks can and do appear in the pool for no discernible reason, *The Swimmers* is an exquisite companion." Khong argued that "the novel's quiet insistence resonates," as the daily laps of Otsuka's swimmers illustrate the ways in which all people live their lives through an accumulation of everyday habits.

Writing for *The Atlantic*, Apoorva Tadepalli likewise focused on the symbolic resonance of swimming laps and on the gap between how Alice and her writerly daughter see the world. Tadepalli argued that Alice's daughter chose to not follow her mother's "patient understanding of what makes a good life, and her tender curiosity about other unremarkable, unambitious people like herself." Seen through this lens, Otsuka's listing of items lost in the pool and of memories lost to Alice's mother may be a type of salvage operation. As Tadepalli puts it, "In dark times, our own as much as Alice's, a focus on these little things can salvage the moments of joy we may otherwise overlook."

However, the novel's unorthodox construction and narrative experimentation proved an issue for some reviewers. In *The Los Angeles Times*, Nina Renata Aron maintained that the book came across as "sometimes twee in its first half," adding that "its often-captivating insularity can also be cloying at times." For Aron, the book improved as it went on, and "sparkle[d]" once its focus shifted from the pool to Alice herself. Aron saw this as indicative of Otsuka's substance and style, something that was also apparent in the author's previous two novels; as Aron wrote, "The heavier the themes, the more Otsuka's language lifts off." As Aron's review demonstrates, *The Swimmers* takes some bold risks, and the transitions among the disparate parts of the novel may alienate some readers.

With *The Swimmers*, Otsuka offers up a powerful meditation on the inevitability of aging and loss. It is a book that will resonate with all sorts of readers, for it looks squarely and unsentimentally at the future that all people must face.

Author Biography

Julie Otsuka's novels include *When the Emperor Was Divine* (2002), which won the Asian American Literary Award and the American Library Association's Alex Award, and *The Buddha in the Attic* (2011), which was as finalist for the National Book Award and the winner of the PEN/Faulkner Award for Fiction. Her third novel, *The Swimmers*, was published in 2022.

Matthew J. Bolton

Review Sources

Aron, Nina Renata. "Review: A Survivor of Internment Sinks into Forgetting in Julie Otsuka's *The Swimmers*." Review of *The Swimmers*, by Julie Otsuka. *The Los Angeles Times*, 2 Mar. 2022, www.latimes.com/entertainment-arts/books/story/2022-03-02/an-internment-survivor-sinks-into-dementia-in-julie-otsukas-haunting-the-swimmers. Accessed 15 Oct. 2022

Corrigan, Maureen. "Still Waters Run Deep in The Swimmers, a Brilliant Novel about Routine and Identity." Review of *The Swimmers*, by Julie Otsuka. *National Public Radio*, 14 Mar. 2022, www.npr.org/2022/03/14/1086009836/the-swimmers-julie-otsuka-review. Accessed 15 Oct. 2022

Khong, Rachel. "Julie Otsuka Dives Into the Underground World of the Community Pool." Review of *The Swimmers*, by Julie Otsuka. *The New York Times*, 11 Feb. 2022, www.nytimes.com/2022/02/11/books/review/julie-otsuka-the-swimmers.html. Accessed 15 Oct. 2022

Tadepalli, Apoorva. "The Big Secret in Our Small Routines: Julie Otsuka's *The Swimmers* Finds the Beauty in a Seemingly Unextraordinary Life." Review of *The Swimmers*, by Julie Otsuka. *The Atlantic*, www.theatlantic.com/books/archive/2022/03/the-swimmers-julia-otsuka-review/623328/. Accessed 15 Oct. 2022

Take My Hand

Author: Dolen Perkins-Valdez
Publisher: Berkley (New York). 359 pp.
Type of work: Novel
Time: 1973–2016
Locale: Alabama

Take My Hand, best-selling author Dolen Perkins-Valdez's third novel, is a work of historical fiction that examines the involuntary sterilizations of Black girls and women that happened in the United States in the 1970s.

Principal characters
CIVIL TOWNSEND, a young nurse working at a family planning clinic in Alabama
ERICA WILLIAMS, a thirteen-year-old girl from a poor family
INDIA WILLIAMS, Erica's eleven-year-old sister
MACE WILLIAMS, the widowed father of Erica and India
TYRELL, Civil's ex-boyfriend
MRS. SEAGER, the White head nurse at the clinic where Civil works
LOU FELDMAN, a Jewish lawyer who takes on the Williams sisters' case

For Dolen Perkins-Valdez, the desire to write fiction has always been fueled by curiosity and the desire to give a voice to the countless Black Americans whose lives were erased from the history of the United States. In an April 2022 interview with Ayesha Rascoe for National Public Radio, she explained this drive, stating, "I'll be reading something that is historical, and then I have a question . . . and this, to me, is very specific about African American history. There are so many silences in the archive there. There are so many stories that need to be told."

This motivation first became evident in Perkins-Valdez's best-selling debut, *Wench* (2010). Following the journey of a young enslaved African American woman who is the mistress of her White enslaver, *Wench* examines the complex power dynamics of interracial relationships in the American South during the antebellum period, which occurred before the US Civil War (1861–5). To accomplish this, the novel is set in Xenia, Ohio, at the Tawawa House—a real summer resort that once existed for White southern plantation owners who wanted to go on vacation with the enslaved Black women they had taken as their mistresses. In her next book, *Balm* (2015), Perkins-Valdez explored what life was like for Black people during the Reconstruction Era, the period after the Civil War during which the US government attempted, with mixed results, to enact several policies intended to help formerly enslaved Black Americans.

Dolen Perkins-Valdez (Courtesy Penguin Publishing Group)

Perkins-Valdez continues to shine a light on the oft-erased experiences of Black Americans throughout US history in her third novel, *Take My Hand* (2022). Although it differs from her previous novels in that it is not set in the nineteenth century, *Take My Hand* proves that the author is not done addressing the myriad ways that Black American women have had their bodily autonomy stolen from them as a result of institutionalized racism. Specifically, *Take My Hand* is a fictional reimagining of the story of the Relf sisters, Mary Alice and Minnie Lee—two Black teenagers who were sterilized against their will by a federally funded family planning clinic in Montgomery, Alabama, in 1973.

One of the special qualities of Perkins-Valdez's writing is the way that she stays quite close to the truth while simultaneously using fiction as a tool to further her readers' understanding of historical events. This tendency is especially evident in *Take My Hand*, which is told from the perspective of a fictional nurse named Civil Townsend. The real clinic responsible for sterilizing the Relf sisters was led by a White woman who attempted to justify the clinic's actions by pointing to the fact that she had a staff of all-Black nurses. Through Civil, Perkins-Valdez aims to understand who these nurses were, the impossible position they were put in, and the conflicted emotions they must have experienced. Perkins-Valdez also uses Civil to speculate how several of these nurses might have helped bring the truth of what the clinic was doing to light.

Throughout *Take My Hand*, Civil proves to be a compelling and well-wrought character. When the novel begins, she is a recent college graduate of Tuskegee University, a historically Black university located in Tuskegee, Alabama, and is the daughter of a doctor who himself is devoted to helping the Black community. Civil is idealistic and believes in the power of birth control to give women control over their own destinies, in part because she is a product of the burgeoning women's liberation movement but also because she herself has recently had an abortion. It is for these reasons that she feels a strong calling to her job at a family planning clinic that provides low-income women with free access to birth control.

Everything changes for Civil, however, after she meets two young patients named Erica and India Williams. Aged thirteen and eleven, the Williams sisters live in abject poverty with their grandmother and father, a handsome widower named Mace. Feeling maternally drawn to the girls, Civil quickly oversteps the boundaries of her job by bringing them home one day so they can bathe, eat, and get new clothes. When she learns that India was put on birth control before she had even started menstruating, Civil begins to question the true morality of the clinic's mission. Her concern quickly grows once she learns that the Depo-Provera birth control shot she has been administering to Black American patients has yet to be approved by the FDA.

One of the most nuanced themes of *Take My Hand* is the dangerous, double-edged sword of good intentions. More specifically, the novel illustrates how harmful it can be for outsiders to interfere in the lives of people they hope to help, even if these outsiders believe they know what is best. This idea is depicted primarily through Civil's employer, which is a federally funded clinic with the ostensible mission to "help" poor Alabaman women prevent pregnancies that they do not have the financial or emotional means for. However, Civil quickly realizes that many of the clinic's patients are unable to truly consent because they are either too young or do not have the educational background to understand what they are agreeing to. For example, in the case of the Depo-Provera birth control shot, these patients are coerced into agreeing to receive an experimental form of birth control with dangerous side effects, including bleeding and possibly a link to cancer. This issue of consent becomes particularly troubling once Civil realizes that the clinic has also been coercing patients into sterilization.

Alternating between the past and present, *Take My Hand* is movingly narrated by Civil as she later relays the story of everything that happened to Erica and India in 1973 to her adult daughter. There are also a handful of sections that take place in 2016 as Civil tries to follow up with what ultimately happened to the girls. Civil's narration has a very honest, human quality to it as she parses her memories as best she can to try to explain her actions from forty years earlier. In the hands of a lesser writer, the novel could easily be no more than a summary of the Relf sisters' case; however, Perkins-Valdez prevents this from happening by fleshing out her characters' worlds and lives. Rather than a vessel to help readers understand a narrative based on a real historical event, Civil comes across as a three-dimensional protagonist with her own problems beyond the workplace, including her father's disappointment in her career, her mother's deteriorating mental health, and the complex feelings that she has toward her ex-boyfriend, Tyrell, as well as the Williams sisters' father, Mace.

Given *Take My Hand*'s focus on the stories of different Black American women, the novel, at its core, is a powerful examination of the way that Black people were still not free from many forms of institutionalized racism even after the gains of the Civil Rights movement in the 1960s. Perkins-Valdez's decision to make Civil a graduate of Tuskegee successfully amplifies this idea, due to the real-life history of the university. It was in 1972, when Civil was a senior, that the university finally stopped the notorious experiment of giving Black men syphilis and leaving it untreated to learn about the disease's effects. These experiments, known as the Tuskegee experiments, were conducted with the help of the United States Public Health Service. Meanwhile, the characters of Erica and India function as stand-ins not only for the Relf sisters but also for the tens of thousands of people—the majority of whom were poor women of color—who were coerced into sterilization by federally funded clinics from the late 1960s through 1973. Ultimately, Perkins-Valdez's message that Black American women's bodily autonomy and reproductive rights have always been under attack remained resonant even at the time of its publication in 2022.

Reception of *Take My Hand* was overwhelmingly positive upon its publication in 2022, with many critics extolling Perkins-Valdez's talent for blending exceptional storytelling with beautiful prose and historical fact. In her review for the *Washington Post*, Tina McElroy Ansa wrote, "Perkins-Valdez paints Montgomery in such rich strokes, you can feel history breathing down your neck through the sounds of ice cream trucks in summer, the drawl of a Southern judge, and Booker T. and the M.G.'s on the record player." Indeed, it is true that one of the most memorable aspects of *Take My Hand* is the way that Perkins-Valdez uses historical details to provide readers with a sensory experience of what Civil's life would have really been like in Montgomery, Alabama, in 1973. In turn, the novel has a transportive quality to it and its pages feel akin to a time machine. Donna Edwards also highlighted this point in her review for the Associated Press, stating, "This is the kind of story you want to build extra time into reading so you can explore the wealth of history it draws upon."

For some critics, however, this focus on history resulted in *Take My Hand* falling slightly short of the high bar that Perkins-Valdez's previous two novels had set. Writing for the *Washington Independent Review of Books*, Carrie Callaghan remarked, "This first foray into the 20th century feels more explicitly drawn from the headlines and, strangely, a little less intimate than her prior work." Callaghan's point is a fair one, as the meticulousness of Perkins-Valdez's historical research is so good that sometimes it outshines the more character-based parts of the story. Still, it is important to note that there are other places in the novel where the storytelling greatly benefits from Perkins-Valdez's tendency to lean more heavily on fact than fiction. This is especially true of parts 2 and 3, which focus more on the court case against the Montgomery clinic and eventual trial. Here, the novel introduces the lawyer character of Lou Feldman and, in turn, begins to boast elements of a legal drama. Perkins-Valdez based Feldman off of Joseph Levin, the White, Jewish lawyer who represented the Relf sisters. The author was able to interview Levin in real life; her research pays off by giving a dynamic realness to the novel's depiction of the Williams' sisters court case.

Standard accounts of US history typically ignore the fact that the government sponsored a sterilization program rooted in eugenics-based ideas that affected tens of thousands people whom the government deemed unfit to have children. Many of the survivors of these programs were poor, young, and Black. *Take My Hand* is not only an important reminder of these events and how recently they occurred, but also an affirmation that every human being is entitled to their own bodily autonomy and reproductive rights.

Author Biography

Dolen Perkins-Valdez is an NAACP Image Awards finalist and the best-selling author of *Wench* (2010) and *Balm* (2015). For *Balm*, she received a DC Commission on the Arts Grant.

Emily E. Turner

Review Sources

Ansa, Tina McElroy. "'Take My Hand' Exposes a Dark Episode in American History." Review of *Take My Hand*, by Dolen Perkins-Valdez. *The Washington Post*, 15 Apr. 2022, www.washingtonpost.com/books/2022/04/15/take-my-hand-dolen-perkins-valdez-book-review. Accessed 14 Dec. 2022.

Callaghan, Carrie. "A Compelling, Fictional Look at the Sordid History of Reproductive Politics." Review of *Take My Hand*, by Dolen Perkins-Valdez. *Washington Independent Review of Books*, 22 Apr. 2022, www.washingtonindependentreviewofbooks.com/index.php/bookreview/take-my-hand-a-novel. Accessed 14 Dec. 2022.

Edwards, Donna. "Eye-Opening Historical Fiction 'Take My Hand.'" Review of *Take My Hand*, by Dolen Perkins-Valdez. Associated Press, 11 Apr. 2022, apnews.com/article/entertainment-book-reviews-arts-and-historical-fiction-9e920c7f598948a-93c9426a298a8ef49. Accessed 14 Dec. 2022.

Review of *Take My Hand*, by Dolen Perkins-Valdez. *Publishers Weekly*, 3 Feb. 2022, www.publishersweekly.com/9780593337691. Accessed 14 Dec. 2022.

Tell Me Everything
The Story of a Private Investigation

Author: Erika Krouse
Publisher: Flatiron Books (New York).
288 pp.
Type of work: Memoir, current affairs
Time: Early 2000s
Locale: Colorado

Part reportage and part memoir, Elizabeth Krouse's Tell Me Everything: The Story of a Private Investigation *chronicles the novelist and short-story writer's work as a private investigator on a landmark sexual assault case involving a college football team in the early 2000s as well as how sexual abuse has affected her personally.*

Principal personages

ERIKA KROUSE, author, private investigator
GRAYSON, the lawyer who hired her to work
as a private investigator; name of the real-life figure changed for the book
X, her unnamed childhood abuser

Erika Krouse had already published a book of short stories—the award-winning *Come Up and See Me Sometime* (2001)—when she met a lawyer, whom she calls Grayson in her 2022 book *Tell Me Everything: The Story of a Private Investigation*, in 2002. Though the two had started chatting because they had both reached for the same novel in a bookstore, Grayson wound up telling her a secret: he was thinking of quitting his job and possibly his entire legal career. Despite her literary success, Krouse was broke and working temp jobs to make ends meet. So, when Grayson, astonished at his own unbidden confession to a stranger, extended an unusual employment offer, she leaped at it, only to consider the ramifications of her decision later. Grayson hired Krouse as a private investigator, a job for which she had no training but had always secretly coveted. "I had wanted to be a PI ever since I read my first Dashiell Hammett book," she writes. "I wanted to be the one who could walk into a room and know what happened there."

However, Krouse insisted that Grayson hire her, not for any perceived skill, but because of her face. It happens all the time, she explains in *Tell Me Everything*. Strangers tell her things—intimate, scary, painful things—because she has a familiar face. A woman once told her she was considering suicide; a man in a diner revealed to her that he had killed his girlfriend. People often mistake her for someone they know, but that does not quite explain the powerful force within her that compels them to tell her their

Erika Krouse

darkest secrets. "Something in my face bore the shape of a key," she writes, "or a steel table on which to lay something heavy."

Working for Grayson, Krouse was finally able to put her seemingly natural abilities to use. Her first days on the job were rough, though; she showed up to an event with a neon green poster board that said, in part, "Please talk to me!!" With her failures apparent, Grayson theorized that he must not have been adequately leveraging her set of skills. Expecting to be fired, instead, she was moved to a different case. It was a Title IX lawsuit against a local university (unnamed in the book) where Krouse had been a graduate student. A rape case, it involved a female student and several football players from the university's Division I football team. Grayson had chosen to approach the case from a surprising angle: he hoped to prove that the university knowingly and systematically supported a larger culture of sexual violence against women. His argument, for which there was no legal precedent at the time, was that pervasive sexual violence and harassment violated female students' rights of protection against discrimination under Title IX. The case felt like a moon shot, especially given the power of the university and the football team, but it was the details of the case that gave her pause. A survivor of sexual assault herself, she wondered if she could devote herself to the case without getting hurt. "Unqualified, and too qualified," she writes, in her sardonic, slightly hard-boiled narrative voice. "I understood rape victims and I understood rapists, and I didn't want to understand either, ever again."

Of course, Krouse agreed to work the case, which makes *Tell Me Everything* an impressive work encompassing both reportage and memoir. Most of the names in the book are pseudonyms, and Krouse writes in an introductory disclaimer that she further altered physical details to obscure the identities of those involved with the case. She also later explains that she "rearranged the timeline to increase clarity and fit into the larger truth of the story" while maintaining "the veracity of the events themselves." The story loses nothing from these capitulations. In her review of the book for *Slate*, Laura Miller noted that memoirs inhabit an uneasy grey area between fact and fiction. "Is it art or confession, and what does it owe to empirical fact?" she wrote. Scorching debate over these questions, she added—most notably spurred by James Frey's 2003 book *A Million Little Pieces*—resulted in "an artistic straitjacket that has funneled literary autobiographers to autofiction and . . . perplexed publishers with readers' demands that they fact-check the details of their authors' personal lives." In this context, Miller wrote, *Tell Me Everything* "is a startlingly fresh book that proves the memoir can do much, much more than just describe, or pretend to describe, what really happened." By interweaving her own personal story, Krouse poignantly illustrates the extraordinary toll of experiencing sexual assault and living within a culture that indifferently condones it.

Krouse's own experience is effectively revealed in small pieces, scattered throughout the book. From the ages of four to seven, she was abused—sexually, physically, psychologically—by an adult man she calls X. (She does not reveal his name, she writes, because he is still alive.) Though his relationship to her is never specified, he is suggested to have been familiar in some way with her mother. Compounding Krouse's trauma was her mother's ambivalence to the abuse, both as it was happening and in the years that followed. Her mother, shockingly cruel at times, maintained that the abuse did not happen, and if it did, it was Krouse's fault. It was an illogical argument, but as Krouse illustrates, a familiar one. From Grayson, Krouse learned that it is part of what is known as the "four-dog defense," so commonly faced by victims of sexual violence. Krouse quotes Grayson's explanation of it: "One, that's not my dog. Two, if that was my dog, he didn't bite you. Three, if my dog bit you, it didn't hurt you. And four, if my dog bit you and hurt you, you provoked him."

Inevitably, Grayson's quest for justice became personal for Krouse. She desperately hoped to win the case, spiraling after each setback. Her boyfriend, a gentle acupuncturist that she had met through a shared passion for martial arts, begged her to walk away, fearing for her mental health. She struggled to find meaning in the abuse—her own and the abuse suffered by the women in the case—in the absence of justice. Reaching out to her estranged family with heartbreaking hope, after decades of pain, her most fervent desire was merely an admission from X and her mother that X had harmed her and that it had been wrong. Recounting several of her interviews to the best of her memory, she compellingly describes how her approach to extracting useful information evolved over time.

Krouse also grappled with the role of the perpetrators in the case. Following Grayson's lead, she began to view the events that transpired not merely as individual instances of harm but as part of a coercive culture of violence and domination that hurts all students. If there are villains in the book, they are the adults who think that sexual violence is a necessary evil in service of winning football games—though one wonders how they came to internalize that idea. It is to Krouse's credit that she is able to consider the perpetrators' complex role in a generational cycle of violence without detracting from the trauma experienced by the victims.

Tell Me Everything received starred reviews from *Kirkus* and *Publishers Weekly*. Both praised Krouse's ability to wrench a rewarding story from a complicated legal battle. "The narrative that emerges is riveting and consistently insightful in its assessment of the psychodynamics of trauma for both victims and offenders," the anonymous reviewer for *Kirkus* wrote. The *Publishers Weekly* reviewer concluded, "The emotional catharsis delivered by the book's end turns this sensational tale into a stunning story of redemption and hope. Readers will be gripped." Other reviewers additionally noted the strength of Krouse's writing itself. Patrick Hoffman, an author and private investigator, praised the author's ability to set a scene, including capturing the beauty of the Colorado landscape. The changing seasons, particularly the punishing winter and rejuvenating spring, provide a visceral backdrop to her developing involvement in the case. The book is not "preachy or didactic," Hoffman wrote. "Instead, we get beautiful sentences that leap out of nowhere," he added. Overall, reviewers praised Krouse's ability to authentically focus on a particular historical incident of sexual violence and effectively combine honest personal perspective to bring further attention to a social issue that remained relevant more than a decade after the case. Setting itself apart from many traditional true crime tales, *Tell Me Everything* is far from a dry recounting of a lengthy legal battle or a sensationalized account of a real-life event. Nuanced, intelligent, and personal, Krouse's book explores what it means, for victims and perpetrators alike, to exist in a culture that often allows sexual violence to occur without accountability.

Author Biography

Erika Krouse is an award-winning novelist and short-story writer. Her books have included *Come Up and See Me Sometime* (2001) and *Contenders* (2015), the latter a novel about a female street fighter. Her short fiction has been featured in such publications as the *New Yorker*, *Ploughshares*, and the *Kenyon Review*.

Molly Hagan

Review Sources

Cary, Alice. Review of *Tell Me Everything: The Story of a Private Investigation*, by Erika Krouse. *BookPage*, Mar. 2022, www.bookpage.com/reviews/tell-me-everything/. Accessed 2 Dec. 2022.

Hoffman, Patrick. "She Became a Private Eye. And Investigated Her Past." Review of *Tell Me Everything: The Story of a Private Investigation*, by Erika Krouse. *The New York Times*, 16 Mar. 2022, www.nytimes.com/2022/03/16/books/review/tell-me-everything-erika-krause.html. Accessed 28 Sept. 2022.

Miller, Laura. "The Unreliable Narrator." Review of *Tell Me Everything: The Story of a Private Investigation*, by Erika Krouse. *Slate*, 14 Mar. 2022, slate.com/culture/2022/03/tell-me-everything-erika-krouse-memoir-review.html. Accessed 28 Sept. 2022.

Review of *Tell Me Everything: The Story of a Private Investigation*, by Erika Krouse. *Kirkus*, 21 Dec. 2021, www.kirkusreviews.com/book-reviews/erika-krouse/tell-me-everything-krouse/. Accessed 28 Sept. 2022.

Review of *Tell Me Everything: The Story of a Private Investigation*, by Erika Krouse. *Publishers Weekly*, 12 Nov. 2021, www.publishersweekly.com/9781250240309. Accessed 28 Sept. 2022.

Thank You, Mr. Nixon

Author: Gish Jen (b. 1955)
Publisher: Alfred A. Knopf (New York). 272 pp.
Type of work: Short fiction
Time: 1970s–2020s
Locales: China, United States, heaven and hell

Thank You, Mr. Nixon is a collection of interlinked short stories that explore the cultural relationship between the United States and China. Featuring a rotating cast of characters—ranging from elderly parents to preteen children—the collection spans generations and continents attempting to understand geographic and political divides.

Principal characters

TRICIA SANG, a former Little Red Guard who writes to Richard Nixon from heaven
OPAL, an older Chinese immigrant who lives in the US with her daughter
GRACE CHEN DE CASTRO, Opal's daughter
GIDEON, Opal's son-in-law
AMARYLLIS CHEN DE CASTRO, Opal's granddaughter
DUNCAN HSU, the underachieving son of Chinese immigrants
BOBBY KOO, an activist who has broken free from expectations
LULU KOO, Bobby's sister
BETTY KOO, Bobby's sister
TINA KOO, Bobby's mother
JOHNSON KOO, Bobby's father
TOM SHORE, a White man from suburban Ohio
TORY SHORE, Tom's wife
ARABELLA LI, a law student who decides to pursue a career defending undocumented immigrants in the United States
RICH LEE, a.k.a., Mr. Crime and Punishment and War and Peace, Arabella's law school classmate and admirer

Gish Jen's ninth book, *Thank You, Mr. Nixon* (2022), is wide-ranging in its characters and settings, and laser-focused in its intention: to explore how relationships and families are shaped and changed by history and capitalism. Consisting of eleven stories, most of which share characters, Jen's collection balances personalities, generational responsibilities, and unexpected failures with large historical moments like China's

Gish Jen

Cultural Revolution and quieter personal moments, for example a child leaving home or a couple deciding to part ways. Along with this, Jen explores what it means to be Chinese and Chinese American, whether through a keen understanding of the relationship between China-born parents and US-born children or the ties one maintains to a place they have never been to and people they have never met. Her language is crisp and clear, allowing the lives and inner emotions of her characters to take precedence across plotlines and international boundaries.

Thank You, Mr. Nixon opens with its title story, a posthumous letter penned by Tricia Sang, a resident of heaven, to former US president Richard Nixon, who is spending the afterlife in hell, specifically at "Ninth Ring Road, Pit 1A." Sang had met Nixon when she was a Little Red Guard in Hangzhou during his famous visit to China in the 1970s. The first US president to ever visit mainland China while in office, Nixon brought a level of fanfare with his visit that shook up the lives of many Chinese citizens. Jen's narrator, and the painful memories she includes in her letter, set a tone for the rest of the book. The reader understands that the lives lived by many of those in the following stories will be difficult and painful, with some moments of joy and humor.

The second story, "It's the Great Wall!," works to further complicate the relationship between Chinese citizens, US citizens, and those of Chinese heritage with a cast of characters spanning the spectrum. Gideon and Grace are an interracial couple; Gideon is a White man whose family is "Caribbean Sephardic Jewish with maybe some Moorish something," while Grace's mother, Opal, was born in China but immigrated to the US. Jen sets up a tension between Gideon and Grace and how they should approach a tour they are expecting to take of China with Opal. Grace wants to take an "Overseas Chinese" tour where everyone speaks Chinese, while Gideon wants to take the "regular American tour." One goal of the trip is to reunite Opal with her two sisters after decades of separation.

The third story, "Duncan in China," follows a twenty-something man from the US named Duncan who is going to China to teach. One of three children born to Chinese immigrants, he will be meeting his relatives who live in China for the first time during his visit. The tensions he experiences and feels during his visit and the awkward meeting between him and his family further lay the groundwork for the collection's themes. The remaining eight stories feature characters from "It's the Great Wall!" and "Duncan in China," adding new voices and situations that further complicate their experiences.

What stands out the most in *Thank You, Mr. Nixon* is how Jen handles the relationships between her characters. Often it seems nearly impossible for many of those connected within one story to truly understand each other, regardless of language and cultural barriers. For example, in "It's the Great Wall!," Gideon, despite his longtime connection to Grace and her mother, insists that the trio buy seats on the more expensive tour made for American tourists. Grace knows that this is not the right tour for her mother, who would feel more comfortable visiting China with the Overseas Chinese tour; however, she gives in to her husband. On the tour, the trio meet a loud, obnoxious couple of "blond Cincinnatians" named Tom and Tory, along with a smug professor and his wife. The group's tour guide, Comrade Sun, and the commune tour guide, Comrade Tu, both have difficulty speaking English and being understood, leading to Opal being enlisted to translate for them and to field the group's questions about Chinese culture and people. The tension created by this scenario—the exhaustion Opal feels, the arrogance, ignorance, and ethnocentrism the other tourists convey—is further heightened when their tour group finds itself in the same cafeteria as a China-born group and Grace recognizes David, an Asian American man she went to high school with in Mamaroneck, New York. Jen's way of conveying Opal's exhaustion and outsider status among the group is done through showing how many hours she spends translating. She is also allowed moments of wit that reveal the truly ridiculous personalities of her tour companions.

Thank You, Mr. Nixon's stories are loosely linked throughout, and Tory and Tom show up in a later story called "A Tea Tale," as do Duncan and his wife, Lingli, the daughter of a woman from the class he taught in "Duncan in China." "A Tea Tale" is most effective because of the precedent Jen sets up when first introducing Tory and Tom. On the tour, they are blissfully ignorant, annoying Americans. The reader learns that they have been so inspired by their trip that they now plan to begin to sell tea at the coffee shop they have owned for years. They find a tea farmer in China and set up an agreement to buy in bulk. The partnership is a disaster, and coincidentally Duncan is opening a tea store half a block from their coffee shop. The tension between Tom and Tory and their China-based tea partners is juxtaposed with the tension between Duncan and his new shop, and allows Jen to skillfully expose the racism Tom and Tory carry. Tom and Tory's adoption of their toddler daughter, Mei, in China, adds an even greater source of tension to the story.

The last story in the collection, "Detective Dog," moves on to the next generation of children growing up in the United States. Betty, one of the three Koo sisters, is living in New York with her husband, Quentin, and their sons Theo and Robert. The setting takes place just after the height of the COVID-19 pandemic and the protests in Hong Kong. Betty and her husband move easily back and forth between their wealthy Manhattan life and the life they had back in Hong Kong. Her parents are extremely wealthy and have given their children every chance. Their eldest daughter, Bobby Koo, got into top US universities and had a high-paying job on Wall Street but then gave it up, ran off with a musician, joined the protests in Hong Kong—as detailed in the collection's sixth story, "Gratitude"—and eventually disappeared in China. News that Bobby's "last letter," written to be sent to her loved ones in the event of her death or arrest, was received by a family member who subsequently ripped it up, causes much heartbreak among the family. This story is particularly poignant because Betty's adopted son Robert is inquisitive and is also much more aware of what is going on around him than Betty realizes. When he writes an extra-credit mystery story about Detective Dog, a dog who solves missing-person cases, she tells him stories about missing people that she knows: her older son, Theo, who has left home but not really disappeared, and her sister Bobby, who has. The story, which was selected for *Best American Short Stories of 2022*, perfectly concludes the narrative arcs of the characters contained within *Thank You, Mr. Nixon*.

Thank You, Mr. Nixon was widely praised by critics. Citing the opening story of the collection, Michael Schaub wrote for NPR, "The story beautifully illustrates a crucial chapter in the relationship between China and its residents, and America and ours. The tensions that arise between the two peoples, especially the ones felt by Chinese Americans, form a throughline in Jen's collection." In a starred review, *Publishers Weekly* stated, "With wry humor, pathos, and punchy dialogue, Jen's uncanny stories easily stand up to her hefty themes. This is a stellar addition to Jen's prolific body of work." For the *Christian Science Monitor*, Erin Douglass wrote, "Jen's stories prove engrossing thanks to her polished prose and multifaceted characters. Equally riveting is the fearless way she dives into fraught, ripped-from-the headlines topics." Jacqueline Houton reviewed the collection for the *Arts Fuse* and, noting that 2022 marked fifty years since Nixon touched down in China, admired the way that Jen was able to bring the personal into a historical context. Houton wrote, "The collection is united by her blend of sharp observation and compassion for her characters. . . . Taken together, the stories have the sweep and scope of a novel, one that's by turns humorous and harrowing and, above all, humane." The collection was also favorably reviewed in the *Boston Globe* and the *Star Tribune*, while Jen was profiled and her book was positively discussed in a story for the *New York Times*.

Author Biography

Gish Jen is the author of nine books, including *Typical American* (1991), *Who's Irish?* (1999), and *The Resisters* (2020). Her work has been included in *The Best American Short Stories* and was selected for *The Best American Short Stories of the Century*. She has been the recipient of awards such as a Lannan Literary Award for Fiction.

Melynda Fuller

Review Sources

Douglass, Erin. "*Thank You, Mr. Nixon* and Other Tales of the Chinese Diaspora." Review of *Thank You, Mr. Nixon*, by Gish Jen. *The Christian Science Monitor*, 4 Feb. 2022, www.csmonitor.com/Books/Book-Reviews/2022/0204/Thank-You-Mr.-Nixon-and-other-tales-of-the-Chinese-diaspora. Accessed 1 Feb. 2023.

Houton, Jacqueline. "Book Review: *Thank You, Mr. Nixon*—East Meets West, Again and Again." *The Arts Fuse*, 1 Feb. 2022, artsfuse.org/246515/book-review-thank-you-mr-nixon-east-meets-west-again-and-again/. Accessed 1 Feb. 2023.

Oldweiler, Cory. Review of *Thank You, Mr. Nixon*, by Gish Jen. *Star Tribune*, 21 Jan. 2022, www.startribune.com/review-thank-you-mr-nixon-by-gish-jen/600138134/. Accessed 1 Feb. 2023.

Review of *Thank You, Mr. Nixon*, by Gish Jen. *Kirkus*, 27 Oct. 2021, www.kirkusreviews.com/book-reviews/gish-jen/thank-you-mr-nixon/. Accessed 1 Feb. 2023.

Review of *Thank You, Mr. Nixon*, by Gish Jen. *Publishers Weekly*, 2 Nov. 2021, www.publishersweekly.com/9780593319895. Accessed 1 Feb. 2023.

Schaub, Michael. "*Thank You, Mr. Nixon* Is a Collection Written with Intelligence, Wit and Grace." Review of *Thank You, Mr. Nixon*, by Gish Jen. *NPR*, 1 Feb. 2022, www.npr.org/2022/02/01/1077296906/thank-you-mr-nixon-is-a-collection-written-with-intelligence-wit-and-grace. Accessed 1 Feb. 2023.

Tuttle, Kate. "Place and Displacement in *Thank You, Mr. Nixon*." Review of *Thank You, Mr. Nixon*, by Gish Jen. *The Boston Globe*, 11 Feb. 2022, www.bostonglobe.com/2022/02/10/arts/place-displacement-thank-you-mr-nixon/. Accessed 1 Feb. 2023.

This Time Tomorrow

Author: Emma Straub (b. 1980)
Publisher: Riverhead Books (New York). 320 pp.
Type of work: Novel
Time: Present day; 1990s
Locale: New York City

In This Time Tomorrow, *best-selling author Emma Straub considers life and familial love in a time-bending story that is both funny and poignant. When a woman named Alice Stern, the daughter of the famous science-fiction novelist Leonard Stern, turns forty, she finds herself thrust back in time to the day of her sixteenth birthday. Alice must figure out how she got there, and what choices she must make to change the course of her life.*

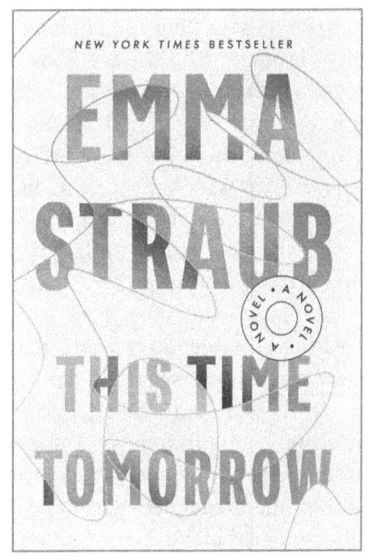

Principal characters
ALICE STERN, a forty-year-old woman who travels back in time
LEONARD STERN, her father, a best-selling science fiction author
SAM, her devoted best friend
TOMMY, her high school crush

This Time Tomorrow (2022) is Emma Straub's fifth novel. Straub's books are often described as "beach reads," a moniker, often derogatory, that she embraces. In fact, her books are literary, but not pretentiously so; previous novels like *The Vacationers* (2014) and *Modern Lovers* (2016) are well-told stories for readers who enjoy well-told stories. *This Time Tomorrow* is no exception.

At the start of the novel, protagonist Alice Stern, daughter of the famous science-fiction novelist Leonard Stern, is turning forty. Alice is ambivalent about birthdays, but the prospect of such a milestone occasion forces her to take stock of her life. She is happy, she decides, or rather, happy enough. She has a good, if unexciting, administrative job at the same Upper West Side prep school she once attended. Furthermore, she is contentedly single and without roommates, paying a blessedly decent rent for the same adorable Brooklyn studio she has inhabited for over a decade, and she has the support of her devoted, lifelong best friend, Sam.

But all is not perfect. Alice's father, Leonard, who raised her as a single dad, is dying in a hospital—the "many neighborhoods" of his body "falling apart in a great, unified chorus"—and Alice cannot help but feel that if her life had unfolded differently, he might not be dying, or at least she might somehow feel better prepared to accept his death. Though their relationship was enviable in many ways, Alice is filled with regret: for not asking more questions about his family or why he never wrote another book after his massive best-selling novel about two time-traveling brothers who solve crimes. Moreover, she regrets not saying "I love you" more, or ever initiating a hug.

Alice cannot help but view her passivity in her relationship with her father as indicative of a larger character flaw. She is happy because she is comfortable; she wonders if she shares this inclination for the path of least resistance with her father. She sees them each, in their own ways, as "stable like a seahorse with its tail looped around some seagrass" and "happier to stay close to what had worked, rather than risking it all on something new." Here, Straub undoubtedly draws from her own experiences with her father, the acclaimed horror novelist Peter Straub, who died in 2022. Explaining this central relationship of the novel, critic Heller McAlpin for NPR wrote, "Regardless of how many autobiographical elements *This Time Tomorrow* does or does not contain, it joins a growing lineup of books in which writer-daughters pay tribute to their fathers."

Emma Straub

On the night of her fortieth birthday, after the unexpected relief of turning down a marriage proposal from her painfully bland boyfriend, Matt, Alice takes a small risk. She returns to one of her teenage haunts, a hidden dive bar in a Manhattan subway station called Matroyshka, named for the stackable Russian dolls, and gets drunk. This small but unexpected choice unleashes a series of events that propel Alice back through time. At the end of the night, she passes out in her father's garden shed at age forty and wakes up in her teenage bedroom on the morning of her sixteenth birthday.

Straub's writing in this novel, as in her previous works, is witty, sharp, and well-paced. Particularly enjoyable in *This Time Tomorrow* are the asides satirizing the absurdity of New York's privileged class. Alice works at a private school on the Upper West Side called Belvedere, and her experience makes her an expert in the varieties of rich people and the expensive schools where they choose to send their children. There are schools for athletes, but also schools for "eating-disordered overachievers" and "tiny Brooks Brothers mannequins who would end up as CEOs." Alice can instantly tell the difference between rich parents with generational wealth "for whom jobs were superfluous," and people like her father, an ill-fitting artist-type, whose lone source of wealth was a single blockbuster novel-turned-television show called *Time Brothers*. These types of wealthy people intermingle and occasionally intermarry, but "it was a farce, the contortions that rich people would make so as to appear less dripping with privilege," Straub writes. Ironically, Alice wields a lot of power over these very influential people. She works in admissions, interviewing and selecting potential students.

"In the real world, and in her own life, Alice had no power," Straub writes, "but in the kingdom of Belvedere, she was a Sith Lord, or a Jedi, depending on whether one's child got in or not."

These kinds of humorous, observant details set Straub's novels apart. *This Time Tomorrow* does not introduce any new concept or special device to time-travel literature, and in fact, it playfully and explicitly invokes other stories about time travel, including popular films like *Peggy Sue Got Married* (1986), *Bill & Ted's Excellent Adventure* (1989), and *Groundhog Day* (1993). However, genre is not really the point, just as it was not the point in Straub's 2016 romantic comedy *Modern Lovers*. As Michiko Kakutani, the famously critical former head critic of the *New York Times*, wrote of that novel, while the plot dynamics felt familiar, "Straub writes with such verve and sympathetic understanding of her characters that we barely notice."

After Alice travels back in time, Straub imparts rich detail in her descriptions of the Upper West Side of the 1990s, before the neighborhood had completely succumbed to the whims of the wealthy people who live there. New York City is Straub's actual hometown, but also a place, if one lives there long enough, in which one can be struck by the relentless passage of time. Then again, Straub writes, "that was New York, watching every place you'd kissed or cried, every place you loved, turn into something else."

It has not been that long since Alice was sixteen—a little over twenty years—and yet it has been a lifetime. She eagerly visits restaurants and shops that, even in such a seemingly short period of time, have long since disappeared. Her neighborhood in 1996 feels familiar but also like another planet. This dissonance is particularly striking when Alice first wakes up in her sixteen-year-old body. Feeling the sensations of her youthful limbs, and looking at her cherub-like face in the mirror, Alice recalls, as an adult, having complained about getting older and sometimes feeling age creaking in her bones. "But on the whole, she'd felt exactly the same as she had when she was a teenager," Straub writes. "She'd been wrong."

Alice's experiences recall the cliché about youth being wasted on the young, but in Straub's hands the concept is tangible, evoking both joy and pain. As her journey through her past progresses, it recalls the last scene of Thornton Wilder's play *Our Town* (1938), in which a young woman dies and returns to an ordinary morning when she was twelve years old. The smell of coffee and her mother's brusque, familiar movements through the kitchen eventually become too much for her to bear.

Indeed, several reviewers of *This Time Tomorrow* also drew comparisons to *Our Town*, indicating the overall favorable critical response. The starred review for *Kirkus* added another comparison: to the "time-travel shenanigans" in Kate Atkinson's novel *Life After Life* (2013). In that novel, each time the main character dies, she begins her life all over again—a concept that Alice, in the book, is too horrified by to contemplate. She desperately hopes she will not be forced to relive her life starting at sixteen. Part of the fun of time-travel stories, though, is watching the characters grapple with their situation, wondering how they got to the past and if they will ever be able to leave it. For Alice, the answers to these questions are surprising. "Even as it rifles through references, *This Time Tomorrow* insists on its own originality," Susan Dominus wrote in her positive review for the *New York Times*. "The novel experimentally cycles through a few forms of narrative, playing on reader expectations."

Most reviewers agreed that the heart of the novel lies in the unique relationship between Alice and her father, Leonard. Alice's mother left the family when she was six, and while both Alice and Leonard are too shy and eccentric to demonstrate their love, they are fiercely attached. This attachment, of course, makes the prospect of losing Leonard all the more unbearable for Alice. When she was a teenager, Leonard was a trusting "cool dad" who let her smoke cigarettes at fourteen—a lesser deal, perhaps, in the 1990s—and always treated her with the respect of a fellow adult. Adult Alice considers the ambivalence inherent in these parental choices, but also revels in the memories of watching *Jeopardy!* with her father, or visiting the gargantuan blue whale that hangs from the ceiling of the American Museum of Natural History. As much as Alice enjoys reliving aspects of her past—sleeping with an unrequited crush, for instance—her travel is really aimed at saving her father. Not only does Alice endeavor to save his life literally—suggesting he quit smoking and start exercising, for instance—but she also encourages him to take the risks that she later wishes he had taken when faced with his death. As Dominus wrote, "What she wants out of time travel is not so much to fix herself, but to unstick her father, who has stalled out romantically and creatively."

This yearning on behalf of her father is not entirely selfless. It also reminds forty-year-old Alice that new beginnings are not just for the young. As an adult in her teenage body, she is in awe of a simple fact about her father. "He had been young, and she had been young—they had been young together," Straub writes. "Why was it so hard to see that?"

Author Biography

Emma Straub is a best-selling author whose novels include *Laura Lamont's Life in Pictures* (2012), *The Vacationers* (2014), *Modern Lovers* (2016), and *All Adults Here* (2020). She also published a book of short stories called *Other People We Married* (2011). Straub, who grew up in Manhattan, owns a bookstore in Brooklyn called Books Are Magic.

Molly Hagan

Review Sources

Dominus, Susan. "A Time-Traveling Daughter Just Wants Some Time with Her Dad." Review of *This Time Tomorrow*, by Emma Straub. *The New York Times*, 17 May 2022, www.nytimes.com/2022/05/17/books/review/emma-straub-this-time-tomorrow.html. Accessed 21 Sept. 2022.

Gage, Eleni N. "The Era-Hopping Narrator of Emma Straub's *This Time Tomorrow* Finds Love Is the Only Thing That Lasts." Review of *This Time Tomorrow*, by Emma Straub. *Oprah Daily*, 6 July 2022, www.oprahdaily.com/entertainment/books/a40080937/emma-straub-this-time-tomorrow/. Accessed 21 Sept. 2022.

McAlpin, Heller. "In *This Time Tomorrow*, Emma Straub Looks at the Pieces That Make a Life." Review of *This Time Tomorrow*, by Emma Straub. *NPR*, 17 May 2022, www.npr.org/2022/05/17/1099085795/in-this-time-tomorrow-emma-straub-looks-at-the-pieces-that-make-a-life. Accessed 21 Sept. 2022.

Review of *This Time Tomorrow*, by Emma Straub. *Kirkus*, 13 Apr. 2022, www.kirkusreviews.com/book-reviews/emma-straub/this-time-tomorrow-straub/. Accessed 21 Sept. 2022.

Review of *This Time Tomorrow*, by Emma Straub. *Publishers Weekly*, 23 Feb. 2022, www.publishersweekly.com/9780525539001. Accessed 21 Sept. 2022.

This Woven Kingdom

Author: Tahereh Mafi (b. 1988)
Publisher: HarperCollins (New York). 512 pp.
Type of work: Novel
Time: Unknown
Locale: Setar, the capital city in the kingdom of Ardunia

In Tahereh Mafi's young adult fantasy novel, equal parts love story and political scheming, Alizeh, a jinn with special powers working secretly as a maid, accidentally meets the human crown prince of Ardunia, Kamran. Once their worlds collide, their curiosity and feelings about each other grow while the kingdom of Ardunia is thrown into turmoil.

Principal characters

ALIZEH, a young jinn woman hiding her true identity by working as a maid
PRINCE KAMRAN, in line to inherit the throne from his grandfather, King Zaal
KING ZAAL, King of Ardunia and grandfather to Prince Kamran
OMID, a destitute boy whom Alizeh befriends
MISS HUDA, the young woman who hires Alizeh to design and sew gowns
HAZAN, minister and personal attendant to Prince Kamran

While Tahereh Mafi has published an acclaimed young adult dystopian series, the *Shatter Me* series (2011–20), and the award-nominated contemporary young adult novel *A Very Large Expanse of Sea* (2018), *This Woven Kingdom* (2022) is her first foray into young adult fantasy novels. Mafi, who is of Iranian American decent, draws from her cultural background, the traditions of Islam, and the *Shahnameh*, an epic Persian poem which portrays the pre-Islamic history of Persia through the escapades of a hero with special powers and abilities. Mafi updates the epic poem by making the hero a heroine, named Alizeh, and endowing her with exceptional physical strength, invisibility, and unique eyes that reveal her origin as a jinn, a race of people who are superior to humans (known as Clay) in speed and strength. After many years of battles between the two races, peace was achieved, but it has been a tenuous and inequitable peace, with jinns in constant danger due to Clay prejudice and jealousy. In *This Woven Kingdom*, Mafi creates a captivating fantasy world based on a strong heroine, an exploration of class struggles, a reliance on folklore and mythology, and a writing style that is both lyrical and sophisticated.

Mafi sets her novel in the imagined country of Ardunia, which is led by King Zaal. With tensions rising between Ardunia and neighboring countries over a lack of fresh

Tahereh Mafi

water and other resources, Prince Kamran, King Zaal's grandson and the kingdom's heir, has spent the last year away fighting in small skirmishes and making sure the country's borders are secure. Prince Kamran has returned at his grandfather's request, and he learns he must make a politically advantageous marriage and prepare to take over the throne. Alizeh, on the other hand, has a much different background. She is poor and without family; both her parents are dead. She is also a jinn and an excellent seamstress. She uses these skills to support herself after her parents' deaths. In the small town where she lived, a Clay dressmaker was jealous of her abilities and reported her to the authorities, accusing her of wrongfully using her jinn powers to get ahead. After nearly being arrested, Alizeh fled, and, thinking she would fare better in a larger city where she could hide in plain sight, she sneaks into the city of Setar, the capital city of Ardunia.

In Setar, Alizeh does her best to conceal the fact that she is jinn and ensure her safety by finding a maid's position. Since all maids are required to wear snodas, or sheer coverings over their eyes and nose, she will be able to obscure her race, which is most evident in the color of her eyes. Alizeh works at Baz House, the home of Prince Kamran's aunt. After a chance encounter with the prince on the street, Kamran and Alizeh become curious about each other. It is these tensions, the personal and the political, that Mafi uses to drive the narrative forward in *This Woven Kingdom*.

In Alizeh, Mafi has created an especially strong and brave heroine, and she is the moral compass of the novel. As a jinn, Alizeh has been gifted with the powers of superhuman strength, speed, and invisibility. jinns can also go days at a time without food with no ill effects, allowing Alizeh to work long hours with little sleep. When Alizeh is hired by the housekeeper at Baz House, she is not hired out of pity for her desperate situation but because jinns are workhorses, and the housekeeper knows she can get twice the amount of work accomplished with Alizeh as she could from a Clay maid. Even with these physical gifts, however, Alizeh fears being alone and understands the perils of walking the city streets at night; these fears are mitigated, though, by knowing her strength and speed allow her to take care of herself in dangerous situations, thereby enabling Alizeh to take risks a Clay woman would not.

Alizeh's most important character trait, however, is her empathy and kindness. In early childhood, Alizeh's parents provided her with masters and tutors and financial stability, but they stressed the importance of compassion. When Alizeh was an adolescent, her parents died, and Alizeh then had to survive with very little money and no secure housing. Rather than becoming bitter about her changed circumstances, Alizeh chooses to be empathetic, kind, and generous. For example, when a young stranger,

Omid, puts a knife to Alizeh's throat, she responds, gently, with, "Unhand me. Do it now and I give you my word I will leave you unharmed." Alizeh recognizes that the young man is poor and probably hungry, and she could have used her strength to do him great physical harm or even kill him. Omid laughs in response because he does not realize how powerful she is, but Alizeh surprises him by swiftly breaking the wrist holding the knife to her throat and then twisting his arm behind his back, dislocating his shoulder. Immediately afterward, however, she returns his knife to him and says, "There are other ways to stay alive. . . . Come to the kitchens at Baz House if you are in need of bread." When Omid asks why Alizeh would offer him food after he has threatened her life, she responds simply, "Because I understand." She knows how it feels to be hungry and alone, and she wants to alleviate that hunger if she can. As the novel progresses, Alizeh encounters many more dangerous situations, but she is always mindful of others, thinking about what they might be feeling or need rather than focusing on her own needs and safety, making her a character with honor and integrity.

In addition to characterization, Mafi also excels at exploring the theme of class conflict and infusing the narrative with myth and folklore. Alizeh is sympathetic to Omid because she understands his struggle for the basic necessities of food, water, and shelter. Alizeh is also sympathetic to the plight of Miss Huda, the young woman who employs Alizeh to create and sew her dresses, work Alizeh completes at night after her maid duties are finished to earn extra money. Alizeh learns that Miss Huda is the love child of her wealthy father and his mistress. Miss Huda lives with her father and his wife, but she is treated differently from his other children. She is ostracized, and she secretly hires Alizeh so she will have a beautiful dress for the ball. Alizeh understands how it feels to be an outsider, and she does her best to help Miss Huda. Mafi contrasts the struggles of Alizeh, Omid, and Miss Huda with the opulent life of Prince Kamran, who, although pressured into choosing a wife for political gain rather than love, nonetheless lives a life of luxury, where he has personal attendants, all the food and elaborate clothing he could want, and a palatial home. On the surface, Prince Kamran and Alizeh would seem to have little in common, yet despite his wealth and privilege, Prince Kamran shows care in his dealings with others and attempts to make thoughtful decisions. He even disguises himself as one of the townspeople so that he might roam the streets unknown and better understand their everyday lives and problems. It is this quality of caring about the needs of others that brings Alizeh and Prince Kamran together, widening the world for both of them and forcing them to make difficult choices about their future roles and responsibilities.

Folklore, Islamic culture, and myth also play an important role in Mafi's novel. Not only does Mafi incorporate elements of the epic Persian poem *Shahnameh* through its characters and narrative structure, but she also references Islamic culture in the naming of characters, the description of the Setar's public baths, and the smoking of shisha, a flavored tobacco smoked in a hookah pipe. Similarly, Mafi integrates the Qur'an as part of jinn culture with Iblees, or the devil, a being of fire who was thrown out of heaven and forced to witness the rise of humanity (Clay) that took his place. Alizeh encounters Iblees several times in the novel, most notably in chapter 2, where Iblees, who speaks in riddles, warns her of an important prophecy, which begins, "There once was a man / who bore a snake on each shoulder." This prophecy plays an important role in the climax of the novel. In addition to Islamic references, numerous reviewers recognized the fairy tale of Cinderella in *This Woven Kingdom*. Alizeh, like Cinderella, is destitute, works as a maid, lives in an attic room, becomes involved with a prince, and prepares for a ball she is destined to attend. Mafi's use of myth and cultural elements contribute significantly to the success of the fantasy world she creates.

The reviews of *This Woven Kingdom* were overwhelmingly positive. *Kirkus* described it as "gut-wrenchingly beautiful," praising the "richly textured, descriptive prose" as well as its enthralling romance. Similarly, Annie Metcalf of *BookPage* stated that the "novel's stand out feature is its language," noting that the lyrical and heightened prose added to the book's fairytale qualities. Almost all of the reviewers commented on how rich and poetic the language is, with Carrie R. Wheadon of *Common Sense Media* adding that it would not be the ideas or mature content that would challenge teen readers but the high level of vocabulary and lyrical descriptions of characters and their dialogue. In addition to praise for the prose and romance, Lacy Baugher Milas for *Paste* described Mafi's worldbuilding as "lush and detailed" in its weaving together of myth and fantasy.

In *This Woven Kingdom*, Mafi has created a fantasy world rich in detail, characterization, and complexity, and one that has an enduring love story, explores real issues, such as class conflict, and incorporates myth and Islamic culture. It is truly a world readers will want to immerse themselves in.

Author Biography

Tahereh Mafi is the author of the acclaimed dystopian young adult novel series *Shatter Me* (2011–14) and the follow-up novella series *Restore Me* (2018–20). Her novel *A Very Large Expanse of Sea* (2018) was long-listed for the National Book Award for Young People's Literature.

Marybeth Rua-Larsen

Review Sources

Derickson, Grace. Review of *This Woven Kingdom*, by Tahereh Mafi. *Seattle Book Review*, Apr. 2022, seattlebookreview.com/product/this-woven-kingdom-this-woven-kingdom-1/. Accessed 19 Oct. 2022.

Metcalf, Annie. Review of *This Woven Kingdom*, by Tahereh Mafi. *BookPage*, 22 Sept. 2022, www.bookpage.com/reviews/this-woven-kingdom/. Accessed 19 Oct. 2022.

Milas, Lacy Baugher. "*This Woven Kingdom*: A Star-Crossed Romance Set in a Rich Persian-Inspired Fantasy World." Review of *This Woven Kingdom*, by Tahereh Mafi. *Paste*, 1 Feb. 2022, www.pastemagazine.com/books/this-woven-kingdom-a-star-crossed-romance-set-in-a/. Accessed 19 Oct. 2022.

Review of *This Woven Kingdom*, by Tahereh Mafi. *Kirkus*, 1 Feb. 2022, www.kirkusreviews.com/book-reviews/tahereh-mafi/this-woven-kingdom/. Accessed 19 Oct. 2022.

Review of *This Woven Kingdom*, by Tahereh Mafi. *Publishers Weekly*, 23 Dec. 2021, www.publishersweekly.com/9780062972446. Accessed 19 Oct. 2022.

Wheadon, Carrie R. Review of *This Woven Kingdom*, by Tahereh Mafi. *Common Sense Media*, 25 Jan. 2022, www.commonsensemedia.org/book-reviews/this-woven-kingdom. Accessed 19 Oct. 2022.

A Thousand Steps into Night

Author: Traci Chee
Publisher: Clarion Books (Boston). 384 pp.
Type of work: Novel
Time: Long ago
Locale: Awara

Set in a world inspired by Japanese mythology, A Thousand Steps into Night *is a fantasy novel by the best-selling American author Traci Chee.*

Principal characters
OTORI MIUKO, a seventeen-year-old girl born into the servant class
GEIKI, a magpie spirit who becomes her best friend
ROHIRO, her father
TUJIYAZAI, a demon prince out for revenge

   Traci Chee is the kind of writer whose work cannot be easily described by one genre. When she first broke into the literary scene, it was with the best-selling fantasy trilogy *The Sea of Ink and Gold* (2016–18), which imagined a world without reading. She then forayed into historical fiction with a novel about a group of young second-generation Japanese Americans who were incarcerated during World War II. Titled *We Are Not Free* (2020), it was a critical success, becoming a National Book Award finalist while also earning a place on *TIME*'s list of the one hundred best young adult novels of all time.
   In her fifth novel, *A Thousand Steps into Night* (2022), Chee provides readers with a genre-mashup tale about a young woman standing up to oppression. Set in the fictional world of Awara, it follows the story of a seventeen-year-old girl of the serving class named Miuko who has always struggled to adhere to society's gendered expectations for her. Instead of having the demure, obedient qualities of an ideal young woman, she is loud, clumsy, and always speaking her mind. Her identity as a woman is further challenged one day when she is kissed by a demon and starts slowly becoming a demon herself. When she is subsequently exiled from her village of Nihaoi, Miuko must find a way to break her curse before her demonic transformation is complete.
   A Thousand Steps into Night is an epic on-the-road adventure. Like the Greek hero Odysseus, fantasy writer J. R. R. Tolkien's character Frodo Baggins, or many other protagonists from these genres, Miuko is sent on a quest that sends her far away from everything she has ever known. Along the way, she encounters monsters, demons, spirits, and feral gods that force her to be brave. However, Miuko's story feels more fresh than imitative of these classic tales. Although her journey is also a coming of

age, the personal growth she undergoes is focused primarily on the evolution of her womanhood in a patriarchal society. This is to say that as Miuko battles literal demons, she does the same with the figurative ones that represent her understanding of what a woman's role in Awara can be.

It is not surprising, then, that the theme of feminism is one of the novel's strongest, and many readers will delight in the imaginative way that Chee uses storytelling to highlight the importance of women taking a stand against sexism in both their personal lives and the world at large. Chee also uses the narrative to address other related issues, including the way that marriage and religion are often used to reinforce male authority and how women sometimes end up doing irreparable harm to womankind by trying to protect the men they love. Arguably, one of the most haunting revelations in the book is about a woman who would cover up all of her son's murders by burying the bodies of his young female victims under the house.

Traci Chee

Because Miuko's story is one about her own personal growth, however, the most powerful feminist subtheme is internalized sexism. When the story begins, Miuko is critical of herself because she does not have the makings of an ideal potential wife, which is the ultimate goal for young women—especially in the serving class. Her ostensible desire to be the marriable type and fulfill her societal duty is exacerbated by the fact that her mother abandoned their family, ostensibly because she wanted a life of adventure rather than domesticity. Miuko resents her mother for leaving and subsequently dislikes any of her own tendencies that might be comparable. This changes over time, of course, as she discovers on her adventure that not fitting into Awara's society may not be a bad thing but, instead, what makes her special. While this idea is not necessarily a new one in storytelling, Chee ensures that Miuko's evolution from internalized sexism to self-acceptance is full of interesting ideas of selfhood and born through exciting events.

A Thousand Steps into Night is a plot-heavy novel that takes countless twists and turns as Miuko's quest to find a cure from becoming an indigo-skinned demon is often derailed by setbacks and side adventures. However, the novel is also a character-driven drama, as most of the novel's cast have unique traits and voices. Chee's talent for crafting memorable characters is most evident in the protagonist herself; in addition to having relatable fears and awkwardness, Miuko is a compelling heroine thanks to the internal battle she is fighting against a growing demonic desire to commit violence and consume the lifeforce of others.

Controlling these desires proves to be especially difficult thanks to the fact that she is being followed by Tujiyazai—a fiery demon prince who has possessed the human form of "the doro," or Awara's future ruler, Omaizi Ruhai. Tujiyazai is a superb antagonist in that he is both terrifying and magnetic, evil but at times almost empathetic. Like Miuko, he too was once wronged by Awara and believes that once her transformation is complete that they will have the power to burn society down together. Tujiyazai and some of the other disturbing characters could easily sink the novel into a dark, hopeless tone, but Chee strikes a balance with some of the other supporting cast. Miuko's father, Rohiro, for example, is a hopeful character who demonstrates that people can err and redeem themselves. More than anyone, however, the novel's sense of optimism is buoyed by the character of Geiki—a shapeshifting magpie spirit whose loyalty and hilarious quips make him the perfect sidekick.

Equally good to Chee's characters is her capacity for fresh, original worldbuilding. Awara is inspired, in part, by historical Japan, as evidenced by many of the small details about the culture, customs, architecture, and food that comprise Miuko's life in Nihaoi and elsewhere in the realm. Meanwhile, its fantasy elements like spirits, demons, Gods, and other supernatural forces are inspired by traditional Japanese folklore. This mashup of history, fantasy, and folklore becomes a world entirely Chee's own, and to ensure that readers do not get lost in her original creation, she provides footnotes that explain Awara's unique rules, expressions, history, and figures.

Because it has so many different elements blended into it, it is difficult to know exactly where to place *A Thousand Steps into Night* in the literary landscape. While some critics have lumped it into the broad category of young adult—which is correct in that it is mostly intended for readers in their formative years—others have designated it as fantasy. However, the novel can also be described as a welcome addition to the growing and more specific subgenre of culturally inspired fantasy. In the 2020s, there has been a movement among writers of color to interweave elements of their culture's folklore, mythology, and storytelling traditions into young adult fantasy. Darcie Little Badger did this in her novel *A Snake Falls to Earth* (2021), which was inspired by traditional Lipan Apache myths, beliefs, and characters. Similarly, young adult author Kat Cho's heroine in *Wicked Fox* (2019) is a modern interpretation of the Korean folklore creature of a "gumiho," or nine-tailed fox. *A Thousand Steps into Night* feels like it belongs alongside these books as Chee, like Little Badger and Cho, successfully used her own cultural background as a springboard for creating an entirely original fantasy landscape with its own unique rules, history, and supernatural forces.

Reviews of *A Thousand Steps into Night* were mostly positive, with many critics extolling Chee for her vivid imaginative writing style. To this point, *Kirkus* concluded that the novel is "a captivating read rich in atmosphere." It is true that the world of Awara is well wrought, layered, and tonally distinct. This is compounded by the creativity with which she renders the many beings that inhabit Awara, including mischievous monkey spirits, Lunar Gods, and lugubrious priests.

Beyond Chee's talent for transporting readers somewhere fantastical, many critics thought that her plotting is excellent. In her review for the *School Library Journal*, Stacey Shapiro wrote that, "Just like Miuko, the story never takes the path that's expected." Here, Shapiro touches on how one of the novel's most enjoyable qualities is its unpredictability. The first part of *A Thousand Steps into Night* can be a bit slow;

however, there is an incredible twist that reinvigorates the narrative in a truly captivating way and furthers Miuko's journey as feeling wholly original. This sense of originality in the plot is refreshing, especially as so much genre fiction has the tendency to recycle well-worn tropes. In fact, subverting one traditional young adult trope, Miuko is never caught in a love triangle nor does her journey have to do with finding romantic love.

While some critics noted that some readers might find its feminist themes overpowering, others argued that the story offered more than just a societal critique. As Wendy Chen wrote in her review for *Tor*, "The narrative was thought-provoking with its ideas around past selves, the ways we come to new understandings of our innate desires, and the role of our own choices in our lives' turning points." Chen is right to point out that the novel succeeds in making Miuko's personal growth something that any person can learn from as they come to terms with who they presently are versus who they used to be. This sense of universality is not limited to just this issue—Miuko's struggles with feeling different, facing antagonists, and maintaining her humanity during dark times are ones that people of all backgrounds are likely to find meaning in.

In addition to its positive critical reviews, *A Thousand Steps into Night* was longlisted for the 2022 National Book Award for Young People's Literature.

Author Biography

Traci Chee is the best-selling author of the young adult trilogy *Sea of Ink and Gold* (2016–18). Her novel *We Are Not Free* (2020), about Japanese American teenagers during World War II, was a National Book Award finalist and won the Printz Honor Award.

Emily E. Turner

Review Sources

Chen, Wendy. "Transformation, Morality, and Demonic Power." Review of *A Thousand Steps into Night*, by Traci Chee. *Tor*, 17 Mar. 2022, www.tor.com/2022/03/17/book-reviews-a-thousand-steps-into-night-by-traci-chee/. Accessed 1 Feb. 2023.

Review of *A Thousand Steps into Night*, by Traci Chee. *Kirkus*, 15 Dec. 2022, www.kirkusreviews.com/book-reviews/traci-chee/a-thousand-steps-into-night. Accessed 1 Feb. 2023.

Review of *A Thousand Steps into Night*, by Traci Chee. *Publishers Weekly*, 27 Jan. 2022, www.publishersweekly.com/9780358469988. Accessed 9 Feb. 2023.

Shapiro, Stacey. Review of *A Thousand Steps into Night*, by Traci Chee. *School Library Journal*, 1 Feb. 2022, www.slj.com/review/a-thousand-steps-into-night. Accessed 2 Feb. 2023.

Time Is a Mother

Author: Ocean Vuong (b. 1988)
Publisher: Penguin Press (New York). 128 pp.
Type of work: Poetry
Time: Present day, some flashbacks

Ocean Vuong's second collection of poetry, Time Is a Mother, *finds the writer grappling with the 2019 death of his mother. Combining poignant descriptions and moments with a modernist sensibility, the poems blend perspective and create an atmosphere of timelessness as Vuong imagines both the past—near and distant—and a future spent without her.*

Ocean Vuong's poetry collection *Time Is a Mother* (2022) takes readers deeper into his feelings of admiration, love, and confusion about his mother, Lê Kim Hồng—many of the themes he developed in his best-selling novel *On Earth We're Briefly Gorgeous* (2019). However, *Time Is a Mother* also takes on themes of grief, fractured identity, and loss. Filled with sometimes abstract personal poems and beautifully lyrical meditations on his mother and what her loss means to him, *Time Is a Mother* marks a new direction for the writer, whose first collection of poetry, *Night Sky with Exit Wounds* (2016), dealt more definitively with concrete ideas delivered in a more formal voice. In his second collection, Vuong further develops his style, this time hovering in a modernist tradition as he eschews punctuation and line breaks and switches perspectives often. His mother's presence is felt throughout the entirety of this collection, and though she had already died from breast cancer at the time of its writing, her life pulses from the pages. The poet's sense of loss, and perhaps even a sense of wonder at the waves of grief that have taken over his life, mark each poem.

The poems of *Time Is a Mother* are divided into four sections, which appear between an opening poem and closing poem that each stand on their own. In the opening poem, "The Bull," the reader comes face to face with the monumental pain and fear one faces when feeling alone in the world. Vuong writes of a beast with "kerosene- / blue eyes" who is standing in the dark of his backyard "Like something prayed for / by a man with no mouth." The speaker of the poem goes on to describe his ambivalent feelings toward the beast: "I didn't want him to / be beautiful—but needing beauty / to be more than hurt gentle / enough to want, I reached for him." These words and this moment act as a prelude to the feelings, and often the images, that fill the rest of the collection.

Vuong's mother shows up most profoundly in poems like "Amazon History of a Former Nail Salon Worker" in the second section and "Dear Rose" in the fourth section. Through the twenty-one months recorded in "Amazon History of a Former Nail Salon Worker," Vuong catalogs the muted collapse of a human life, the lost vitality of a body. In March, which begins the poem, the order includes items that denote a busy life, full of work and perhaps some fun: a four-pack of Advil, Sally Hansen Pink Nail Polish, an "I Love New York" T-shirt. Even in August, just a few months later, the itemized order shows a life in progress: a floral print summer dress, an Adirondack lawn chair. However, by January the worker's life has taken a new turn. No items are ordered that month and the next, February, finds her ordering a folding walker.

Ocean Vuong

By the poem's end, she is ordering Chemo-Glam cotton scarves, back braces, and an eternity urn. The progression from active life to preparation for an end is made all the more poignant by the inclusion of orders for Wrigley's Doublemint Gum and Burt's Bees lip balm.

In "Dear Rose" the speaker addresses Ma but also uses language to travel through time, perspective, and place. A poem that draws heavily on the meta, "Dear Rose" begins with an epigraph from philosopher Roland Barthes taken from his own book about his mother's death. Throughout the poem, Vuong evokes his mother's memory, recalling an afternoon when she made fish sauce from fermenting anchovies. The bodies of the anchovies are quickly woven into themes of death and decay as Vuong writes, "you must bear the scent of corpses / salted & crushed a year in a jar tall / as a boy they drop with slick / thumps like bullets." The fish sauce and Vuong's mother are pulled into thoughts about identity and belonging. As the poet recalls his mother telling him about those in Vietnam who "nearly killed [her] / . . . for being white" and called her "traitor" and "ghost girl" for having a relationship with the speaker's "white soldier" father, it becomes hard to tell which pronouns refer to the speaker and which refer to his mother. The poem concludes with an echo to the earlier images of anchovies as corpses, but now the poems in the collection themselves are the corpses, each a remnant of his mother's death.

Time Is a Mother is notable for its usage of distinct images to portray feelings of pain and grief. A continuing theme through the collection is the idea of whole bodies breaking open or being undone. In the first section, the poem "Beautiful Short Loser" juxtaposes Jaxson, a character who has undergone top surgery, with Vuong's uncle, who hanged himself with a belt after working at the Colt factory for fifteen years. As the poem concludes, Vuong contrasts his uncle's decision "to leave this world, intact" with Jaxson's surgery in which "taking a piece of my friend away from him made him more whole." The people in Vuong's sphere, like anyone, have complicated relationships with their bodies.

In "You Guys," another poem in the first section, the protagonist is brushing his teeth, speaking to "you guys" in the background. It soon appears that the speaker may be addressing a pair of crushed white rabbits they have left in the bathtub. The combined imagery of foam in the narrator's mouth, his pleas for the "guys" to wait a little longer, and the dead rabbits evoke a lack of completion or doneness.

As Vuong continues to build his body of work, his importance as a literary voice becomes more and more clear. Writing from the perspective of an immigrant, as a child of an immigrant mother, as a queer poet, and as someone reconciling his identity within an ever-more-complicated landscape in the US, his words carry extra weight for both the reader and the literary record at large. Like the titles that came before *Time Is a Mother*, Vuong and his mother's identities are carefully considered, often fractured by their experiences in the US. At one point in "Dear Rose," the concluding poem of the fourth section, Vuong recalls his mother hiding during the Vietnam War, starving in a cave and longing for slivers of chicken dipped in fish sauce. Her physical sacrifice is on display in his work, whether he's describing her work in a nail salon in *On Earth We're Briefly Gorgeous* and its effects on her body or the trauma she experienced in her young adult life in this collection of poems. So often throughout the collection, Vuong's words ricochet almost out of control, as bodies, both the speaker's and those of others, break or bend under strain. As a counter, perhaps, other poems enter into dream worlds where the dead are still living, can still be reached, or can still reach him. In the poem "Künstlerroman," he seems to watch himself in rewind on a dreamed-up video, collecting literary accolades but ultimately ending up inside a scene of destruction. Caskets line the way to this finale. In each of Vuong's works, the body is the most tender and the most horrifying thing imaginable.

Critical response to *Time Is a Mother* was overwhelmingly positive and it debuted on the New York Times Best Sellers list in April 2022. In her review for NPR, Thúy Đinh wrote, "Aesthetically complex yet emotionally accessible, *Time Is a Mother* at once innovates and affirms the existing poetic tradition, bringing to mind John Ashbery's *Paradoxes and Oxymorons*." In a review for *The Observer*, Kadish Morris stated, "Still, underneath the macabre scenes is an innocent curiosity and thirst for truth and beauty. These ghost poems are about the cavernous corners of loss, grief, abandonment, trauma and war, but that doesn't result in nihilism or apathy for life; in fact, Vuong approaches death like an entrance rather than an ending." In a starred review, *Publishers Weekly* stated, "Vuong's powerful follow-up to *Night Sky with Exit Wounds* does more than demonstrate poetic growth: it deepens and extends an overarching project with 27 new poems that reckon with loss and impermanence." The collection was also positively reviewed in *Library Journal* and the *Chicago Review of Books*, among other outlets.

Author Biography

Ocean Vuong is the author of the best-selling novel *On Earth We're Briefly Gorgeous* (2019), the critically acclaimed poetry collection *Night Sky with Exit Wounds* (2019), and the poetry collection *Time Is a Mother* (2022). His honors include a 2019 MacArthur Fellowship, the Stanley Kunitz Prize for Younger Poets from the *American Poetry Review*, a Whiting Award, and the T. S. Eliot Prize.

Melynda Fuller

Review Sources

Chaffa, Mandana. "Portrait of the Artist Transforming Grief in *Time Is a Mother*." Review of *Time Is a Mother*, by Ocean Vuong. *Chicago Review of Books*, 11 Apr. 2022, chireviewofbooks.com/2022/04/11/portrait-of-the-artist-transforming-grief-in-time-is-a-mother/. Accessed 13 Oct. 2022.

Chandonnet, Henry. "Poetry Review: *Time Is a Mother*—Grieving through Language." Review of *Time Is a Mother*, by Ocean Vuong. *The Arts Fuse*, 17 Apr. 2022, artsfuse.org/254373/poetry-review-time-is-a-mother-grieving-through-language/. Accessed 13 Oct. 2022.

Đinh, Thúy. "In *Time Is a Mother*, Poet Ocean Vuong Reflects on Life, and Time, without His Mom." Review of *Time Is a Mother*, by Ocean Vuong. *NPR*, 5 Apr. 2022, www.npr.org/2022/04/05/1090996745/in-time-is-a-mother-poet-ocean-vuong-reflects-on-life-and-time-without-his-mom. Accessed 13 Oct. 2022.

Gorham, Luke. Review of *Time Is a Mother*, by Ocean Vuong. *Library Journal*, 1 Mar. 2022, www.libraryjournal.com/review/time-is-a-mother-2133939. Accessed 13 Oct. 2022.

Morris, Kadish. "*Time Is a Mother* by Ocean Vuong Review—Writing That Demands All of Your Lungs." Review of *Time Is a Mother*, by Ocean Vuong. *The Observer*, Guardian News and Media, 11 Apr. 2022, www.theguardian.com/books/2022/apr/11/time-is-a-mother-by-ocean-vuong-review-writing-that-demands-all-of-your-lungs. Accessed 13 Oct. 2022.

Review of *Time Is a Mother*, by Ocean Vuong. *Publishers Weekly*, 17 Mar. 2022, www.publishersweekly.com/978-0-593-30023-7. Accessed 13 Oct. 2022.

A Tiny Upward Shove

Author: Melissa Chadburn (b. 1976)
Publisher: Farrar, Straus and Giroux (New York). 352 pp.
Type of work: Novel
Time: 1990s
Locales: Seaside, California; Los Angeles; Vancouver

A Tiny Upward Shove, journalist Melissa Chadburn's gut-punch of a debut novel, is shocking for its brutal violence but also its vivid beauty. In it, a teenager named Marina, who is selling sex to maintain her heroin addiction, is murdered by serial killer Willie Pickton. In her dying moments, she reaches out to the aswang, a mysterious and vengeful spirit from Filipino folklore.

Principal characters
MARINA SALLES, a Black Filipina teen growing up in Los Angeles
LOLA VIRGIE, her grandmother
MUTYA, her mother
ALEX, her best friend and lover
WILLIE PICKTON, her killer, based on a real-life Canadian serial killer of the same name
ASWANG, a spirit creature from Filipino folklore, who must eat human flesh to remain immortal

In *A Tiny Upward Shove*, journalist Melissa Chadburn's astonishingly vivid but also disturbing debut novel, the main character, a teenage girl named Marina Salles, is murdered by pig farmer Willie Pickton on the first page, becoming his last victim. Marina will not be reborn, or otherwise given a second chance at life. Her death, sadly, is irreversible, but in her last moments, she receives one small mercy—a chance to save others, including her beloved girlfriend, Alex, if not herself. With her last breath, Marina, who is Black and Filipina, or "Blackapina," as she describes herself, invokes a shape-shifting spirit creature from Filipino folklore called the *aswang*. Usually depicted as a kind of vampire, the *aswang* maintains their immortality by eating human flesh. But Chadburn's Aswang also has a mission. They have been called to take care of Marina's "unfinished business." It is a tough call for the hungry Aswang. As much as they "need to taste that raunchy yellow man who killed Marina," they also must remind themselves that Marina had stronger desires. Killing Willie "is not a hunger Marina ever felt.... This is a hunger only we vengeful feel," Aswang says. Among other exquisitely rendered political ideas in the book, Chadburn considers the concept of vengeance.

After Aswang leaps up from the world of the dead to inhabit Marina's body, they pull up Marina's memories beginning with her peaceful early life living with her mother, Mutya, and her grandmother, Lola (*lola* means "grandmother" in Tagalog), in Seaside, California. Aswang goes on to recall Marina's life with Mutya in Los Angeles, their violent separation, years spent languishing in the foster care system, and Marina's descent into addiction and sexual exploitation. The memories are narrated by the omniscient, foul-mouthed Aswang. The synergy of this dual narration—Marina's thoughts and memories in Aswang's voice—gives the book its force and in truth, makes it possible to bear. *A Tiny Upward Shove* can be a challenging read for its repeated, graphic descriptions of rape and abuse, but Chadburn finds moments of redemption in unexpected places. The abuse suffered by and at the hands of the characters is relentless, "lurid and hard to read," Erin Somers wrote in her review for the *New York Times*. "But the book is rescued by a joy evident in the writing, something ablaze at its core. It burns." The fire is Aswang, a promise that there is more to the world than suffering.

Melissa Chadburn

Interspersed among Marina's memories, all of them alive with detail, are passages from Aswang, as they fulfill the quest left unfinished when Marina died. The exact nature of this quest unfolds over the course of the novel. But it could also be argued that Aswang, who has come to generations of Salles women, has unfinished business of their own. Stepping out of the garbage pile onto which Pickton had carelessly thrown Marina's body, Aswang hears the spirit voices of the other women Pickton has murdered. "Pulsing through the trees, I heard their voices. Anita killed by Willie's bare hands; Jordan strangled with a belt around her neck; and Elaine, her final breath on a slaughtering hook." Together the women's voices, whose parts have been scattered in the mud, whose spirits have merged with the trees, urge Aswang to kill Willie: "*Gethimgethimgethim*, a schoolyard chant, pushing me on all sides."

These are the "throwaway" women, as Chadburn describes them in the book. It is a purposefully flippant phrase Chadburn has used before, in her work as a journalist and activist, driven by rage over the way that society considers some deaths worthy of mourning but not others. In the book's afterword, Chadburn shares some of the names of the girls, womxn, and two-spirit people, many of them Indigenous and/or sex workers, who were killed by the real Willie Pickton. Some readers will be aware of this prior to reading, others will not; it is no spoiler to know that Chadburn lightly fictionalizes the real life of Pickton, who was a victim of abuse before becoming an abuser himself. Pickton was arrested in 2002, and later confessed to killing forty-nine people and hiding their bodies on his farm. Chadburn also writes about her investigative work unearthing the redacted files of children who died while in the care of the Los Angeles County child welfare system. These children, abused and neglected by both loved ones and the state, are also among the "throwaways," human beings too poor or otherwise needy to be worth protecting. Chadburn incorporates some of their stories into the book as well.

While it would be unfair to draw specific connections between Marina's life and Chadburn's, it is worth noting that Chadburn has published essays about growing up in poverty with a single mother and spending her teenage years in the Los Angeles County foster care system. Her intimacy with these experiences is evident. After one horrific night, thirteen-year-old Marina is taken from her mother and becomes a ward of the state. Chadburn illustrates how the programs and restrictions meant to ensure safety for both Marina and Mutya only serve to make them more vulnerable, forcing them toward more dangerous paths. In one scene, Marina tries to explain the arbitrary bureaucratic benchmarks she must meet to free herself of the system to Lola Virgie, who, maddeningly, cannot take her in because she lives in a different county. Marina tells her that she must complete a number of programs to be eligible for emancipation at sixteen. Phone calls to her Lola or Mutya should keep her tethered to her real life, but they only serve to further alienate her from it.

Through her characters, Chadburn builds a powerful argument that drug addiction, sexual exploitation, and violence are, in overwhelming part, symptoms of the larger disease of poverty. As Marina observes numerous times, if her mother (or Lola) had enough money to adequately care for them, Marina would have never been taken into foster care in the first place. Mutya is a complicated character, both loving and aloof, but Marina is right. Mutya's faults as a mother are exacerbated by her poverty, and in turn, poverty thwarts her attempts to prove to the state that she is capable of becoming a better mother. Mutya has her own programming to attend, and while she is no enthusiastic student, the schedule and location of the classes seem designed to further thwart her. Mutya, despairing, exhausted and broke, gives up. Here, Chadburn illustrates how grinding poverty and its related afflictions can warp the mind. In her grief, Mutya embraces a fiercely religious mindset, casting her failures as God's will. It is the only solace she can find as her life unravels around her.

Teenage Marina, meanwhile, looks to meet her basic needs in more reckless ways—arguably, just as the teenage Mutya did. Inspired by the other girls at the foster home, she begins performing sex acts for money. But her need for love is more difficult to satisfy; Chadburn observes that Marina, so estranged from tenderness, cannot even articulate this need, though she sees it in others. When kids fight at the foster home, Marina notices that some of them will wait for an orderly to intervene, holding them back and pinning them down, as if that twisted version of intimacy had been the point all along. When Marina wonders if sex work will offer her the affection she craves, Chadburn writes: "She needed so badly to be touched. She wanted the fastest cheapest way to feel wanted. She wanted the fastest cheapest way to exist. Yet somehow, at the same time, if you'd asked her, she would have told you that she did not want to exist. She did not want to be touched."

Marina eventually finds true tenderness, or more accurately, true love, with Alex, another girl at the foster home. It is, as a reviewer wrote in a starred review for *Kirkus*, "a short moment of sweetness in Marina's journey to her fate." Other reviews, all of them positive, strike a similar note, casting *A Tiny Upward Shove* as a brutal story with enough moments of respite to keep the reader engaged. Bethanne Patrick, for the *Los Angeles Times*, wrote that at one point, she was tempted to abandon the novel, but then questioned her impulse. "Lucky me: privileged enough years ago to say 'That's enough,'" when confronted with a particularly upsetting passage about abuse, she wrote. She goes on to urge the reader: "Pick the novel back up again, as I did. There are payoffs and compensations, even in the most cursed lives. . . . Chadburn has written a stunning debut novel about the hardest things, drawing on style, study and tough experience to make it impossible for us to look away."

Author Biography

Melissa Chadburn is a Filipina American journalist and activist. Her work has been published in the *New York Times*, *Los Angeles Times*, the *Paris Review*, the *New York Review of Books* and *McSweeney's*. *A Tiny Upward Shove* is her first novel.

Molly Hagan

Review Sources

Patrick, Bethanne. "Review: A Murdered L.A. Woman Gets Her Revenge in a Shocking, Redemptive Debut Novel." Review of *A Tiny Upward Shove*, by Melissa Chadburn. *Los Angeles Times*, 13 Apr. 2022, www.latimes.com/entertainment-arts/books/story/2022-04-13/a-tiny-upward-shove-melissa-chadburn-book-review. Accessed 18 Sept. 2022.

Review of *A Tiny Upward Shove*, by Melissa Chadburn. *Kirkus Reviews*, 4 Feb. 2022, www.kirkusreviews.com/book-reviews/melissa-chadburn/a-tiny-upward-shove/. Accessed 18 Sept. 2022.

Review of *A Tiny Upward Shove*, by Melissa Chadburn. *Publishers Weekly*, 14 Feb. 2022, www.publishersweekly.com/978-0-374-27775-8. Accessed 18 Sept. 2022.

Somers, Erin. "Young Women and Their 'Unfinished Business'." Review of *A Tiny Upward Shove*, by Melissa Chadburn. *The New York Times*, 11 May 2022, www.nytimes.com/2022/05/11/books/a-tiny-upward-shove-melissa-chadburn-acts-of-service-lillian-fishman-sedating-elaine-dawn-winter.html. Accessed 18 Sept. 2022.

Stout, Caitlin. "Breaking the Cycle of Violence in *A Tiny Upward Shove*." Review of *A Tiny Upward Shove*, by Melissa Chadburn. *Chicago Review of Books*, 19 Apr. 2022, chireviewofbooks.com/2022/04/19/breaking-the-cycle-of-violence-in-a-tiny-upward-shove/. Accessed 18 Sept. 2022.

Tomorrow, and Tomorrow, and Tomorrow

Author: Gabrielle Zevin (b. 1977)
Publisher: Knopf (New York). 416 pp.
Type of work: Novel
Time: 1980s–2010s
Locales: Cambridge, Massachusetts; Los Angeles

Gabrielle Zevin's 2022 novel, Tomorrow, and Tomorrow, and Tomorrow, *is an emotionally absorbing story about video game designers making it big in the late 1990s and early 2000s. Zevin follows main characters (MCs in gaming parlance) Sadie, Sam, and Marx through worlds both virtual and real to tell a story about the importance of play, the creative process, and the power of true friendship.*

Principal characters

SAMSON "SAM" MASUR, a.k.a. Mazer, a Harvard student who develops a bestselling video game
SADIE GREEN, his childhood friend, who develops the video game with him
DOV MIZRAH, a professor who has an affair with Sadie
MARX WATANABE, his roommate, who becomes the producer of his video game

Gabrielle Zevin's novel *Tomorrow, and Tomorrow, and Tomorrow* (2022) takes its title from William Shakespeare's classic tragedy *Macbeth* and the lines spoken by its titular character as he laments the endless days and the monotonous experience of time—its "petty pace from day to day" in contrast to the "brief candle" that constitutes a human life. In her novel, Zevin, an award-winning novelist and screenwriter, contrasts references to Shakespeare and poet Emily Dickinson with more modern references to classic arcade games like *Donkey Kong* and the beloved PC game *Oregon Trail*, resulting in a work that is both fresh and modern as well as literary.

When the novel *Tomorrow, and Tomorrow, and Tomorrow* begins, Sam Masur is a reclusive young student at Harvard in the 1990s. He is arduously making his way through a crowded subway station, doing his best to disguise the limp he acquired from a traumatic childhood injury that all but destroyed one of his feet. Zevin's references to the digital world are front and center right from the start as she describes Sam's trajectory in the manner of a video game. Sam thinks of himself as the "doomed amphibian" in the classic arcade game *Frogger*, thwarted by each passing body. "Occasionally, someone would hastily leave, creating gaps in the crowd," Zevin writes. "The gaps should have been opportunities of escape for Sam, but somehow, they immediately filled with new humans." When the crowd finally does part, it reveals a different kind of escape, one from the loneliness that consumes him, despite the support and devotion of his handsome, charming roommate, Marx. Against what will be revealed to be his nature, Sam calls out to a familiar face: "SADIE MIRANDA GREEN!" he yells. "YOU HAVE DIED OF DYSENTERY!"

This unusual greeting is a reference to the 1990s PC game *Oregon Trail*, but it is also a poignant inside joke. Sadie, now a student at the Massachusetts Institute of Technology (MIT), turns to greet him; a simple moment, but the way Zevin describes it, the reader will understand its import. This itself is reminiscent of a video game, evoking the balance of chance and choice so inherent to play, and, as Zevin suggests, to life in general. It was lucky that Sam saw Sadie that day, but calling out to her made all the difference.

Gabrielle Zevin

Through Zevin's engaging prose, readers learn that Sam and Sadie first met when they were around eleven years old at a children's hospital in Los Angeles in the 1980s. Sadie is there to visit her teenage sister, Alice, who is being treated for cancer. Sam is there for his foot. They encounter one another in the hospital's playroom, where without preamble or introduction, they bond over games of *Super Mario Bros*. The nurses are, in Sadie's mind, unusually moved by this friendship. As it turns out, Sam, following his accident, the details of which Zevin unfolds over the course of the novel, has not spoken a single word in six weeks. Sadie is asked to return in hopes of drawing Sam out of his shell; encouraged by her mother and the nurses, she tallies the hours as community service for her upcoming bat mitzvah. The two form a genuine friendship, but Sam's discovery that Sadie is hanging out with him in order to rack up hours of community service precipitates their first break. The next time they speak, it is many years later in the subway station, though they have seen each other from afar at various school competitions over the years.

Zevin's narrative leapfrogs through time, and occasionally offers tantalizing details from the future, portents of success but also of tragedy. The reader knows early that Sam and Sadie's friendship will be turbulent, but not when or how or why. These questions propel the story, providing a necessary engine to a long and intricate saga spanning decades. Sam and Sadie's relationship is powerful. It is also plutonic. Zevin's choice to center the novel on a non-romantic relationship, particularly one between a man and a woman, is admirable, emphasizing the depth of love that can be found in it. As Pippa Bailey wrote in her review for the *Guardian*, "Their relationship is a joining of minds and of worlds that is both purer and sweeter than any base physical attraction." Through Sam and Sadie, Zevin also renders the particular joys and pains of artistic collaboration. As Sadie tells Sam later in the book, lovers are "common," but "true collaborators in this life are rare."

Zevin has played with time and narrative in her books before, though she explored the concept more literally in her best-selling young adult novel, *Elsewhere*. In that work, a fifteen-year-old girl named Liz dies, only to find herself in a mysterious place called Elsewhere. There, time runs backward, and Liz is forced to live her life in reverse in hopes of being reborn in the real world. But for a teenager so intent on reaching the benchmarks of maturity, the prospect of becoming younger is excruciating. *Tomorrow* similarly illustrates the multifaceted anguish of time's passage. As mentioned earlier, the theme is in the title, a line from *Macbeth* in which the titular character laments the monotonous experience of time. Sam and Sadie struggle with this notion in their own individual ways, but both find solace in the endless rebirth available to them in virtual worlds, and the intimacy they find with one another through play. As Zevin writes, "To allow yourself to play with another person is no small risk. It means allowing yourself to be open, to be exposed, to be hurt. . . . Many years later, as Sam would controversially say in an interview with the gaming website *Kotaku*, 'There is no more intimate act than play, even sex.'"

After their fortuitous meeting in the train station, Sam and Sadie endeavor to create a video game together. Marx, Sam's wealthy and altogether faultless, roommate, funds the project and takes on the role of producer. Zevin captures the frustration and exhilaration of a team learning to work together. Their youth serves them in many ways—their energy, their relative ignorance of the challenges they face—but hinders them in others. They know how to describe what they want, but they do not yet know how to manifest it. As Sadie, the group's exacting artist, observes at one point, it is difficult to soldier through the period in which one's taste exceeds one's talent. Sadie faces a particularly challenging choice in making *Ichigo*, the blockbuster game that will ultimately launch their successful company, Unfair Games. Having broken up with her domineering but brilliant former professor, Dov, she ponders whether to rekindle their relationship in service of his much-needed help.

Zevin explores each character with nuance and complexity, investigating how their otherness draws them to gaming and also makes it difficult to survive the industry. Both Sam and Marx are Asian American. Sam is continually stymied by the chronic pain of his foot, an added feature that sets him apart and which becomes a long-term disability. As Zevin describes him, Sam's taste in games, in contrast to Sadie's, springs from his ever-present desire to escape his own body.

Tomorrow was praised by gamers and non-gamers alike. Tom Bissell, an author and video game designer who reviewed the book for the *New York Times*, found joy in the novel's dozens of game references, ranging from *Metal Gear Solid* to *Harvest Moon*. "Zevin gets a lot of the detail-y things about game development right, among them the centrality of having a good producer . . . along with much of the terminology," Bissell remarked. He further noted that while producer Marx, a non-creative, is occasionally maligned by the other characters as an NPC—"non-player character," a gaming reference suggesting insignificance—he is also the glue that holds the team together. Meanwhile, Maureen Corrigan for *NPR*, who professed to know little about gaming, still found much to love because, as with a book as beloved as *Moby Dick*, full of obscure references to the whaling industry, "when a novel is powerful enough, it transports us readers deep into worlds not our own," she wrote. Similarly, another reviewer wrote in a starred review for *Kirkus* that "readers who recognize the references will enjoy them, and those who don't can look them up and/or simply absorb them. Zevin's delight in her characters, their qualities, and their projects sprinkles a layer of fairy dust over the whole enterprise."

For those who are gamers, reviewers like Bissell made several interesting observations about Zevin's rendering of the game-making process. While he praised her facility with the language, he also noted that the book lacks the "unadorned realities of game-making," referring to the tedium and exhaustive trial-and-error process of making a game that works. There are failures in the book, but not technical ones, nor major overhauls involving core concepts. Bissell conceded that a true-to-life novel about game development would be boring, but also made note of something even non-gamers might sense while reading Zevin's book. "The professional parts of her game creators' lives seem far too easy, while the personal parts often seem far too hard," Bissell remarked.

Several reviewers made note of an intriguing latter section of the book that takes place entirely in an online role-playing game called *Pioneers*. After so much talk of playing and making games, it is an exhilarating experience to find oneself inside of one, watching Sam and Sadie's numerous inspirations find new life in a strange world. In *Pioneers* and in the novel itself, Zevin illustrates the "literary" potential of games, as Bissell called it. Non-gamers, he wrote, "will wonder what took them so long to recognize in video games the beauty and drama and pain of human creation."

Author Biography

Gabrielle Zevin is best-known for her novel *The Storied Life of A. J. Fikry* (2014)—which was adapted for film in 2022—and the young adult novel *Elsewhere* (2005), which was named one of *Time Magazine*'s "100 Best YA Books of All Time." Zevin is also a screenwriter; her screenplay of the film *Conversations with Other Women* earned her an Independent Spirit Award nomination for best first screenplay.

Molly Hagan

Review Sources

Bailey, Pippa. "*Tomorrow, and Tomorrow, and Tomorrow* by Gabrielle Zevin Review—When Game Boy Meets Game Girl." Review of *Tomorrow, and Tomorrow, and Tomorrow*, by Gabrielle Zevin. *The Guardian*, 18 July 2022, www.theguardian.com/books/2022/jul/18/tomorrow-and-tomorrow-and-tomorrow-by-gabrielle-zevin-review-when-game-boy-meets-game-girl. Accessed 12 Sept. 2022.

Bissell, Tom. "How to Design a Beautiful, Cruel Universe." Review of *Tomorrow, and Tomorrow, and Tomorrow*, by Gabrielle Zevin. *The New York Times*, 8 July 2022, www.nytimes.com/2022/07/08/books/review/tomorrow-and-tomorrow-and-tomorrow-gabrielle-zevin.html. Accessed 12 Sept. 2022.

Corrigan, Maureen. "The Immersive Novel *Tomorrow* Is a Winner for Gamers and N00bs Alike." Review of *Tomorrow, and Tomorrow, and Tomorrow*, by Gabrielle Zevin. *NPR*, 28 July 2022, www.npr.org/2022/07/28/1114196664/video-game-novel-tomorrow-and-tomorrow-and-tomorrow-gabrielle-zevin. Accessed 12 Sept. 2022.

Review of *Tomorrow, and Tomorrow, and Tomorrow*, by Gabrielle Zevin. *Kirkus Reviews*, 13 Apr. 2022, www.kirkusreviews.com/book-reviews/gabrielle-zevin/tomorrow-and-tomorrow-and-tomorrow/. Accessed 12 Sept. 2022.

Review of *Tomorrow, and Tomorrow, and Tomorrow*, by Gabrielle Zevin. *Publishers Weekly*, 30 Mar. 2022, www.publishersweekly.com/9780593321201. Accessed 12 Sept. 2022.

The Trayvon Generation

Author: Elizabeth Alexander (b. 1962)
Publisher: Grand Central Publishing (New York). 160 pp.
Type of work: Biography, current affairs, memoir
Time: Twentieth century, twenty-first century
Locale: The United States

The Trayvon Generation is a treatise about the generational impact of White supremacy and anti-Black racism on the lives of Black families with a focus on Black youth under the age of twenty-five that author Elizabeth Alexander defines as the Trayvon Generation.

Principal personages

CLINT SMITH III, American writer, poet, and scholar
LUCILLE CLIFTON, American poet, poet laureate of Maryland (1979–82)
JOHN HOPE FRANKLIN, American scholar and historian
ZORA NEALE HURSTON, American author, anthropologist, and filmmaker
W. E. B. DU BOIS, American sociologist and historian
ALICE WALKER, American novelist, poet, and activist
DAWOUD BEY, American photographer and educator
CHANDRA MCCORMICK, American photographer

In *The Trayvon Generation* (2022), Elizabeth Alexander draws on her extensive skills as a poet, scholar, social justice advocate, and mother to provide a critical assessment of what she refers to as "the thorny truth" that although society is more integrated in the twenty-first century, "the war against Black people feels as if it is gearing up for another epic round." Alexander intricately weaves iconic paintings, poetry, films, and photos, with history and contemporary social, political, and cultural issues to illustrate how racial violence in America systemically robs Black youth of their humanity and how Black people have witnessed and responded to this legacy of racial violence for centuries. She employs the work of a star-studded cast of prominent artists, scholars, authors, and activists to tell a compelling story of generational risk, trauma, and resilience in the lives of Black Americans under the age of twenty-five, including her own two sons, a cohort she has dubbed the Trayvon Generation.

The book is written in three parts. In the first paragraph of part 1, Alexander makes the focus of the book strikingly clear to readers. She opens with the pronouncement that "the problem of the twenty-first century remains the color line." This powerful,

Elizabeth Alexander

unapologetic decree sets the tone in preparing the reader for what is to come. She also makes her own position transparent at the beginning of part 1, declaring that "White supremacy is not the creation of Black people. I both lament and am enraged that this work is undone, and that our young people still have it to wrestle with." She provides ample evidence of the color line problem examining history, societal issues, cultural clashes, political endeavors, and literature as well as reflecting on her personal experiences as an educator and mother of two young adult Black males. She uses artistic expressions throughout the book to not only to portray disparate social realities, but to also convey a message of hope and future possibilities. It is her bold, unequivocal truth-telling that drives the book, making it both gripping and painful to absorb at times.

In part 1 she tackles the destructiveness of racial ideologies that motivate violence and place Black people's humanity at risk while they engage in everyday life like shopping in a grocery store, jogging down a street, reading in the library, praying in a church, driving a car, or sleeping at home in one's own bed. Using the poem "Your National Anthem" (2018) by Clint Smith III, Alexander illustrates what she refers to as "the perennialness and sorrow of race in America." She recognizes the power of words and hate speech spread at "the highest levels of governance" to purposely falsify, harm, misinform, and divide the nation while she simultaneously encourages readers to, instead, use words responsibly to build bridges of hope. She does not, however, naïvely believe that talking is the only solution. She acknowledges the "great societal head fake" to always look to and expect Black people, who did not create the problem, to explain and solve the problem of race in America. A best-selling, award-winning poet herself, Alexander lauds the language of poetry and its power to activate peoples' collective humanity and instinct to share stories with one another and chronicle their lives across cultures in ways that can facilitate solutions. She illustrates her perspective using the experiences of Black poets who have used poetry to remember, memorialize, and chronicle Black history habitually *not* found in American history books, archives, and commemorative sites.

In the second chapter, titled "*here lies*," Alexander offers readers a dynamic critique of the prolific American landscape of Confederate and other monuments, statues, and commemorative markers found in a multitude of public spaces. In her analysis, these symbols of remembrance "[teach] us many things, the greatest of which is that Black people are inferior to white people." She further asserts "No other people in the United States are so extensively portrayed in a built public history that asserts their subhumanity." The overwhelming evidence she offers to illuminate her assertions is irrefutable. She notes that the Confederate monuments were erected several decades after the Civil War to "express and instantiate the ideology of white supremacy." Additionally, Alexander links the timing of the dedication and rededication of many Confederate monuments with the civil rights movement, the US Supreme Court's efforts to desegregate public schools, and the assassination of Dr. Martin Luther King. She contends that the magnitude and scale of Confederate remembering is essentially to maintain racial distortions, myths, and lies and to frame future ideas and values that perpetuate White superiority and Black subordination in America in much the same way that earlier maps of the world distorted the size of Europe and North America as much larger than Africa or Latin America—a distortion that was taught as fact without question or scrutiny in many classroom settings. Again, Alexander draws on the mission of Black poets and artists' remembering and memorializing, specifically Maryland's poet laureate Lucille Clifton's poem "why some people be mad at me sometimes" to illustrate counter narratives that "refuse and refute" the lies that Confederate and other monuments depict about history. In contrast, Clifton and other Black poets affirm and memorialize the "history itself, the stories and names otherwise lost, distorted, or minimized."

In the third chapter of part 1, titled "*shock of delayed comprehension*," Alexander uses her own experiences in the Corporation Room at Yale to further illustrate and underscore the pervasiveness with which portraits, paintings, and photographs have been used in much the same way as monuments to reinforce the myth of White superiority as normal. Often prominently featured at universities like Yale over an extended period without comment, these images visually and symbolically honor White men who display their wealth by posing with an unnamed enslaved person positioned subordinately relative to the White man in the image. Alexander argues that such images convey the message "*Slavery was normal*" and that "white supremacy is matter-of-fact, casual, and ordinary."

Alexander's expert knowledge as an African American literature and culture scholar is on full display in the fourth chapter of part 1, titled "*a tale of two textbooks*." She centers the contributions of historian John Hope Franklin's texts *From Slavery to Freedom* (1947), a canonical Black studies textbook, and *Land of the Free* (1966, cowritten with John W. Caughey and Ernest R. May), which focused on civil rights and the history of people of color to illustrate the educational reach of systemic racism through censorship of school textbooks. She then links efforts by right-wing critics to ban *Land of the Free* from being taught in California schools, an attempt at silencing critical Black consciousness and history, with contemporary "deliberate distortions and manufactured fear surrounding critical race theory" demonstrating the generational impact of racial inequities. Alexander also recognizes the generational impact of Black resilience and reclamation when she states that "attempting to see things as they really are with the unflinching critical eye is, at the end of the day, the way Black people have strategized and survived."

In the last chapter of part 1, titled "*cemetery for the illustrious negro dead*," Alexander demonstrates the breadth and depth of generational racism in the death, destruction, and demolition of Black bodies, enterprise, and communities. She also documents efforts to ritualize, memorialize, and remember in ways that "over the years, cemeteries themselves tell stories and become history." She examines the force of "urban renewal" that pushed Black people out of their homes and communities, the bulldozing of Black cemeteries, the gutting, destruction, and racial gentrification of Black neighborhoods to "make a model community for white people" and the physical and symbolic ways Black people memorialize loss. The artistry of choreographer Alvin Alley's remarkable ancestral tribute "Revelations," the life of Zora Neale Hurston and her 1945 letter to W. E .B. Du Bois to "propose a cemetery for the illustrious Negro dead," and the work of Alice Walker to find Hurston's unmarked grave stand out as markers of Black remembering and perseverance in the face of violence. Alexander brilliantly weaves the actions of the living with the dead and the spirit world to demonstrate the dehumanization of Black people and their efforts to collectively remember, memorialize, and reclaim their humanity. She ends part 1 with the evocative, critical question, "I wonder, do I really believe that cultural expression can somehow shape a world where our children are safer?"

It is a fitting end to part 1 of the book and sets the stage for the title chapter that comprises part 2. It opens with photographer Dawoud Bey's *Martina and Rhonda* (1993), which features splintered photo images of two young Black women sitting side by side. The gripping narrative of the opening paragraph eulogizes, in powerful lyrical imagery, the lives of Black youth lost to the violence of racism beginning with the phrase, "This one," after which Alexander describes the graphic circumstances in which the youth was murdered. She invokes their names and commemorates their lives.

In part 3, Alexander turns her attention to the issue of mass incarceration, opening with a black and white photo of *Daddy'O, The Oldest Inmate in Angola State Penitentiary* (2004), by Chandra McCormick. Alexander provides a comprehensive look at the Louisiana State Penitentiary, also known as Angola, which "houses the largest population of lifers on planet Earth" in plantation style with "Black men picking cotton, or okra, while white correctional officers ride on horseback to oversee their work."

In the next chapter of part 3, titled "*whether the negro sheds tears,*" Alexander centers a letter sent to W. E. B. Du Bois in 1905 by the researcher Alvin Borgquist of Clark University in Massachusetts in which he questions "whether the negro sheds tears" and "if so, under what general conditions." Alexander links this and other absurd attempts to dehumanize Black people with the details of George Floyd's murder as conveyed through the trial of his murderer, former Minneapolis police officer Derek Chauvin. She ends the chapter with another powerful poem, each line starting with the phrase "In tears."

The title of the last chapter, "*there are black people in the future,*" a reference to artist Alisha B. Wormsley's billboard in a racially gentrifying neighborhood of Pittsburgh and others, is a signal of hope, determination, and possibility. Alexander reminds the reader that "Black people today are the product of people who survived, who were not meant to flourish," and that "Black flourishing and futurity occur against the odds." She reminds Black people to claim their inheritance carrying "not only the hopes and dreams of a generation but also the will and ingenuity to survive."

Media critics responded with rave starred reviews to *The Trayvon Generation*. It received a starred review from *Kirkus*, which described it as "a dynamic critique on the sprawling effects of racism and its effects on today's youth." The anonymous *Kirkus* reviewer also noted that "Alexander paints a vivid portrait of a societal landscape that is fundamentally different depending on race, class, and other demographic makers, weaving together prose, poetry, and artwork." Similarly, Alexander was applauded by reviewer Mitchell S. Jackson, writing for the *New York Times*, for "a profound and lyrical meditation on race, class, justice, and their intersections with art." Jackson observed that Alexander "[disabuses] white readers of their innocence" as "she explores the 'didactic violence' of monuments; degraded, divisive language; and other insidious harms of white supremacy." Jackson recognized Alexander's personal experiences as a mother of young Black males as a driving force in the book. "Her awareness that no accomplishment or prestige or lineage nor even the greatest parental love can secure her son's or any other Black lives from the perils of white supremacy works as the vital pulse of the last half of the book." In her review for the *Boston Globe*, correspondent Joshunda Sanders framed *The Trayvon Generation* as a "beautiful, relevant book" in which "the poet redefines the proximity of Black identity to loss as an opportunity to create new rituals and a new paradigm." Undoubtedly, *The Trayvon Generation* will affirm and confirm the lived experiences of some readers. Other readers may be taken aback, jarred, or shocked. Some readers may find it a hard emotional read while others may find it hard to put down.

Author Biography
Elizabeth Alexander is an award-winning and best-selling author, renowned American poet, educator, and cultural advocate. She serves as president of the Andrew W. Mellon Foundation.

Valandra, MBA, MSW, PhD

Review Sources
Jackson, Mitchell S. "In the Face of Black Pain, Elizabeth Alexander Turns to Art." Review of *The Trayvon Generation*, by Elizabeth Alexander. *The New York Times*, 31 Mar. 2022, www.nytimes.com/2022/03/31/books/elizabeth-alexander-the-trayvon-generation.html. Accessed 29 Sept. 2022.
Review of *The Trayvon Generation*, by Elizabeth Alexander. *Kirkus*, 15 Jan. 2022, www.kirkusreviews.com/book-reviews/elizabeth-alexander/the-trayvon-generation/. Accessed 29 Sept. 2022.
Sanders, Joshunda. "Reclaiming Black Life, and Joy, in *The Trayvon Generation*." Review of *The Trayvon Generation*, by Elizabeth Alexander. *The Boston Globe*, 31 Mar. 2022, www.bostonglobe.com/2022/03/31/arts/reclaiming-black-life-joy-trayvon-generation/. Accessed 29 Sept. 2022.
Schlichenmeyer, Terri. Review of *The Trayvon Generation*, by Elizabeth Alexander. *The Washington Informer*, 6 Apr. 2022, www.washingtoninformer.com/book-review-the-trayvon-generation-by-elizabeth-alexander/. Accessed 29 Sept. 2022.

The Treeline
The Last Forest and the Future of Life on Earth

Author: Ben Rawlence
Publisher: St. Martin's Press (New York). Illustrated. 320 pp.
Type of work: Nature, science
Time: Present day
Locales: Wales, Scotland, Norway, Russia, Alaska, Canada, and Greenland

In The Treeline, *author Ben Rawlence focuses on a deep study of seven tree species of the boreal forest in an effort to bring greater clarity to the fundamental habitat changes already underway due to climate change. This work of ecojournalism is a call to action as well as a sobering account of the irreversible damages that are already underway.*

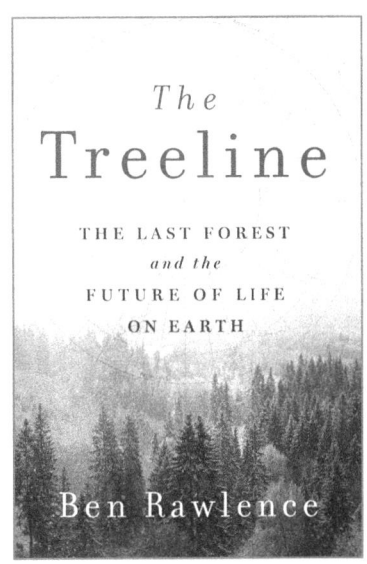

Principal personages

BEN RAWLENCE, the author and narrator
CATHERINE ATTLA, a Koyukon elder whose work is used as a resource in "the oral history of global warming"
DIANA BERESFORD-KROEGER, an Irish Canadian climate change scientist
THOMAS MACDONNELL, a conservation manager for Wildland Ltd.
HALLGEIR STRIFELDT, a Sámi member and town manager of Alta, Norway
NADEZHDA TCHEBAKOVA, a scientific modeler employed at the Sukachev Institute in Krasnoyarsk, Russia

Writer and activist Ben Rawlence concludes *The Treeline: The Last Forest and the Future of Life on Earth* (2022) with a call to action: "We must prepare our children for uncertainty but not as victims. We and they are stewards, still charged with an ancient responsibility. . . to create the future with every step in full recognition of the fact that every move you make, however large or small, matters." These words of moral obligation and the call for small steps toward a more hopeful future are all that Rawlence can offer as a salve to the larger, dire message of his research. Through firsthand observations of travel to extreme arctic habitats accompanied by data from scientific research concerning six tree species, *The Treeline* aims to convince the reader that catastrophic global warming and civilization-shifting climate change are inevitable and already underway. Rawlence argues that the future of the current generation of children will be indelibly marked by these changes as they unfold, and that the next generation will almost surely face an existential fight for survival. The fate of humanity is the most

Ben Rawlence

urgent topic of the book, but Rawlence meditates just as deeply on the long historical durée of ancient trees, such as the yew with which he opens the text. The *Taxus baccata*, or yew, are "refugees from another era with a life cycle so much longer than human timescales," a fact that allows Rawlence to imagine a post-Anthropocene world in which some species of trees might survive and usher in a new planetary era.

The Treeline is part scientific study, part disaster tourism, and part combat journalism. Periodically throughout the book, Rawlence refers to how his ability to complete the study relied on his past experiences reporting on conflict areas in Africa. The travel-based structure of the text is marked in interesting ways by the onset of the global COVID-19 pandemic in 2020. Rawlence completes a remarkable journey to Ary Mas, the northernmost forest in the world, located in the Russian Taiga, just before global travel ceases with the onset of the pandemic. Due to travel shutdowns, he continues his conversations with scientists and cultural leaders via Zoom. The quick-moving devastation of the pandemic and the quickening pace of climate change become two forces moving within and throughout the text in uncomfortable and threatening ways. As Rawlence resumes travel to the remotest locations of the planet, the habitual solitude of these locations is weighed down by the isolation and trauma of the present alongside the accelerating signs of the start of catastrophic climate change and the future suffering it will bring about. As critics noted, *The Treeline* is a dense text, full of scientific research and critical social history, accompanied by the observed and damning evidence of human-induced climate change that is already transforming the most remote regions of the planet. The intellectual, psychological, and social weight of the text are perhaps appropriate: through them, Rawlence seeks to convey the profound moral imperative that every living adult must step up and shoulder this burden, taking every viable step to prevent the future annihilation of humanity and the many species on Earth with whom we share this planet. He states unequivocally: "if there is a tipping point in earth's climate equilibrium, we have already left it far behind."

If Rawlence is clear on the urgency of the problem, he is also pointed in clarifying the forces to blame. Throughout *The Treeline*, Rawlence carefully spools a history of human civilization that celebrates ancient ways of living in symbiosis with the environment and, specifically, seeks to gain knowledge from Indigenous cosmologies. By looking to the practices of First Nations and Indigenous communities, including fundamental spiritual tenets and rules of interaction with flora and fauna, Rawlence foregrounds a way of thinking that rejects a colonial and consumer mentality toward the landscape. This colonial mentality is, of course, easily recognized in the conventional discovery and settlement stories of the Americas. Confronting the enduring mystique of the "untouched wilderness," Rawlence reflects, "No 'untouched wilderness' is either untouched or wild to those who call it home... [it] has been shaped by millennia of human guardians." The conceptual counterpoint to these ideas of untouched wilderness lies in the "civilized" landscape, for which Rawlence's own United Kingdom serves as an example. Opening the book with the treeless rolling hills of Scotland, Rawlence reminds his readers that this "ruined landscape" is the byproduct of centuries of extractive cultural behaviors, which have approached the environment as something to be commodified. Yet, while some organizations work to return portions of the Scottish landscape to wilderness, others oppose such actions for economic and cultural reasons. Importantly, Rawlence emphasizes that a significant change in mindset toward cultural history is of the essence: "How we see the present and the future often depends on our understanding of the past. What is natural? What is being restored? Meanwhile, as humans debate ecological history, global warming gathers force, threatening to render our meager response irrelevant."

In search of alternative knowledge-seeking, Rawlence speaks with Indigenous peoples in Canada, Russia, Alaska, and Norway. He also offers erudite deep dives into the physical, cultural, and linguistic violence that has been done to these groups, as well as the ways in which their current efforts to reengage with traditional lifeways have also increased their physical health and mental well-being while reinvesting in rich relationships with local habitat. Yet, these communities work to resurrect and rediscover their heritage of relationship with the environment in the context of a planet in which habitats are changing. A particularly poignant example of this complex balance is found when Rawlence travels to Canada to explore the case study of the *Populus balsamifera*, the balsam poplar. There, he meets Diana Beresford-Kroeger, a scientist whose research into trees and climate change offers one of the direct sets of evidence that Rawlence places before the reader in *The Treeline*. Compellingly, his visit with Beresford-Kroeger is followed in the account by a visit to Thunder Lake, with Anishinaabe people who are both its traditional and current stewards. These travels take place within Pimachiowin Aki, "the land that gives life," which was designated as a UNESCO World Heritage Site in 2018, in recognition both of its environmental significance and of the cultural relationship that the First Nations peoples have to the ecosystem. Here Rawlence explores in detail the ways in which the inhabitants of this site are seeking to "reforge a harmonious relationship between humans and mother earth" based on the principle that Rawlence's hosts share with him: "If the land gets sick, we get sick." He reflects: "It seems so obvious, so simple. How could we ever have forgotten?" Rawlence presents these Indigenous cultural tenets as the crucial piece to recapturing a healthier relationship with our planet, but he cannot present them as capable of preventing the damage that is already underway. Even in Pimachiowin Aki, the habitat is transforming. Moose and other animals are changing their patterns, the spruce trees are ill; climate change is underway.

In its exploration of climate change through a boreal forest perspective, *The Treeline* is organized through focused consideration of seven tree species, from which the story spins out to explore its larger narratives of cultural history and the science of climate change. The book opens with a prologue focused on the *Taxus baccata* (yew) in Wales. The chapters then move sequentially to: *Pinus sylvestris* (Scots pine) in Scotland, *Betula pubescens* (downy birch) in Norway, *Larix gmelinii*, (Dahurian larch) in Russia, *Picea glauca/Picea mariana* (white spruce/black spruce) in Alaska, *Populus balsamifera* (balsam poplar) in Canada, and *Sorbus groenlandica* (Greenland mountain ash) in Greenland. The book closes with an epilogue titled "Thinking Like a Forest," in which Rawlence invites the reader to a shift in mentality, recognizing that for the human race to survive it needs to reconnect with its biosphere and origins as a species of the forest. However, the ideas in this section are not presented as a solution to climate change. Arguing that "the last generation to know a stable climate with seasonal cycles and familiar species . . . has already been born," Rawlence presents this concept of "thinking like a forest" as part of the vital "struggle to limit the damage and prepare for what is coming." He invites the reader to quickly move from recognition and acceptance of the terrible realities of climate change to action—if only "to participate: to explore, experience, to get lost or find your way."

Rawlence received widespread praise for *The Treeline*. In a review for the *Washington Independent Review of Books*, Julie Dunlap wrote: "*The Treeline* is much more than a grand adventure with a grim message. Elegant writing on the latest research and traditional worldviews reveals glimmers of hope in dark, frozen forests." Similarly, *Publishers Weekly* found that "nature lovers and travelers alike will find this a lovely paean to a rapidly changing landscape." However, some criticism was leveled at the accessibility of the book's subject matter for those who are not well-versed in the larger movement into which *The Treeline* fits. Adrienne Ross Scanlan, in a review for the *New York Journal of Books*, remarked, "While a resource for a naturalist or activist, it's easy to imagine a reader new to these issues left with only overwhelming loss over an unavoidable fate." Even so, *The Treeline* is an important addition to the critical subject of climate change and its devastating effects on the planet.

Author Biography

Prior to *The Treeline*, Ben Rawlence published two books: *Radio Congo: Signals of Hope from Africa's Deadliest War* (2012) and *City of Thorns: Nine Lives in the World's Largest Refugee Camp* (2016). Rawlence previously worked as a researcher for the Africa division of Human Rights Watch. He is also a cofounder of Black Mountains College, an institute dedicated to fighting climate change.

Julia A. Sienkewicz, PhD

Review Sources

Dunlap, Julie. Review of *The Treeline: The Last Forest and the Future of Life on Earth*, by Ben Rawlence. *Washington Independent Review of Books*, 17 Feb. 2022, www.washingtonindependentreviewofbooks.com/index.php/bookreview/the-treeline-the-last-forest-and-the-future-of-life-on-earth. Accessed 11 Nov. 2022.

Klinkenborg, Verlyn. "The Forest's Eye View: Two New Books Investigate the Ways in Which Deforestation Affects Climate Change, and Climate Change Affects Forests." Review of *The Treeline: The Last Forest and the Future of Life on Earth*, by Ben Rawlence. *The New York Review of Books*, 21 July 2022, www.nybooks.com/articles/2022/07/21/the-forests-eye-view-ever-green-the-treeline/. Accessed 11 Nov. 2022.

Radbill, Olivia. Review of *The Treeline: The Last Forest and the Future of Life on Earth*, by Ben Rawlence. *EcoLit Books*, 24 Mar. 2022, ecolitbooks.com/2022/03/24/book-review-the-treeline/. Accessed 11 Nov. 2022.

Review of *The Treeline: The Last Forest and the Future of Life on Earth*, by Ben Rawlence. *Publishers Weekly*, 8 Oct. 2021, www.publishersweekly.com/9781250270238. Accessed 21 Dec. 2022.

Scanlan, Adrienne Ross. Review of *The Treeline: The Last Forest and the Future of Life on Earth*, by Ben Rawlence. *The New York Journal of Books*, www.nyjournalofbooks.com/book-review/treeline-last-forest. Accessed 11 Nov. 2022.

True Biz

Author: Sara Nović (b. 1987)
Publisher: Random House (New York). 400 pp.
Type of work: Novel
Time: Present day
Locale: Ohio

True Biz is a coming-of-age story that celebrates the American Deaf community while examining the sociopolitical challenges it continues to face within the hearing world. It is author Sara Nović's third book.

Principal characters
CHARLIE SERRANO, a deaf teenage girl who transfers from a public high school to the River Valley School for the Deaf
KAYLA, her roommate at River Valley
SLASH, her former love interest, an older hearing boy
AUSTIN WORKMAN, her love interest, a popular boy at River Valley
FEBRUARY WATERS, the headmistress of River Valley, a child of deaf adults

About two-thirds of the way through *True Biz* (2022), the novel's teenage deaf heroine, Charlie, asks her roommate, Kayla, to explain the different types of prejudices that she faces as a Black person who is deaf. Kayla's immediate response is to send Charlie a pre-written email with links to information—her "white people primer." Kayla then signs to Charlie in American Sign Language (ASL): "Lesson two is next time do your own research. I'm not on a teacher's salary yet."

It is a brief exchange, and yet a powerful reminder that members of disenfranchised communities should not be the ones burdened with educating others on their discrimination. In turn, the scene also provides insight into why the novel's author, Sara Nović, who is deaf, might have taken it upon herself to write a novel that could very well be described as a "hearing people primer." In addition to writing fiction, Nović also teaches Deaf studies and therefore is adept at providing an in-depth look at the history, language, joys, and challenges of her community. It is easy to imagine that her motivation in explaining these topics in detail is perhaps to spare other deaf people from having to do the same in their everyday lives.

Indeed, *True Biz*, which takes its name from the exclamation unique to ASL meaning "real talk" or "definitely," is an engaging piece of literature in the way that it presents the contemporary Deaf experience in the United States. At its core is a fictional narrative about three people whose lives intersect at a boarding school for deaf children. However, between the alternating chapters of their stories, Nović weaves in

Sara Nović

short, nonfiction sections that cover topics about deafness relevant to the plot. In the beginning of the novel, for example, when the character of Charlie is learning ASL, Nović intersperses sections about the basics of ASL, its unique grammar, history, and how Jim Crow segregation led to the development of Black American Sign Language, or BASL.

Beyond providing context and deepening readers' understanding of what the characters are going through, these sections are likely to pique interest in learning more about ASL and different Deaf cultures. It is for good reason—as *True Biz* unfolds, the importance of hearing people acting as allies for people who are deaf becomes harrowingly clear. Like the real people whom Nović discusses in her nonfiction history lessons, her characters are all grappling with what seems to be a timeless issue: the movement to force deaf people to assimilate to the hearing world.

The challenges that deaf people face is one of the novel's most poignant themes and is evidenced in all three of the book's main characters. For Charlie, she has felt a profound sense of alienation throughout the entirety of her life because her mother, a hearing woman, has always been obsessed with making her daughter "normal" by forcing a cochlear implant on her as a child. When Charlie is first introduced in the novel, she is miserable, friendless, and failing all of her classes because her cochlear implant does not work effectively. When she arrives at the fictional River Valley School for the Deaf at the beginning of the novel, it is the first time she feels like she has belonged anywhere. Finally, she is able to learn about her own community's language, culture, and history.

Meanwhile, the character of Austin serves both as Charlie's love interest as well as her foil. He is the member of a proud multigenerational deaf family on his mother's side while his father, who is hearing, works as an ASL interpreter. Unlike Charlie, he grew up in the Deaf community and knows nothing else but acceptance and validation, and subsequently he is one of the most popular students at River Valley. However, when Austin's parents give birth to his baby sister who is hearing, for the first time in his life his sense of identity, belonging, and self-worth are challenged.

Finally, there is the character of February, who is a child of deaf adults (CODA) and is the headmistress of River Valley. Devoted to helping her students, and Deaf culture as a whole, thrive, her story arc begins when she learns that the school will likely be shut down due to budget cuts. Ultimately, Nović uses February as a catalyst for a larger conversation about the history of Deaf erasure at an institutional level in the United States. In some of the short, nonfiction sections interspersed between the novel's narrative, Nović provides horrifying history lessons on how deaf people were sterilized in the name of eugenics, sent to insane asylums, and sometimes forbidden from using sign language to communicate with each other.

A large part of what makes *True Biz* such a compelling read is its firm stance on the debate of whether deafness is a disability that should be "fixed" by medicine and science. Throughout the novel, Nović demonstrates that she passionately believes it is not a disability. Using the setting of River Valley, a kind of Hogwarts for deaf children, she not only shines a light on the richness and diversity of Deaf culture but also on how deaf people's lives are just as fulfilling as those of hearing people. In turn, it becomes easier to understand how gaining the ability to hear is not an aspiration for all deaf people as it would require them to lose their cultural identity and connection to deaf friends and family while also putting them at risk for serious health problems that can come with malfunctioning cochlear implants.

Although Nović successfully captures the beauty of Deaf culture, she ensures that all of her characters are multidimensional beings with just as many flaws as strengths. In turn, she succeeds in upturning any myopic, infantilizing stereotypes about deaf people somehow being "purer" or more innocent. Just like hearing teenagers, Charlie, Austin, and their friends struggle in school, gossip, have sex, drink, and get into trouble. Nović's decision to present them this way infuses the novel with a powerful rawness and honesty.

One of the most interesting aspects of *True Biz* is its presentation of activism. When she is not at River Valley, Charlie spends time with an older ex-boyfriend nicknamed Slash. A member of an anarchy-inspired punk rock band called The Robespierres, Slash is seemingly always looking for ways to create chaos in American institutions. As Charlie learns more about the history of Deaf oppression and begins grappling with the potential closing of River Valley and her mother's decision for her to get another cochlear implant, she finds inspiration in Slash and decides to take radical action herself—something that Nović seems to condone as an unfortunate necessity for change.

Reception of *True Biz* was primarily positive. After being selected by actor Reese Witherspoon's popular book club, the novel quickly became a New York Times Best Seller. It was also relatively well received by critics, many of whom extolled the author for her storytelling style. As Taryn Allen wrote for the *Chicago Reader*, "Nović's writing is smooth and easy, even while jumping between perspectives. She balances dialogue in ASL, spoken English, and over text, with italics and alignment indicating who's communicating. It's interesting to read Deaf characters written by a Deaf author, as the use of sound as a key sense and descriptor is altered, but it's no disadvantage." Indeed, the way that Nović breaks literary conventions like punctuation and formatting to capture the different ways that her characters communicate with one another makes for an especially enjoyable read. By removing quotation marks entirely, she ensures that spoken English and ASL feel equally important on the page while also demonstrating that there is often a fluidity among the languages as many deaf and CODA characters like Charlie and February alternate between the two depending on to whom they are speaking.

Some critics were less favorable in their reviews of the novel, arguing that it was too ambitious in the scope of what it aimed to accomplish. "Nović addresses a lot of topics here, from eugenics and racism to teen romance and middle-aged marital strife. The resulting narrative has an odd shape," the anonymous reviewer for *Kirkus* stated, explaining that the first half of the novel is quite slow while the ending feels rushed. "The lessons in ASL and Deaf history interspersed throughout the text may keep the reader's interest more than the story alone would."

It is true that there are places in *True Biz* where Nović's attempts to strike a balance between the novel's plot and its nonfiction "lessons" can feel more clunky than seamless and therefore could possibly take readers out of the story. However, the novel's content is typically so engaging that most will not notice. Additionally, it is also true that the ending might frustrate those who are looking for a clearer conclusion and takeaways. That said, it is important to note here that the pace of the ending aligns to the characters' actions while amplifying a feeling of suspense that is necessary for the plot. Furthermore, by leaving the last few scenes slightly open-ended, Nović ensures that the characters have what feels like a new beginning rather than an ending.

Despite its few minor flaws, *True Biz* is a groundbreaking novel in its depiction of Deaf life in America. Maile Meloy touched on this idea in her *New York Times* review, stating, "Great stories create empathy and awareness more effectively than facts do, and this important novel should—true biz—change minds and transform the conversation." Meloy's argument here that the book is significant in the ways that it will make hearing readers more aware and empathetic to the alienation and erasure that Deaf people face was likewise argued by Penny Parrish in her review for the *Fredericksburg Free Lance-Star*. "This book is important," wrote Parish. "It made me care, made me better understand, and made me more aware of the importance of human connection for all of us."

In addition to revolving around well-crafted, relatable characters, *True Biz* is compelling and will educate many about the richness, diversity, and value of Deaf culture. Through its story, hearing readers will likely no longer see deafness as a disability but rather as an identity in need of their allyship and protection. Especially as, according to Nović, the only real obstacle that stands in deaf people's way is the hearing world's attempt to force them to assimilate.

Author Biography

Sara Nović is an educator, translator, and the award-winning author of three books. Her work has earned her an American Library Association Alex Award. She is also a prolific writer of essays on Deaf culture, appearing in publications like the *New York Times*, *Slate*, and the *Guardian*, and articles about sports, particularly the New York Mets.

Emily E. Turner

Review Sources

Allen, Taryn. "True Biz? There's a Lot to Learn in Sara Nović's New Book." Review of *True Biz*, by Sara Nović. *Chicago Reader*, 16 May 2022, chicagoreader.com/arts-culture/true-biz-theres-a-lot-to-learn-in-sara-novics-new-book/. Accessed 21 Dec. 2022.

Meloy, Maile. "At a School for the Deaf, Signs of Change Are Clear." Review of *True Biz*, by Sara Nović, *The New York Times*, 15 Mar. 2022, www.nytimes.com/2022/03/15/books/review/true-biz-sara-novic.html. Accessed 20 Nov. 2022.

Parrish, Penny A. "Book Review: Deaf Author Uses Vivid Characters to Tackle Important Issues in 'True Biz.'" *Fredericksburg Free Lance-Star*, 23 Apr. 2022, fredericksburg.com/entertainment/book-review-deaf-author-uses-vivid-characters-to-tackle-important-issues-in-true-biz/article_8ee14c61-32c3-530f-ae9b-4cc03d0ef21c.html. Accessed 20 Nov. 2022.

Review of *True Biz*, by Sara Nović. *Kirkus*, 26 Jan. 2022, www.kirkusreviews.com/book-reviews/sara-novic/true-biz. Accessed 20 Nov. 2022.

Trust

Author: Hernan Diaz (b. 1973)
Publisher: Riverhead Books (New York). 416 pp.
Type of work: Fiction
Time: 1920s and 1930s
Locale: New York City; Grand Tour sites in Europe; Switzerland

Across four interconnected but contradictory narratives, Trust *follows the story of the marriage of an elite New York City couple and probes themes of truth and fiction, morality and finance, and mental illness.*

Principal characters
BENJAMIN RASK, character in *Bonds*; a speculative investor and purported mathematics genius who may be the richest man in the United States
HELEN (BREVOORT) RASK, his wife; a philanthropist with a special interest in music
HAROLD VANNER, author of *Bonds*
ANDREW BEVEL, a speculative investor who may be the richest man in the United States
MILDRED BEVEL, Andrew's wife; a philanthropist with a special interest in music
IDA PARTENZA, author of *A Memoir, Remembered*; a writer who worked for Andrew

Trust has been characterized as a novel in four parts, though reviewers have accurately noted that its structure is quite experimental—the text consists of four distinct types of writing bound together through their interconnected, if contradictory, fictional arc. As Hillary Kelly described the work in a review for the *Los Angeles Times*, it consists of "a novel within a novel followed by an autobiography in progress followed by a memoir and finally a primary source." Across these four sections of the book, author Hernan Diaz presents and re-presents a cast of characters, telling and retelling the life story of a New York city investor and his wife in the years spanning the 1920s and the Great Depression. Much of the reading enjoyment of *Trust* relies on the surprising revelations that unfold between the different formats.

The book opens with a text entitled "Bonds: A Novel" and credited to the author Harold Vanner. Later in *Trust*, it is clarified that *Bonds* is a published novel that is referred to in other sections. The novel-in-the novel follows the life story of Benjamin Rask and Helen Rask. Both descend from old-money families in New York state. While Helen's family has fallen on hard financial times, Benjamin has amplified his vast inherited wealth through investments in the stock market. Furthermore, Helen's father has succumbed to mental illness, and during a family grand tour he was institutionalized in Switzerland. After Benjamin and Helen marry, the novel follows the extreme growth of their wealth during the Roaring Twenties, tracing Helen's work in philanthropy and Benjamin's cutthroat investing brilliance, and then Helen's declining health in the 1930s. The title "Bonds" consciously incorporates both the idea of the ties that bind family members to one another and the financial product.

The second, third, and fourth parts of *Trust* all relate to the stories of Andrew and Mildred Bevel, who the reader can quickly ascertain inspired the characters of Benjamin and Helen Rask in *Bonds*. The second section, "My Life," takes the form of an unfinished autobiography, *My Life*, by Andrew Bevel. Certain narrative sections are fleshed out, while elsewhere it includes telegraphic notes about details to be filled in later.

Hernan Diaz

The third section of the book, "A Memoir, Remembered," refers to the title of a memoir attributed to a woman named Ida Partenza, who presents herself as a renowned writer who is looking back at her early life. In this section, Ida intermixes details of her own life story with remembrances of her work for Andrew, who had engaged her to help him write his autobiography as a way to counter what he saw as Vanner's thinly disguised libel against him and Mildred in *Bonds*. Ida views *Bonds* as "evidence," and sees herself job as a "detective" to uncover the truth about Mildred by studying Vanner's depiction of Helen.

The concluding section, "Futures," which is attributed to Mildred Bevel, is presented as a primary source Ida discovered in the archives while working on *A Memoir, Remembered*. It is fragmentary and the evidence it presents could be interpreted multiple ways, but it certainly offers contradictory, even shocking, alternative information about the Bevel/Rask characters, inviting the reader to review evidence from earlier sections and reflect on the truth or fiction of other versions of the tale. Part of *Truth*'s hold over the reader lies in the fact that the second, third, and fourth parts of the book are each written with the voice of a first-person narrator, though how much the reader should trust the authority of these narrative voices is ultimately one of the central questions of the novel.

Among the themes Diaz raises, reviewers have recognized the concepts of "trust" and "financial capital" as the most important. Across the four sections of the novel, it becomes apparent that the reader cannot lay too much trust in any one version of the tale, but may pick and choose which aspects of the account they believe. Gender roles and biases also play a strong role in this expectation of trust—the novel adopts different versions of authorial voice from the 1920s, each upholding sexist notions of female inferiority or great-man heroism. Yet because none of the accounts emerges as authoritative and the fictional construct of some is even laid bare, *Trust* could be said to confront and critique gender bias—at least in certain limited ways.

Within the larger metaphor of trust, mental illness plays a central role. In "Bonds: A Novel" Helen's mental illness is displayed in graphic and highly sensationalized terms. Elsewhere in *Trust*, the text revisits the same events and characters and variously hides or silences this narrative of mental illness. Still, the reader is left with questions—is Helen's condition, described alternately as schizophrenia or mania, a factor in the central narrative of the novel? If so, which aspects of the story are objectively impacted by the disease and which are not? This question is made murkier by the historical fiction aspect of the text, as references use 1920s vocabulary and medical concepts, leaving modern readers likely horrified by the treatments of that time but also with little clarity on the nature of the actual suffering involved.

The treatment of finance in *Trust* has perhaps received the greatest critical attention as a theme in the novel. The novel is concerned with the moral authority of inherited wealth, the question of blame or even criminality in experimental stock market trades, and the mathematical mystery and beauty of the stock market itself. All of this ties most fundamentally to the question of how the pursuit of money ties to ideas of morality. If fantastically wealthy individuals are also effective and enthusiastic philanthropists, does this buy them moral righteousness? Are they obligated in any way to help others or responsible for the damages that they cause to others? The stakes are high, as *Trust* centers around the question of the role played by its central couple in the onset of the Great Depression. In "Bonds," Vanner accuses Benjamin Rask of triggering the Great Depression single handedly and eschewing any obligation to help offset the damage. In his autobiography, Andrew Bevel repeatedly asserts his own moral authority as an investor, which is built on the morality of his father and grandfather, while blaming the Federal Reserve and government policies for the Great Depression. This question of financial blame remains unresolved, and a dark horse arises toward the end of the book that changes these stakes further, but what remains throughout is a fascination with finance itself, presented throughout the novel with its own mystique. Ida Partenza is the daughter of an Italian anarchist and self-described exile who discusses Marx's thoughts on money with her—notions that she uses to good effect in her job interview at Bevel Investments, "Why work at a place that makes one thing when I could work at a company that makes all things? Because that's what money is: *all* things. Or at least it can become all things. It's the universal commodity by which we measure all other commodities." Ida's conclusion takes this even further—money is, itself, a divinity and the investment banks of Wall Street are its temples. Within such a mindset in which god is money, how might morality be judged? If readers can answer that question, then they may hold the key to understanding the central quandaries of the novel.

Trust met with strongly positive critical reception, winning the Kirkus Prize, making the longlist for the Booker Prize, and finding a place on annual best-books lists from more than thirty outlets. It also made the New York Times Best Sellers list. Reviewers have found *Trust* to be an intellectually deep novel, one that employs meditations on truth and fiction alongside thoughts on finance and morality in order to unveil the structural mechanisms of capitalism. For example, writing for the *New York Times*, Michael Gorra noted that the circularity of the novel's narrative arc reflects the self-referential quality of capital in economics. He observed that *Trust* "recognizes the human costs of a great fortune, even though its characters can see nothing beyond their own calculations; they are most guilty when most innocent, most enthralled by the abstraction of money itself." Many critics also focused on the larger metaphor of "trust" that is woven across the text. As Jane Hu, a reviewer for the *Atlantic*, observed, Diaz does not attempt to produce an authoritative version of the narrative, but instead asks "readers to speculate on what is 'real' and what is 'fake.'" With its fictional primary source materials, memoir, autobiography and novel-within-a novel, *Trust* in many ways establishes a house of cards or an adult "choose your own adventure," as readers can decide which aspects of the text they find meaningful.

Author Biography
Hernan Diaz's first novel, *In the Distance* (2017), was a Pulitzer Prize for Fiction finalist and won the William Saroyan International Prize for Writing. Diaz has also received the Whiting Award and a Guggenheim fellowship, as well as fellowships from the Rockefeller Foundation Bellagio Center and the New York Public Library's Cullman Center for Scholars and Writers, among others.

Julia A. Sienkewicz, PhD

Review Sources
Chakraborty, Abhrajyoti. "*Trust* by Hernan Diaz Review—Unreliable Tales of a Manhattan Mogul." Review of *Trust*, by Hernan Diaz. *The Guardian*, 26 July 2022, www.theguardian.com/books/2022/jul/26/trust-by-hernan-diaz-review-unreliable-tales-of-a-manhattan-mogul. Accessed 4 Feb. 2022.
Corrigan, Maureen. "You Can't 'Trust' This Novel. And That's a Very Good Thing." Review of *Trust*, by Hernan Diaz. *Fresh Air*, NPR, 12 May 2022, www.npr.org/2022/05/12/1098478246/herman-diaz-trust-novel-review. Accessed 4 Feb. 2022.
Gorra, Michael. "The Secrets of an American Fortune, Told Four Ways." Review of *Trust*, by Hernan Diaz. *The New York Times*, 28 Apr. 2022, www.nytimes.com/2022/04/28/books/review/trust-hernan-diaz.html. Accessed 4 Feb. 2022.
Hu, Jane. "We Tell Ourselves Stories about Money to Live." Review of *Trust*, by Hernan Diaz. *The Atlantic*, 26 May 2022, www.theatlantic.com/books/archive/2022/05/hernan-diaz-trust-book-review-capitalism/629950/. Accessed 4 Feb. 2022.
Kelly, Hillary. "Review: Hernan Diaz's Jigsaw-Puzzle Novel Aims to Debunk American Myths." *Los Angeles Times*, 29 Apr. 2022, www.latimes.com/entertainment-arts/books/story/2022-04-29/hernan-diaz-trust-book-review. Accessed 4 Feb. 2022.
Sidhu, Hardeep. Review of *Trust*, by Hernan Diaz. *Harvard Review*, Harvard University, 9 Aug. 2022, harvardreview.org/book-review/trust/. Accessed 4 Feb. 2022.

The Twist of a Knife

Author: Anthony Horowitz (b. 1955)
Publisher: Harper (New York). 384 pp.
Type of work: Novel
Time: Early twenty-first century
Locales: London, England, and surrounding locales

The author's fictional alter ego Anthony Horowitz is arrested for the murder of a theater critic who panned his new play, forcing him to ask for help from Daniel Hawthorne, a detective with whom Horowitz had previously collaborated on three true-crime novels based on Hawthorne's investigations.

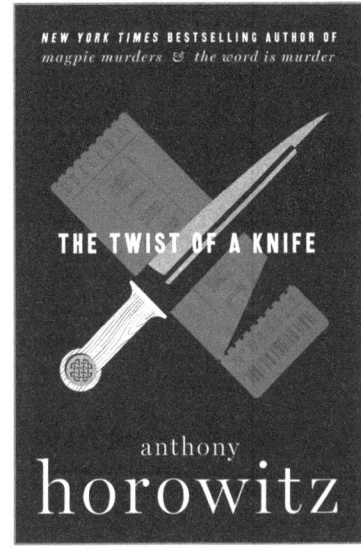

Principal characters
ANTHONY HOROWITZ, an award-winning writer
DANIEL HAWTHORNE, a private detective, formerly a detective inspector with the Metropolitan police
HARRIET THROSBY, a theater critic
EWAN LLOYD, a director
SKY PALMER, an actor
TIRIAN KIRKE, an actor
JORDAN WILLIAMS, an actor
AHMET YURDAKUL, a producer
MARTIN LONGHURST, Yurdakul's accountant
CARA GRUNSHAW, a detective inspector with Scotland Yard

The Twist of a Knife (2022) is the fourth installment in Anthony Horowitz's series of detective stories featuring detective Daniel Hawthorne and writer Anthony Horowitz—a fictionalized version of author Horowitz himself. The novel joins a long list of publishing credits from one of Great Britain's most prolific authors and one of its most versatile. Horowitz has published young adult fiction and novels for adults; his work in television includes the scripts for the long-running series *Poirot* and *Midsomer Murders*; he also created the acclaimed series *Foyle's War*. At the behest of the Arthur Conan Doyle Estate, he has written two novels based on the tales featuring Sherlock Holmes and has also been commissioned by the Ian Fleming Estate to write new novels featuring James Bond. Horowitz's two novels in his Susan Ryeland series, *Magpie Murders* (2016) and *Moonflower Murders* (2020), have been best sellers. The initial installment of his series featuring detective Daniel Hawthorne, *The Word is Murder*, was first published in the UK in 2017 and released in the US the following year. This novel was followed by *The Sentence Is Death* in 2018 and *A Line to Kill* in 2021.

Like its predecessors, *The Twist of a Knife* contains many of the conventional elements one associates with detective fiction. The action centers on a group of people involved in the production of Horowitz's play, *Mindgame*. After a successful run in other cities, *Mindgame* premieres at the Vaudeville Theatre in London's West End. In the audience for the inaugural performance is Harriet Throsby, a theater critic, who writes a vicious review. At the opening-night after-party, one of the cast, Sky Palmer, finds an advance copy of Throsby's review on her phone. She shares it with the producer, director, fellow cast members, and Horowitz, all of whom are outraged. The following day, Throsby is murdered in her home. Evidence points strongly toward Horowitz as the murderer, and he is swiftly arrested by Detective Inspector Cara Grunshaw. He panics, knowing that Grunshaw would love to see him convicted of this crime. She would consider it payback for his role in leading her to arrest the wrong person on a previous case, an error for which she was publicly humiliated. Knowing he needs help, Horowitz calls on private detective Daniel Hawthorne for assistance. Readers learn that the two have a history of working together. They met years earlier, when Hawthorne, interested in profiting from his work, had approached Horowitz to write a series of books based on the detective's cases. They have had a rocky relationship, and *The Twist of a Knife* opens with Horowitz telling Hawthorne that their true-crime fiction collaboration is ending; however, when Horowitz gets into trouble, he believes Hawthorne is the one person who can help him escape a prison sentence.

Anthony Horowitz

Released on bail but subject to rearrest, Horowitz joins Hawthorne in an investigation to identify Throsby's killer. They learn quickly that everyone associated with the play—director Ewan Lloyd; actors Sky Palmer, Tirian Kirke, and Jordan Williams; producer Ahmet Yurdakul; and even Yurdakul's accountant, Martin Longhurst—has a motive for killing the critic. Determining who had the opportunity becomes more problematic, however, as each suspect seems to have an airtight alibi. While Hawthorne and Horowitz conduct interviews and search for clues that might reveal the murderer, Grunshaw and her associates at Scotland Yard methodically gather evidence that supports her belief that Horowitz committed the crime. Just before Horowitz is rearrested, however, Hawthorne gathers all of the suspects at the Vaudeville Theatre and exposes the real murderer.

On one level, this novel is an homage to the tradition of mystery and detective fiction that stretches back to Conan Doyle's tales featuring Sherlock Holmes through the golden-age whodunits of Agatha Christie, Dorothy L. Sayers, and Ngaio Marsh. For example, the relationship between Hawthorne and Horowitz mirrors that of Conan

Doyle's Holmes and his associate and "biographer" Dr. John Watson. Reviewer Carol Memmott also pointed out parallels between the plot of Horowitz's novel and the thrillers of Alfred Hitchcock. *The Twist of a Knife* is a variation of the closed-circle mystery, in which circumstances suggest that the murderer must be one of a small number of suspects identified either by profession or locale (such as in a country house mystery). The plot recalls Marsh's *A Vintage Murder*, in which her Inspector Roderick Alleyn solves the murder of a member of a traveling troupe of actors. The ending of Horowitz's novel reprises those often used by Agatha Christie in her novels. Horowitz calls attention to the parallel by having Hawthorne tell the character Horowitz that he has called the suspects together to reveal the killer; in that way, Hawthorne explains, Horowitz will have materials to create a dramatic ending for the novel Hawthorne expects him to write about this adventure. Like many of these classic tales, the backstory revealing the relationship between the detective and the chronicler of his adventures is given to readers piecemeal over several tales. Horowitz, however, is careful to provide sufficient details to afford those not familiar with previous novels to understand the relationship between the fictional Horowitz and Hawthorne.

The best mystery novels depend not only on complex plotting and genre conventions but also on complex characterization, particularly involving the fictional detective. Horowitz's Hawthorne is a composite of many of the legends of the genre. Like Conan Doyle's Holmes, he tends to be secretive about his past (and, like Watson, the character Horowitz becomes something of a voyeur in his attempts to learn more about his colleague). Like Christie's Hercule Poirot, he is fastidious in his dress and his personal affairs—two qualities that fascinate the fictional Horowitz. Yet Hawthorne has a violent streak reminiscent of Dashiell Hammett's Sam Spade. Hawthorne was dismissed from the police force for tossing a handcuffed suspect accused of crimes against children down a flight of stairs at Scotland Yard. He seems remarkably callous and even cynical, considering virtually anyone capable of committing crimes—even murder—if driven by circumstances. His treatment of others is often rude—especially in his dealings with Horowitz, whom he insists on calling Tony despite repeated pleas by Horowitz to call him Anthony, as others do. Of course, the novel is narrated in the first person by the fictional Horowitz, so readers' perceptions of Hawthorne are often colored by Horowitz's judgments.

The real-life Horowitz is no conventional mystery writer, and like his other novels in the genre, *The Twist of a Knife* is a highly unconventional mystery. Part of the pleasure in reading this novel and others in the series comes from recognizing the many references to actual people and events and trying to discern what is real and what is made up. Horowitz draws on his own past experiences as a writer to create the fictional backstory for the series. The real Horowitz wrote a thriller titled *Mindgame*, which was adapted for the stage in 1999 and, after performances outside London, ran for several performances at the Vaudeville Theatre in 2000 (and in revivals in New York in 2008 and in London again in 2018). He also wrote the other works for which his protagonist claims credit in the series. In *The Twist of a Knife*, Horowitz's wife, Jill Green, a British television executive, plays an important cameo role. Comments about actors, producers, and writers who populate writer Horowitz's world give an aura of reality to the fictional Horowitz's adventures. A cynical reader might consider this technique cheating, as Horowitz has ready-made materials on which to work his creative imagination. It would be equally fair to say, however, that he is simply following the age-old advice given to writers who wish to create successful works of fiction: write what you know. Horowitz knows much about the theater and about writing mysteries, and this knowledge allows him to create convincing plots that contain enough suspense to keep readers wondering about the killer while maintaining an air of plausibility that heightens the tension felt by the narrator as the police build their case against his fictional alter ego.

As has been the case with reviews of earlier books in the Horowitz/Hawthorne series, *The Twist of a Knife* has been well received. *New York Journal of Books* reviewer Toni V. Sweeney applauded Horowitz's ability to maintain readers' interest and create suspense throughout this "witty and descriptive" narrative. Tom Nolan of the *Wall Street Journal* called the novel part of a "gleefully written series," and in his summary of the year's best mysteries judged it the best of Horowitz's books featuring Hawthorne. The reviewer for *Kirkus* recommended it highly, as did *Library Journal*'s Bill Anderson, who concluded his brief critique with the observation that "readers of character-driven novels will love the twists and turns" of a novel that provides an "unexpected reveal." In her lengthy review for the *Washington Post*, Carol Memmott praised Horowitz for creating a work of "dry humor" that pays homage to the traditions of detective fiction from which he draws while remaining "wholly original."

Author Biography

Anthony Horowitz is the author of young adult novels and several series of detective fiction. He is also a prolific writer for television, most notably as the creator of the popular series *Foyle's War*. In 2014 he was awarded the Order of the British Empire (OBE).

Laurence W. Mazzeno

Review Sources

Anderson, Bill. Review of *The Twist of a Knife*, by Anthony Horowitz. *Library Journal*, Sept. 2022, pp. 117–18. *Literary Reference Center Plus*, search.ebscohost.com/login.aspx?direct=true&db=lkh&AN=158645474&site=lrc-plus. Accessed 3 Feb. 2023.

Hertzel, Laurie. Review of *The Twist of a Knife*, by Anthony Horowitz. *Star Tribune*, 3 Dec. 2022, www.startribune.com/review-a-twist-of-the-knife-by-anthony-horowitz/600232169/. Accessed 2 Feb. 2023.

Memmott, Carol. "Whodunit? In Anthony Horowitz's New Novel, the Villain May Be the Author." Review of *The Twist of a Knife*, by Anthony Horowitz. *The Washington Post*, 29 Nov. 2022, www.washingtonpost.com/books/2022/11/29/anthony-horowitz-novel/. Accessed 2 Feb. 2023.

Nolan, Tom. "Mysteries: Anthony Horowitz's *The Twist of a Knife*." *The Wall Street Journal*, 11 Nov. 2022, wsj.com/articles/mysteries-book-review-anthony-horowitz-the-twist-of-a-knife-11668179494/. Accessed 2 Feb. 2023.

Sweeney, Toni V. Review of *The Twist of a Knife*, by Anthony Horowitz. *New York Journal of Books*, 19 Nov. 2022, www.nyjournalofbooks.com/book-review/twist-knife-novel. Accessed 2 Feb. 2023.

Under the Skin
The Hidden Toll of Racism on American Lives and on the Health of Our Nation

Author: Linda Villarosa (b. 1959)
Publisher: Doubleday (New York). 288 pp.
Type of work: Current affairs, history, medicine
Time: 1700s–Present day
Locales: New York City; Montgomery, Alabama; New Orleans; Jackson, Mississippi; West Virginia

In Under the Skin, *Linda Villarosa provides a comprehensive and well-supported investigation into systemic racial disparities that have roots in slavery and continue to impact African Americans' medical care, overall health, and living conditions.*

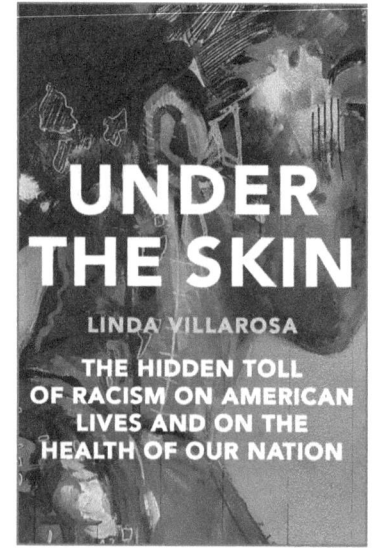

Principal personages
HAROLD FREEMAN, MD, director of surgery, Harlem Hospital
DAVID WILLIAMS, PhD, professor of public health, Harvard University
HEATHER MILLER, MD, patient with high-risk pregnancy and childbirth
ARLINE GERONIMUS, ScD, professor of public health, University of Michigan
CEDRIC STURDEVANT, community health worker, Jackson, Mississippi

Linda Villarosa began writing about the health of African Americans in the 1980s when she wrote and edited articles about nutrition and fitness for *Essence*, the popular Black-owned magazine whose readership then consisted primarily of Black women. Over the following decades, her journalistic work moved to reflect her growing understanding of systemic and structural racial disparities that impact the health of African Americans. *Under the Skin,* a National Association for the Advancement of Colored People (NAACP) Image Award nominee, is a comprehensive compilation of Villarosa's research, investigative reporting, and insight on health threats that disproportionately affect Black communities. Her journalistic skill, activist's spirit, experience, and compassion combine powerfully in this work to convincingly link three critical factors to racial health disparities: historical racial discrimination that has shaped American society, the stress that racism heaps upon the Black body, and structural and interpersonal biases that lead to inequitable treatment in the health care system.

Over eight chapters the book moves across a spectrum of debate, myth, scientific evidence, and reports of personal experience to explain that Black Americans 'live sicker and die quicker' than White Americans even of the same economic level.

Linda Villarosa

Villarosa states, "Even when income, education, and access to health care are matched, African Americans remain disadvantaged and racial disparities in health cut lives short." *Under the Skin* presents eyewitness accounts, gives voice to survivors of questionable medical practices, and cites a mountain of research to support the argument that systemic racism causes health and health care disparities that negatively affect Black Americans. Villarosa is a master of uncovering the humanity hidden in health statistics through storytelling that rings with immediacy, authenticity, and truth.

Villarosa begins *Under the Skin* with the story of the evolution of her personal beliefs about the well-documented crises of diabetes, heart disease, hypertension, and many other serious ailments that disproportionately affect Black communities. In 1985 her perspective and her work as a health writer at *Essence* were greatly affected by her close reading of the US Department of Health and Human Services Office of Minority Health's *Report on the Secretary's Task Force on Black and Minority Health*, produced under HHS Secretary Margaret Heckler and known as the Heckler Report. An analysis of the existing data about race, disease, and mortality published by the federal government, the Heckler Report was influential as the first-ever comprehensive report of the health status of Black Americans and other minoritized Americans and was thus the source of motivation and purpose for Villarosa in her role as a provider of health information for her Black readers and their communities. Determined to fix the health crisis so alarmingly documented in the Heckler report, Villarosa redoubled her journalistic efforts to inform and advise Black communities about how to take better care of themselves. Laboring under her long-held assumption that the crisis could be resolved through more responsible behaviors of Black people, an assumption that was only strengthened by the Heckler Report, Villarosa edited articles about nutrition, diet, and exercise for the magazine under the banner of "self-health." During that period Villarosa also assumed that the health crisis in Black communities was primarily linked to poverty and a lack of education and encouraged her readers to help the less privileged and less educated in their lives to make healthy lifestyle changes.

By 1991 Villarosa had begun to question those assumptions after meeting Dr. Harold Freeman, a physician at Harlem Hospital and coauthor of an article published a year earlier in the *New England Journal of Medicine* on racial health disparities in Harlem. His insights into what he called a national tragedy of racial health disparities were profoundly influential in helping Villarosa see the error in her thinking regarding the issues affecting Black communities. Dr. Freeman's work showed that the health crisis in Harlem affected middle-class, educated Black people, not just their poorer neighbors, disproving poverty as the sole cause of widespread and persistent health problems among Black people. While this expanded Villarosa's vision about the causes of the Black health crisis, she was not yet ready to challenge the medical system, although she remained dedicated to her mission of providing information for effective self-help as a way to empower her Black readers. The true turning point in her work came from the wrenching experience of witnessing the disrespectful and discriminatory care her Black, well-educated, affluent father received as a seriously ill patient at a veterans' hospital. She and her mother had to intervene emphatically to ensure he was cared for with the skill and dignity every patient deserves. "We made them 'see' him, beyond his race and the ravages of his illness." This personal experience powerfully reinforced what she was learning from her involvement with the National Black Women's Health Project and the work of Black scholars and physicians who were advancing theories on the role racism plays in the health and medical treatment of Black bodies. Villarosa's journalistic focus then shifted from a perspective of self-help and empowerment to one of critical analysis of systemic factors that affect African American health and the quality of medical care they receive.

Under the Skin recounts the origins and long-term impact of myths explaining how Black bodies and White bodies differ and how the medical establishment's belief in those myths has resulted in the disrespectful and dangerous treatment of Black patients. In the eighteenth and nineteenth centuries, White doctors, scientists, and even statesmen developed and spread antiscientific theories about Black people to both give substance to the notion of White supremacy and justify the brutality of slavery. These wildly invalid theories asserted that Black bodies were created to withstand extreme conditions and assaults and were therefore fit for backbreaking labor and cruel treatment. In a detailed chapter, Villarosa summarizes the fallacies, naming the people, including Thomas Jefferson, who asserted them. She cites Jefferson's influential 1785 book *Notes on the State of Virginia* in which he invented physiological and psychological differences of Black people, including a greater ability to withstand heat, weak lungs that benefit from hard work, less need for sleep, hypersexuality, intellectual inferiority and the limited ability to feel tenderness and human emotions such as grief compared to White people. During the same historical moment, Benjamin Moseley, a member of London's Royal College of Physicians, similarly described Black people as all but lacking human sensibilities. Villarosa then skillfully and convincingly demonstrates how this influential historical misinformation has permeated American consciousness to the degree that physicians and others continue to hold fallacious beliefs about Black bodies, which often leads to inappropriate, neglectful, or otherwise dangerous treatment of Black patients and Black communities.

The book covers the major areas of Villarosa's investigative health reporting from the 1980s to 2021, and she uses documented evidence to make the disturbing point that many of the inequities addressed in articles earlier in her career regarding AIDS/HIV, maternal mortality, and environmental health risks have yet to be remedied. In the twenty-first century the United States spends more on health care than other comparable nations, but the money the nation spends does not lead to a healthier population. The United States does worse than other developed, wealthy nations on global health indicators including infant mortality, maternal mortality, and life expectancy. The racial health gap is a key factor in this reality. The author supports such assertions about health care in the United States with documented evidence.

Although *Under the Skin* primarily addresses the ways in which Black Americans are disadvantaged, Villarosa shows how gaps in the health care system affect other Americans as well. In a chapter titled "Discrimination and Ill-Treatment Can Harm Every Body," the author describes her visit to West Virginia to talk to White Appalachians about their health and their lives. Her report from Appalachia shows how this largely White region is disproportionately affected by extremely high rates of heart disease, obesity, alcoholism, drug overdose, and suicide and provides context to explain the prevalence of these health problems. Villarosa references the work of Arline Geronimus on 'weathering' to support her assertion that poor health can result from the damage bodies of any color experience when exposed to the discrimination, ill-treatment, and disregard that many people in Appalachia experience. According to Geronimus, weathering is what happens when a body sustains high levels of health-threatening stress produced by the high effort of coping with unrelenting adversity.

Villarosa closes the book on a hopeful note by devoting the final chapter to promising new practices in community health, medical education, and health care facilities aimed at eliminating racial health disparities. She also highlights the efforts of medical students, community health workers, elected officials, and others who have educated themselves to recognize and address racial health inequities. The chapter presents detailed accounts of the efforts of citizens who are working against a resistant, slow-to-change system to improve the health of their neighbors through community-based health worker programs. These programs train community members to provide resources and appropriate, compassionate care and advocacy for sick people.

Reviews of *Under the Skin* were overwhelmingly positive. The descriptor 'meticulous' appeared frequently in reviews in reference to Villarosa's perceptive critical analysis; thorough, well-researched reporting; and richly detailed storytelling. Jerald Walker, the reviewer for the *Washington Post*, opened his review with the story of his wife's inadequate and dismissive treatment by medical staff during a pregnancy crisis. Walker, who identified himself and his wife as Black, reviewed the book from a personal perspective that poignantly illustrated and underscored the multiple dire messages of *Under the Skin*. His wife's story could have been one of Villarosa's case studies. *Guardian* reviewer Charles Kaiser focused part of his review on Villarosa's reporting on the history of mythmaking about Black bodies, and how the shadow of long-ago debunked mythology has survived in the medical establishment as racist stereotypes that can make medical attention dangerous for Black people. For Kaiser, the most dismaying information in the book describes the reality that racism is alive and affecting the training of future physicians at some of our nation's most prestigious institutions. Kaitlyn Greenidge reviewed *Under the Skin* for the *New York Times* the week after a draft was leaked from the Supreme Court suggesting the Court's intention to overturn *Roe v. Wade*. That may be why she opened her review with a summary of Villarosa's report of two Black Alabama girls who were forcibly sterilized in 1973 and whose stories figure prominently in *Under the Skin*. She wrote, "Some women and activists on social media have predicted that '*The Handmaid's Tale* will become a reality,' conveniently forgetting that it already has been for generations of American women who are not white." Greenidge praised Villarosa for illuminating the effects of the cruel legacy of medical maltreatment of Black people in contemporary times.

Author Biography
Linda Villarosa is a celebrated journalist who has received awards from organizations such as the New York Association of Black Journalists, the Arthur Ashe Institute, the American Medical Writers' Association, Lincoln University, the National Lesbian and Gay Journalists' Association, the National Women's Political Caucus, and the Callen-Lorde Community Health Center. Villarosa contributed an article on myths about physical racial differences to the award-winning 1619 Project, which examined the legacy of slavery. She is a professor in residence at the City University of New York and teaches journalism, Black studies, and medicine at the City College of New York in Harlem.

RoAnne Elliott

Review Sources
Greenidge, Kaitlyn. "The Roots of Black Pain in America." Review of *Under the Skin: The Hidden Toll of Racism on American Lives and on the Health of Our Nation*, by Linda Villarosa. *The New York Times*, 8 June 2022, www.nytimes.com/2022/06/08/books/review/under-the-skin-linda-villarosa.html. Accessed 18 Jan. 2023.

Kaiser, Charles. "*Under the Skin* Review: US Healthcare, Racism and a Terrible Toll Taken." *The Guardian*, 3 July 2022, www.theguardian.com/books/2022/jul/02/under-the-skin-review-us-healthcare-racism-linda-villarosa. Accessed 7 Feb. 2023.

Review of *Under the Skin: The Hidden Toll of Racism on American Lives and on the Health of Our Nation*, by Linda Villarosa. *Kirkus Reviews*, 4 Apr. 2022, www.kirkusreviews.com/book-reviews/linda-villarosa/under-the-skin-racism/. Accessed 18 Jan. 2023.

Walker, Jerald. "Racism's Ill Effects on the Health-care System—and the Body Itself." Review of *Under the Skin: The Hidden Toll of Racism on American Lives and on the Health of Our Nation*, by Linda Villarosa. *The Washington Post*, 10 June 2022, www.washingtonpost.com/outlook/2022/06/10/racisms-ill-effects-health-care-system-body-itself/. Accessed 18 Jan. 2023.

The Verifiers

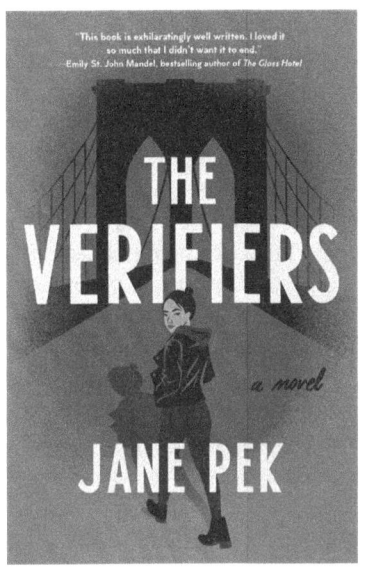

Author: Jane Pek
Publisher: Vintage Books (New York). 368 pp.
Type of work: Novel
Time: Present day
Locale: New York, New York

Set in New York City, Jane Pek's debut novel, The Verifiers, is a complex murder mystery involving the online matchmaking industry.

Principal characters
CLAUDIA LIN, a newly hired verifier at Veracity, an online identity verification firm
CHARLES LIN, her older brother
CORALINE LIN, her older sister
MAX, her roommate, an artist
REBECCA "BECKS" RITTEL, her immediate superior at Veracity
KOMLA ATSINA, head of Veracity
IRIS LETTRISTE, a.k.a. Flora or Fauna, a Veracity client
SARAH REAVES, Iris's sister
CHARRETTER, someone Iris flirts with on Soulmate
JUDE KALMAN, a.k.a. Captain Bubbles, Iris's ex

In interviews, Jane Pek has confessed to being an avid mystery reader. In her first novel, The Verifiers (2022), it is obvious she has learned well the conventions of the genre. Better still, she has updated the old-fashioned detective agency trope for the twenty-first century and brought it to life, supplanting the plodding gumshoe approach with the ease and speed of discovery generated through the use of proprietary technology designed for researching and investigating a growing modern phenomenon: online dating.

For better and worse, the internet is supplanting former methods of getting to know someone who just might become a permanent fixture. Electronics have streamlined the process. Instead of waiting and hoping for a chance encounter—at church, school, a bar, the gym, or a library—that might produce a suitable partner, a mate seeker in contemporary society can be proactive. There are dozens of platforms where subscribers can access profiles of hundreds or thousands of prospective candidates for romance and initiate correspondence with some, or many.

The problem is, online or face-to-face, people are still people. They hide secrets. They deceive. They do not always tell the truth. When a long-term commitment is at stake, a subscriber is wise to be cautious about accepting information at face value. To allay consumer fears, a whole subindustry has sprung up to fact-check given data on individuals of interest.

Jane Pek shows how it all works, briskly and humorously in The Verifiers, through the distinctive voice of her creation, narrator and protagonist Claudia Lin. The author's skill is evident from the start. The novel's well-constructed opening line begins what will become an active, thoughtful plot: "I can tell right away that Iris Lettriste isn't like the others."

In a dozen words, Pek accomplishes several tasks. Two people are mentioned: the observant first-person narrator, who will soon be introduced more fully, and Iris Lettriste. The reader's curiosity is instantly aroused, a necessary component for a story blurbed on the back cover as "a clever and thought-provoking mystery."

Jane Pek

Questions spring to mind. Who is Iris? Why is she not like the others, whoever they may be?

The second line explains why Iris is different and adds new elements to be considered: "Everyone else walks into Veracity wearing some residue of embarrassment"—but not Iris, apparently. (What is Veracity? Why are people generally ashamed to be there?) The following passages move from general to specific, showing symptoms of embarrassment: "Their gazes skitter about, their sentences are potholed with *ums* and *wells*. They overexplain. They worry that we'll judge them, or they get preemptively angry because they assume we do."

In quick order, readers receive more specifics. They learn about Veracity, a small company on the third floor above a spa at a townhouse in Tribeca. The firm consists of three full-time employees—Komla Atsina, the head of the company; his assistant and Claudia's supervisor, Rebecca "Becks" Rittel; and newest hire, twenty-something Claudia Lin—plus Squirrel, a part-time IT specialist. Veracity is promoted as "a start-up that conducts independent research for dating platforms." Their business is verifying for clients the accuracy of information potential matches have given in profiles on matchmaking sites. This is a major concern, because people lie, to themselves and others, particularly when romance is involved, to appear more desirable than they are. They upload photos from several years ago, when they were several pounds lighter and their "skin hadn't yet had to negotiate with gravity." They claim skills and interests they hope will appeal to possible mates. They fudge their education, airbrush their background, inflate their income, expand their qualifications, erase their crimes. As Komla, who, according to Claudia, is "harder to read than Finnegans Wake," explained at her hiring, verifiers do not solve crimes. They do not "intervene in the course of events beyond reporting their findings to their clients." Veracity should be viewed as a "personal investments advisory firm."

After a few weeks working at Veracity, Claudia knows better. It is obvious clients think of them as a

dating detective agency. She takes that perception to heart with Iris, the first client for Claudia, who envisions herself as a sleuth. Iris (screen name: Flora or Fauna), a lawyer in her mid-thirties, wants Veracity to verify Charretter, whom she has been chatting and flirting with on the Soulmate Messenger platform. Though Komla suggests such an investigation would be a waste of time and money, Iris insists. For a significant fee, Veracity agrees to take her case for six weeks, to review Charretter's activity on Soulmate and check if he is active on other matchmaking sites. Because it is a case with low outcome expectations, it is given to newbie Claudia, who, since coming on board at Veracity has been tasked with reading industry magazines and setting up training profiles.

According to Charretter's profile, he is thirty-five and works in advertising. He averages three to six online contacts per week. He chats on Soulmate Messenger with four or five women at a time. Veracity obtained access to his data via Match Insights, "a vendor that consolidates customer data across matchmakers, and resells it to businesses in the industry." Claudia reads transcripts of chats between Charretter and Iris and takes notes, comparing the exercise to Literary Analysis 101 in college, where she parsed *Pride and Prejudice* or *Anna Karenina* or *Othello*. There are many such literary references in *The Verifiers*, including to Oscar Wilde, Henry David Thoreau, Jane Austen, and others, which neatly summarize milestones in Claudia's progress on the case and reinforce her reputation as a dedicated reader. Claudia periodically refers to famous fictional detectives: Arthur Conan Doyle's Sherlock Holmes, Agatha Christie's Hercule Poirot, Georges Simenon's Maigret. Her favorite detecting inspiration, however, is the fictitious Inspector Yuan series, cozy mysteries set in Ming Dynasty China (1368–1644). Claudia's encyclopedic recall of the detective's actions in the series even help her out of later jams.

All three members of Veracity are present when their findings are presented during a meeting with Iris, who requests a second verification—with cost no object—on Jude Kalman, also known as Captain Bubbles on Soulmate, whom she dated a few times before he became incommunicado, then resurfaced months later.

Becks takes over the Charretter account and assigns the Jude Kalman case to Claudia. She is set up with an application installed on her phone, Finders Keepers, that can track people's movements via their cell phones. The app takes advantage of the fact that when people sign up with a dating platform, they give consent to have their current location accessed with GPS.

Claudia researches Kalman, follows him on Finders Keepers, plots his movements on a spreadsheet, and ultimately does in-person surveillance. She discovers that Kalman has a wife and child. Ready to report these findings to Iris, Veracity schedules a meeting. Iris does not show. They soon learn that Iris is dead and was not the person they thought she was.

That is the heart of the mystery that unravels over the course of *The Verifiers*. Claudia defies direct orders and after work conducts her own investigation into what happened to Iris and Iris's sister Sarah Reaves. There are clues to be found, red herrings to eliminate, obstacles to overcome, suspects to consider, physical perils to dodge, plot twists to survive, and conclusions to draw before the end is reached. Meanwhile, there is considerable entertainment to be had. The burgeoning online dating industry, for example, is taken to task on several issues, especially invasion of privacy, data harvesting, and the proliferation of shady subcontractors and con artists that attach themselves to profitable matchmakers, the Big Three as they are called in the novel.

One sub-thread is a celebration of New York City. Claudia bicycles everywhere, initiating an urban travelogue that moves from her apartment in Gowanus, where she lives with her roommate Max, to her job site in Manhattan, to Flushing, where her mother, an immigrant from Taiwan, lives. Her bicycle, in fact, becomes an important plot point later in the novel.

Likewise, Claudia's family provides subplots, side trips, comic relief, and pathos. Claudia regularly interacts with her siblings: her overworked brother, Charles, and her beautiful, arrogant sister, Coraline, who "always treated male infidelity like I would milk going bad: sniff to confirm, toss, pick up a new bottle." Although Claudia came out as a lesbian to her siblings years ago, she has not been able to tell her mother, who wants her to date "a nice Chinese boy"; the Inspector Yuan mysteries are one of the few things they bond over. Claudia reminisces about her absent father, whom she has not seen in years.

Critics enthusiastically approved of *The Verifiers*. A reviewer for *Kirkus* called it a "cool, cerebral, and very funny debut novel," singling out "Claudia's engaging voice: She keeps the narrative moving at a fast-paced clip" and the "entertaining secondary characters." Doreen Sheridan, writing for *Criminal Intent*, agreed on all particulars. "*The Verifiers* is a really terrific debut novel that melds a borderline techno thriller mystery with a contemporary comedy of manners. . . . Claudia is smart, funny, self-aware."

Oline H. Cogdill for the South Florida Sun-Sentinel described The Verifiers as a "lively debut" that "works well as a look at modern matchmaking, as a paean to crime fiction, a story of a tightly knit Asian family and a young woman navigating her attraction to other women." Cogdill ended the review with a closing line that should fire the author's and publisher's imagination related to series extension: "The Verifiers is a sharp debut, leaving room for more of Claudia's escapades." Publishers Weekly echoed the thought: "This nuanced novel will leave readers eagerly awaiting Pek's next book."

Author Biography
A lawyer for an investment firm, Jane Pek has published short fiction that was anthologized in *The Best American Stories* in both 2020 and 2021. *The Verifiers* is her first book.

Jack Ewing

Review Sources

Cogdill, Oline H. "Book Reviews: 'Local Gone Missing' in a Seaside British Town; Austen Meets Holmes in 'Verifiers.'" Review of The Verifiers, by Jane Pek, and Local Gone Missing, by Fiona Barton. South Florida Sun Sentinel, 7 July 2022, www.sun-sentinel.com/entertainment/theater-and-arts/books/fl-et-books-local-gone-missing-verifiers-20220707-7ca6uondb5co5i6iwrusy4athi-story.html. Accessed 5 Jan. 2023.

De Mariaffi, Elisabeth. "Elisabeth de Mariaffi Recommends Three of Her Favourite Thriller and Mystery Reads." Review of The Verifiers, by Jane Pek, et al. CBC Radio, 13 May 2022, www.cbc.ca/radio/thenextchapter/full-episode-may-14-2022-1.6451089/elisabeth-de-mariaffi-recommends-three-of-her-favourite-thriller-and-mystery-reads-1.6451112. Accessed 5 Jan. 2023.

Sheridan, Doreen. "Book Review: *The Verifiers* by Jane Pek." *Criminal Intent*, 3 Mar. 2022, www.criminalelement.com/book-review-the-verifiers-by-jane-pek/. Accessed 5 Jan. 2023.

Review of The Verifiers, by Jane Pek. Kirkus, 30 Nov. 2021, www.kirkusreviews.com/book-reviews/jane-pek/the-verifiers-pek/. Accessed 5 Jan. 2023.

Review of *The Verifiers*, by Jane Pek. *Publishers Weekly*, 29 Nov. 2021, www.publishersweekly.com/978-0-593-31379-4. Accessed 5 Jan. 2023.

Victory. Stand!
Raising My Fist for Justice

Authors: Tommie Smith (b. 1944) and Derrick Barnes
Illustrator: Dawud Anyabwile (b. 1965)
Publisher: Norton Young Readers (New York). 208 pp.
Type of work: Graphic nonfiction, memoir
Time: 1944–present
Locales: Mexico City, Texas, California

Victory. Stand! Raising My Fist for Justice presents the inspiring life story of the athlete and activist Tommie Smith in a graphic novel format aimed at young adult readers. Centered around the 1968 Olympic Games, at which Smith won a gold medal and raised a gloved fist on the podium in an iconic protest for civil rights, the book also covers Smith's childhood and later life with particular attention to issues of racial justice throughout.

Principal personages

TOMMIE SMITH, a Black athlete and civil rights activist
DADDY, his father, a sharecropper with deep religious faith and a firm work ethic
MULLA, his mother, a tireless homemaker
HARRY EDWARDS, a sociologist and civil rights activist concerned with the treatment of Black athletes
JOHN CARLOS, Smith's teammate and fellow protester at the 1968 Olympics

Victory. Stand! Raising My Fist for Justice (2022) is a work of autobiographical graphic nonfiction by track-and-field star Tommie Smith, who penned his tale with the help of award-winning writer Derrick Barnes and acclaimed illustrator Dawud Anyabwile. Aimed at readers from middle school up, it transcends mere sports memoir to provide a compelling look at deep issues of race and society. Along with fascinating and often inspiring details of Smith's life, it offers an engaging look at the challenges that have long faced Black American athletes and the way sports have intersected with the civil rights movement. The graphic novel format reinforces these powerful themes with dynamic black-and-white imagery that effectively propels the narrative and draws the reader into the action.

The story opens with Smith at the 1968 Summer Olympic Games in Mexico City. The 1968 Games were notable for several reasons, including for being the first-ever Olympics held in a Spanish-speaking country, but they are perhaps most remembered

Tommie Smith

for an iconic act of protest by Smith and his teammate John Carlos. *Victory. Stand!* is in many ways focused on that protest, but it uses a nonlinear structure to build up to this central event. The first panels of the book show Smith about to compete in the final race of the 200m sprint competition. His narration reveals that he had injured a thigh muscle as he crossed the finish line in the semifinals not long before, putting his performance in the final at risk. It also hints at the bigger tensions surrounding him at the time, noting that when he first felt a sharp pain he thought he might have been attacked by "the people who had been making threats on my life." Smith goes on to foreshadow that "If we did what we had planned, there was no telling what the backlash would be." But before any of that is further explained, the starting pistol goes off and Smith bursts forward, focused only on the race.

The narrative then jumps back to Smith's early childhood. He grew up in the tiny town of Acworth, Texas, the seventh of twelve children in a poor sharecropping family. They had no running water or other amenities in their home, and the entire family worked hard to make ends meet. Smith notes that he was energetic from a young age and would draw on his parents' tireless work ethic throughout his life.

The book continues to cut back and forth between scenes from the Olympics and the story of Smith's formative years. When he was seven, in the early 1950s, his family moved to California to forge a better life. There, his almost-preternatural athletic ability quickly emerged, nurtured by a series of supportive school coaches. However, he was also bullied by White classmates, denied opportunities because of institutionalized racism, and forced to contend with the everyday indignities suffered by Black Americans in that era. Smith earns a scholarship to San José State University, where he continues to establish himself as an athletic star, especially in track and field. He also meets sociologist Harry Edwards, whose social activism helps him begin to consider what he, as an athlete, can contribute to the burgeoning civil rights movement. One important lesson comes in 1965, when a group of Black football players threatens to boycott an All-Star game unless it is moved from its planned venue in the South to a more progressive locale and wins that concession.

As one of the top sprinters in the country, Smith sets records and qualifies for the US national team for the 1968 Olympics. He also deepens his activism, becoming involved in the Black Power movement and especially Edwards' organization, the Olympic Project for Human Rights (OPHR). In the days leading up to their arrival in Mexico City, Smith and fellow US sprinter John Carlos discuss how to draw attention to the injustices of racial discrimination in the US and abroad. The high-profile international Olympic Games would provide an effective spotlight, they reason, but by the time of the final 200m sprint, they still have not yet fully decided what their protest will look like.

Overcoming the extreme pain of his injury, Smith crosses the finish line first. Not only does he win the Olympic gold medal, he also sets a new world record of 19.83 seconds. Coming in second is Australian runner Peter Norman, with the third-place bronze medal going to Carlos. The victory assures that an act of protest will be even more visible, and Smith makes final preparations. Though he knows there will likely be repercussions for making a statement, he feels a moral obligation to do so.

Before ascending the podium, Smith and Carlos decide to remove their shoes to symbolize the poverty facing many Black Americans. Smith wears a black scarf while Carlos dons a beaded necklace to subtly reference the horrors of lynching, and Carlos also defies the Olympic dress code by unzipping his jacket to represent the average worker. Both Americans as well as Norman wear OPHR buttons. The most dramatic and eye-catching part of the protest, however, comes as the three athletes stand on the podium. Smith and Carlos each thrust a black-gloved fist in the air and bow their heads for the eighty seconds it takes for the US national anthem to play. "We had to be seen because we were not being heard," Smith writes of that now-iconic pose. "Those fists in the air were dedicated to everyone at home, back in the projects in Chicago, Oakland, and Detroit, to everyone in the boroughs of Queens and Brooklyn, to all of the brothers and sisters, mothers and fathers, in Birmingham, Atlanta, Dallas, Houston, St. Louis, New Orleans, to everyone struggling, working their fingers to the bone on farms across America, to everyone holding out hope that things will get better."

Victory. Stand! reaches a peak with the triumph and defiance of the protest, but the story does not end there. As Smith expected, there is considerable backlash from the US Olympic Committee and many others. He and Carlos are summarily sent home from the Olympics, and amidst a storm of media opprobrium and hate mail, their athletic careers never fully rebound. Smith largely turns his attention to furthering his education and activism. He also finds work coaching at Oberlin College and then Santa Monica College, where he remains for almost three decades.

Over time, attitudes evolve, and the public perception of Smith and Carlos's Black Power protest becomes more positive. In 2005 a statue depicting the two with fists in the air is mounted on the San José State campus. In 2016 they are guests of the first Black US president, Barack Obama, at the White House. Three years later they are inducted into the US Olympic and Paralympic Hall of Fame. This helps make the overall tone of *Victory. Stand!* hopeful and inspirational.

Derrick Barnes

Smith, Barnes, and Anyabwile do not shy away from clearly describing the more difficult themes, however. The book confronts the realities of anti-Black racism at every turn, from the sharecropping system that kept people in poverty to the ongoing fight for true equality in the twenty-first century. It seamlessly weaves information about important historical events in with Smith's more personal story. For example, readers will learn about the Great Migration that saw millions of Black families like Smith's move out of the South in search of opportunity; the Jim Crow laws that made it impossible for Black athletes to find lodging and food when traveling to events; and the assassinations of John F. Kennedy, Medgar Evers, and Martin Luther King Jr. Many galvanizing moments in the civil rights movement are mentioned, including the 1963 murders of four young Black girls at a Birmingham church and the 1964 shootings of three Freedom Rider college students who were working to register Black voters.

Dawud Anyabwile

Such historically evocative storytelling helped *Victory. Stand!* become a finalist for the 2022 National Book Award and garner near-universal praise from critics. In a review for *Teen Librarian Toolbox*, Amanda MacGregor captured the general consensus: "The story isn't an easy or comfortable read, nor should it be. It's a hard, honest look at the horrors of the era, the discrimination and outright hatred that Smith faced, and the continued struggles he faced after the Olympics on the long path to him eventually being widely recognized as a courageous and inspiring role model," she wrote. "An amazing celebration of resiliency, strength, and determination, Smith's incredible story shows how far we have come and how far we have yet to go." Similarly, Thomas Maluck opined for *School Library Journal*, "There is nothing saccharine about this view into the past, but there is plenty worth remembering and considering."

Many critics also highlighted how Anyabwile's artwork contributes to the book's powerful message. Starred reviews in both *Publishers Weekly* and *Kirkus* drew attention to the illustrations, with the latter noting that the art's "realism echoes the visual influences of the Black Power period." The *Kirkus* reviewer was one of many to also mention *Victory. Stand!*'s potential to inspire readers of all ages, concluding that "This evocative undertaking extends histories of 20th-century Black struggles for new generations, reminding us to continue to be brave, courageous, and organize for change." In a review for the *New York Times*, Matt De la Peña noted that sports memoirs are often mistakenly dismissed, arguing that readers with preconceived notions would be ignoring this universally engaging work at their own peril. "Timely and timeless, Smith's *Victory. Stand!* is a must read not just for sports fans but for everyone," he wrote.

Author Biographies

Tommie Smith set world records and won an Olympic gold medal as a sprinter, played professional football, and worked as a coach and college teacher. Well known for his activism, his honors include the Arthur Ashe Award for Courage and the Courage of Conscience Award from the Peace Abbey Foundation. He published the autobiography *Silent Gesture* (2007) with coauthor David Steele.

Derrick Barnes is an acclaimed author known for his work aimed at young readers. His picture book *Crown: An Ode to the Fresh Cut* (2017) earned several awards, including a Newbery Honor, the Kirkus Prize for Young Readers, and a Coretta Scott King Author Honor.

Illustrator Dawud Anyabwile received an Emmy Award and several comic book industry awards for his art. Along with various comics, he illustrated works by such authors as James Patterson, Kwame Alexander, and Walter Dean Myers.

Mari Rich

Review Sources

De la Peña, Matt. "Sports Stories That Transcend Sport." *The New York Times*, 7 Oct. 2022, www.nytimes.com/2022/10/07/books/review/victory-stand-tommie-smith-call-him-jack-the-story-of-jackie-robinson-black-freedom-fighter.html. Accessed 15 Jan. 2023.

MacGregor, Amanda. Review of *Victory. Stand! Raising My Fist for Justice*, by Tommie Smith, Derrick Barnes, and Dawud Anyabwile. *Teen Librarian Toolbox*, School Library Journal, 23 Sept. 2022, teenlibrariantoolbox.com/2022/09/23/book-review-victory-stand-raising-my-fist-for-justice-by-tommie-smith-derrick-barnes-dawud-anyabwile/. Accessed 15 Jan. 2023.

Maluck, Thomas. Review of *Victory. Stand! Raising My Fist for Justice*, by Tommie Smith, Derrick Barnes, and Dawud Anyabwile. *School Library Journal*, 23 Sept. 2022, www.slj.com/review/victory-stand-raising-my-fist-for-justice. Accessed 15 Jan. 2023.

Review of *Victory. Stand! Raising My Fist for Justice*, by Tommie Smith, Derrick Barnes, and Dawud Anyabwile. *Kirkus*, 22 June 2022, www.kirkusreviews.com/book-reviews/tommie-smith/victory-stand/. Accessed 15 Jan. 2023.

Review of *Victory. Stand! Raising My Fist for Justice*, by Tommie Smith, Derrick Barnes, and Dawud Anyabwile. *Publishers Weekly*, 30 June 2022, www.publishersweekly.com/978-1-324-05215-9. Accessed 15 Jan. 2023.

The Violin Conspiracy

Author: Brendan Slocumb
Publisher: Anchor Books (New York). 352 pp.
Type of work: Novel
Time: Present day
Locales: Charlotte, North Carolina; New York City; Moscow, Russia

Unfolding after the theft of a Stradivarius violin, owned by Ray McMillian, The Violin Conspiracy *follows the frantic and global search for the violin while Ray continues to prepare to compete in the important Tchaikovsky Competition in Moscow. Alongside the narrative of the theft, the novel unspools Ray's family history and his struggles to be recognized as a high-performing Black professional in the majority-White world of classical music.*

Principal characters

RAYQUAN "RAY" MCMILLIAN, the central protagonist, a professional violinist
NICOLE, his girlfriend, a fellow professional musician
JANICE STEVENS, his violin instructor and mentor
GRANDMA NORA, his maternal grandmother who gifts him the violin
POPPOP, his great-great-grandfather who owned the violin, Grandma Nora's grandfather
AUNT ROCHELLE, his maternal aunt
ANDREA MARKS, the woman who claims ownership of his violin
DANTE MARKS, the man who claims ownership of his violin

In the opening chapter of Brendan Slocumb's debut novel, *The Violin Conspiracy* (2022), Ray McMillian becomes the victim of a crime when his Stradivarius violin, valued at $10 million, is stolen from its case and exchanged with a single Converse Chuck Taylor sneaker and a ransom note for $5 million in Bitcoin. Ray is a professional violinist whose career has been skyrocketing since his family heirloom violin was authenticated as a Stradivarius less than two years prior. As a Black performer, Ray has faced an uphill climb for recognition and the instrument's theft immediately punctures his self-esteem. He has failed as a steward of the most precious object: an instrument of enormous financial value but also an irreplaceable personal tie to his Grandma Nora, who had gifted it to him six years prior. Moreover, the timing could not be more unfortunate. Ray has just over a month left before he is scheduled to compete in the Tchaikovsky Competition at the Moscow State Tchaikovsky Conservatory, a ten-day-long event that is likened to "The Music Olympics."

Like many details in the book, this event blends fact and fiction, placing the realities of the international music world into the narrative. The International Tchaikovsky Competition is a real-life premiere competitive venue in classical music that was first held in 1958, though many readers of the novel may not be aware of its existence. Similarly, Brendan Slocumb explains in the author's note with which he concludes the book, that many of the race-based incidents that Ray experiences throughout the novel are drawn from Slocumb's own struggles as a Black musician in the classical music world—a world in which incidents of racism and discrimination are quite common for musicians of color. While the more sensational fictional aspects of the story may keep the reader engrossed in the novel—the crime, the search, the tension of international competition, the historical tie to slavery and its impact over the generations—Slocumb's authentic voice concerning the role of race in the life of a professional classical musician is certainly the novel's greatest contribution. Slocumb emphasizes that this narrative will surely resonate with the "1.8 percent of musicians performing in classical symphonies [who] are Black," but it also seeks to create greater empathy among White readers. As Slocumb further reflects in his author's note, "When I share these stories with friends who don't look like me, I get the same reaction: 'Things like that don't happen. It's not really like that.'" This novel encapsulates his response: "They do. It is."

Brendan Slocumb

Two plotlines run through *The Violin Conspiracy*. The first, already introduced, is the story of the violin's theft and Ray's attempt—with the help of the FBI and an insurance company investigator—to recover the instrument. The crime is the dominant plotline, as the structure of the novel is organized around it, including the framing of many of the chapters and the beginning and concluding narratives of the book. Even when the logistics of the search for the violin are not foregrounded in the story, its loss palpitates within the narrative. Ray is psychologically and professionally linked to the instrument. Although he procures a spectacular loaner instrument almost immediately, this does not keep him from the psychological and emotional trauma of the loss. With such high stakes at play, he fears being revealed as an imposter whose musical skill is only the result of a spectacular instrument. Even as it is clear to the reader, and to Ray's colleagues and mentors, that his capacity as a musician remains undiminished by the loss of the violin, he struggles mightily to confront this deficiency. His ultimate perseverance and personal strength provide a personal story arc of heroism and achievement made possible only by the theft.

The second plotline, though subsidiary, is arguably more important. Embedded within *The Violin Conspiracy* are chapters that discuss the six preceding years that led up to Ray's professional success—the years in which he began to play the violin and received the instrument from his grandmother. Ultimately, this plotline unspools to tell the deep history of Ray's instrument, which brings the history of enslavement, abolition, racism, and reparations to the foreground of the story. While Ray's mother is unsympathetic to his musical talent and tries to push her son to quit high school and get a low-paying job that will contribute to the household expenses, his Grandma Nora not only believes in his ability but inspires him with stories of the musical ability of her grandfather, PopPop, who was enslaved and played the fiddle. Grandma Nora's stories of her grandfather's music were foundational in Ray's own childhood memories. After playing his poor-quality high school loaner violin for his grandmother, Ray realizes that "Maybe—now he couldn't remember—he'd first gotten interested in the violin because Grandma Nora talked about it all the time." That Christmas, his grandmother surprises him with the gift of her PopPop's fiddle, which had been stowed away in the attic ever since his death. The instrument is in terrible shape. Given its personal significance, Ray spends all his savings to get it repaired, overcoming clear racism and hostility from the music shop technician to get the work completed.

Years later, after Grandma Nora's death, Ray gets the violin repaired and cleaned again. His mentor believes that he has probably outgrown the capacity of his instrument, but he hopes that his violin will be sufficient if it is properly rehabilitated. His devotion pays off, as the instrument proves to be a rare and highly valuable Stradivarius violin, an identification that is quickly authenticated by a rare instrument appraiser in New York City. This astonishing find sets in motion both the best and the worst experiences of Ray's young life. On the positive side, his career rapidly accelerates, with a speed that he realizes is not only because of his musical skill, but also from the curiosity that arises from a Black violinist who owns an ancestral Stradivarius. While touring, he meets Nicole, who quickly becomes both serious girlfriend and musical companion. But, the discovery of the violin's heritage also leads to two extraordinary crises. His mother and most of her siblings object to Ray's sole ownership of the violin and sue Ray in the hopes of capitalizing on what they perceive to be their inheritance. Even more sinisterly, two strangers, Andrea and Dante Marks, lay claim to the violin. They are descendants of the man who had enslaved Ray's PopPop and have a family story of the violin and how an ancestor had imported it from Italy. The Marks assert that Ray's family obtained the violin by theft and that they are its rightful owners. Soon enough, Ray finds himself subject to two lawsuits—one from his own family and the other from the White family with whom his ancestry would always be intertwined. Worse yet, the Marks family does not stop at legal action. They confront Ray in person on more than one occasion and, once, nearly succeed in convincing responding police officers that Ray has stolen the violin from them. Of course, the Marks' claim to Ray's instrument seems feeble, mean-spirited, and unlikely outside of the space of a novel, but that is beside the point. Through this plotline, Slocumb invites the reader to consider the legacy of slavery from a distinct perspective. Though Ray and his family have grown up poor and though the stories that are eventually revealed about PopPop's enslavement are gruesome, they have somehow managed to emerge from these wounds with a clear heritage—the legacy, memory, and violin of their enslaved ancestor. Uniquely within his family, Ray understands and treasures this gift. Using his musical talent, he remembers, celebrates, and uplifts the memory of his great-great-grandfather. Conversely, of course, the harassing presence of the Marks family reminds the reader that even across multiple generations, the damage of slavery lingers—continuing to mark both enslavers and enslaved.

Some reviewers of *The Violin Conspiracy* noted that the novel has its weaknesses, observing that the ultimate resolution of the crime plot is neither engrossing nor particularly surprising. Further, several critics commented on the uneven writing of the book. Both of these commentaries are justified. Despite these downsides, however, the novel was received warmly for both its confrontations with racism and its evocative descriptions of classical performance. In her review for *Library Journal*, Jane Jorgenson wrote that "the novel brings an unflinching eye to the sometimes-cutthroat world of classical music, its very white culture, and the challenges a talented young Black violinist might face in that world." Bethanne Patrick noted in her review for NPR that *The Violin Conspiracy* is rare in its successful combination of polemic and fiction, specifically highlighting its convincing exploration of the reality that "the high-toned world of classical music suffers from, and because, of racism." Indeed, Slocumb's infusion of first-person experience—both with the professional classical music world and as a person of color within it—is what gives the novel its greatest value. The book stands out for bringing the reader deeply into the professional realm of classical music and affirming that issues of race and violence exist in the concert hall as well as on city streets.

Author Biography

Brendan Slocumb is a concert violinist and a teacher who has taught music to children of all ages. He graduated from the University of North Carolina at Greensboro. *The Violin Conspiracy* is his debut novel.

Julia A. Sienkewicz, PhD

Review Sources

Barone, Joshua. "*The Violin Conspiracy* Is a Musical Thriller with Some Unexpected Notes." Review of *The Violin Conspiracy*, by Brendan Slocumb. *The New York Times*, 1 Feb. 2022, www.nytimes.com/2022/02/01/books/review/the-violin-conspiracy-brendan-slocumb.html. Accessed 13 Nov. 2022.

Jorgenson, Jane. Review of *The Violin Conspiracy*, by Brendan Slocumb. *Library Journal*, 1 Feb. 2022, www.libraryjournal.com/review/the-violin-conspiracy-2133633. Accessed 2 Dec. 2022.

Murray, Victoria Christopher. "*The Violin Conspiracy* Could Be One of the Year's Big Crowd-Pleasers." Review of *The Violin Conspiracy*, by Brendan Slocumb. *The Washington Post*, 2 Feb. 2022, www.washingtonpost.com/books/2022/02/02/violin-conspiracy-brendan-slocumb/. Accessed 13 Nov. 2022.

Patrick, Bethanne. "Thriller *The Violin Conspiracy* Addresses Racism in Classical Music." Review of *The Violin Conspiracy*, by Brendan Slocumb. *National Public Radio*, 7 Feb. 2022, www.npr.org/2022/02/07/1078283114/thriller-the-violin-conspiracy-addresses-racism-in-classical-music. Accessed 13 Nov. 2022.

Plesh, J. N. "*The Violin Conspiracy*: A Different Kind of Crime Story." Review of *The Violin Conspiracy*, by Brendan Slocumb. *The Southern Review of Books*, 15 July 2022, southernreviewofbooks.com/2022/07/15/the-violin-conspiracy-brendan-slocumb-review/. Accessed 13 Nov. 2022.

The Vortex
A True Story of History's Deadliest Storm, an Unspeakable War, and Liberation

Authors: Scott Carney (b. 1978) and Jason Miklian (b. 1977)
Publisher: Ecco (New York). 498 pp.
Type of work: History, novel
Time: 1968–72
Locales: Pakistan, Bangladesh, the United States

The Vortex offers a "novelistic" account of one of the deadliest storms in history—a 1970 cyclone that devastated much of Bangladesh, at the time part of Pakistan known as East Pakistan, and set the stage for Bangladeshi independence.

Principal personages

YAHYA KHAN, Pakistani general and president of Pakistan (1969–71)
ZULFIKAR ALI BHUTTO, president of Pakistan (1971–73)
HAFIZ UDDIN AHMAD, top soccer star from East Pakistan who later fought in the civil war
CANDI ROHDE, American aid worker
MOHAMMED HAI, son of a prominent East Pakistani politician and cyclone survivor
NEIL FRANK, prominent American meteorologist
RICHARD NIXON, president of the United States (1969–74)

As its lengthy subtitle suggests, *The Vortex: A True Story of History's Deadliest Storm, an Unspeakable War, and Liberation* tells a complicated story, showing how the massive cyclone that devastated East Pakistan in November 1970 led to massive political destabilization, a civil war, and the establishment, in late 1971, of the independent nation of Bangladesh. The cyclone itself arose and ended rather quickly, but the enormous devastation it left in its wake led to turmoil in practically every sphere of Pakistani life. In a work they describe as a piece of "narrative nonfiction," authors Scott Carney and Jason Miklian manage to convey a strong sense of the personalities and events they describe, although they concede that they found themselves required "to make judgments at times about motivations and states of mind that are not preserved in the historical record" to provide "clarity and to better bring out the essence of events." For example, they compress some long, complicated events into "single narrative moment[s]," and elsewhere they "extrapolate minor pieces of dialogue, mannerisms, and presumable emotional responses" in scenes where the people involved could not

Scott Carney

recall details of conversations that happened decades earlier. For the sake of transparency, the authors use the notes section that concludes the book to document instances in which they made up certain details, instead of using footnotes easily visible at the bottom of each page or in visibly numbered endnotes. As a result, readers never quite know when a claim is being documented unless they flip to the end of the book and look for the appropriate page number.

Some readers may, therefore, wish that Carney and Miklian had chosen a more conventional historical approach to the fascinating story they have to tell and that they had made the people they describe sound less like characters in a novel and more like figures in a standard work of historical narrative. However, the story they do tell is undeniably fascinating, and some readers may find themselves less interested in the novelized parts of the narrative and more interested in the meatier, obviously factual passages, which are intriguing enough in their own right. For some readers, ironically, the book may seem less interesting when the authors try to make it *more* interesting by adding commentary, personal judgments, and invented details not documented in the historical record. These, however, are minor qualms about a book that is obviously the result of years of dedicated primary and secondary research. In creating this work, the authors read and cited all the sources they consulted, and they were able to interview most of the important surviving people involved.

The book opens with a stunningly vivid depiction of the cyclone, which killed an estimated three hundred thousand to five hundred thousand people, and describes some of the people who were either killed by it or who had their lives totally decimated by its fury and deadly aftermath. The overarching narrative of the cyclone is fleshed out through vivid anecdotes. For example, few readers will be able to forget the story of the ship that haplessly sailed right into the storm and whose passengers were never heard from again. Equally unforgettable is the story of a lone survivor who, as the waters rose higher and higher into his family's home, managed to jump from the house's roof onto a nearby tree and cling there literally for his life. Although he urged his family members to follow his lead, no one else did so. This survivor later found the drowned bodies of his loved ones floating inside the storm-ravaged house. Multiply his story by the hundreds of thousands or even millions, and one has some sense of just how awful this unusually destructive cyclone was, not only in its impact on individual people but on life in East Pakistan in general.

Carney and Miklian take time to describe why East Pakistan had long felt neglected by the rest of the country. Most of the wealth and power had long been allotted to West Pakistan, which was divided from East Pakistan by Indian territory. The central

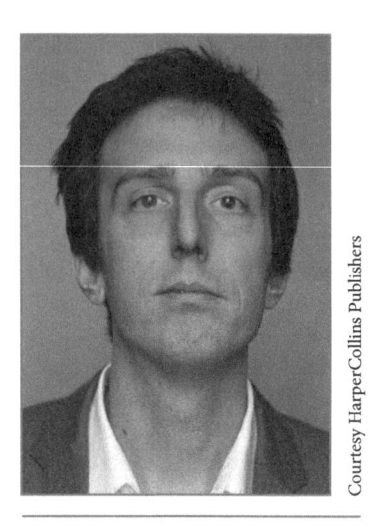

Jason Miklian

government, located in the capital of Islamabad in West Pakistan, tended to look down on or completely ignore the Bengali-majority population of East Pakistan. An independence movement had been steadily brewing in East Pakistan by the time of the cyclone, but, as Carney and Miklian demonstrate, the sheer incompetence and perhaps even malevolence of the Pakistani government when trying to deal with the results of the cyclone helped deepen East Pakistan's desire for independence. In March 1971, armed conflict broke out, marking the official start of Bangladesh's war of independence.

The authors manage to populate this divisive political landscape with larger-than-life heroes and villains. The book demonstrates how politicians in the west, from the president on down, were often corrupt and venal—so much so that some readers may sometimes find themselves wondering if some of the stories related about these individuals are too bad to be credible. The fact that Yahya Khan, the president of Pakistan at the time of the cyclone, was also an ally of Richard Nixon, who was then president of the United States, sometimes makes it appear as if the narrative is being used to suit a particular political line. On the other hand, Democratic senator Edward "Ted" Kennedy of Massachusetts, who traveled to Pakistan and reported on the Pakistani Army's brutal actions, somewhat predictably emerges as a saint among a crew of generally despicable American and West Pakistani political figures.

There is no denying, however, that the book is almost cinematic in the way it builds suspense, describes characters, depicts battles, and recounts both grim tragedies and occasional triumphs. The authors manage to make politics—both national and international—anything but boring. They also weave in a narrative about Pakistan's secret assistance to Nixon in making his historic reestablishment of relations between the US and China in the early 1970s that only adds to the literal and figurative intrigue. The sheer brutality of Pakistan's efforts to crush the rebellion in the east is often sickening. The leaders of the central government's army take a brutal approach to dealing with the Bangladeshi independence movement, and one comes away from the book wondering how any country could have survived under a leadership so unscrupulous, greedy, and self-serving. A central villain of the story is Yahya Khan, who served as president of Pakistan during some of the tempestuous years Carney and Miklian depict. He had started out as a talented military officer whose military government suspended Pakistan's constitution in 1969; however, according to Carney and Miklian, Khan also seemed genuinely committed to giving Pakistan its very first free and democratic elections. Carney and Miklian depict Khan's presidency as a deeply flawed one, marred by his luxurious and hedonistic habits. Khan's successor, Zulfikar Ali Bhutto, also emerges as particularly unscrupulous and dishonest.

Starting in 1971 the government of Pakistan, desperate to prevent East Pakistan from seceding, began committing atrocities that many contemporary observers and later academics described as a genocide. Intellectuals were rounded up and quickly slaughtered; entire villages were terrorized or destroyed; soldiers who had been part of the national Pakistani Army were abruptly arrested or killed outright. Waves of refugees, still suffering from the after-effects of the cyclone and now threatened by war and genocide, had to flee for help to neighboring India, which had its own reasons to want to see Pakistan break apart but which also had to deal with the consequences of the flood of asylum seekers. To make matters even more complicated, the US, China, and the Soviet Union all got involved in this complicated situation. At one point, as the authors describe, a US warship and a Soviet submarine even engaged in a tense stand-off that could easily have resulted in nuclear war.

The Vortex received mostly positive reviews from critics upon its publication in 2022, though some reviewers expressed reservations about the work's blending of fact and fiction. C. Uday Bhaskar, writing for the *Financial Express*, felt that Carney's "eye of [an] investigative journalist" perfectly complimented Miklian's "[rigor] of the academic," and that the work "fill[ed] a gap" in a key period of Southeast Asian history. However, while Bhaskar felt the authors effectively tackled some key events of this period, including the US government's morally dubious support of Pakistan, he felt that some "salacious asides" about Khan and other figures detracted from the book's moral weight. Mahir Ali, who reviewed the book for the *Wire*, an independent Indian publication, pointed out some notable omissions from the book's historical narrative, which Ali alleged was "peppered with inaccuracies." Despite these reservations, Ali still felt the book was "highly readable" and a "useful jumping point for further exploration," as long as readers remained aware of the book's fictional elements.

As the volume reaches its final pages, Carney and Miklian draw conclusions that seem implied throughout, especially the conclusion that climate disasters can result in wholly unpredictable consequences for governments and nation-states, especially when these are already unstable to begin with. The concept of the butterfly effect, the idea that the mere flapping of a single butterfly's wings in one part of the world can help set the stage for a brutal storm somewhere else, may occur to some readers, who will in any case long remember the meteorological, political, and military chaos that Carney and Miklian describe in such shattering detail.

Author Biography
Scott Carney is a freelance investigative journalist and commentator with anthropological training. His previous books include *The Red Market* (2011), *The Enlightenment Trap* (2015), *What Doesn't Kill Us* (2017), and *The Wedge* (2020).

Jason Miklian is a researcher, entrepreneur, and writer.

Robert C. Evans, PhD

Review Sources

Ali, Mahir. "Book Review: A Disturbing Account of the 1970 East Pakistan Storm and Its Political Fallout." Review of *The Vortex: A True Story of History's Deadliest Storm, an Unspeakable War, and Liberation*, by Scott Carney and Jason Miklian. *The Wire*, 4 Apr. 2022, thewire.in/books/vortex-1970-east-pakistan-cycline-political-crisis. Accessed 29 Dec. 2022.

Bhaskar, C. Uday. "In the Eye of a Storm." Review of *The Vortex: A True Story of History's Deadliest Storm, an Unspeakable War, and Liberation*, by Scott Carney and Jason Miklian. *Financial Express*, 31 July 2022, www.financialexpress.com/lifestyle/in-the-eye-of-a-storm-book-review-the-vortex-the-true-story-of-historys-deadliest-storm-and-the-liberation-of-bangladesh-by-scott-carney-jason-miklian/2611750/. Accessed 29 Dec. 2022.

Dikshit, Sandeep. "Scott Carney and Jason Miklian's *The Vortex* Is Based on the Wild Theory of a Cyclone Splitting Pak." Review of *The Vortex: A True Story of History's Deadliest Storm, an Unspeakable War, and Liberation*, by Scott Carney and Jason Miklian. *The Tribune*, 24 July 2022, www.tribuneindia.com/news/reviews/story/scott-carney-jason-miklians-the-vortex-is-based-on-the-wild-theory-of-a-cyclone-splitting-pak-415091. Accessed 29 Dec. 2022.

Roig-Franzia, Manuel. "How a Devastating Cyclone Led to a Genocide and a New Nation." Review of *The Vortex: A True Story of History's Deadliest Storm, an Unspeakable War, and Liberation*, by Scott Carney and Jason Miklian. *The Washington Post*, 15 Apr. 2022, www.washingtonpost.com/outlook/2022/04/15/how-devastating-cyclone-led-genocide-new-nation/. Accessed 29 Dec. 2022.

Varadarajan, Tunku. "*The Vortex* Review: A Storm of Political Violence." Review of *The Vortex: A True Story of History's Deadliest Storm, an Unspeakable War, and Liberation*, by Scott Carney and Jason Miklian. *The Wall Street Journal*, 18 Mar. 2022, www.wsj.com/articles/the-vortex-book-review-east-pakistan-bangladesh-bhola-a-storm-of-political-violence-11647614824. Accessed 29 Dec. 2022.

Walking the Bowl
A True Story of Murder and Survival among the Street Children of Lusaka

Authors: Chris Lockhart (b. 1967) and Daniel Mulilo Chama (b. 1976)
Publisher: Hanover Square Press (Toronto). 304 pp.
Type of work: Anthropology, current affairs
Time: Present day
Locale: Lusaka, Zambia

This nonfiction work examines the tenuous experience of impoverished children living in one of the world's fastest-growing cities. Despite being a carefully researched anthropological study, it has the gripping narrative arc of a novel, painting detailed portraits of several young people who find themselves connected to a murder investigation.

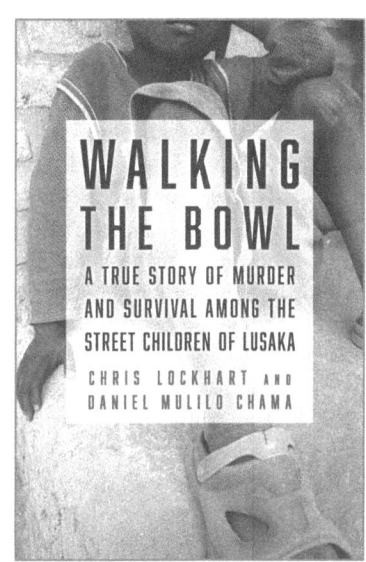

Principal personages
LUSABILO, a scavenger leader at Chunga Dump in Lusaka, Zambia
TIMO, an ambitious drug dealer
KAPULA, a sixteen-year-old prostitute
MOONGA, an eight-year-old new arrival to Lusaka
KAKU, head of Bullet, Lusaka's most violent gang
CHEELO, Kaku's lieutenant
SEVEN SPIRITS, a drug lord
THE OUTREACHER, coauthor Daniel Mulilo Chama, a former street kid who is now a social worker
THE WHITE MAN, coauthor Chris Lockhart, the Outreacher's academic colleague

The preface of *Walking the Bowl: A True Story of Murder and Survival among the Street Children of Lusaka* (2022) addresses the work's central issue: "To call attention to the growing problem of street children around the world." A major part of the problem is that street kids are largely ignored by society. Governments are often blind to them, except as impediments to order. Laws generally do not account for them, except in negative fashion so miscreants can be punished for minor violations, such as loitering. To many average people, urban street kids have become part of the scenery, an obstacle to be stepped around.

The children themselves, living in survival mode, also tend to be elusive. As authors Chris Lockhart and Daniel Mulilo Chama note in Walking the Bowl's preface, it is not certain how many kids live on their own on the streets worldwide; estimates range wildly, from tens of millions to 150 million or more, and are fiercely debated by researchers. Efforts to gather more information about this young, highly vulnerable population face serious obstacles. Many studies are essentially slap-dash affairs, with unskilled data collectors hired for the occasion who spend a relatively short period of time conducting formulaic interviews or surveys, which are intended, above all, to generate statistics that can easily be quantified and categorized. Lockhart and Chama acknowledge that such data can have value. However, they warn that it also risks missing the human element, the lived experience of street children as individuals.

For Walking the Bowl, Lockhart and Chama took a different approach. As explained in the preface (and in even more scholarly detail after the main text), the book is the result of immersive anthropological field work with street children in Lusaka, the capital of the south-central African nation of Zambia. A team of workers spent more than five years recording interviews, taking photos, hand-drawing illustrations and maps, and transcribing field notes. The focus is on real people, a collection of youngsters with genuine human strengths and weaknesses. This deeply humanist approach also extends to the way the book is structured and written. "An academic writing style was totally incompatible with our desire to pursue and tell a story about a specific event involving a particular group of children," Lockhart and Chama note. Instead, they craft a compelling, suspenseful narrative that often reads like a mystery novel despite being research-based nonfiction. In many cases, actual words spoken by participants are used in dialogue. The tone is also deftly balanced between the differing perspectives of its coauthors, as Lockhart, a White outsider, often was more pessimistic about the conditions they witnessed than Chama, himself a former Lusaka street child.

The work's strong narrative drive is, in part, due to an unforeseen development that occurred during the research phase: a child was found murdered, and, unusually, a serious police investigation was launched. Lockhart and Chama quickly turned their attention to the significant impact this incident had upon various segments of local society, especially the street children themselves. The ripple effect of the murder and investigation makes a compelling plot arc and provides a natural structure for the book.

Walking the Bowl paints a vivid portrait of Lusaka. Beginning in the late twentieth century, the city experienced rapid, massive population growth. By the 2010s, when Lockhart and Chama began their study, many poor residents—including tens of thousands of children from toddlers to teens—spilled to the outskirts of the city, where they subsist however they can. Some street children shelter in the notorious landfill known as Chunga Dump, picking over hundreds of tons of garbage delivered daily to salvage edible food and discarded items that can be repurposed or sold. Others live in makeshift huts in sprawling slums or empty lots and get by through begging, crime, prostitution, or other unsavory means.

It is in this environment that the prologue opens with Lusabilo, an eleven-year-old "quasi leader of Chunga Dump's scavenger kids," discovering on a heap of trash the mutilated dead body of a boy with a teardrop-shaped birthmark on his forehead. Lusabilo dubs the body "the Ho Ho Kid," based on the laughing reaction of a younger scavenger who does not speak the same language. After reporting the body to an adult scavenger called Mama B, Lusabilo returns to find Cheelo, a lieutenant of the prominent Bullet gang, inspecting the corpse. Cheelo leaves when more adults arrive, and eventually the police take away the body, but Lusabilo is nervous that "the Ho Ho Kid was about to become a bigger and more complicated problem than he could ever imagine."

Daniel Mulilo Chama

Lusabilo's premonition proves correct when, a week later, a social worker nicknamed the Outreacher (Chama) comes to fetch him to talk to the police. It turns out the Ho Ho Kid was the illegitimate son of an important political official and a "a concubine of some repute, a highly prized sugar baby known in the right circles for her charm and beauty." The police are pressured to solve the crime, fast. At the police station, Lusabilo is immediately treated as a suspect despite the Outreacher's protests. After being confined in an overcrowded cell and threatened with torture, he desperately mentions seeing Cheelo and even lies that he saw Bullet leader Kaku around the dump as well. Lusabilo is finally released after agreeing to gather more information about the Bullet gang, a perennial foe of law enforcement in Lusaka, and its possible connection to the murder.

In quick order, three other primary individuals are introduced whom the Ho Ho Kid's death will affect, directly or indirectly. One is Timo, an older teen who has spent half his life in Chibolya Township, a large slum covered with dwellings made from scraps, where drugs of all kinds—from marijuana ("dagga") to crack cocaine and heroin—are widely available. He is the head of a network selling the glue that is a popular inhalant but has aspirations of moving up in the drug-dealing hierarchy. Timo hopes to eliminate a chief rival to demonstrate his ruthlessness, a qualification that should earn him a responsible position with Lusaka's major drug lord, known only as Seven Spirits.

Kapula, a teenaged prostitute and "street wife" of Timo, is another central figure. She is saving her brothel earnings in hopes that she can leave sex work behind and move to the country with her younger brother to start a new life. She is also worried because her brother has gone missing. Meanwhile, their beautiful mother, a "slay queen," or mistress of an older, wealthy man who flies her around the world, posts photos of her lavish lifestyle on social media so she will not be associated with her slumming children or other poor relatives.

The third important figure is Moonga, age eight, a former rock breaker in a lead mining town who hopes to attend school. After being orphaned, he traveled by bus to Lusaka to search for an aunt he had never met but quickly finds himself fending for himself. Joining a beggar gang, he becomes one of many street children addicted to a heady mixture of glue and gasoline inhaled from bottles. Moonga recounts meeting a boy with a tear-shaped birthmark, deepening the mystery interconnecting each part of the book.

With setting and major players established, *Walking the Bowl* unfolds in murder-mystery fashion. Persons of interest in the crime are observed as they interact with the police and each other. Some are elevated to suspects while others are proven innocent, and the tension builds steadily as more and more information emerges. Ultimately, the motive behind the crime is revealed and the actual culprit is exposed. Yet while the murder investigation provides the book's backbone, there are more universal themes at play in this tightly structured work. Who killed the Ho Ho Kid, and why, are central questions that provide an entry point to broader considerations of life on the streets of Lusaka and beyond.

As the title implies, a major thread throughout the book is the concept of "walking the bowl," drawn from an African legend about a generous headsman. Walking the bowl is akin to "paying it forward": doing kindnesses for others, like feeding the hungry or helping the needy, without expecting a reward. Some people portrayed walk the bowl in creative ways. They are rays of hope that light up an otherwise dark, bleak landscape. The Outreacher and his colleague and friend, known as the white man (Lockhart), debate what meaning such small acts of goodness have in the context of so much poverty and pain.

By focusing on the conditions endured by street children, *Walking the Bowl* naturally also turns an eye to related matters. The cruelty and indifference of law enforcement come under especially close scrutiny. While Lockhart and Chama maintain an overall neutral tone appropriate for anthropology, it will be hard for readers not to see the corrupt Zambian police, who dehumanize street children as merely "a collection of hooligans, vandals, petty thugs, and societal eyesores," as a major part of the problem. Indeed, this implicit critique extends to the entire society, where corruption is "so embedded in the economic, legislative, and judicial structures" that it is seen as normal. The authors also indicate how more subtle factors contribute to the reality of Lusaka's streets. For example, they explain how the city's very urban design—with wide streets, open spaces, and low-density housing specified by European city planners to serve a small White minority—has proved inadequate to accommodate the growing population. Such information adds to the richly detailed portrait of a place and its people, though readers hoping for prescriptive answers to the social problems described will be left wanting.

There were relatively few mainstream evaluations of *Walking the Bowl*, but those that did appear were very positive. The anonymous critic for *Publishers Weekly* deemed it a "riveting and deeply reported portrait of life on the margins" in a starred review. Writing for the *New York Times*, Ellen Barry called it "a fluid, elegant crime story, without an ounce of excess, all the more powerful because it is true." She emphasized the way the book has the literary qualities of "a clean arc of ascending action, a handful of vivid characters, an ending that snaps shut like a purse," which make for a page-turning read, although she also noted that this led to "an unsettling sense, at times, that I was hearing a writer's imagination at work." In a review for *Bookreporter*, Barbara Bamberger Scott perhaps best summed up the work's potential impact: "*Walking the Bowl* should be read and studied by anyone genuinely dedicated to real reform and wishing to be educated about the actual conditions of the world's abandoned and often forgotten children."

Author Biography
Medical anthropologist Chris Lockhart has published various academic pieces and worked on development efforts in Africa, with a focus on health and human rights. He also coauthored the book *I Am Not Your Slave* (2020), a memoir by human trafficking survivor Tupa Tjipombo.

Daniel Mulilo Chama grew up as a street child in Lusaka before training as a social worker. He has worked for a group of nonprofit organizations on outreach efforts to street children.

Jack Ewing

Review Sources
Barry, Ellen. "An 8-Year-Old Street Child Is Killed, and a World Opens Up." Review of Walking the Bowl: A True Story of Murder and Survival Among the Street Children of Lusaka, by Chris Lockhart and Daniel Mulilo Chama. The New York Times, 13 Feb. 2022, www.nytimes.com/2022/02/13/books/review/walking-the-bowl-chris-lockhart-daniel-mulilo-chama.html. Accessed 16 Jan. 2023.

Scott, Barbara Bamberger. Review of Walking the Bowl: A True Story of Murder and Survival Among the Street Children of Lusaka, by Chris Lockhart and Daniel Mulilo Chama. Bookreporter, 25 Feb. 2022, www.bookreporter.com/reviews/walking-the-bowl-a-true-story-of-murder-and-survival-among-the-street-children-of-lusaka. Accessed 16 Jan. 2023.

Review of Walking the Bowl: A True Story of Murder and Survival Among the Street Children of Lusaka, by Chris Lockhart and Daniel Mulilo Chama. *Publishers Weekly*, 19 Oct. 2021, www.publishersweekly.com/978-1-33542-574-4. Accessed 16 Jan. 2023.

The White Girl

Author: Tony Birch (b. 1957)
First published: *The White Girl*, 2019, in Australia
Publisher: HarperVia (New York). 272 pp.
Type of work: Novel
Time: 1960s
Locale: Deane, Australia

Aboriginal artist Odette Brown lives in fear that the Welfare Board will take her light-skinned, blonde granddaughter, Sissy, away from her, especially when Odette begins to experience health problems. Set in a small Australian town in the 1960s, Birch's novel follows Odette as she searches for a way to protect the one person she has left.

Principal characters
ODETTE BROWN, an Aboriginal artist
CECILY ANNE BROWN, a.k.a. Sissy, her granddaughter
LILA BROWN, her daughter
HENRY LAMB, a local junkman
AARON KANE, a local bully
BILL SHEA, a retiring police officer
SERGEANT LOWE, a new police officer
JOHN HAROLD HAINES, a.k.a. Jack Haines, an Aboriginal man who lives in the capital

Tony Birch is an Aboriginal Australian author and activist. His activism for Aboriginal people in his home country is evident not only in many of his short stories and his 2011 novel, *Blood*, but it reappears as a major concern in *The White Girl*. In this novel, sixty-three-year-old Odette Brown, an Aboriginal woman living in the small town of Deane, has spent her whole life struggling as a result of the laws created by White settlers, but now, that struggle becomes even more difficult as she fights to keep the only family she has left.

Child custody issues are also a major theme of the book. The novel begins with Odette remembering the birth of her now twelve-year-old granddaughter, Cecily, also known as Sissy. When Odette's daughter, Lila, had given birth to Sissy, Odette immediately knew their lives would be questioned because Sissy was "a light-skinned Aboriginal baby." Lila refused to identify her child's father, and within a short time, she disappeared from Odette and Sissy's lives, trusting her mother to be a better parent to her child than she felt capable of being. As a result, "Odette had no choice but

Tony Birch (Courtesy HarperCollins Publishers)

to engage in a game of cat and mouse with the Welfare authorities" if she wanted to keep her grandchild.

Odette's fear about losing her grandchild was partially based on her own childhood experience. As a child, Odette was placed on a mission, where she was allowed to see her family only on Sundays during church services, and where she watched friends and cousins die of diseases brought by the White settlers: "whooping cough, measles, and fever." The religious mission's goal was to convert Aboriginal people "into God-fearing Christians," and Odette's father encouraged his daughter to show just enough enthusiasm to be mistaken for one of them. This was a skill she employed with most of her interactions with White people.

Odette is not the only character who has dealt with child custody issues. Delores Reed, a passing acquaintance, tells her the sad tale of her own children having been taken from her and placed in a home attached to a convent. Delores tells Odette that the children in that place "are half-caste or quarter-caste. Sometimes a bit less. But they're all treated the same. The church finds homes for them. With white families." Odette learns later that Delores's children were taken away without the other woman's knowledge. Delores's heart was broken. Later in the story, Odette learns of a boy named Jimmy Brown, who had attempted to escape the mission home where he had been placed. After several attempts, the boy met a horrible end because "in the eyes of the institution, Jimmy had to be broken."

In addition to the child custody issues Birch confronts, the author also notes various other restrictions forced on Aboriginal people. For instance, their time in the town was limited to only certain times and days. Odette remembers that "during mission times, any Aboriginal person found within the town boundary without permission was given a warning. A second offense resulted in a night or two in the cells. Any *habitual absconder* who refused to comply with the law was likely to be sent away to prison." If they wanted to leave the area, they had to get approval from local law enforcement.

Unfortunately for Odette and Sissy, there is a new law officer in the area. Bill Shea, the retiring police officer, has lived in the area most of his life, so he knows Odette and the other locals. As a result, he often overlooks the legal restrictions. Sergeant Lowe, however, is more power-hungry. Changing times and attitudes have stirred up unrest for both White and Aboriginal people, and Odette learns that resistance movements have led to stricter observation. Odette's friend Millie tells her, "I heard they've been handpicked, and I reckon this new copper is one of them. They want to keep us in our place." Among other things, "some coppers have been doing the old count again. Names. Age. Color. Blood. The lot." If this news is not problematic enough, Odette learns that the new officer in a neighboring area has been photographing children, especially those with lighter skin. Sergeant Lowe illustrates that Deane is changing as well when he begins to show an unusual interest in Sissy. After he threatens Odette, telling the older woman, "She is a smart young lady, your granddaughter. I would not want to see a girl with such potential slip back. It is my duty to uplift children such as Cecily, and I will not fail her," the older woman knows she will need to take charge of her destiny as well as that of her grandchild.

This leads the pair on a journey away from the home they have always known. In order to leave the area, Odette has to ask the local police for permission. Sergeant Lowe is never going to give that permission, but Bill, remembering a childhood friendship, secretly delivers papers to her. At this point, Odette dresses Sissy in a white lace dress and newly polished dancing shoes in hopes that she will pass as a White girl. The two depart for the capital city in search of answers.

Through Odette's story, Birch brings awareness to the ways White settlers and their descendants have historically oppressed Aboriginal people in Australia. Abuse of the land leaves all of the citizens of the Deane area in desperate need. For instance, the local river had been mostly dried up, because, as Odette told her granddaughter, "White people got even greedier than we thought possible. . . . Between the farmers and the politicians, we were left with nothing. Our people have been hurting since." The land and people were further devastated by mining. The totality of the novel further demonstrates the ways systemic racism overwhelmed every aspect of the Aboriginal people's lives. Odette's father had once told her to "excuse the ignorance of the white people," which he justified as being *for your own sake more than theirs. . . . If you can't get them people out of your head, they will hold you down for the rest of your life.*"

Several additional serious conflicts are introduced in the story: rape, bullying, and suicide. Though Odette has never known who impregnated her daughter, Lila's response to Sissy's birth and physical appearance foreshadows the identity of the baby's father. Sissy herself is accosted by a local bully, Aaron Kane, and is only barely saved from assault. Aaron also threatens Henry Lamb, a man with an intellectual disability who has done nothing to provoke Aaron's anger. Three separate characters die by suicide, further showing the dire circumstances found in the community.

Positive themes are also central to *The White Girl*. The love of family is clearly illustrated through Odette and Sissy's relationship. Odette is willing to seek out Lila out even after she abandoned them because Odette still loves Lila and holds onto hope that she will be ready to take on parenting Sissy if Odette's health declines more. Sissy's love for Odette is shown throughout the story as well with her refusal to take full advantage of her light skin if that means her grandmother will be disrespected.

Kindness to others is another upbeat note in the story. These instances are sometimes just snapshots or moments, like the woman who gave Odette a place to stay when Odette first searched for Lila, or Henry Lamb, who builds a birthday bike for Sissy and later provides transportation as the two leave town. Other instances of kindness are longer lasting, like Jack Haines and his family. Odette and Sissy first meet Jack on their trip to the capital city. His knowledge of the way the city works helps the women when they are overwhelmed by the differences between Deane and the metropolis. Days later, Odette collapses in the hotel bathroom, and one of the Aboriginal women working behind the desk takes care of her and contacts Jack, the only one whose personal information Odette had with her. Jack and his wife step in to provide aid beyond what Odette could have expected.

The novel received glowing reviews. Joanna M. Burkhardt of the *Library Journal* wrote that the author "creates a moving tribute to the courage and determination of Indigenous Australians" while the *Publishers Weekly* reviewer noted the tone as "sad yet heartening." *Publishers Weekly* also commented on Birch's "brisk pace and lush prose," proclaiming, "Readers will feel the pull of this harrowing story." Carol Haggas of *Booklist* affirmed the novel's positive attributes by calling *The White Girl* "a poignant novel that keenly demonstrates how the strength of family bonds can shatter societal biases." Meanwhile, the reviewer from the *New Yorker* commented on the novel's social issues, lauding Birch's ability to show "how Australia's policies dehumanized not only the Indigenous people they sought to control . . . but also the white people who were complicit in enforcing them." Elayne Clift of the *New York Journal of Books* also praised the skill in Birch's writing, claiming the novel as "among the most compelling novels by indigenous writers." Clift went on to compare it to Keri Hulme's *The Bone People* and Leslie Marmon Silko's *Ceremony* in the way that it "captures the strength, character, and suffering of native peoples everywhere." Clift also called Odette and Sissy's trip "archetypal," promoting the older woman's story as a successful hero journey. Indeed, the overall consensus among all was a strong recommendation of Birch's novel.

Author Biography
Australian author Tony Birch is the writer of best-selling novels, short stories, and poetry. His work won several awards, including the Victorian Premier's Literary Award for Indigenous Writing, for his 2015 novel *Ghost River*; the 2017 Patrick White Literary Award, the New South Wales Premier's Literary Awards Indigenous Writers' Prize for *The White Girl*; and the 2022 Christina Stead Prize for fiction. His 2011 novel *Blood* made the shortlist for the Miles Franklin Award. Birch is also a climate justice activist and a professor.

Theresa L. Stowell, PhD

Review Sources
Burkhardt, Joanna M. Review of *The White Girl*, by Tony Birch. *Library Journal*, Sept. 2022, p. 43. *Literary Reference Center Plus*, search.ebscohost.com/login.aspx?direct=true&db=lkh&AN=158645135&site=lrc-plus. Accessed 1 Feb. 2023.
Clift, Elayne. Review of *The White Girl*, by Tony Birch. *New York Journal of Books*, www.nyjournalofbooks.com/book-review/white-girl-novel. Accessed 1 Feb. 2023.
Haggas, Carol. Review of *The White Girl*, by Tony Birch. *Booklist*, 15 Feb. 2022, p. 22. *Literary Reference Center Plus*, search.ebscohost.com/login.aspx?direct=true&db=lkh&AN=155170310&site=lrc-plus. Accessed 1 Feb. 2023.
Review of *The White Girl*, by Tony Birch. *Kirkus Reviews*, 26 Jan. 2022, www.kirkus-reviews.com/book-reviews/tony-birch/the-white-girl/. Accessed 1 Feb. 2023.

Review of *The White Girl*, by Tony Birch. *The New Yorker*, 11 Apr. 2022, p. 57. *Literary Reference Center Plus*, search.ebscohost.com/login.aspx?direct=true&db=lkh&AN=156059678&site=lrc-plus. Accessed 1 Feb. 2023.

Review of *The White Girl*, by Tony Birch. *Publishers Weekly*, 31 Jan. 2022, pp. 48–49. *Literary Reference Center Plus*, search.ebscohost.com/login.aspx?direct=true&db=lkh&AN=154940241&site=lrc-plus. Accessed 1 Feb. 2023.

The World Keeps Ending, and the World Goes On

Author: Franny Choi (b. 1989)
Publisher: Ecco (New York). 144 pp.
Type of work: Poetry

The World Keeps Ending, and the World Goes On explores the concept of apocalypse, bringing together history and speculative futures to contextualize the many issues facing the world today and imagine how humanity might cope with or even overcome them.

Franny Choi's 2019 poetry collection *Soft Science* was a major hit in poetic circles; it was nominated for numerous book awards and received favorable attention from outlets such as the *New York Times*, the *Paris Review*, and NPR. *The World Keeps Ending, and the World Goes On* (2022) was, therefore, a highly anticipated release—in fact, it appeared on lists of most anticipated books of 2022 in *LitHub*, *Vulture*, and *Time*.

Where *Soft Science* focused on a personal longing for connection, the scope of *The World Keeps Ending* is wider, taking in all of history and all of the globe. Its thesis is that while modern times may seem full of unprecedented calamities and many feel that humanity is on the brink of complete destruction, in truth the past is full of disasters and atrocities, many of which also felt like the end of the world to those who experienced them. In fact, in a way they *were* the end of the world, or the end of *a* world—especially when it comes to the experiences of marginalized people, whose ways of life have often been destroyed by imperialism and genocide. Choi enumerates some of these apocalypses in the collection's title poem: the apocalypses of "the bombed mosque," of "pipelines legislating their way / through sacred water," of "dogs and slave catchers"; the apocalypse that "began / when Columbus praised God and lowered his anchor."

But in some way those worlds went on; the descendants of these people are still alive and carrying on bits and pieces of those worlds into their future. Thus, *The World Keeps Ending* argues, modern catastrophes might bring about drastic change and great suffering yet might still allow humanity to struggle through and continue living in a world that still bears a faint resemblance to the one that came before. This idea is explored in poems such as "Dispatches from a Future Great-Great-Granddaughter," whose speaker tells her ancestor, "What I want you to know is that we're okay. Hurting / but okay." Some of the collection's future-set poems even dare to imagine a better world, such as "Field Trip to the Museum of Human History," whose speaker is a twelve-year-old viewing artifacts of "Ancient American society," such as handcuffs and nightsticks, and shuddering at the thought that her ancestors lived in a society that maintained order through casual violence.

As that example suggests, *The World Keeps Ending* states that "dystopia," too, is "the word for what's already happened / so many times." This line comes from one of four poems titled "Upon Learning That Some Korean War Refugees Used Partially Detonated Napalm Canisters as Cooking Fuel." The series of poems relates horrifying realities of the Korean War but ultimately celebrates the resilience of Koreans in taking something that was meant to kill them and turning it into sustenance. Like cataclysms, repressive societies are not the exclusive territory of an imagined future; they are a past and present reality for many people around the world, including in the United States. But people in those societies have still found ways to survive, and even thrive, despite the efforts of those in power.

Franny Choi

Many poems draw on Choi's Korean heritage; her ancestors lived through Japanese imperialism and then the Korean War, which remains an unresolved frozen conflict. The poem "Demilitarized Zone" is one that focuses on this topic; it describes a trip to the titular area of the Korean peninsula, where the speaker seeks to piece together family records from both sides of the de facto border. The country's division was also the end of a world, and the demilitarized zone is a reminder of that, not so much a scar as a still-open wound. The irony of its name is foregrounded in the poem, which euphemizes the speaker's experiences in the same way that the name euphemizes the very much militarized nature of the region: the train conductor "does not have a gun," the river "is not full of bodies," the taxi stand "is not pockmarked with mines." But the speaker's fantasy of reuniting the halves of her genealogical record, though currently not possible in reality, still expresses hope for some kind of mending: "Together," she says of herself and the records clerk, "we demilitarize my family."

Some poems are more personal, such as "Grief Is a Thing with Tense Issues," in which the speaker is attempting to come to terms with her mother's mortality, preparing for the fact that she will have to mourn her mother eventually. But these interlink with the larger apocalyptic themes: "I Have Bad News and Bad News, Which Do You Want First?" reveals that the speaker fears for her mother's safety because her mother works in health care and is constantly exposed to COVID-19. "How to Let Go of the World" discusses the accidental death of the speaker's first love but also ties it to the despair of a friend who is contemplating suicide due to fears regarding the effects of climate change.

The collection ends with "Protest Poem," inspired by the 2020 protests following the killing of George Floyd. The poem is a testimony to the power of anger—or "rage

/ and its promises"—and expresses a belief that a better world is possible, but only if people are willing to fight for it, to "make paradise" from the "ruins" of the old world. "It's okay / if you don't believe me," the speaker says; in the end, what matters is not the words of the poem but its energy, its force, "a wave / that stutters / at the air until / the plate glass / cracks."

Critics received *The World Keeps Ending* just as warmly as *Soft Science*. *Time* magazine named it one of its one hundred must-read books of 2022, *Vulture* listed it as one of the ten best books of the year, and it was featured in NPR's 2022 "Books We Love." Many reviewers commented on the way the poems' use of language, which is characterized by repeated words and driving rhythms, reinforces the collection's themes. Writing for the *Poetry Foundation* website, Rebecca Morgan Frank stated that "repetition is the pulse of this book in subject and practice." In a starred review for *Library Journal*, Diane Scharper wrote, "Choi's use of alliteration, enjambment, and repetition lend a chantlike feel to her work." Stephanie Burt, a reviewer for *Believer*, described the repetition as "words recurring as grief does," and a starred review for *Publishers Weekly* described its effect as "dizzying."

Some noted that the emphasis on form was unusual for modern poetry and felt that this was to the collection's benefit. Annelie Hyatt wrote for the *Columbia Journal of Literary Criticism* that *The World Keeps Ending*'s "balance between authenticity and good form" was a "breath of fresh air," and that the collection was "angry without being sloppy, profound without relapsing into truisms." In addition, Hyatt noted that the formal consistency among poems enables Choi to "cover great swathes of content without any poem feeling out of place." A reviewer for the website *The Poetry Question* stated that the way Choi "leans into structure throughout the collection . . . serves to highlight her commentary on the systemic failings" that have led to the many ills of the modern world. That review also made note of her use of chiasmus and palindromic poems to explore temporality, calling the effect "haunting."

The collection's potential to grant perspective on the world's problems and perhaps provide some hope for the future to those who have struggled with despair is also something that many reviewers lauded. Frank wrote that the "paradox of how we can live in this disastrous world" in *The World Keeps Ending* is resolved "if not [quite] hopefully, at least not in disaster." Meanwhile, Hyatt wrote that "Choi's eloquent thoughts about the present moment are valuable in understanding it more clearly," and Burt described the images of "how something might come after us and look back at us" as "the best parts of Choi's new volume."

The poems of *The World Keeps Ending* are well crafted and full of striking images, but the true beauty of the collection is only evident when it is looked at as a whole. Though the poems about the past may seem to dwell on terrible events, their parallels to the poems about events in the present day reveal a message: if humanity could survive those past events, it will likely also find a way to survive the catastrophes it now faces. Meanwhile, the poems about the future range from cautiously optimistic to outright utopian, and the final poem exhorts the reader to make the difficult but necessary attempt to chart a course to that future.

Author Biography
Franny Choi is the author of the poetry collections *Floating, Brilliant, Gone* (2014) and *Soft Science* (2019), the latter of which was a finalist for a Lambda Literary Award. She is also the author of the chapbook *Death by Sex Machine* (2017) and the plays *Mask Dances* (2011) and *Family Style* (2017).

Emma Joyce

Review Sources
Burt, Stephanie. Review of *The World Keeps Ending, and the World Goes On*, by Franny Choi. *Believer*, 9 Dec. 2022, www.thebeliever.net/a-review-of-the-world-keeps-ending-and-the-world-goes-on. Accessed 15 Feb. 2023.

Frank, Rebecca Morgan. Review of *The World Keeps Ending, and the World Goes On*, by Franny Choi. *Poetry Foundation*, 1 Nov. 2022, www.poetryfoundation.org/harriet-books/reviews/159102/the-world-keeps-ending-the-world-goes-on. Accessed 15 Feb. 2023.

Hyatt, Annelie. Review of *The World Keeps Ending, and the World Goes On*, by Franny Choi. *Columbia Journal of Literary Criticism*, c-j-l-c.org/portfolio/the-world-keeps-ending-and-the-world-goes-on-by-franny-choi. Accessed 15 Feb. 2023.

Review of *The World Keeps Ending, and the World Goes On*, by Franny Choi. *The Poetry Question*, 1 Nov. 2022, thepoetryquestion.com/2022/11/01/review-the-world-keeps-ending-and-the-world-goes-on-franny-choi-ecco. Accessed 15 Feb. 2023.

Review of *The World Keeps Ending, and the World Goes On*, by Franny Choi. *Publishers Weekly*, 13 Oct. 2022, www.publishersweekly.com/9780063240087. Accessed 15 Feb. 2023.

Scharper, Diane. Review of *The World Keeps Ending, and the World Goes On*, by Franny Choi. *Library Journal*, 1 Nov. 2022, www.libraryjournal.com/review/the-world-keeps-ending-and-the-world-goes-on-1791625. Accessed 15 Feb. 2023.

Yonder

Author: Jabari Asim (b. 1962)
Publisher: Simon & Schuster (New York). 272 pp.
Type of work: Novel
Time: Mid-nineteenth century
Locale: The American South

The novel Yonder *offers a powerful evocation of the horrors of slavery and the promise of freedom while focusing on the humanity of enslaved people.*

Principal characters

WILLIAM, one of the Stolen, or enslaved people, who lives on the plantation Placid Hall
MARGARET, a Stolen woman who loves William
CATO, a sensitive and intellectual Stolen man who falls in love with Pandora
PANDORA, a Stolen woman who works in the kitchen at Placid Hall
CUPID, an enslaved man who serves as foreman at Placid Hall
ZANDER, a young Stolen man who dreams of flying
RANSOM, an itinerant preacher and freeman
GUINEA JACK, an old man who advises William
RANDOLPH "CANNONBALL" GREENE, the White owner of Placid Hall

Yonder (2022), the first novel for adults by acclaimed writer Jabari Asim, is a striking addition to the realm of literature scrutinizing the horrors of chattel slavery in the United States. While the subject has been tackled before, including in other esteemed works of fiction, Asim in many ways presents a fresh approach. Notably, he makes a series of choices regarding language that work cumulatively to defamiliarize the setting of the antebellum American plantation. Rather than speaking of "slaves" and "masters," his protagonists refer to themselves as the "Stolen" and to their White enslavers as "Thieves." The setting is also intentionally vague in terms of exact geography. The result is to make Placid Hall, the plantation overseen by the White Cannonball Greene, an island of cruel reality surrounded by a dreamlike zone of possibilities. One of the tensions that runs through the first half of the novel is whether its protagonists will leave the known world of the plantation and venture across the unknown and dangerous territory that lies between them and Canada. In a similar vein, *Yonder* combines brutal depictions of the sufferings of enslaved people with elements of magical realism. It is a powerful combination that allows Asim to evoke and subvert readers' assumptions about this grim period in American history.

The novel is told by a rotating series of first-person narrators, each of them one of the Stolen who lives on or around the ironically named Placid Hall. William, the first narrator, comes to the plantation after saving Cannonball Greene's young son from being trampled by a runaway horse. Greene's gratitude lends William a degree of status on the plantation, so that even Greene's cruel Stolen enforcer, Cupid, does not dare to touch him. William is well aware of the horrors of slavery despite this relative privilege, and he struggles with whether to seek freedom or try to make the best of life on the plantation. Greene has paired him off with Margaret, in the hopes that the two will produce children whom Greene will own. Although William loves Margaret, he does not want to bring a child into a world of bondage. He faces a terrible choice, for if he and Margaret do not produce children soon, Greene will almost certainly separate them. William's natural tendency for introspection is deepened by his relationship with an old man named Guinea Jack, a spiritual adviser who, like several characters in the novel, may not be entirely of this world.

Jabari Asim

Switching points of view between chapters allows Asim to quickly introduce and characterize his cast of protagonists. Cato is a young man with an intellectual bent who, before he was put out to work in the fields, was briefly made the project of a Thief woman who taught him to read. Pandora's childhood is even more of a study in contrasts, for she was raised inside a plantation house as the playmate of a young Thief girl. When that girl died, her mother sold Pandora to a brothel, where she would see "the worst of men, the foulest of their appetites and capabilities." Zander is the youngest of the narrators, a boy who dreams of flying to Africa and who still possesses an innocence that plantation life and the outrages of slavery must eventually take from him. Ransom is a freeman, an itinerant preacher who travels from plantation to plantation. There are a series of layers to his work and to his identity. Although he presents himself as a Christian preacher, Ransom also leads the Stolen in secret naming rituals and other rites that seem to be drawn from their African heritage and pre-slavery culture. Moreover, he is a leader of the Chariot, a version of the Underground Railroad that helps guide enslaved people to the free North and to Canada.

Asim occasionally includes chapters in a third-person perspective as well, focusing on characters such as Cannonball Greene and the slavecatcher Norbrook. The shift from the intimacy of first-person narration to the objectivity of the third-person view creates a narrative distance between the reader and the Thief characters who propagate the system of slavery. The reader observes these characters, rather than hearing directly from them. When writing of Greene or his psychopathic wife, for example, Asim employs a droll, understated irony: "Greene often marveled that Providence had blessed men like him with an entire continent of pliant, soulless beings, strong in body but empty in mind." Greene's White supremacist thoughts and beliefs are their own indictment. The gulf between how Greene sees himself and how the reader sees him helps keep the morally reprehensible nature of enslavement front and center. It also subtly suggests that while slavery sought to dehumanize Black people, the enslavers themselves are the ones who fail to demonstrate their essential humanity.

The plot of *Yonder* is propelled by a series of escalations and challenges, as the protagonists engage in the fierce moral calculus of determining how best to keep themselves and their loved ones from torture and death. When William and Cato stand up to the bullying foreman Cupid, for example, they set in motion a series of events that will have disastrous ramifications for all of the Stolen people on Placid Hall. Although Asim does a good job of giving each main character a story arc and making each one sympathetic to the reader, it is arguably William who has the most choices to make and who goes through the most profound changes. Although William is distrustful of Ransom, fearing at different points that the preacher has designs on Margaret or that he plans to betray the Stolen to the Thieves, he also knows that the preacher offers the only viable way out of bondage. William's relationship with the elder Guinea Jack further complicates his relationship to freedom and enslavement. Jack, like Ransom, retains a connection to traditional African culture and religion, and offers William a vision of life outside of the enslavement system. When William accepts Cupid's old job as Greene's overseer, Jack rejects him, saying, "You're doing exactly what the Thief wants you to do, to forget who the real enemy is and do his sordid work for him." William's temptation, ultimately, is to make a life of accommodation for himself, reconciling himself to the enslavement system and helping to prop it up. Particularly because Asim has shown graphic depictions of Stolen people being punished, tortured, beaten, and killed, this is no easy decision. William's eventual choice to join the other Stolen in an attempted journey to freedom is a moral victory that lies at the heart of the novel.

While the narrative structure helps move the story forward quickly through a series of overlapping perspectives, it carries with it an inherent challenge. A diverse collection of characters should not only think, speak, and act differently, but should also read differently on the page as they each take on the role of narrator. Asim, at times, struggles with this aspect of the narration, and the reader may find themselves flipping back to the chapter heading—which lists the character's name—to remind themselves of who is speaking. This becomes particularly true when the principal characters begin their journey to the north. Their experiences are so closely aligned during their journey that the device of shifting perspective serves less purpose than in the earlier sections of the book.

Nevertheless, the protagonists' freedom-seeking journey is a gripping section of the novel. As they travel north, the Stolen must overcome various hardships and challenges and must make crucial choices about who to trust. Asim depicts their flight and the terrible choices they face in taut and harrowing terms. Beyond the plantation, moreover, the magical realism that has been hinted at becomes an ever-more potent presence in the world. One example is the legendary Swing Low, a protective spirit that defends freedom seekers. In a similar vein, two characters who are separated from the group are taken in by the People, a group who look like the Stolen but who live free and harmonious lives in the hidden depths of the forest. With their trackless passages through the forest, their healing skills, and their intricately designed cabins and canoes, the People are reminiscent of an idealized American Indian tribe. The time in the almost utopian society of the People serves as a counterpoint to the injustices of Placid Hall and of the United States in general. While the episode teeters on the edge of a deus ex machina intervention, with a new and quasi-magical group of people appearing just in time to save the protagonists, it contributes to the interesting layering of magical realism and sharp social commentary.

Yonder was well received by many critics, including starred reviews in both *Kirkus* and *Publishers Weekly*. Writing for the *New York Times*, Vanessa Riley praised Asim's representation of "the spiritual resilience of enslaved people" and concluded that "with his handling of Black love, showing how it existed amid the worst circumstances, tender and memorable, Asim delivers a fresh, sweeping, must-read tale." In a review for the *Washington Post,* Evangeline Lawson similarly praised the way that Asim "brilliantly takes the horrific details of the Black American experience of slavery and breathes life into them." Lawson further saw the book as particularly timely "given the current cultural climate, with people challenging the importance of teaching about slavery within the broader scope of American history."

Yonder is a welcome addition to an already extensive literature about the lives of enslaved people. With his engaging narrative structure, his subtle repurposing of words, and his fusion of grim reality with magical realism, Asim offers a new perspective on one of the darkest passages of American history.

Author Biography
An author and cultural critic, Jabari Asim is known for his focus on the Black American experience, with works spanning nonfiction, poetry, and children's literature. He was nominated for the 2001 Pulitzer Prize in Criticism and earned a Guggenheim Fellowship, among other honors.

Matthew J. Bolton

Review Sources
Lawson, Evangeline. "Yonder is a Vital Addition to Our Literature about Slavery." Review of *Yonder*, by Jabari Asim. *The Washington Post*, 22 Feb. 2022, www.washingtonpost.com/books/2022/02/04/yonder-is-vital-addition-our-literature-about-slavery. Accessed 14 Nov. 2022.

Riley, Vanessa. "In Yonder, Escape from Slavery Comes with a Magical Twist." Review of *Yonder*, by Jabari Asim. *The New York Times*, 11 Jan. 2022, www.nytimes.com/2022/01/11/books/review/yonder-jabari-asim.html. Accessed 14 Nov. 2022.

Review of *Yonder*, by Jabari Asim. *Kirkus*, 27 Oct. 2021, www.kirkusreviews.com/book-reviews/jabari-asim/yonder-asim/. Accessed 19 Dec. 2022.

Review of *Yonder*, by Jabari Asim. *Publishers Weekly*, 23 Sept. 2021, www.publishersweekly.com/9781982163167. Accessed 19 Dec. 2022.

You Don't Know Us Negroes and Other Essays

Author: Zora Neale Hurston (1891–1960)
Editors: Henry Louis Gates Jr. (b. 1950) and Genevieve West
Publisher: Amistad (New York). 464 pp.
Type of work: Essays
Time: 1922–ca. 1959
Locales: Plateau (African Town), Alabama; Harlem, New York; and Live Oak, Florida

Henry Louis Gates Jr. and Genevieve West have chosen fifty of acclaimed author Zora Neale Hurston's essays in this collection, covering issues such as folklore, art, race, gender and politics. Though many of the essays were previously published, there are several pieces that appear for the first time in this volume.

Principal personages

CUDGO LEWIS, a.k.a. Kossula-O-Lo-Loo-Ay and Cudjo Lewis, member of the Takkoi people in Nigeria; survivor from the final shipload of enslaved Africans taken to the US aboard the Clotilda.
FANNIE HURST (1885–1968), Jewish American writer who was popular in the post–World War I era.
MARCUS GARVEY (1887–1940), Jamaican activist during the Harlem Renaissance.
RUBY MCCOLLUM, a married Black woman accused of murdering her lover
C. LEROY ADAMS, McCollum's lover; a White male physician and politician

In addition to writing novels and short stories, famed author Zora Neale Hurston was a prolific essayist. *You Don't Know Us Negroes and Other Essays*, edited by scholars Henry Gates Louis Jr. and Genevieve West, contains essays Hurston wrote throughout her life, and serves as a culmination of her deepest thoughts about the world in which she lived. In the introduction, Gates and West prepare readers to immerse themselves in Hurston's previously published and never-before seen essays that range in topic from "inner logic of Black cultural forms, social institutions, and behavior" to African American language and "folk cultural forms." The table of contents further categorizes the essays into five parts, titled "On the Folk," On Art and Such," "On Race and Gender," "On Politics" and "On the Trial of Ruby McCollum."

In "Part One: On the Folk," editors Gates and West compile eight essays relating to the history and language of African Americans. One of the most intriguing is "The Last Slave Ship," in which Hurston shares thoughts about her interviews with Kossula O-Lo-Loo-Ay, also known as Cudgo (Cudjo) Lewis, whom she described as "the last survivor of the last boat-load of black men and women who had been set down stark naked on American soil." In this piece, she writes about the rivalry between two West African kingdoms, Takkoi and Dahomey, which led to the murder and enslavement of the former by the latter. As she tells Lewis's story, Hurston shares the betrayal, attempted escapes, conditions on the infamous slave ship the *Clotilda*, and the lasting humiliation felt by those of the Takkoi kingdom. Hurston's skill in sharing the heart of the people is clear as she ends the essay with a note that Lewis "felt his uprooting deeply. If I ever went to Africa, he said, I must tell his people where he was. Kossula never knew that not one survivor of Takkoi was known to be alive." She would later use this essay, along with the interviews and notes she collected while living near Lewis, to write her novel *Barracoon*, a fictionalized retelling of his life.

Henry Louis Gates Jr.

"Part Two: On Art and Such" also includes eight essays, this time focused on artistic endeavors. According to the editors' notes, *American Mercury* intended to publish the section's opening essay, "You Don't Know Us Negroes," in 1934, but never did, and the essay subsequently remained unpublished during Hurston's lifetime. In it, she fearlessly argues that Black writing up to that point had been more like "oleomargarine," the "fictionalized form of butter" in its inauthentic depictions of Black life. While she felt that Black authors meant well, she lamented their need to cater to White editors and producers who were unable to see past the minstrelsy and vaudeville caricatures that dominated popular American depictions of Black life. She condemns the use of biblical scenes, "hoodoo dance," and the use of mulatto characters as villains. As she censures the publishing world, she mocks those earlier writers by ironically framing her criticism with skillful, ironic use of the very stories she censures. Another essay, "Fannie Hurst," shares a story about Hurston's friendship with Hurst, a White writer, to acclaim the other woman's skill as "a blend of woman and author." In the essay "Art and Such," which was not published during Hurston's life, she likewise promotes other Black artists of the day and her own work while lamenting the "cruel waste" of Black genius during slavery as well as the "Race Men and Women and other champions of 'Race Consciousness'" whose object in the three decades after slavery was "to 'champion the Race'" and who produced writing that lacked the "drama, analysis, characterization and the universal oneness necessary to literature.

The next two parts of the collection, "Part Three: On Race and Gender" and "Part Four: On Politics," deal with societal issues. "The Emperor Effaces Himself" showcases Hurston's humor and acts as a satirical roast of Marcus Garvey, the man, without criticizing his political views. Another humorous piece is the short essay "Noses." This is followed by two more serious essays, "How It Feels to Be Colored Me" and "Race

Genevieve West

Cannot Become Great Until It Recognizes Its Talent," before Gates and West include "Now Take Noses," a continuation on the ideas of the earlier essay. "The 'Pet Negro' System," is a parody of a sermon on the need to excuse White Southerners for their hypocrisy in treating a few Black individuals favorably while practicing anti-Black racism in general. Hurston shares her opinion of educational issues in "The Rise of Begging Joints," where she expresses concern over the inadequate higher education options for Black students unable to get into or afford top colleges and universities, including "Class A" historically Black universities and colleges. In "Court Order Can't Make Races Mix," she mulls over *Brown vs. Board of Education's* desegregation policies and reveals that she took issue with the ruling for its implicit judgment of White or integrated schools as inherently better than all-Black schools.

Other essays in this section elucidate Hurston's own, often unpopular, political views. "Crazy for This Democracy," in part critiques the hypocrisy of the United States and other democracies around the world that extoll freedom and liberty but do not extend it to their "non-Caucasian" populaces or colonies. In "I Saw Negro Votes Peddled," Hurston rails against the manipulation of Black voters. "Mourner's Bench: Why the Negro Won't Buy Communism" critiques the racist saviorism behind Communist efforts to attract Black Americans and other people of color around the world to the party.

The book concludes with Part 5, titled "On the Trial of Ruby McCollum." The pieces in this section differ from the earlier parts because they are all focused on a specific event, the trial of McCollum for the murder of Dr. C. LeRoy Adams, in Live Oak, Florida. Gates and West note, "In 1952, [Hurston] essentially became a beat reporter for the *Pittsburg Courier*." Thus, the tone and form of these articles offer a slightly different perspective on Hurston as a writer and observer. To understand the essays, it is significant to know about the trial. McCollum was an African American woman from a prosperous family. Adams, a physician and politician, was McCollum's lover (or rapist) and the father of at least one of her children. McCollum admitted that she walked into his office and shot him. There were many potential causes for her action, but, unsurprisingly, McCollum's jury consisted only of White men and she was found guilty.

The thirteen essays in this final section share Hurston's thoughts about the case, the judge, McCollum's motives, media coverage, and public reception of the case. The first of these, "Zora's Revealing Story of Ruby's 1st Day in Court!" presents snippets of Hurston's observations as she sat in the segregated section of the courtroom. The author's irritation with the process is highlighted in sentences presented in all-capitals that mimic headlines. In "Trial Highlights," which appears about halfway through the section, Hurston highlights the opening hour of one day of trial. "Ruby Bares Her Love Life" is a transcription of McCollum's interrogation by her own defense attorney with additional questions from the judge. "The Life Story of Mrs. Ruby J. McCollum!" features an apparently incomplete, serialized, and sympathetic biography of McCollum in ten installments with a beginning date of February 28, 1953. The collection ends with Hurston's essay "My Impressions on the Trial." Appalled by the reactions of both White people and Black people over the trial, she called it "a smothering blanket of silence" and "a mass delusion of mass illusion." She was disgusted by the way Ruby's neighbors fawned over the deceased doctor and publicly decried the fact that he had fathered one of her children, clinging to a superficial motive of an unpaid medical bill. Clearly, in Hurston's eyes, this trial would never be fair because too much was cloaked in "silence."

Hurston's lasting popularity and skill as a writer is clearly illustrated in the glowing reviews this collection received. *Booklist* reviewer Aryssa Damron noted that the essays show off Hurston's "acerbic wit, her crisp prose, and the breadth of her artistic ability and interests." The reviewer for *Kirkus* repeated this view, praising Hurston "trenchant, acerbic commentaries on Black life" and concluding that the collection presents "vigorous writings from a controversial and important cultural critic." The critic for *Publishers Weekly* claimed the collection is "showstopping," adding that Hurston's "pride in the richness of Black American life is evident throughout" and her "work stands out for its wit and range." Jordannah Elizabeth, writing for the *New York Amsterdam News*, lauded Hurston as a "deeply profound Black writer" and the collection as "indispensable literary work for the Black book collector and Black literary enthusiast." The *National Review*'s Timothy Sanderfur pointed out the ways the essays show that Hurston was "a writer who, above all else, thought for herself," and noted that "The essays gathered here are delightful examples of her eloquence and charm." Trudier Harris, writing for the *New York Times*, expanded upon this by pointing out Hurston's daring opinions as "unapologetic and unbridled." Harris further argued, "Despite facing sexism, racism and general ignorance, Hurston managed to produce a written legacy that, thanks to enduring collections like this one, will engage readers for generations to come."

Author Biography
Renowned Harlem Renaissance author and ethnographer Zora Neale Hurston published four novels during her lifetime: *Jonah's Gourd Vine* (1934), *Their Eyes Were Watching God* (1937), *Moses, Man of the Mountain* (1939), and *Seraph on the Suwanee* (1948). She also published the folklore collections *Mules and Men* (1935) and *Tell My Horse* (1938) and the autobiography *Dust Tracks on a Road* (1942). *Barracoon: The Story of the Last "Black Cargo"*, based on her conversations with Cudjo Lewis in 1927, was published posthumously in 2018.

Theresa L. Stowell, PhD

Review Sources

Damron, Aryssa. Review of *You Don't Know Us Negroes and Other Essays*, by Zora Neale Hurston. *Booklist*, 12 Dec. 2021, p. 12. *EBSCOhost*, search.ebscohost.com/login.aspx?direct=true&db=a9h&AN=153919995&site=ehost-live. Accessed 16 Nov. 2022.

Elizabeth, Jordannah. "New Collections from Literary Titans Zora Neale Hurston, Stanely Crouch Emerge." *New York Amsterdam News*, 22 Sept. 2022, p. 22. *EBSCOhost*, search.ebscohost.com/login.aspx?direct=true&db=a9h&AN=159240848&site=ehost-live. Accessed 16 Nov. 2022.

Harris, Trudier. "In Her Own Words." Review of *You Don't Know Us Negroes and Other Essays*, by Zora Neale Hurston. *The New York Times*, 14 Jan. 2022, www.nytimes.com/2022/01/14/books/review/you-dont-know-us-negroes-zora-neale-hurston.html. Accessed 16 Nov. 2022.

Review of *You Don't Know Us Negroes and Other Essays*, by Zora Neale Hurston. *Kirkus*, 1 Dec. 2021. *EBSCOhost*, search.ebscohost.com/login.aspx?direct=true&db=a9h&AN=153812330&site=ehost-live. Accessed 16 Nov. 2022.

Review of *You Don't Know Us Negroes and Other Essays*, by Zora Neale Hurston. *Publishers Weekly*, 22 Nov. 2021, p. 96. *EBSCOhost*, search.ebscohost.com/login.aspx?direct=true&db=a9h&AN=153670637&site=ehost-live. Accessed 16 Nov. 2022.

Sanderfur, Timothy. "Singing a Song to the Morning." Review of *You Don't Know Us Negroes and Other Essays*, by Zora Neale Hurston. *National Review*, 21 Feb. 2022, pp. 39–40. *EBSCOhost*, search.ebscohost.com/login.aspx?direct=true&db=a9h&AN=155026301&site=ehost-live. Accessed 16 Nov. 2022.

Young Mungo

Author: Douglas Stuart (b. 1976)
Publisher: Grove Press (New York). 390 pp.
Type of work: Novel
Time: 1993
Locale: Glasgow, Scotland

Douglas Stuart's second novel focuses on the story of Mungo Hamilton, a sensitive teenager living on the margins of society in Glasgow, Scotland, as he navigates young love and family dysfunction.

Principal characters
MUNGO HAMILTON, a sensitive teenager
HAMISH HAMILTON, his older brother, a criminal
JODIE HAMILTON, his ambitious older sister
MAUREEN "MO-MAW" BUCHANAN HAMILTON, his widowed, alcoholic mother
JAMES JAMIESON, his love interest, a racing pigeon breeder

Douglas Stuart's *Young Mungo* (2022) could, in some senses, be considered a spiritual sequel to his award-winning debut novel, *Shuggie Bain* (2020). In the latter, a sweeping urban epic focused on the relationship between a young boy and his mother in working-class Glasgow, Scotland, Stuart drew heavily on his own experiences dealing with poverty, his mother's addiction, and his own sexuality. *Young Mungo* focuses on an entirely new cast of characters, but they have a familiar quality: people wracked by desperation, trying to cope with adversity in various ways.

Young Mungo also shares a similar context with *Shuggie Bain*'s timeline and setting. By the opening of *Young Mungo*, Margaret Thatcher, who served as prime minister of the United Kingdom from 1979 to 1990, has been out of office for a couple of years. Yet many in the UK continue to feel the deleterious effects of her economic policies, which have been widely criticized as hostile toward working-class people. The apparent failures of Thatcher's policies are felt especially in metropolitan areas where public housing, inhabited by many unemployed persons, is concentrated. This political and economic context perfectly suits the novel's setting in the early 1990s. Stuart's focus is still on Glasgow, Scotland's largest city, a gritty industrial community and seaport. At the time of the novel's events, a chasm of inequality separates the city's haves and have-nots, and sectarian violence between Protestants and Catholics can flare up at any time. Though many local landmarks are noted in passing, the action is centered on the poverty-stricken East End of the city. The focus is on the residents of a dilapidated, government-built tenement. This is where the Hamilton family lives.

Douglas Stuart

Readers are quickly introduced—and leisurely exposed—to a full range of individual strengths and weaknesses of surviving members of the Hamilton clan. There is no mature adult male present. The patriarch, who was involved with the Protestant gangs, is long gone, stabbed to death in a fight years earlier. The head of the family is Maureen "Mo-Maw" Hamilton, a thirty-four-year-old widow and mother to three teenagers. She does not like to admit that fact, and typically dresses and acts younger (and uses her maiden name, Buchanan) when she is trying to meet and date new men. Mo-Maw's struggles with alcoholism often lead her to stay away from home for weeks at a time, neglecting her children and other responsibilities. Despite this behavior, Mo-Maw has moments of clarity and wisdom, such as when she humorously contemplates the violence of the past, present and future: "Aye, well, it's aw fun and games till someone loses an eye, eh?"

Her oldest child, Hamish, a short but tough young man of eighteen, is involved in multiple criminal enterprises and harbors strong homophobic and anti-Catholic beliefs. He deals speed and hashish cut with tobacco, and also engages in insurance fraud. He runs a vicious gang of children and adults, called Billies, who specialize in stealing car radios and fighting with the rival Catholic gang. Hamish and his companions regularly raid construction sites to steal tools, commit wanton acts of vandalism, and otherwise cause mischief. Hamish lives near the Hamilton household with his teenaged girlfriend, Sammi-Jo, who recently gave birth to a daughter and is learning how to nurse. He also acts as surrogate father to his sensitive younger brother, Mungo, and is determined to toughen him up and help him survive.

Jodie, Mo-Maw's daughter, is gainfully employed at an Italian restaurant. She has grown tired of her mother's antics and often hurls sharp insults at Mo-Maw. Jodie, noted for a distinctive, annoying laugh that escapes at inappropriate times, hopes to better her situation by attending university.

While the entire Hamilton family is important, the novel truly centers on the family's youngest child, Mungo, who was born after his father died. A handsome boy, he is gentle, not angry and bitter like his siblings; as a result, he is his mother's favorite. Mungo, named after Glasgow's patron saint, is quite different from other boys in his neighborhood and faces occasional exclusion and bullying.

Through his thoughts and actions, Mungo is revealed as sensitive and naive (he has barely left his own neighborhood during his young life). He is an artistic loner who draws complicated patterns in his sketchbook. He is high-strung, a condition that spawns a facial tic he cannot always control. His sexuality is indeterminate until—well into the story—he spots a good-looking young neighbor, James Jamieson, who maintains a hand-built coop where he breeds pouter pigeons. There is mutual attraction between Mungo and James, and over time a casual relationship slowly blossoms into love. The affection is illustrated by Mungo's observation of his boyfriend: "He looked like an oil painting, as though the heavens were smiling down on him." There are many such lyrical passages scattered throughout, like gemstones sparkling among gravel. The transformation of two young men into a single unit serves as the novel's driving force.

However, the conservative, judgmental neighborhood often proves a hostile place for Mungo. Neighborhood bullies, including Hamish, often harass individuals they suspect are gay or otherwise different. For example, Mungo's family and neighbors have long shunned another tenant, "Poo-Wee-Chickie" Calhoun, for decades, since Calhoun is not married and is viewed as effeminate. As a result, Mungo and James try to avoid being caught together in compromising situations. In addition to worrying about homophobia in their neighborhood, the boys must also worry about religious tensions. Mungo is Protestant and James is Catholic, which could be a major issue in a sharply divided city where restless boys and disgruntled men, armed with bottles and bricks and knives, are ready any time to cause trouble. They gather "like colour-blocked moths . . . jumpy and unpredictable with adrenaline . . . full of love and rage, eager to stab and maim."

Mungo is forced to consider the possible reactions of his family members to his relationship with James. Mungo feels that Jodie will be accepting, as she has long protected and defended her younger brother, but knows that Mo-Maw would be unpredictable, depending upon her condition. Most of all, he knows that Hamish would be enraged and vindictive if he were to find out. Mungo fears his brother might hurt James in an effort to salvage the Hamilton family's reputation.

The cover of the North American first edition of *Young Mungo* adds to the novel's unsettling ambiance. The cover depicts a red-lipped young man submerged from the nose down in dark water. The image provides a subtle, intriguing metaphor—and foreshadows events to come—before the book is opened. By contrast, the cover of the European version, published by Picador, shows a closeup of two young men engaged in a passionate kiss, focusing attention on the theme of gay romance.

The structure of *Young Mungo* is unusual but effective. The novel starts in the recent past with a section consisting of a single chapter, entitled "The January Before." This construction accomplishes several authorial purposes. It sets several characters into motion, provides background for the action that lies ahead, and establishes a tense, menacing atmosphere. The remaining twenty-seven chapters fall under the heading "The May After." The story moves forward and backward in time, intertwining two separate, sometimes overlapping storylines together to paint a harsh but rich and thoughtful saga that alternates between awful acts and moments of beauty. Ultimately, *Young Mungo*, like Stuart's first novel, gives new definition and a Glaswegian stamp to Russian author Leo Tolstoy's famous opening in his 1878 novel *Anna Karenina*: "Happy families are all alike; every unhappy family is unhappy in its own way."

Notably, the novel makes heavy use of Scots dialect, which some linguists and speaker consider to be a language distinct from English. The unfamiliarity of this language could prove challenging to readers outside of Scotland. To those who have not sampled prominent modern Scottish writers who write in this dialect, such as Irvine Welsh (*Trainspotting*, 1993) or James Kelman (*How Late It Was, How Late*, 1994), Stuart's prose may seem hard to grasp at first. Dialogue that reproduces the pronunciation of Scots dialect—"cannae" (cannot), "oot" (out), "fitba" (football/soccer)—is liberally peppered with local terms for everyday things. Nouns like "smirr" (light drizzle) and "bothy" (a basic shelter) and "teuchter" (someone from the Highlands) are struck against verbs like "scunner" (to feel disgust), "clipe" (to inform on someone), and "shoogle" (to shake or wobble) to create linguistic sparks. Fortunately, the author is such a skillful storyteller that it does not take long to fall into the rhythm, grasp this new language through context, and become totally immersed in Stuart's vision of Glasgow.

Most critics were overwhelmingly positive about *Young Mungo*. Maureen Corrigan, writing for *NPR*, called it "a nuanced and gorgeous heartbreaker of a novel." She especially appreciated the author's "precisely observed and often wry style," concluding that it is "hard to imagine a more disquieting and powerful work . . . about the perils of being different." Alex Preston, in a review for the *Guardian*, agreed, noting how the author "brilliantly summons a family, brings them to vivid life on the page, makes us love them for all their faults" and describing *Young Mungo* as a "finer novel than its predecessor." Preston concluded that *Young Mungo* confirmed its author "as a prodigious talent."

However, some critics qualified this praise. One mildly negative comment came from Molly Young in her review for the *New York Times*; she commended the novel's "world of exquisite detail" but faulted Stuart's occasional "excess." In particular she questioned Stuart's "[insistence] on telling what he has already shown," and wondered whether this represented "condescension" towards readers who did not understand the novel or "self-doubt" toward his own writing. Similar comments came from Stuart Kelly for the *Scotsman*, who called *Young Mungo* "a form of self-plagiarism." While praising the "fluent" prose, Kelly critiqued the book's "tendency towards the easy image" and craved more "freshly-minted" passages, suggesting that the novel simply "reshuffled" the themes Stuart first explored in *Shuggie Bain*. Yet despite these critiques, many readers will find *Young Mungo* a worthwhile effort, blending the tender and the disturbing in a sharply realistic exploration of family and identity.

Author Biography

Douglas Stuart's first novel, *Shuggie Bain* (2020), a best-seller, won the Booker Prize and garnered many other domestic and international honors, including British Book of the Year. Stuart's short fiction has appeared in a number of publications, including the *New Yorker*.

Jack Ewing

Review Sources

Charles, Ron. "*Young Mungo* Seals It: Douglas Stuart Is a Genius." *The Washington Post*, 5 Apr. 2022, www.washingtonpost.com/books/2022/04/05/young-mungo-douglas-stuart/. Accessed 21 Sept. 2022.

Corrigan, Maureen. "Brace Yourself for Young Mungo, a Nuanced Heartbreaker of a Novel." Review of *Young Mungo*, by Douglas Stuart. NPR, 29 Mar. 2022, www.npr.org/2022/03/29/1089215299/book-review-young-mungo-douglas-stuart. Accessed 21 Sept. 2022.

Kelly, Stuart. Review of *Young Mungo*, by Douglas Stuart. *The Scotsman*, 5 Apr. 2022, www.scotsman.com/arts-and-culture/books/book-review-young-mungo-by-douglas-stuart-3642230. Accessed 21 Sept. 2022.

Preston, Alex. "*Young Mungo* by Douglas Stuart Review—Another Weepy from a Writer on a Roll." *The Guardian*, 3 Apr. 2022, www.theguardian.com/books/2022/apr/03/young-mungo-by-douglas-stuart-review-another-weepy-from-a-writer-on-a-roll. Accessed 21 Sept. 2022.

Young, Molly. "Young Mungo Explores Love and Violence in Emotional Technicolor." Review of *Young Mungo*, by Douglas Stuart. The New York Times, 3 Apr. 2022, www.nytimes.com/2022/04/03/books/review-young-mungo-douglas-stuart.html. Accessed 21 Sept. 2022.

Category Index

Anthropology
Walking the Bowl (Chris Lockhart and Daniel Mulilo Chama), 677

Autobiography
Free (Lea Ypi), 197
The Naked Don't Fear the Water (Matthieu Aikins), 410

Biography
Buster Keaton (James Curtis), 94
Camera Man (Dana Stevens), 108
Civil Rights Queen (Tomiko Brown-Nagin), 123
Her Country (Marissa R. Moss), 226
His Name Is George Floyd (Robert Samuels and Toluse Olorunnipa), 231
Last Call at the Hotel Imperial (Deborah Cohen), 308
River of the Gods (Candice Millard), 494
The Trayvon Generation (Elizabeth Alexander), 628

Current Affairs
My Seven Black Fathers (Will Jawando), 405
The Naked Don't Fear the Water (Matthieu Aikins), 410
Tell Me Everything (Erika Krouse), 592
The Trayvon Generation (Elizabeth Alexander), 628
Under the Skin (Linda Villarosa), 652
Walking the Bowl (Chris Lockhart and Daniel Mulilo Chama), 677

Diary
Gathering Blossoms under Fire (Alice Walker), 202

Education
How to Raise an Antiracist (Ibram X. Kendi), 242

Essays
Body Work (Melissa Febos), 65
Happy-Go-Lucky (David Sedaris), 212
I'll Show Myself Out (Jessi Klein), 264
Rogues (Patrick Radden Keefe), 499
Serious Face (Jon Mooallem), 517
You Don't Know Us Negroes and Other Essays (Zora Neale Hurston), 695

Fiction
Trust (Hernan Diaz), 643

Graphic Nonfiction
Ducks (Kate Beaton), 177
Rise (Jeff Yang, Phil Yu, and Philip Wang), 490
Victory. Stand! (Tommie Smith and Derrick Barnes), 662

Graphic Novel
Ain't Burned All the Bright (Jason Reynolds), 5
Swim Team (Johnnie Christmas), 578

History
Bad Mexicans (Kelly Lytle Hernández), 37
Buster Keaton (James Curtis), 94
Camera Man (Dana Stevens), 108
Civil Rights Queen (Tomiko Brown-Nagin), 123
Free (Lea Ypi), 197
Half American (Matthew F. Delmont), 207
Index, a History of the (Dennis Duncan), 282

Last Call at the Hotel Imperial (Deborah Cohen), 308
The Last Slave Ship (Ben Raines), 313
Legacy of Violence (Caroline Elkins), 328
The Nineties (Chuck Klosterman), 429
Rise (Jeff Yang, Phil Yu, and Philip Wang), 490
River of the Gods (Candice Millard), 494
South to America (Imani Perry), 556
Under the Skin (Linda Villarosa), 652
The Vortex (Scott Carney and Jason Miklian), 672

History of Science
The Song of the Cell (Siddhartha Mukherjee), 551

Letters
The Letters of Thom Gunn (Thom Gunn), 346

Literary Criticism
Constructing a Nervous System (Margo Jefferson), 137

Literary History
Index, a History of the (Dennis Duncan), 282

Literary Theory
Body Work (Melissa Febos), 65

Medicine
The Song of the Cell (Siddhartha Mukherjee), 551
Under the Skin (Linda Villarosa), 652

Memoir
All Down Darkness Wide (Seán Hewitt), 10
Also a Poet (Ada Calhoun), 28
Body Work (Melissa Febos), 65

Constructing a Nervous System (Margo Jefferson), 137
Corrections in Ink (Keri Blakinger), 141
Deaf Utopia (Nyle DiMarco with Robert Siebert), 159
Ducks (Kate Beaton), 177
Easy Beauty (Chloé Cooper Jones), 182
Free (Lea Ypi), 197
How to Raise an Antiracist (Ibram X. Kendi), 242
I Cried to Dream Again (Sara Kruzan and Cori Thomas), 250
I'll Show Myself Out (Jessi Klein), 264
I'm Glad My Mom Died (Jennette McCurdy), 268
The Impossible City (Karen Cheung), 278
The Invisible Kingdom (Meghan O'Rourke), 291
Left on Tenth (Delia Ephron), 323
Lost & Found (Kathryn Schulz), 356
The Man Who Could Move Clouds (Ingrid Rojas Contreras), 367
Mean Baby (Selma Blair), 371
Mother Noise (Cindy House), 396
The Movement Made Us (David J. Dennis Jr. with David J. Dennis Sr.), 400
My Seven Black Fathers (Will Jawando), 405
The Naked Don't Fear the Water (Matthieu Aikins), 410
Red Paint (Sasha taqʷšəblu LaPointe), 485
Shy (Mary Rodgers and Jesse Green), 531
Solito (Javier Zamora), 546
South to America (Imani Perry), 556
Stay True (Hua Hsu), 564
Tell Me Everything (Erika Krouse), 592
The Trayvon Generation (Elizabeth Alexander), 628
Victory. Stand! (Tommie Smith and Derrick Barnes), 662

CATEGORY INDEX

Miscellaneous
Rise (Jeff Yang, Phil Yu, and Philip Wang), 490

Music
Her Country (Marissa R. Moss), 226

Natural History
Otherlands (Thomas Halliday), 467

Nature
An Immense World (Ed Yong), 273
The Treeline (Ben Rawlence), 633

Novel
Afterlives (Abdulrazak Gurnah), 1
All My Rage (Sabaa Tahir), 14
All This Could Be Different (Sarah Thankam Mathews), 23
Babel (R. F. Kuang), 32
Big Girl (Mecca Jamilah Sullivan), 42
Black Cake (Charmaine Wilkerson), 47
Black Cloud Rising (David Wright Faladé), 52
The Book Eaters (Sunyi Dean), 70
Book Lovers (Emily Henry), 75
The Books of Jacob (Olga Tokarczuk), 80
Booth (Karen Joy Fowler), 85
The Bullet That Missed (Richard Osman), 90
Call Me Cassandra (Marcial Gala), 99
Calling for a Blanket Dance (Oscar Hokeah), 103
The Candy House (Jennifer Egan), 113
Carrie Soto Is Back (Taylor Jenkins Reid), 118
The Colony (Audrey Magee), 128
Companion Piece (Ali Smith), 133
The Daughter of Doctor Moreau (Silvia Moreno-Garcia), 150
Daughter of the Moon Goddess (Sue Lynn Tan), 155

Demon Copperhead (Barbara Kingsolver), 164
Dinosaurs (Lydia Millet), 169
The Door of No Return (Kwame Alexander), 173
Either/Or (Elif Batuman), 187
Fellowship Point (Alice Elliott Dark), 192
Horse (Geraldine Brooks), 237
I Must Betray You (Ruta Sepetys), 254
The Kaiju Preservation Society (John Scalzi), 296
Kaikeyi (Vaishnavi Patel), 300
Killers of a Certain Age (Deanna Raybourn), 304
The Last White Man (Mohsin Hamid), 318
Lessons (Ian McEwan), 338
Lessons in Chemistry (Bonnie Garmus), 342
Lucy by the Sea (Elizabeth Strout), 361
The Memory Librarian (Janelle Monáe, Alaya Dawn Johnson, Danny Lore, Eve L. Ewing, Yohanca Delgado, and Sheree Renée Thomas), 376
Memphis (Tara M. Stringfellow), 381
Moon Witch, Spider King (Marlon James), 386
Moth (Melody Razak), 391
A New Name (Jon Fosse), 415
Nightcrawling (Leila Mottley), 425
Nona the Ninth (Tamsyn Muir), 434
Notes on an Execution (Danya Kukafka), 439
Nothing More to Tell (Karen M. McManus), 449
Now Is Not the Time to Panic (Kevin Wilson), 454
The Ogress and the Orphans (Kelly Barnhill), 458
Olga Dies Dreaming (Xochitl Gonzalez), 462
Our Missing Hearts (Celeste Ng), 472

Properties of Thirst (Marianne Wiggins), 476
The Rabbit Hutch (Tess Gunty), 480
The School for Good Mothers (Jessamine Chan), 504
Sea of Tranquility (Emily St. John Mandel), 509
The Seven Moons of Maali Almeida (Shehan Karunatilaka), 526
Siren Queen (Nghi Vo), 536
Small World (Jonathan Evison), 541
The Stardust Thief (Chelsea Abdullah), 560
The Summer of Bitter and Sweet (Jen Ferguson), 573
The Swimmers (Julie Otsuka), 582
Take My Hand (Dolen Perkins-Valdez), 587
This Time Tomorrow (Emma Straub), 601
This Woven Kingdom (Tahereh Mafi), 606
A Thousand Steps into Night (Traci Chee), 611
A Tiny Upward Shove (Melissa Chadburn), 619
Tomorrow, and Tomorrow, and Tomorrow (Gabrielle Zevin), 623
True Biz (Sara Nović), 638
The Twist of a Knife (Anthony Horowitz), 647
The Verifiers (Jane Pek), 657
The Violin Conspiracy (Brendan Slocumb), 667
The Vortex (Scott Carney and Jason Miklian), 672
The White Girl (Tony Birch), 682
Yonder (Jabari Asim), 691
Young Mungo (Douglas Stuart), 700

Philosophy
Body Work (Melissa Febos), 65

Poetry
Ain't Burned All the Bright (Jason Reynolds), 5
All the Flowers Kneeling (Paul Tran), 19
Customs (Solmaz Sharif), 146
The Hurting Kind (Ada Limón), 246
Inheritance (Elizabeth Acevedo), 287
Time Is a Mother (Ocean Vuong), 615
The World Keeps Ending, and the World Goes On (Franny Choi), 687

Psychology
Body Work (Melissa Febos), 65

Science
An Immense World (Ed Yong), 273
Otherlands (Thomas Halliday), 467
The Song of the Cell (Siddhartha Mukherjee), 551
The Treeline (Ben Rawlence), 633

Short Fiction
Bliss Montage (Ling Ma), 60
The Haunting of Hajji Hotak and Other Stories (Jamil Jan Kochai), 217
Heartbroke (Chelsea Bieker), 221
If I Survive You (Jonathan Escoffery), 259
Lesser Known Monsters of the 21st Century (Kim Fu), 333
Liberation Day (George Saunders), 351
Night of the Living Rez (Morgan Talty), 420
Seeking Fortune Elsewhere (Sindya Bhanoo), 513
Seven Empty Houses (Samanta Schweblin), 521
Stories from the Tenants Downstairs (Sidik Fofana), 568
Thank You, Mr. Nixon (Gish Jen), 596

CATEGORY INDEX

Short Stories
Blank Pages and Other Stories (Bernard MacLaverty), 56

Sociology
Camera Man (Dana Stevens), 108
How to Raise an Antiracist (Ibram X. Kendi), 242
My Seven Black Fathers (Will Jawando), 405
The Nineties (Chuck Klosterman), 429

Travel
South to America (Imani Perry), 556

Verse Novel
The Door of No Return (Kwame Alexander), 173
Nothing Burns as Bright as You (Ashley Woodfolk), 444

Title Index

Afterlives (Abdulrazak Gurnah), 1
Ain't Burned All the Bright (Jason Reynolds), 5
All Down Darkness Wide (Seán Hewitt), 10
All My Rage (Sabaa Tahir), 14
All the Flowers Kneeling (Paul Tran), 19
All This Could Be Different (Sarah Thankam Mathews), 23
Also a Poet (Ada Calhoun), 28

Babel (R. F. Kuang), 32
Bad Mexicans (Kelly Lytle Hernández), 37
Big Girl (Mecca Jamilah Sullivan), 42
Black Cake (Charmaine Wilkerson), 47
Black Cloud Rising (David Wright Faladé), 52
Blank Pages and Other Stories (Bernard MacLaverty), 56
Bliss Montage (Ling Ma), 60
Body Work (Melissa Febos), 65
The Book Eaters (Sunyi Dean), 70
Book Lovers (Emily Henry), 75
The Books of Jacob (Olga Tokarczuk), 80
Booth (Karen Joy Fowler), 85
The Bullet That Missed (Richard Osman), 90
Buster Keaton (James Curtis), 94

Call Me Cassandra (Marcial Gala), 99
Calling for a Blanket Dance (Oscar Hokeah), 103
Camera Man (Dana Stevens), 108
The Candy House (Jennifer Egan), 113
Carrie Soto Is Back (Taylor Jenkins Reid), 118

Civil Rights Queen (Tomiko Brown-Nagin), 123
The Colony (Audrey Magee), 128
Companion Piece (Ali Smith), 133
Constructing a Nervous System (Margo Jefferson), 137
Corrections in Ink (Keri Blakinger), 141
Customs (Solmaz Sharif), 146

The Daughter of Doctor Moreau (Silvia Moreno-Garcia), 150
Daughter of the Moon Goddess (Sue Lynn Tan), 155
Deaf Utopia (Nyle DiMarco with Robert Siebert), 159
Demon Copperhead (Barbara Kingsolver), 164
Dinosaurs (Lydia Millet), 169
The Door of No Return (Kwame Alexander), 173
Ducks (Kate Beaton), 177

Easy Beauty (Chloé Cooper Jones), 182
Either/Or (Elif Batuman), 187

Fellowship Point (Alice Elliott Dark), 192
Free (Lea Ypi), 197

Gathering Blossoms under Fire (Alice Walker), 202

Half American (Matthew F. Delmont), 207
Happy-Go-Lucky (David Sedaris), 212
The Haunting of Hajji Hotak and Other Stories (Jamil Jan Kochai), 217
Heartbroke (Chelsea Bieker), 221
Her Country (Marissa R. Moss), 226

His Name Is George Floyd (Robert Samuels and Toluse Olorunnipa), 231
Horse (Geraldine Brooks), 237
How to Raise an Antiracist (Ibram X. Kendi), 242
The Hurting Kind (Ada Limón), 246

I Cried to Dream Again (Sara Kruzan and Cori Thomas), 250
I Must Betray You (Ruta Sepetys), 254
If I Survive You (Jonathan Escoffery), 259
I'll Show Myself Out (Jessi Klein), 264
I'm Glad My Mom Died (Jennette McCurdy), 268
An Immense World (Ed Yong), 273
The Impossible City (Karen Cheung), 278
Index, a History of the (Dennis Duncan), 282
Inheritance (Elizabeth Acevedo), 287
The Invisible Kingdom (Meghan O'Rourke), 291

The Kaiju Preservation Society (John Scalzi), 296
Kaikeyi (Vaishnavi Patel), 300
Killers of a Certain Age (Deanna Raybourn), 304

Last Call at the Hotel Imperial (Deborah Cohen), 308
The Last Slave Ship (Ben Raines), 313
The Last White Man (Mohsin Hamid), 318
Left on Tenth (Delia Ephron), 323
Legacy of Violence (Caroline Elkins), 328
Lesser Known Monsters of the 21st Century (Kim Fu), 333
Lessons (Ian McEwan), 338
Lessons in Chemistry (Bonnie Garmus), 342

The Letters of Thom Gunn (Thom Gunn), 346
Liberation Day (George Saunders), 351
Lost & Found (Kathryn Schulz), 356
Lucy by the Sea (Elizabeth Strout), 361

The Man Who Could Move Clouds (Ingrid Rojas Contreras), 367
Mean Baby (Selma Blair), 371
The Memory Librarian (Janelle Monáe, Alaya Dawn Johnson, Danny Lore, Eve L. Ewing, Yohanca Delgado, and Sheree Renée Thomas), 376
Memphis (Tara M. Stringfellow), 381
Moon Witch, Spider King (Marlon James), 386
Moth (Melody Razak), 391
Mother Noise (Cindy House), 396
The Movement Made Us (David J. Dennis Jr. with David J. Dennis Sr.), 400
My Seven Black Fathers (Will Jawando), 405

The Naked Don't Fear the Water (Matthieu Aikins), 410
A New Name (Jon Fosse), 415
Night of the Living Rez (Morgan Talty), 420
Nightcrawling (Leila Mottley), 425
The Nineties (Chuck Klosterman), 429
Nona the Ninth (Tamsyn Muir), 434
Notes on an Execution (Danya Kukafka), 439
Nothing Burns as Bright as You (Ashley Woodfolk), 444
Nothing More to Tell (Karen M. McManus), 449
Now Is Not the Time to Panic (Kevin Wilson), 454

The Ogress and the Orphans (Kelly Barnhill), 458

TITLE INDEX

Olga Dies Dreaming (Xochitl Gonzalez), 462
Otherlands (Thomas Halliday), 467
Our Missing Hearts (Celeste Ng), 472

Properties of Thirst (Marianne Wiggins), 476

The Rabbit Hutch (Tess Gunty), 480
Red Paint (Sasha taqʷšəblu LaPointe), 485
Rise (Jeff Yang, Phil Yu, and Philip Wang), 490
River of the Gods (Candice Millard), 494
Rogues (Patrick Radden Keefe), 499

The School for Good Mothers (Jessamine Chan), 504
Sea of Tranquility (Emily St. John Mandel), 509
Seeking Fortune Elsewhere (Sindya Bhanoo), 513
Serious Face (Jon Mooallem), 517
Seven Empty Houses (Samanta Schweblin), 521
The Seven Moons of Maali Almeida (Shehan Karunatilaka), 526
Shy (Mary Rodgers and Jesse Green), 531
Siren Queen (Nghi Vo), 536
Small World (Jonathan Evison), 541
Solito (Javier Zamora), 546
The Song of the Cell (Siddhartha Mukherjee), 551
South to America (Imani Perry), 556
The Stardust Thief (Chelsea Abdullah), 560
Stay True (Hua Hsu), 564
Stories from the Tenants Downstairs (Sidik Fofana), 568
The Summer of Bitter and Sweet (Jen Ferguson), 573
Swim Team (Johnnie Christmas), 578
The Swimmers (Julie Otsuka), 582

Take My Hand (Dolen Perkins-Valdez), 587
Tell Me Everything (Erika Krouse), 592
Thank You, Mr. Nixon (Gish Jen), 596
This Time Tomorrow (Emma Straub), 601
This Woven Kingdom (Tahereh Mafi), 606
A Thousand Steps into Night (Traci Chee), 611
Time Is a Mother (Ocean Vuong), 615
A Tiny Upward Shove (Melissa Chadburn), 619
Tomorrow, and Tomorrow, and Tomorrow (Gabrielle Zevin), 623
The Trayvon Generation (Elizabeth Alexander), 628
The Treeline (Ben Rawlence), 633
True Biz (Sara Nović), 638
Trust (Hernan Diaz), 643
The Twist of a Knife (Anthony Horowitz), 647

Under the Skin (Linda Villarosa), 652

The Verifiers (Jane Pek), 657
Victory. Stand! (Tommie Smith and Derrick Barnes), 662
The Violin Conspiracy (Brendan Slocumb), 667
The Vortex (Scott Carney and Jason Miklian), 672

Walking the Bowl (Chris Lockhart and Daniel Mulilo Chama), 677
The White Girl (Tony Birch), 682
The World Keeps Ending, and the World Goes On (Franny Choi), 687

Yonder (Jabari Asim), 691
You Don't Know Us Negroes and Other Essays (Zora Neale Hurston), 695
Young Mungo (Douglas Stuart), 700